Protective Security

Creating Military-Grade Defenses for Your Digital Business

Jim Seaman

Apress®

Protective Security: Creating Military-Grade Defenses for Your Digital Business

Jim Seaman
Castleford, UK

ISBN-13 (pbk): 978-1-4842-6907-7   ISBN-13 (electronic): 978-1-4842-6908-4
https://doi.org/10.1007/978-1-4842-6908-4

Managing Director, Apress Media LLC: Welmoed Spahr
Acquisitions Editor: Susan McDermott
Development Editor: Laura Berendson
Coordinating Editor: Jessica Vakili

Distributed to the book trade worldwide by Springer Science+Business Media New York, 233 Spring Street, 6th Floor, New York, NY 10013. Phone 1-800-SPRINGER, fax (201) 348-4505, e-mail orders-ny@springer-sbm.com, or visit www.springeronline.com. Apress Media, LLC is a California LLC and the sole member (owner) is Springer Science + Business Media Finance Inc (SSBM Finance Inc). SSBM Finance Inc is a **Delaware** corporation.

For information on translations, please e-mail booktranslations@springernature.com; for reprint, paperback, or audio rights, please e-mail bookpermissions@springernature.com.

Apress titles may be purchased in bulk for academic, corporate, or promotional use. eBook versions and licenses are also available for most titles. For more information, reference our Print and eBook Bulk Sales web page at http://www.apress.com/bulk-sales.

Any source code or other supplementary material referenced by the author in this book is available to readers on GitHub via the book's product page, located at www.apress.com/978-1-4842-6907-7. For more detailed information, please visit http://www.apress.com/source-code.

Printed on acid-free paper

I want to thank Susan McDermott and Jessica Vakili, at Apress, for their assistance and to Michael Gioia for his diligent feedback, as technical reviewer, to help me to bring this very personal project to life.

Table of Contents

About the Author

Jim Seaman has been dedicated to the pursuit of security for his entire adult life. He served 22 years in the RAF Police, covering a number of specialist areas including physical security, aviation security, information security management, IT security management, cybersecurity management, security investigations, intelligence operations, and incident response and disaster recovery. He has successfully transitioned his skills to the corporate environment and now works in areas such as financial services, banking, retail, manufacturing, ecommerce, and marketing. He helps businesses enhance their cybersecurity and InfoSec defensive measures and works with various industry security standards.

About the Technical Reviewer

Michael Gioia is an information security leader with 17 years of experience delivering security solutions across several industries. He was an officer in the US Air Force and has worked in higher education, the Department of Defense, retail food services, and security consulting. He has performed most of his information security work in higher education as an Information Security Officer at Eastern Illinois University, Rose-Hulman Institute of Technology, and currently at Bentley University. Michael holds various professional certifications including Certified Information Security Manager (CISM) from ISACA, Certified Information Systems Security Professional (CISSP) from ISC2, GIAC Security Leadership Certification (GSLC) from SANS, and Payment Card Industry Professional (PCIP) from the PCI Security Standards Council.

Tribute To

It goes without saying that I couldn't miss the opportunity of honoring all those who have undergone assimilation into the Armed Forces and have served their country, in any of the military services, and especially my fallen RAF Police colleagues (honored through the RAF Police Memorials, as depicted in Figures 1[1] and 2[2]).

Figure 1. *RAF Police Memorial*

[1]www.warmemorialsonline.org.uk/memorial/255129
[2]www.rafpa.com/

IN MEMORY OF	IN MEMORY OF
CPL DAVID JOHN SHEPHERD	CPL BRENT JOHN MCCARTHY
P8407151	30059891
RAF POLICE	RAF POLICE
WHO DIED IN KUWAIT ON	WHO DIED IN AFGHANISTAN ON
19TH MAY 2003	12TH MAY 2012
FIAT JUSTITIA	*FIAT JUSTITIA*

Figure 2. *RAF Police Memorials*

Although my long, challenging, and rewarding career provided me with an exceptional foundation, within the Protective Security field, I would also like to take the opportunity of paying tribute to others, outside of the Royal Air Force and the military, who had been extremely supportive of me and who I have the upmost respect for.

My late father despite (for as long as I can remember) suffering from Crohn's disease[3] managed to run a successful business, provide for his family, and do charitable work (former President of the Castleford and Pontefract District Lions Club, as depicted in Figure 3). Unfortunately, just before I was due to begin my 10-week residential counter intelligence training course, he had started with what he had thought to be his fourth flare-up of Crohn's disease.

---

[3]www.mayoclinic.org/diseases-conditions/crohns-disease/symptoms-causes/syc-20353304#:~:text=Crohn's%20disease%20is%20a%20type,digestive%20tract%20in%20different%20people

Figure 3. *Maurice Seaman*

I remember, at the outset of the course, during the instructor's briefing, we were told to let him know if there were any personal issues that might impact us during the course. Now, normally, I would not have mentioned anything, but on this occasion something in my head encouraged me to mention about my dad being ill.

A few weeks later, my dad's condition worsened, and he had to be admitted to hospital. Knowing that he had been through this before and having faith that the hospital staff would be able to successfully treat his condition, and make him better again, I continued on with the course.

However, just 2 weeks later, one Wednesday afternoon returning from my lunch break, I would receive the shocking news that things had gotten worse and that I needed to get back home. Immediately, the course instructor made arrangements for me to get on the very next train, to take me home.

I wasn't able to get back home in time to see my father, before he had died. It turns out that, on this occasion, my dad hadn't been suffering with another flare-up of Chrohn's disease but that this time he had had colon cancer. In fact, the very same morning that they had discovered the tumors, he had died that afternoon.

Now, circumstances dictated that I did not really have time to dwell on the situation, as by the time that I got to my parents' home, I automatically assumed the organizer role. Back then, it was an accepted thing for a serviceman from Yorkshire not to show their emotions. Consequently, I spent the next few days helping to organize affairs and to prepare things for my dad's funeral on the following Monday.

Later that week, I received a call from my course instructor, informing me that I needed to be back at the RAF Police School on Tuesday morning to sit the final exam of the course. Should I not be able to do so, I would need to restart the course and to redo the 5 weeks again.

Attending my dad's funeral was his sister (my aunty) and my Uncle Ian (as depicted in Figure 4), who offered to drive me to a railway station 2 hours, closer to the RAF Police School.

Figure 4. *Uncle Ian*

My uncle was always incredibly supportive and could always make me feel better, and all through the 2-hour drive, on the afternoon after my dad's funeral, he managed to keep my spirits up. However, once I had been dropped at the railway station, had boarded the train, and taken a seat, it was not long until being alone in my thoughts all the emotions of that day and week came flooding over me.

I did manage to get back to the RAF Police School and did manage to pass the final exam, but without my uncle's kindness and support, I do not know how I ever could have achieved such a thing.

Over the next few years, my Uncle Ian would become my go-to person (almost like a surrogate father), whom I knew would show an interest in what I had been up to and who I could always rely on. In fact, whenever I would be passing in the vicinity of my aunty and uncle's home, I would also try and drop in to see them.

The first time I did this, I knew the junction of the motorway (near to where they lived) but could not remember exactly where their home was. Consequently, I drove around trying to remember landmarks from when I had last been there, when I was a teenager. I drove around for around 30 minutes with no luck, until out of desperation I stopped and asked an elderly couple, tending to their garden, if they happened to know my aunty and uncle.

This turned out to be a stroke of luck, as they had known them through working together many years ago but didn't know their address but would look it up for me in their telephone directory.

Subsequently, every time I was driving down to RAF Brize Norton for my overseas deployments (Basra, Iraq; Kandahar and Camp Bastion, Afghanistan), I would surprise my aunty and uncle by stopping off at their home, using it as a safe place to break up the long drive. I would always be greeted with a warm welcome; invariably my uncle would be watching sports on the television, and my aunty would offer me a cup of tea, biscuits, and a sandwich.

The first time I did this, my uncle would be a little confused and surprised to hear me ask him to move his car around so that I could back my car onto his driveway (right up to his garage door) and then ask him to park his car directly in front of my car. Although not understanding why, he obliged to this request.

Having had good conversations and a catch-up with my aunty and uncle, and being refreshed, I would then continue my journey to RAF Brize Norton. Of course, before I departed, I showed my uncle the reason for my unusual request. I will never forget his face, after he saw what had been in my vehicle (all the items needed for my overseas deployment), and why I had made the special request. Every time, from then on, he would remind me of this.

As I said, after my father's sudden death, my uncle became incredibly special to me, and he would become the last remaining male figure in my life that I knew I could trust and rely on.

This would certainly be appreciated, a few years later, when my aunty and uncle offered to accompany and support me on a visit to RAF Brize Norton to allow me to show my respect at the repatriation of Corporal Brent McCarthy (as depicted in Figure 5[4]), an RAF Policeman who had been killed during overseas operations in Helmand province, Afghanistan.

---

[4]www.dailymail.co.uk/news/article-2888559/Police-hunting-rogue-Afghan-policeman-shot-dead-British-soldier-posing-picture-arrest-suspect.html

Figure 5. *Cpl Brent McCarthy, RAF Police*

Having finished my career in the RAF Police, I had never considered that I might need to attend another repatriation (having served one tour in Iraq and two tours in Afghanistan, I had attended many repatriations), but, although something I was extremely uncomfortable with, I felt it was something that I needed to do.

Consequently, I had turned to my Uncle Ian for advice and support, where he and my aunty offered to go with me.

Unknown to me, at the time, the next funeral I was to attend was to be the one for my Uncle Ian. A few years later, I had sent a text to my Uncle Ian wishing him a Merry Christmas and asking him how he was, and he had replied that everyone was okay and that he was only suffering from a few stomach problems but had an appointment to see his doctor.

The following March, I received a call informing me that my Uncle Ian had terminal cancer and been admitted into palliative care, at a local hospice. I had not been able to see my father in hospital before he had died, so I was determined that this was not going to happen again.

Despite being warned of what I would see, I had not been fully prepared for what was to greet me. Cancer had made my uncle a shadow of the man that he had been before. However, despite everything, I was glad that I managed to get to see him. Despite all the painkilling drugs and medical equipment, I still managed to see a glimpse of my Uncle Ian's character still coming through.

Despite everything that I experienced, throughout my military service, I was truly humbled by the service that the palliative care team provided to my uncle and would like to include a tribute to all emergency services workers, who are repeatedly called upon to deal with such situations as part of their job roles.

The loss of my father and my Uncle Ian, both to cancer, has also had a significant impact on my life, after which I stopped using a microwave and eating meat, owing to their links with cancer:

- **Facts About Microwave Ovens That Will Make You Never Want To Use One Again**[5]

- **Can eating meat cause cancer?**[6]

- **Ingestion of fight-or-flight response chemicals**[7]

I saw a documentary, in which they said that if an animal shows signs of intelligence, then, at the point of slaughter, they are highly likely to produce "fight-or-flight" response chemicals. Anyone then eating this meat will be ingesting these chemicals as well.

Note Choosing not to eat meat has been a decision that was personal for me, and I have made this conscious decision based upon events that have happened to me and from the research I have carried out.

Although I was not aware of it at the time, I strongly believe that the decision I made, as a teenager, to join the Royal Air Force Police changed my life, putting me on a path that provided me with a purpose, values, and unique challenges to help build the firm foundations I needed for later in my life.

---

[5]https://realfarmacy.com/microwave-free-year-microwave-cooking-trading-cancer-convenience/

[6]www.worldwidecancerresearch.org/stories/2021/january/can-eating-meat-cause-cancer/

[7]www.britannica.com/science/fight-or-flight-response

These experiences I have successfully passed on to one of my nephews, who is now pursuing a successful career as a Ground Technician in the Royal Air Force.

Unfortunately, for another of my nephews (as depicted in Figure 6[8]), I was not able to convince him of the benefits that military service could provide him, before the pressures of being a young adult resulted in him taking his own life. Consequently, I have taken the opportunity of including him in this "Tribute To" section of my book.

Figure 6. *Richard Clarke*

---

[8]www.justgiving.com/crowdfunding/RichardClarke

Acknowledgments

Additionally, thank you to Luana for her continued support, over the past year, patiently tolerating my daily military- and security-related stories. As a result, she probably feels that she knows so much content of both my first book (PCI DSS: An Integrated Data Security Standard Guide) and this book that she could transition away from her chosen profession of psychology. Seriously though, her professional input proved to be invaluable for including psychological perspectives into Chapter 12.

CHAPTER 1

Introduction

The Royal Air Force has a well-earned reputation for excellence in delivering air and space power, and a proud history of success.

While capable aircraft, weapons and support elements are fundamental to that reputation and success, it is you – as individuals, leaders, and as part of a team – who ultimately make the difference and give the Royal Air Force its competitive edge.

It is only through your endeavors that we can be a truly agile, adaptable, and capable Air Force.

Our work is often done in challenging and hazardous circumstances. Success in these circumstances can only be achieved by motivated, capable, and self-disciplined individuals driven by exceptional leadership at all levels of the Service.

By the very nature of the air and space environment, we must be pioneering in approach, pragmatic in delivery, courageous, fair and just.

Mike Wigston, CBE ADC

The Royal Air Force Ethos, Core Values and Standards

Air Publication 1

3rd Revision

October 2019[1]

---

[1] www.raf.mod.uk/recruitment/media/3897/20200703-raf_ap1_2019_rev_3_page_spreads.pdf

© Jim Seaman 2021
J. Seaman, *Protective Security*, https://doi.org/10.1007/978-1-4842-6908-4_1

Figure 1-1. *Air Chief Marshal*

Background

No doubt, many of you will agree that 2020 has been incredibly challenging for many organizations across the globe. Having to respond to the pandemic, many businesses needed to change their ways of working to ensure minimal disruption to their operations.

At the same time, with so many companies rapidly moving to remote working practices, the criminals have seen this as an exceptional opportunity for them to profit from these disruptions and changes to the normal ways of working, with many companies having to rapidly adjust to remote working models.

Suddenly, these organizations needed to be more mobile and flexible while no longer having the traditional security protections of having their personnel work out of the relative sanctity of their corporate infrastructures.

Additionally, we observed changes to the way that the business' customers would interface with them – increasingly relying on their perceived safe and secure virtual environments.

Consequently, while we all observed the dramatic impact of a business being ill-prepared for the pandemic (natural disaster), we also saw the impact of these dynamically changing environments and habits. This provided the criminals with significant increased attack vectors, with which they could seek to exploit and profit from.

In essence, these criminals were like "wildlife predators," seeking any opportunities to gorge themselves, by targeting the weakest or most vulnerable members of the herd (as depicted in Figure 1-2[2]).

---

[2]https://spencercoursen.medium.com/are-you-safety-fit-38ddd8acab0f

Figure 1-2. *On the hunt*

During the year, while the business leaders were trying to deal with the challenges and impacts of the pandemic, the number of reported cyber-attacks appeared to continue relentlessly, with the criminals appearing to have little or no concern for the victims of their attacks.

Just check out some of the statistics and trends seen during the 2020 pandemic.

Hackmageddon Statistics[3] (as depicted in Figures 1-3 to 1-9)

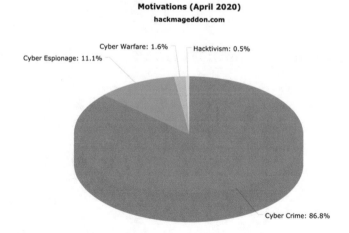

Figure 1-3. *Cyber-crime motivations, April 2020*

---

[3]www.hackmageddon.com/category/security/cyber-attacks-statistics/

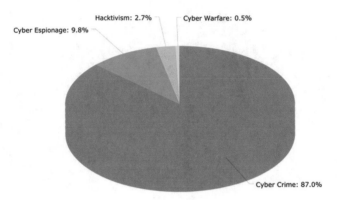

Figure 1-4. *Cyber-crime motivations, May 2020*

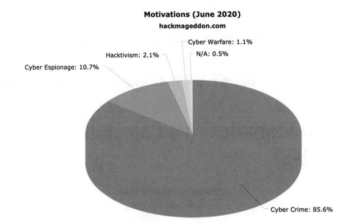

Figure 1-5. *Cyber-crime motivations, June 2020*

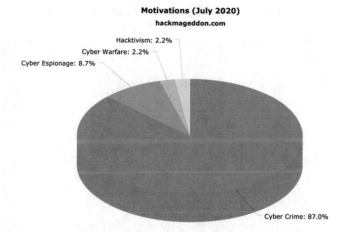

Figure 1-6. *Cyber-crime motivations, July 2020*

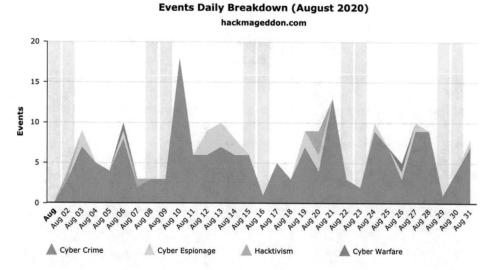

Figure 1-7. *Cyber-crime motivations, August 2020*

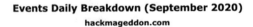

Figure 1-8. *Cyber-crime motivations, September 2020*

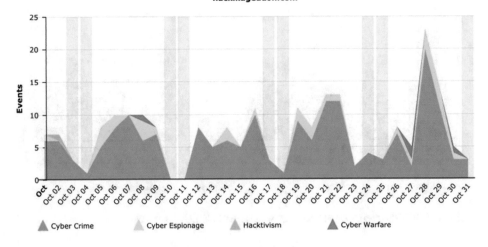

Figure 1-9. *Cyber-crime motivations, October 2020*

Fintech News Statistics[4]

- **85%** of people posting puppy photos are trying to scam you.

- **43%** of data breaches are cloud-based web applications.

- **67%** of data breaches resulted from credential theft, human error, or social attacks.

- Fewer than **1 in 20** breaches exploit weaknesses.

- **70%** of breaches are caused by external actors.

- Organized crime gangs account for **55%** of attacks.

- **37%** of credential theft breaches used stolen or weak credentials.

- **25%** involved phishing.

- Human error accounts for **22%**.

- Ransomware is found in **27%** of malware incidents – **up from 24% in 2019**.

- **18%** of organizations reported a ransomware attack.

- **41%** of customers would stop buying from a business victim of a ransomware attack.

- **9 million** EasyJet customers had their data hacked.

- A hacker leaks **40 million** user records from the Wishbone app.

- There is a cyber-attack every **39 seconds**.

- **75%** of cyber-attacks start with an email.

- **21%** of online users are victims of hacking.

- **11%** of online users have been victims of data theft.

- **72%** of breaches target large firms.

- **10%** of organizations receive cryptocurrency mining malware.

- **80%** of hacking breaches involve brute force or stolen credentials.

---

[4]www.fintechnews.org/the-2020-cybersecurity-stats-you-need-to-know/

14 Most Alarming Cybersecurity Statistics in 2020[5]

1. Americans are more worried about being a victim of cybercrime than being a victim of violent crime.

    Specifically, Americans are more worried about identity theft and being hacked:

    - *__71%__ of Americans are worried about having their personal or financial information hacked.*

    - *__67%__ of Americans are worried about being a victim of identity theft.*

    By contrast:

    - *__24%__ are worried about being a victim of terrorism.*

    - *__22%__ are worried about being attacked while driving, __20%__ about being sexually assaulted, and __17%__ about being murdered.*

    - *__7%__ are worried about being assaulted at the workplace.*

2. There were more than **1.76 billion records leaked in January 2020** alone.

3. Ransomware is expected to cost businesses and organizations **$11.5 billion in 2020**.

4. Microsoft Office extensions are the most malicious file extensions used by email hackers.

5. The main cause of data breaches is malicious or criminal attacks – and they are responsible for **48%** of all data breaches.

6. The global average cost of a data breach is **$3.6 million** – and it keeps increasing every year.

7. The global cost of cybercrime is expected to **exceed $2 trillion in 2020**.

---

[5]https://thebestvpn.com/cyber-security-statistics-2020/

8. **Mobile malware** is on the rise, but **grayware**[6] could pose a more dangerous risk to mobile users.

9. **Cryptojacking**[7] is one of the more serious cyber threats to watch out for in 2020.

10. The number of groups using destructive malware increased by **25%** in 2018.

11. Around **7 out of 10** businesses are not prepared to respond to a cyber-attack.

12. Phishing emails are responsible for about **91%** of cyber-attacks.

13. A staggering **92%** of malware is delivered via email.

14. More than **76%** of cyber-attacks are financially motivated.

In summary, it is fair to say that 2020 has clearly shown that the protection of a business needed to be far more than concentrating on securing a finite type of asset and that the focus needed to be on ensuring that proportionate measures are applied for the protection of the assets that they identify as being valuable to them and their customers.

Consequently, I would like to introduce you to the term "Protective Security" and to see how this might be beneficial to your organization. By looking into the origins of the words "Protective" and "Security," you can see why this might be more appropriate to your business:

Protective (adj.)[8]

"affording protection, sheltering, defensive," 1660s, from protect + -ive. As a noun from 1875.

Related: Protectively; protectiveness. Protective custody is from 1936, translating German Schutzhaft, used cynically by the Nazis. The notion is "adopted or intended to afford protection."

---

[6]www.logixconsulting.com/2019/12/24/what-is-grayware-2/
[7]www.investopedia.com/terms/c/cryptojacking.asp
[8]www.etymonline.com/word/protective#etymonline_v_36598

Security (n.)[9]

mid-15c., "condition of being secure," from Latin securitas, from securus "free from care" (see secure). Replacing sikerte (early 15c.), from an earlier borrowing from Latin; earlier in the sense "security" was sikerhede (early 13c.); sikernesse (c. 1200).

Meaning "something which secures" is from 1580s; "safety of a state, person, etc." is from 1941. Legal sense of "property in bonds" is from mid-15c.; that of "document held by a creditor" is from 1680s. Phrase security blanket in figurative sense is attested from 1966, in reference to the crib blanket carried by the character Linus in the "Peanuts" comic strip (1956).

This book will provide you with some valuable insights into the subject of Protective Security, along with some examples of the application during my 22-year RAF Police career. This will cover such engagements as

- Dog handler

- Special weapons protection

- Security and policing shift supervisor

- Air transport security

- Counter intelligence

- Computer security

- Counter terrorism

- Overseas security deployments

Inspiration for This Book

I have always been a strong believer in "fate" and that everything happens for a reason *(some are good, some are bad)* and that these events help to shape every one of us.

---

[9]www.etymonline.com/search?q=security

I recall one such an event that happened to me, after I had started to transition across from military service life to the corporate sector. I had recently started with a new security consultancy firm, in the role of a Payment Card Industry Qualified Security Assessor (QSA). After an extremely short onboarding period, I was tasked to visit a large retailer, based in the south of England, to deliver a gap assessment of their payment card operations.

It had been the last week of December when I set off on the 6-hour train journey, on the Sunday evening, to be at the client first thing Monday morning. Now, I was very new to the Payment Card Industry Data Security Standard (PCI DSS) but had over 22 years' experience of protecting the RAF's mission-critical assets. With the mindset that PCI DSS was the baseline of mitigation security controls, I engaged in my very first solo client engagement.

I remained at the client for the remainder of the week, interviewing personnel, observing their processes, and reviewing documentation, so that I had gathered sufficient information to provide the client with a status of their payment card operations, against the PCI DSS, and to provide them with a suggested road map to help them improve.

During the week, the heavens had opened, and it had rained continuously all week, and, as a result, on completion of the onsite engagement, my return train journey was to be disrupted. However, despite this disruption proving to be a negative experience, it proved to be extremely beneficial for the way I looked at my life moving forward.

On my day of departure, I boarded my return train. Unfortunately, the week's heavy rain had meant that just 1 hour along the journey, the train would be stopping, and I would be transferred (due to the trainline being flooded) to complete a leg of the journey by coach.

The flooding had caused several earlier trains cancelled. Consequently, during this first 1-hour train journey, the train had been "packed to the rafters," with only standing room (outside the public toilet facilities) available. I managed to find myself a small corner space (adjacent to the door of the public toilet) and set up my small suitcase as an impromptu seat and tried to get comfortable for the train journey.

The next thing I knew, a young male *(around the same age as when I had first started my career in the RAF Police)* had thrown his bag to the floor, in front of the toilet door, and had collapsed onto it – appearing to almost fall instantaneously asleep. Before too long, people were needing to get past him to use the toilet facilities.

As we came to a stop at an exceedingly small rural train station, along the way, the young male was awoken by someone wanting to use the toilet facilities. The young male was clearly disoriented, as he and his large bag alighted the train and stood looking completely lost on this small and remote rural station platform.

I shouted out to the young male, "*Hey pal, where are you heading for*"

He replied, "*I need to get on a connection for Stoke on Trent!*"

Now, this station was not the station where the connection was to be, and it was, in fact, another 30-minute train journey before we would get to the right train station. Stoke-on-Trent was still at least another 5-hour, or so, train journey.

I beckoned him to get back on the train and urgently shouted,
"*This is the wrong station, quick, get yourself back on the train!*"

He managed to get himself back on the train before it departed, and I gave up my corner space so that the young male could settle down, out of the way, while we continued the train journey. The young male thanked me for helping him.

Around 1 hour later, we arrived at the main train station (Exeter), where we were to board the waiting coaches, to allow the passengers to continue our journeys home. The coach journeys were the only means for the train journeys to be diverted around the impassable flooded part of the railway. The coaches would act as a tributary connection between two main train stations (Exeter and Bristol). On the coach's arrival at Bristol, the passengers would then be able to reconnect to a train that went to their destination.

As I departed the train, at Exeter, it was apparent that this young male was completely disoriented, confused, and not knowing what to do or where he needed to go.

I said to him, "*Come with me, I'll take you to the waiting coaches so
that you can get to Bristol.*"

He replied, "*Okay, thank you!*"

I escorted him to the correct coach, made sure that his bag was placed into the baggage compartment, got him onto the coach, and sat in the seat next to him.

This coach transfer would take around 2 hours, and, during this time, after a short sleep, the young male woke up and engaged in conversation with me.

He said, "*Thank you for helping me, I'm not feeling 100% and so
I'm not sure how I would have managed to get home.*"

I replied, "*It's no bother, I'm happy to help.*"

He then asked, "*What have you been doing down here?*"

I politely replied, "*Oh, just some work. What about you?*"

His reply was to be a bit of a shock, for someone who had spent 20 years cocooned within the RAF Police.

He said, "*I'm on the way back home, after being kicked out of a residential drug rehabilitation center! The center had a three-strikes and out policy and I had been play fighting with some of the other residents, got a little carried away and set off a fire extinguisher.*

We all got reprimanded but I already had two previous strikes against me, so they told me to pack my bags, got me a one-way rail ticket and dropped me at local train station!

I'm now feeling the effects of the methadone wearing off, which is why I'm not one hundred percent and I really am grateful that you helped me, this morning!"

This proved to be a reality check for me, as I took a moment to reflect upon how, despite several ups and downs, my life had turned out.

He went on to say, "*I've really blown an opportunity to make a change to my life and I'm worried that when I go back home, that I will end up getting back with the wrong crowds.*

My elder brother is in prison, after turning to crime to feed his habit. At some points, my brother would be so bad that I would have to help him prepare his drugs before I went off to school."

I explained, "*I believe that life is like travelling down a one-way street, you can't turn around and go back.*

Every so often, you will be faced with forks in the road, where you need to decide which road to take (right, left, or straight on).

Should you make the wrong decision, you need to make the best of what you can, learn from it and remain observant, so that you can take the next junction to get yourself back onto a better path.

> *When you get back home, take the weekend to reflect on things*
> *and then on Monday, write a letter to the rehabilitation center,*
> *apologizing for your actions and explaining that you appreciate the*
> *opportunity this provides for you to make a real direction change*
> *for your life."*

To this day, I do not know what made me come up with this analogy, but it is a value that I have held with me ever since.

We eventually arrived at Bristol station, which is where our paths parted. However, I ensured that this young man got on the right train for Stoke-on-Trent, and I wished him well for the future and to stay safe. I then boarded the next train to take me back home.

For me, a career in the RAF Police was to be the thing that really helped me through my early adult years, providing me with plenty of challenges and opportunities to develop – both professionally and personally. (You can discover more of my military career journey by reading Appendix A.)

In Defense of the Crown

Using a combination of autoethnographic research and security industry references, the aim of this book is to introduce you to the term "Protective Security" and to explain the potential benefits these principles could bring to your business.

I had first discovered this term, after being taught about it, during my 10-week residential RAF Police Counter Intelligence training course.

Almost 14 years after joining the Royal Air Force (RAF), and going on to become an RAF Police dog handler, I would be instructed on the RAF Police's method for protecting their mission-critical assets and to become qualified as a counter intelligence (CI) operation. The entire 10-week training and examinations revolved around the application of the guidance provided in the Defence Manual of Security, Joint Services Publication 440 (JSP 440) *(which has subsequently been published on the WikiLeaks website[10])*.

Now, for almost a decade (and, in fact, throughout my 22-year career), the protective efforts were focused around ensuring that this was proportionate to the perceived value of an asset in support of their associated mission statement.

---

[10]https://wikileaks.org/wiki/UK_MoD_Manual_of_Security_Volumes_1%2C_2_and_3_
  Issue_2%2C_JSP-440%2C_RESTRICTED%2C_2389_pages%2C_2001

The JSP 440[11] consisted of over 2300 pages.

For almost a decade, I would continue to develop my knowledge and skillsets, applying the principles and guidance from the JSP 440 in the protection of the military's mission-critical assets.

It is worth noting that throughout the circa 2300 pages of the JSP 440 *(dated October 2001)*, there is not a single mention of the term "Cyber" or "Cybersecurity."

- **Cyber**[12]

- *word-forming element, ultimately from cybernetics (q.v.).*

  - *It enjoyed explosive use with the rise of the internet early 1990s.*

However, despite the omission of these terms, the military were still able to safeguard their mission-critical assets through volumes 1, 2, and 3 (as depicted in Figure 1-10).

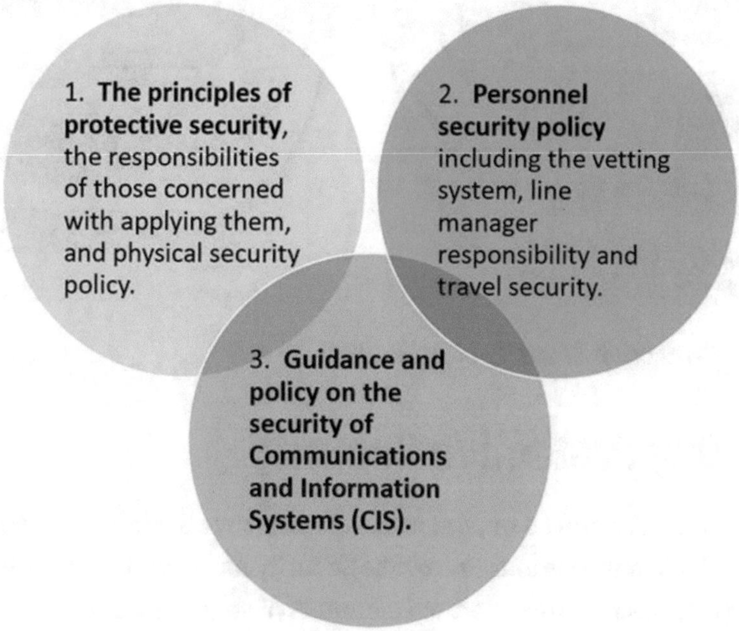

1. **The principles of protective security,** the responsibilities of those concerned with applying them, and physical security policy.

2. **Personnel security policy** including the vetting system, line manager responsibility and travel security.

3. **Guidance and policy on the security of Communications and Information Systems (CIS).**

Figure 1-10. *Components of the JSP 440*

[11]https://file.wikileaks.org/file/uk-mod-jsp-440-2001.pdf
[12]www.etymonline.com/search?q=cyber

Volume 1 – Protective Security

The JSP 440 started by providing guidance on how an establishment should be safeguarding its critical assets, which are essential to the mission statement. The content of the Protective Security section consisted of 14 subsections (as depicted in Figure 1-11).

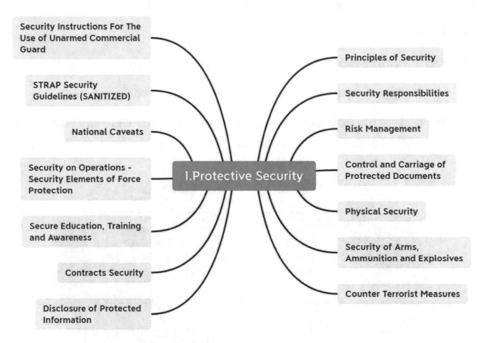

Figure 1-11. *Protective Security components*

Modern-Day Protective Security

Much as technology has moved on, the world of Protective Security has evolved, and should you look at the various Protective Security frameworks, you will find that Protective Security has now incorporated elements of volumes 2 and 3.

For example:

- **UK Protective Security Management Systems**[13] (as depicted in Figure 1-12)

---

[13]www.cpni.gov.uk/system/files/documents/55/90/PSeMS_Guidance_Checklist_Case_ Studies_November_2018.pdf

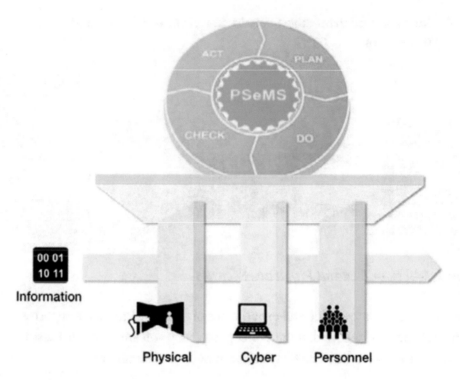

Figure 1-12. *UK Protective Security*

- **Australian Protective Security Framework**[14] (as depicted in Figure 1-13)

Governance

Each entity manages security risks and supports a positive security culture in an appropriately mature manner ensuring: clear lines of accountability, sound planning, investigation and response, assurance and review processes, and proportionate reporting.

Read more...

Information security

Each entity maintains the confidentiality, integrity and availability of all official information.

Read more...

Personnel security

Each entity ensures its employees and contractors are suitable to access Australian Government resources, and meet an appropriate standard of integrity and honesty.

Read more...

Physical security

Each entity provides a safe and secure physical environment for their people, information and assets.

Read more...

Figure 1-13. *Australian Protective Security*

---

[14]www.protectivesecurity.gov.au/

- **New Zealand Protective Security Requirements**[15] (as depicted in Figure 1-14)

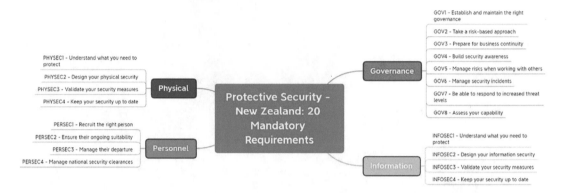

Figure 1-14. *New Zealand Protective Security*

Based upon my knowledge and experiences of applying Protective Security principles, I strongly believe that this concept can help you and your business to formulate more effective defenses against your ever-present threats.

Transitioning from Military Service

Finally, I hope that through reading this book you may glean a better insight into what life in the service is like and gain a better impression of the values and skillsets that military service leavers bring with them.

There is a saying:

You can take the person out of the military, but you will never take the military out of the person.

And why would you want to remove those unique experiences and skillsets that can only ever be gained through military service?

Military veterans are highly adaptable, resilient, and resourceful, which can prove to be invaluable to most businesses. They are quick to learn and are quick to see opportunities, where many might see these as impregnable barriers. They leave military service with enhanced training and experiences, which are directly transferable to many businesses.

---

[15]https://protectivesecurity.govt.nz/about-the-psr/overview/

Their adaptability, resilience, and leadership skills can be extremely beneficial in helping influence and guide others within your company.

Please do not just look at military service leavers as being ex-members of a "war machine" but as an asset, which has received exceptional levels of investment that could potentially give an organization or business an edge over competitors.

I must confess that although I was ready for a new challenge and thought that I was fully ready to leave the military service, the transition came as a huge shock to my system and is something that I struggle with.

Life outside of the military service can be an extremely challenging and isolating experience. Unless you have experienced life in the military, it is awfully hard to understand how different this life can be.

I get that! As a business leader or senior manager, how can you appreciate the benefits a military service leaver might bring to your business and how are these skills transferable to your company?

After reflecting on my career, I am shocked at how far I have come and how much I have changed, since joining the Royal Air Force. Even more astonishing for me is how many of these unique experiences and skillsets gained through my 22 years of military service have been so beneficial during almost a decade in the corporate sector.

Imagine how frustrating it might be to try and convey these exceptional qualities into a two-page curriculum vitae (CV)/resume? Every military service leaver will have gained different qualities through their distinct roles and sometimes extraordinary situations that they may have faced.

For me, my military career turned out to be something completed different to my initial aspirations of becoming an RAF Police dog handler. However, life was not always a "bed of roses" and, at times, life could be particularly demanding; I faced situations and experiences that I could never have imagined but that could only have ever happened because I had taken up a career in the RAF Police.

For example, can you ever imagine the following situations occurring outside of military life?

After many years of being involved in practical exercises where aircraft crashes were simulated, which were deigned to help adequately prepare us to respond to such an event happening. Then, late one October morning, I would be going about delivering my daily counter intelligence duties, when I would receive that call which we never wished to receive.

A private light aircraft had needed to use the RAF airfield to make an emergency landing, after getting into difficulties. However, as the aircraft made its approach to land on the runway, as the wheels had touched down, the throttle had become stuck in the open position. As a result, the aircraft had overshot the runway and had flipped over onto its roof in an adjacent farmer's field (just outside the perimeter fence).

Immediately, the RAF station's emergency services team's incident response drills kicked in. The fire and ambulance service responding to deal with any occupants of the plane, whilst the RAF Police cleared the route to the downed aircraft and established a secure cordon. In this incident, miraculously, the pilot walked away from this incident with only minor cuts and bruises.

Another unexpected incident happened to me during my first counter intelligence field team (CIFT) deployment to Afghanistan. Not long after starting our normal duties, my colleague and I were called in to speak with the Force Protection commanding officer. On arrival, we were briefed about a sensitive incident that had occurred, during the previous night, and which needed our assistance.

An unidentified local national had been accidentally killed by an escalation drill's ricocheted warning shot. As we had established highly commendable engagements with the local nationals, the commanding officer wanted us to handle the arrangements to sensitively return the deceased to their family.

However, the first thing we had to do was to identify the deceased and to confirm whether he had any insurgent or terrorist associations. This could only be achieved through biometric scanning, which involved us having to go to the morgue and having to retina and fingerprint scan the deceased.

There was no record of any insurgent or terrorist associations, and we were able to identify him from his personal effects. The next day, we would spend all day liaising with the family of the deceased to ensure that the deceased could be returned safely and with sensitivity.

These are just some of the examples of some of the unique situations that members of the military are trained to deal with and which prove difficult qualities to translate across to the corporate world.

Despite my long and rewarding RAF Police career, I have learned that my knowledge needs to be continually refreshed. Consequently, I am constantly learning from the experiences of my peers, adding to my professional reading library (as detailed in the Bibliography), and attending various learning courses, while taking the opportunity to learn from successful people from the business.

In fact, I have encountered individuals who have failed to appreciate the unique qualities and experiences I brought to their business. I can recall one individual who really did not understand me and who rejected nearly everything that I recommended and was completely defensive of every observation. Nearly every day became a battle, when all I was trying to do was make improvements and to ensure that the key stakeholders were fully informed as to the risks.

Note   Notwithstanding that the intentions of most of my security industry peers are for the protection of the company that employs them, many of them still face similar problems to the ones that I faced. This is more often the case when the reporting chain does not allow for independence (e.g., reporting into the Head of IT), the strategy is not aligned to the business context, or the business value is not appreciated.

However, despite all these barriers, I struggled on for approximately 18 months. Then, having just returned from lunch (with my line manager), I was called into Human Resources. Here, I was met by a member of Human Resources and my line manager to be informed that my role was being made redundant.

The letter of redundancy cited the European Union general data protection regulation (EU GDPR) as the reason for making the role redundant.

Although confused as to the rationale behind this business decision, as I was the organization's only Information Security specialist and a major component is the need for security, resilience, and data protection (as depicted in Figure 1-15[16]), I was relieved that my line manager battles wouldn't need to continue.

---

[16]https://gdpr-info.eu/

Article 5: Principles relating to processing of personal data

(f) processed in a manner that ensures appropriate **security** of the personal data, including protection against unauthorised or unlawful processing and against accidental loss, destruction or damage, using appropriate technical or organisational measures ('integrity and confidentiality').

Art. 32: Security of processing

1.   Taking into account the state of the art, the costs of implementation and the nature, scope, context and purposes of processing as well as the risk of varying likelihood and severity for the rights and freedoms of natural persons, the controller and the processor shall implement appropriate technical and organisational measures to ensure a level of **security** appropriate to the risk, including inter alia as appropriate:

(a) the pseudonymisation and encryption of personal data;

(b) the ability to ensure the ongoing confidentiality, integrity, availability and resilience of processing systems and services;

(c) the ability to restore the availability and access to personal data in a timely manner in the event of a physical or technical incident;

(d) a process for regularly testing, assessing and evaluating the effectiveness of technical and organisational measures for ensuring the **security** of the processing.

2.   In assessing the appropriate level of **security** account shall be taken in particular of the risks that are presented by processing, in particular from accidental or unlawful destruction, loss, alteration, unauthorised disclosure of, or access to personal data transmitted, stored or otherwise processed.

Figure 1-15.   *Extract from EU GDPR*

And Finally…

The use of autoethnographic research, in this book, has made this something of a personal one for me.

The book is firmly rooted in the experiences I have had throughout my military service life and how they shaped me.

I have included an appendix, where I provide a recap of my journey. I hope this will provide an interesting insight for those who are interested in experiencing what military life is like and for my security professional peers (who also come into this field from a military background), and I hope you will be able to appreciate how some of my experiences will mirror your own.

Additionally, for those business key stakeholders, I hope that by reading this book you will gain a greater appreciation of the unique skillsets *(something to be embraced rather than seen as an enigma)* that service leaders can bring to your organization.

Whether you are from a military background or not, I hope that you find the content and insights helpful in learning a little more about the term "Protective Security."

When I set out to author this book, unhelpfully, I thought that there were a variety of different interpretations of the term "Protective Security" and that if you search Wikipedia for this term, you would only find a redirect to Bodyguard (as depicted in Figure 1-16[17]), "Protective Security Command,"[18] "Protective Security Units,"[19] or "Protective Security Officer" *(note that this takes you to a police community support officer (PCSO) reference[20] (which is something completely different)).*

Figure 1-16. *"Protective Security" wiki search*

Consequently, as well as authoring this book, I also decided to try and author an appropriate reference for Wikipedia. A copy of the draft can be seen on the Wikitia website (as depicted in Figure 1-17[21]).

---

[17]https://en.wikipedia.org/wiki/Bodyguard
[18]https://en.wikipedia.org/wiki/Protective_Security_Command
[19]https://en.wikipedia.org/wiki/Protective_security_units
[20]https://en.wikipedia.org/wiki/Police_community_support_officer#Australia
[21]https://wikitia.com/wiki/Protective_Security

Figure 1-17. *Wikitia – Protective Security*

During the research for this book, I developed the BRIDGES acronym (as depicted in Figure 1-18), which helps to convey the key components of Protective Security and how they relate to each other.

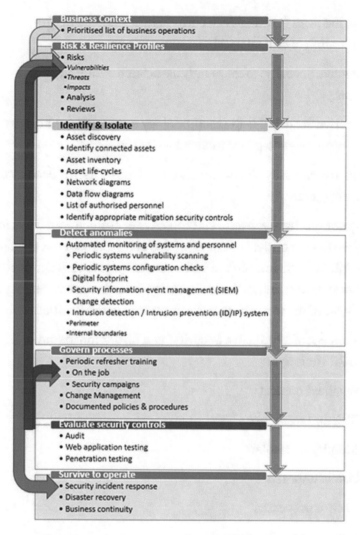

Figure 1-18. *BRIDGES acronym*

Key Takeaways

- The security industry has lapsed into "buzz" terms, such as Cybersecurity, resilience, and so on, whereas Protective Security is an all-encompassing term.

- The term "Protective Security" is an umbrella term, where the focus is around the proportionate protection of business valued assets, to bring the risks to within acceptable tolerances.

- Often, the term "Protective Security" is associated with the safeguarding of critical national infrastructure.

- "Protective Security" is frequently associated with Bodyguard services.

- "Protective Security" is the methodology used by the military to proportionately safeguard their valued assets.

- "Protective Security" incorporates all the "buzz" terms used by the corporate sector.

- Many nations have introduced Protective Security frameworks for the safeguarding of critical national infrastructures. However, the same principles can be introduced within the corporate environment to help ensure that proportionate security measures are implemented to safeguard those assets that are important to the business.

- The concept of "Protective Security" can be demonstrated using the **BRIDGES** acronym:

  - **B**usiness context

  - **R**isk and resilience

  - **I**dentify and isolate

  - **D**etect anomalies

  - **G**overn processes

  - **E**valuate security controls

  - **S**urvive to operate

CHAPTER 2

What Is Protective Security (PS)?

Courage is the greatest of all virtues, for without it there are no other virtues.... Anyone can be brave for five minutes. You will not only be braver than the men you lead; you will be brave for longer.

As a Leader, you will go on being brave when others falter; brave not only in danger, but brave in hardship, in loneliness and, perhaps most difficult of all, in those long periods of inactivity, of boredom that come at times to all soldiers. In failure, too, you will show your courage.

We can all be brave when we are winning. I'm a hell of a General when everybody is whooping along, and the enemy is on the run. But you won't always be winning. If you have ever been a British General at the start of a war you would know what I mean.

You'll find some day when things are bad, whether you're the Commanding General or the Platoon Commander, there will come a sudden pause when your men stop and look at you. No one will speak; they will just look at you and ask, dumbly, for leadership.

Their courage is ebbing; you must make it flow back – and it is not easy. You will never have felt more alone in your life!

Field Marshal Viscount William Slim of Burma

Chief of the Imperial Staff

Governor General of Australia, 1953

From Courage and Other Broadcasts, 1957

© Jim Seaman 2021
J. Seaman, *Protective Security*, https://doi.org/10.1007/978-1-4842-6908-4_2

Figure 2-1. *Uncle Bill[1]*

Introduction

It may seem strange to be referencing a famous quote, regarding courage, when introducing the topic of Protective Security. However, courage comes in two types – physical and moral.

Moral courage is not so easy.

Moral courage in Protective Security (and its everyday application) requires the insistence on the prompt and willful adherence to the policies and procedures, and with this being the heart of an effective Protective Security program.

As a Digital Business, you will employ appropriate technologies to help develop new value within your business models, customer experiences, and the internal capabilities that support your core operations. This includes both digital-only brands and the more traditional businesses that are seeking to transform their organization with innovative digital technologies.

As a result, you will increasingly have assets that are deemed to be valuable to these digital operations and need to be adequately protected, and these assets might be external (e.g., in the cloud), internal (e.g., on premise), virtual, or physical. The modern digital business will be increasingly attractive to opportunist criminals and must ensure that all their attack vectors (as depicted in Figure 2-2) are adequately protected.

Figure 2-2 shows the potential opportunities that criminals will look to exploit, to enable the infiltration of a business' operations/environment and the exfiltration of sensitive data.

---

[1] www.business-live.co.uk/retail-consumer/new-book-reveals-financial-problems-5818911

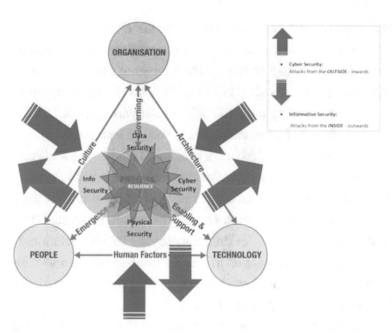

Figure 2-2. *Attack vectors*

Additionally, this shows the holistic elements that contribute to an effective Protective Security strategy, incorporating multiple popular "Buzz" terms that are often used within the security industry.

The criminals will look for holes or misalignments in an organization's integrated security programs, identifying opportunities in poor governance practices, misconfigured technologies, or bad practices.

One such, real-life, example of this happened to me and my team during a deployment to RAFO Thumrait, in support of Operation Enduring Freedom.

Military Example

At the start of February 2002, approximately 5 weeks into my detachment to RAFO Thumrait, I was in mid-shift cycle *(having completed 2-day shifts)* and was a couple of hours into my first night shift of that set of shifts.

It was approximately 2230 hours when I was manning the RAF Police Operations desk, alone within the RAF Police Portacabin. All was peaceful, with my shift colleagues busy manning static and mobile posts but not having any issues that they needed to deal with at that time.

Suddenly, this peace was interrupted by a loud knock on the Portacabin door. I shouted for them to come in and out of the darkness from outside; into the lights from the Portacabin, I saw a high-ranking officer wearing a flying suit. Out of respect for the officer, I immediately stood up from my chair and brought myself to attention. The officer identified himself as being the officer commanding (OC) the tactical airlift command element (TALCE) before telling me to relax. He appeared to be extremely agitated and anxious, so I proceeded to ask him how I could be of assistance to him.

I could not have predicted his response. He went on to inform me that the UK Prime Minister had tasked him to make four of his Hercules C130J aircraft available to transport hundreds of Afghanistan nationals from Kabul to Mecca, in support of their pilgrimage.[2]

In the events leading up to this tasking, the minister for civil aviation, Dr Abdul Rahman, had been beaten and stabbed to death while in a public area within Kabul airport.[3] Initially, this murder had been blamed on the pilgrims who had been having to have extended waits for their flights to Mecca.

Remember that this task came less than 6 months since the Al Qaeda had hijacked domestic aircraft and flown them into the World Trade Center and the Pentagon in the United States.

Clearly, OC TALCE was extremely concerned about the safety of his aircraft and his aircrew personnel. Consequently, he requested the RAF Police to provide air transport security (ATSy) and Air Marshal support for this task.

Now, none of the deployed RAF Police personnel had ever been tasked to carry out such a mission before, and none of the deployment training had prepared any of us for such a request, and, added to this, the RAF Police had just had a change of senior management *(the incumbent Flight Sergeant just happened to be my Flight Sergeant from the United Kingdom (RAF Linton-On-Ouse)).*

> *Although this tasking was not guaranteed to go ahead, as the senior rank on shift that night, I immediately started planning a strategy that would help minimize the risk to the aircraft, aircrew, my RAF Police colleagues, and of course to myself.*

---

[2] www.theguardian.com/world/2002/feb/18/september11.afghanistan

[3] www.afghanistan-analysts.org/en/reports/war-and-peace/
the-start-of-impunity-the-killing-of-dr-abdul-rahman/

Now, the OC TALCE had requested that each aircraft be manned by two members of the RAF Police, for each leg of the flights (*two manning the flight from Kabul, Afghanistan, to Seeb, Oman, and two manning the flight from Seeb, Oman, to Mecca, Saudi Arabia*). This could prove to be a significant problem, given that the entire RAF Police detachment, in Thumrait, at that time consisted of only 15 personnel, and we still needed to be able to provide an effective Protective Security contingent to safeguard all the other critical military assets.

I was able to make all the required plans, including the commandeering of a mobile Rapiscan X-ray machine (which was being loaded onto an aircraft in Thumrait to return to the United Kingdom) and redeploying it to Kabul airfield. I and one other would fly out on the first aircraft to set up the passenger processing operation and to process every passenger before they board the RAF Hercules aircraft (as depicted in Figure 2-3[4]).

Figure 2-3. *Sensitive airlift*

---

[4]www.iwm.org.uk/collections/item/object/205217163

Unlike the processing of passengers for standard military flights, this was an extremely high-risk engagement, and, as such, the processes needed to be enhanced to ensure that it was proportionate to meet this higher threat.

Regarding the RAF Police personnel limitations, I had the idea of taking half the RAFO Thumrait RAF Police detachment and utilizing personnel from the other Omani RAF Police detachment at RAFO Seeb. With my strategic approach in mind, I sought the counsel of my immediate supervisor (Flight Sergeant), as I would need his approval and for him to reach out for the support from the Seeb detachment.

The strategy was approved, and I and seven others, from the RAFO Thumrait detachment, were put on standby for this mission *(nicknamed "Operation Certain Death")*. With the strategy agreed, I completed the rest of that night shift and on returning to the shift tent accommodation prepared my "Go Bergen,[5]" as I waited for the "Go, No Go!"

As you can imagine, the nervousness and anticipation meant that it took many hours before I managed to get any sleep, after that night shift. However, after what seemed like only an hour or two of sleep, we received the news that this mission had been given the green light. That very same night, under the cover of darkness, my seven other team members and I would be boarding the first outbound Hercules aircraft (as depicted in Figure 2-4[6]) for Seeb and then onward to the Kabul airfield. On arrival at Seeb, we met the other members of the RAF Police detachment who would be joining the mission.

---

[5]A packed military issue bag, with all the clothing and equipment needed for this task (aka Jump Bag).
[6]www.eliteukforces.info/air-support/47-Squadron/

Figure 2-4. *C-130J Cockpit*

We all received our mission briefing, and I divided us up into teams of two and allocated the teams to aircraft 1 to 4. The first outbound aircraft would have onboard the first pair who had been allocated the Air Marshal responsibilities for the first leg flight (Kabul to Seeb) and me and another experienced ATSy RAF Police from the Seeb detachment. My team would remain in Kabul to supervise the setting up of the passenger processing facility, processing the passenger for all four flights, to ensure that no potential hazardous items *(whether accidentally or deliberately)* could be taken onto the aircraft.

As we flew from Seeb to Kabul, the nearer we got to our destination, the greater the levels of anxiety grew. Beyond the constant sound and throbbing of the aircraft engines, I'm sure that I could hear the sounds of unknown items glancing off the body of the aircraft – perhaps even so low that we were clipping the tops of trees.

As we got closer to the final approach, we received our disembarkation briefing. As soon as the rear doors opened, we were to sprint down the loading ramp and to get some distance from the aircraft *(avoiding running off the hard surface, as there was a high risk of unexploded ordnance in the softer ground)*, as the large aircraft presented an easy target for opportunist rocket-propelled grenade (RPG) attacks.

We got the signal to don our helmets and body armor, then everything went pitch black, the aircraft suddenly raised its nose, the engines made a loud roar, and then the aircraft made an extremely aggressive descent, with the aircraft accelerating and the engines getting louder and louder. Seconds later, the aircraft abruptly leveled out, the engines appeared to almost fall silent, and with a hard jolt the aircraft had touched down on the runway. The interior instantly became dimly illuminated, the engines roared to slow the aircraft, and almost instantly the aircraft had ground to a halt.

Next, the tailgate started to open *(this could easily have been likened to emerging from Herman Melville's Moby Dick)*, and past the aircraft's dim interior lights, I could make out the faint indications of movement as a sea of blackness. Even before the tailgate had fully opened, the aircrew were instructing us to move. The adrenaline started to increase, and the muscles became flooded with newly oxygenated blood. I felt like a race horse waiting for the stall door to open. Even before the tailgate was fully down, completely disoriented and almost blind from the lack of light, we sprinted out of the plane into this expansive dark abyss of nothingness. All we could hope was that there would be someone there to assist and instruct us where we should go. Once we had vacated the tailgate, we were like grains of rice being dropped from a cup, from a great height – erratically, we'd run in all different directions! Fortunately, the groundcrew were well versed in seeing this happen and were there to herd us all back to safety!

Seconds later, the receiving ground staff managed to collect all the spilled contents of the aircraft and to instruct us on a safe place to go. One of my first thoughts I remember was feeling the distinctly different feel of Kabul's winter air –5C (23F), the icy cold chill stinging against the exposed skin of my face – the polar opposite to the temperature inside the aircraft or my experiences from the previous 5 weeks at Thumrait, where the average temperatures would be an average of 28C (82F) in the daytime and a pleasant 14C (57F) during the nights.

While out in the open, everything remained virtually pitch black, so we carefully followed the instructions from the resident groundcrew. Before long, we were to enter the relative safety and comfort of a nearby building. Here, we immediately set about organizing the passenger processing, ensuring that we had a defined filter between the unprocessed (untrusted), in-process, and postprocess (trusted) passengers and that no one could move between these segmented environments.

Having established the passenger processing topology and drinking a couple of paper cups worth of hot steaming, strong, black coffee, we started the process of sanitizing the Afghani passengers, ready for them to board the first aircraft. Now, although many were very elderly males, there were a handful of younger passengers traveling on the aircraft, and so we had to be especially vigilant for the presence of items that might present a threat to the aircraft and aircrew. Additionally, many of these passengers may never have flown on an aircraft *(especially not a military aircraft)* and may not have been through passenger processing before. Consequently, many dangerous or suspicious items were confiscated from these passengers (e.g., small mystery glass vials, such as depicted in Figure 2-5[7]).

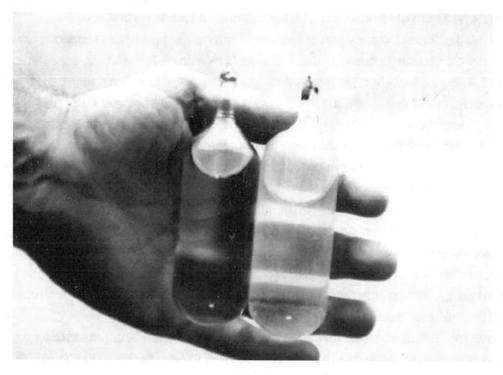

Figure 2-5. *Mystery glass vials*

---

[7]www.thefirearmblog.com/blog/2014/02/27/kgb-afgan-refugees-mystery-glass-vials/

After a short period of time, we had examined all the passengers' carry-on and hold baggage and searched the passengers to ensure that they were not in possession of any contraband items, so that they could board the first departing C-130J aircraft *(accompanied by two of my RAF Police colleagues)*. This process was repeated for the next three aircraft but with the final aircraft having my colleague and I onboard, as their Air Marshal detail. However, time pressures were on us, as all four aircraft needed to have all the passengers processed and boarded, enabling all the aircraft to depart under the cover of darkness.

Finally, we were ready, and I boarded the final aircraft prior to the passengers so that I was placed between them and the flight deck. My colleague joined after the final passenger had boarded and taken their seats, sitting at the back of the craft nearer to the tailgate and maintaining a line of sight, diagonally across from me.

Very soon, everybody was securely aboard, and our aircraft was ready to depart. The departure was a reverse of our arrival, and in the complete darkness and still of the night and after a short transit to the runway, the pilot put the engines to full throttle, and, seemingly, he put the Hercules C-130J aircraft into an almost vertical takeoff.

Initially, during the early part of the flight, many of the passengers remained anxious, impatient, and restless, meaning that I needed to remain on full alert. However, soon after the aircrew had given the passengers something to eat and drink, they had all fallen asleep, and even I was struggling to keep my eyes open in the heavy and hot onboard atmosphere. In order to help me keep awake, I decided to get up and move around a little, but eventually even I would succumb to the sleep demon, dropping in and out of conscious. It turns out that the aircrew had decided, for safety reasons, that they would reduce the oxygen levels and increase the temperature of the air.

Anyhow, we completed the flight, handing over the aircraft and passenger responsibilities to the next crew and RAF Police, for the second leg. This exercise was repeated again the next day, and by the end it was deemed to be a successful mission, meeting the political objectives and the aircrew goals, safely getting the passengers to their destination, and ensuring that these mission-critical assets were able to return to fulfil their primary mission.

The conclusion of this task resulted in the RAF Police team being awarded a Provost Marshal's commendation, in recognition for all their efforts (as shown in Figure 2-6).

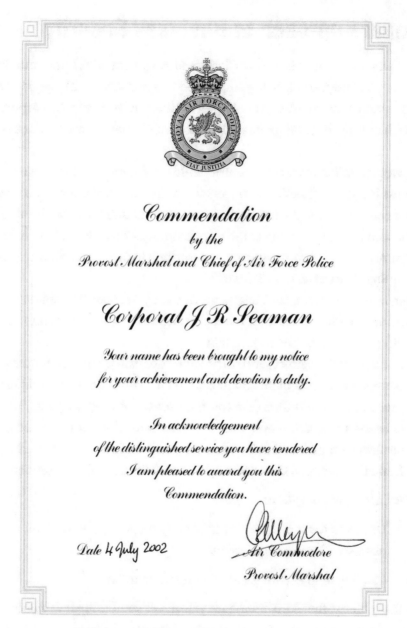

Figure 2-6. *Provost Marshal Commendation*

It is experiences such as this, and others, that have helped me to appreciate the value of Protective Security and how this might be translated across for the benefit of today's digital business.

Traditional Approach to Business Security

Since 2005, I was spending every other Christmas away in hostile, hot, sandy, and dusty environments, so in July 2011 (having completed 22+ years' service) I decided to turn the page and start a new chapter in my life – transitioning across to the corporate sector. Believe me when I say that both personally and professionally this is not as easy as it sounds.

Having worked in the Protective Security industry for more than 22 years, I struggled to get business leaders and senior managers to understand and appreciate just what these 22 years entailed, and still to this day, I'm sure that many will not be able to comprehend and appreciate some of the responsibilities that came with this. This is clearly a common experience, as succinctly described in Jason McAdam's LinkedIn article "Civvy Street: Survive, then Thrive."[8]

However, one of the greatest struggles for me, early on, was the apparent apathy I saw from business leaders and senior managers regarding them understanding the value of safeguarding their critical business assets.

Surely, it should make perfect sense to provide adequate protection for those assets that your business is most reliant on and those, which if compromised, could have the greatest impact on the organization (aka common sense). However, instead, I hear and see instances where such leaders only want to do the bare minimum they need, often relying on the term "compliant" and focusing on nuances of Protective Security (e.g., Cyber Security, Information Security, Data Security, Network Security, Cyber Resilience, etc.):

- **Definition of compliant**

    - Disposed to agree with others or obey rules, especially to an excessive degree; acquiescent

    - Meeting or in accordance with rules or standards

Within the military, the word compliant was never something that would be used in association with the protection of mission-critical/essential assets.

---

[8]www.linkedin.com/pulse/civvy-street-survive-thrive-jason-mcadam/?trackingId=KFg3aN rFQpGzaoxTROe1dw%3D%3D

Consequently, I would like to provide business leaders and senior managers with an alternative approach, which has often been associated with the protection of National Infrastructure.

Protective Security

This concept of Protective Security is defined[9] as being

The organized system of defensive measures instituted and maintained at all levels of command with the aim of achieving and maintaining security.

The term is often associated with the protection of National Infrastructures; however, I believe that the same principles can be applied in support of enhanced business protection. Consequently, the concept of Protective Security incorporates the elements from all the commonly used nuances:

- **Cyber Security**[10] – The ability to protect or defend the use of cyberspace from cyber-attacks

- **Information Security**[11] – The protection of information and information systems from unauthorized access, use, disclosure, disruption, modification, or destruction to provide confidentiality, integrity, and availability

- **Cyber Resiliency**[12] – The ability to anticipate, withstand, recover from, and adapt to adverse conditions, stresses, attacks, or compromises on systems that use or are enabled by cyber resources

Additionally, this has been developed through my military experiences and training as well as through an alignment with several respected resources (e.g., Centre for the

---

[9]www.thefreedictionary.com/protective+security#:~:text=The%20organized%20system%20 of%20defensive,See%20also%20physical%20security%3B%20security.
[10]https://csrc.nist.gov/glossary/term/Cyber_Security
[11]https://csrc.nist.gov/glossary/term/information_security
[12]https://csrc.nist.gov/glossary/term/cyber_resiliency

Protection of National Infrastructure (CPNI),[13] MI5,[14] International Organization for Standardization (ISO),[15] Australian Government,[16] New Zealand Government,[17] etc.).

The Protective Security concept being to focused on what assets are deemed important to the business and then applying proportionate defensive measures to help ensure that the risk and resilience profiles (as depicted in Figure 2-7[18]) remain within the organization's tolerances.

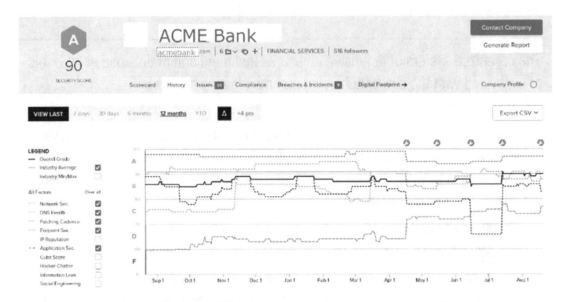

Figure 2-7. *Risk and resilience profile*

To help explain this concept, I have developed the acronym **BRIDGES** (as shown in Figure 2-8) to explain the elements that come together to help an organization apply adequate defenses, in defense of their valued assets. Remembering that rarely are two businesses the same, this approach will need to be adapted to suit each individual organization.

---

[13]www.cpni.gov.uk/advice

[14]www.mi5.gov.uk/what-we-do

[15]www.isotc292online.org/

[16]www.protectivesecurity.gov.au/resources/Pages/relevant-australian-and-international-standards.aspx

[17]https://protectivesecurity.govt.nz/

[18]assistance@cyberrescue.co.uk

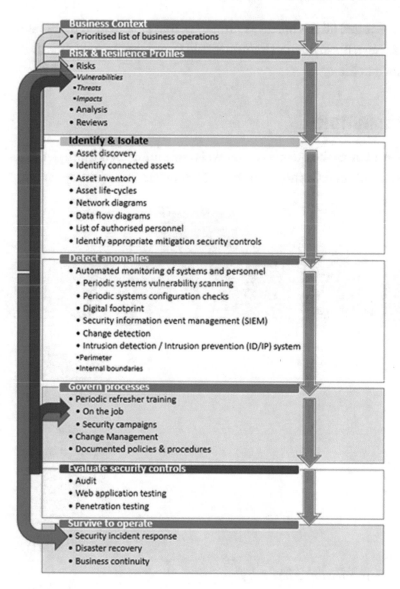

Business Context
- Prioritised list of business operations

Risk & Resilience Profiles
- Risks
  - *Vulnerabilities*
  - *Threats*
  - *Impacts*
- Analysis
- Reviews

Identify & Isolate
- Asset discovery
- Identify connected assets
- Asset inventory
- Asset life-cycles
- Network diagrams
- Data flow diagrams
- List of authorised personnel
- Identify appropriate mitigation security controls

Detect anomalies
- Automated monitoring of systems and personnel
  - Periodic systems vulnerability scanning
  - Periodic systems configuration checks
  - Digital footprint
  - Security information event management (SIEM)
  - Change detection
  - Intrusion detection / Intrusion prevention (ID/IP) system
  - Perimeter
  - Internal boundaries

Govern processes
- Periodic refresher training
  - On the job
  - Security campaigns
- Change Management
- Documented policies & procedures

Evaluate security controls
- Audit
- Web application testing
- Penetration testing

Survive to operate
- Security incident response
- Disaster recovery
- Business continuity

Figure 2-8. *BRIDGES*

Business Context

This is your starting point, where input is needed from key stakeholders as to what they believe is important to the business and which of the company's processes would be the most impactful on the organization, in the event they are compromised as the result of a deliberate or accidental action.

Having identified all the business processes that are deemed to be valuable to the organization, next, these need to be prioritized in order of importance and agreed upon by the key stakeholders.

Military Example

In the Royal Air Force, the business context is communicated through the defined mission statements and Group, Station, and Squadron roles (as depicted in Figure 2-9).

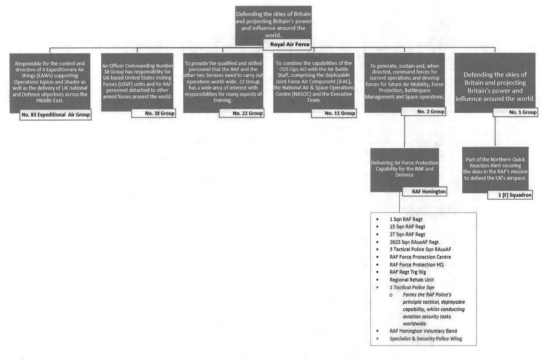

Figure 2-9. *RAF mission hierarchy*

Each of the RAF elements has assigned missions and roles that support the overall RAF mission.[19]

As a business, there should be similar interactions between the various departments, each with their own missions, values, and objectives that are designed to support the success of the business. Where a business department is impacted in being able to fulfil these objectives, then this will represent a potential risk to the operational effectiveness of the business.

Risk and Resilience Profile

Taking each of these processes, by order of priority, the objective of this element is to create an initial baseline for risks (inherent) and resilience. This is the starting point, where an organization can start to understand their risk and resilience profiles.

These profiles will remain live and will need to be reevaluated in response to any significant changes or situational developments. The NIST SP800-37 *(Risk Management Framework for Information Systems and Organizations: A System Life Cycle Approach for Security and Privacy)*[20] provides authoritative guidance for risk management and, at Appendix F of the document, describes a significant change as being

---

A significant change is defined as a change that is likely to substantively affect the security or privacy posture of a system. Significant changes to a system that may trigger an event-driven authorization action may include, but are not limited to:

- Installation of a new or upgraded operating system, middleware component, or application;

- Modifications to system ports, protocols, or services;

- Installation of a new or upgraded hardware platform;

- Modifications to how information, including PII, is processed;

- Modifications to cryptographic modules or services; or

- Modifications to security and privacy controls.

---

[20]https://csrc.nist.gov/CSRC/media/Publications/sp/800-37/rev-2/draft/documents/ sp800-37r2-draft-fpd.pdf

Significant changes to the environment of operation that may trigger an event-driven authorization action may include, but are not limited to:

- Moving to a new facility;

- Adding new core missions or business functions;

- Acquiring specific and credible threat information that the organization is being targeted by a threat source; or

- Establishing new/modified laws, directives, policies, or regulations.

When creating the resilience profile, it is important to understand the factors that may impact the resilience of a business process or asset ability to bounce back, as per NIST's definition of resilience[21]:

The ability to maintain required capability in the face of adversity.

The ability to prepare for and adapt to changing conditions and withstand and recover rapidly from disruption.

Resilience includes the ability to withstand and recover from deliberate attacks, accidents, or naturally occurring threats or incidents.

---

[21]https://csrc.nist.gov/glossary/term/resilience#:~:text=The%20ability%20to%20
maintain%20required%20capability%20in%20the%20face%20of%20adversity.&text=2%20
%5BSuperseded%5D%20INCOSE14-,The%20ability%20to%20prepare%20for%20and%20adapt%20
to%20changing%20conditions,naturally%20occurring%20threats%20or%20incidents.

As depicted in the CPNI's diagram (Figure 2-10[22]), risk management for Protective Security involves eight defined steps.

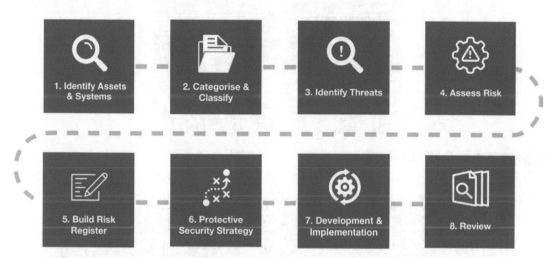

Figure 2-10. *CPNI risk management process*

Military Comparison

The RAF's Hawk T1 (as depicted in Figure 2-11[23]) and Hawk T2 (as depicted in Figure 2-12) training aircraft has a less critical role in the service. However, depending on where it is operating, when deployed on an overseas training exercise, it might be deemed to have a higher risk profile, based upon the associations of the use of this aircraft, by other countries, in a fighter role.[24]

---

[22]www.cpni.gov.uk/rmm/protective-security-risk-management

[23]www.raf.mod.uk/aircraft/hawk-t1/

[24]www.airforce-technology.com/projects/hawk/

Figure 2-11. *RAF Hawk T1*

Figure 2-12. *RAF Hawk T2*

Consequently, local environmental factors might increase the threat to these aircraft when overseas.

If you think of this in terms of your business assets, are there local considerations which could impact the risk value of an asset?

- For example, where you have a "Flat Network," where connected assets could impact your most sensitive business assets, are these deemed as a higher category asset?

Do you consider the aggregation principle, where several lower classified assets[25] are in the same region/area, so that if that region/area was to be compromised, the impact on the business objectives by the collective could be greater?

- This would likely result in the local considerations being a factor for a lower-value asset being deemed as a higher category item.

Identify and Isolate

Every asset has a value to the *business (or to the opportunist criminal)*, can have an aggregated value, or can impact a more valued asset. Consequently, it is essential that each department is aware of their assets and their value to the business. Without this, it is virtually impossible to correctly identify the proportionate defensive measures needed to appropriately reduce the risk and resilience profiles.

Take, for instance, the scenario of a frontline battle unit. They need to be able to defend a military base or attack the enemy and consequently require operational weapon systems (as depicted in Figure 2-13[26]), but which assets would need to be protected?

- The weapon system itself?

- The ammunition?

- The ammunition magazines?

- The optical sighting system?

- The spare parts?

- The correct lubrication oils?

- The weapon cleaning kit *(maintenance)*?

---

[25]https://assets.publishing.service.gov.uk/government/uploads/system/uploads/attachment_data/file/715778/May-2018_Government-Security-Classifications-2.pdf
[26]http://armamentresearch.com/british-enfield-sa80-part-5-sa80-a1vsa2/

Figure 2-13. *L85A2 (SA80)*

Each of these items, if compromised, could potentially impact the operational effectiveness of this weapon.

Once you have identified and categorized the assets for importance, it might be appropriate to isolate some of the higher-value assets and processes from the less important assets.

NIST[27] defines an asset as being

A major application, general support system, high impact program, physical plant, mission critical system, personnel, equipment, or a logically related group of systems.

---

[27]https://csrc.nist.gov/glossary/term/asset#:~:text=NIST%20SP%20800%2D160%20
under,achieve%20organizational%20mission%2Fbusiness%20objectives.

Military Example

In the military, you will see that every military establishment has a segmented architecture to reduce the risks and to restrict the movements between the lower-value and higher-value environments. You wouldn't expect anyone, just based on being a member of the military, to be able to have uncontrolled access into an armory and weapon store or to be able to just walk straight up to any frontline, mission-critical, aircraft (as depicted in Figure 2-14[28]).

Figure 2-14. *Camp Bastion segmented architecture*

The same should apply to your business environments. Consequently, assets should be isolated, based upon their role and importance, and never rely on single perimeter defenses.

- Can you prevent unauthorized insiders or criminals breaching your perimeter from easily gaining access to your valued assets?

- What damage can they do to your business once inside your perimeter?

- Do you test the effectiveness of your defensive systems?

- Do these risks exceed your risk appetites?

---

[28]www.lensculture.com/projects/150970-camp-bastion

Remember, Protective Security is defined as having an organized system of defenses.

Detect Anomalies

Having established a baseline as what is normal, it is now a case of developing a security toolset that will help you to quickly identify any ABNORMAL activities that could increase the risk to your business. Essentially, you want to be monitoring your systems and users for signs of early unauthorized or malicious activities, so that you are able to quickly respond to ensure you are able to minimize the damage being done.

Unauthorized individuals will be looking to gain a persistent presence within your corporate environment, so that they can identify opportunities for infiltration and exfiltration (as depicted in Carbon Black's Cognitive Attack Loop[29] (Figure 2-15) and Lockheed Martin's Cyber Kill Chain[30] (Figure 2-16)).

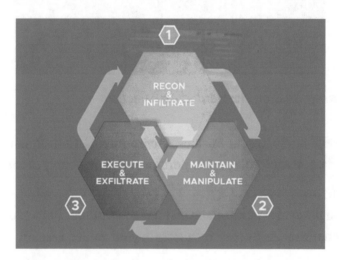

Figure 2-15. *Cognitive Attack Loop*

[29]www.carbonblack.com/blog/introducing-the-cognitive-attack-loop-and-its-3-phases/
[30]www.lockheedmartin.com/en-us/capabilities/cyber/cyber-kill-chain.html

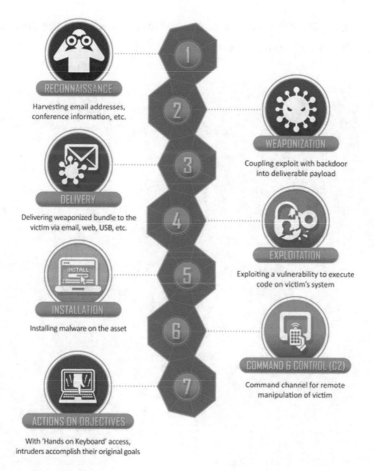

Figure 2-16. *Cyber Kill Chain*

Consequently, aligned with the category and importance of your business valued assets, you need to establish a process for detecting such anomalies and to detect for new instances (e.g., rogue devices, firewall/router rulesets, system misconfigurations, systems with missing updates, vulnerabilities, etc.) that a malicious individual would look to leverage.

This is not about having more security tools but, instead, making the best use of the tools you already have and ensuring that if you have any gaps in the monitoring capabilities, any additional tools are an enhancement to the existing abilities.

In the military, the monitoring resources are all fed back into the central managed Operations Center (as depicted in Figure 2-17[31]).

Figure 2-17. *Kandahar Airfield, Afghanistan*

When considering the effectiveness of your detection capabilities, it is important to remember that this should not only be a technical solution. A good security culture helps to increase your "eyes and ears" capability, with your employees knowing that security is a team effort in the protection of the business.

---

[31]www.wikiwand.com/en/Kandahar_International_Airport

Military Example

During my first ever counter intelligence field team (CIFT)[32] deployment, I was tasked to team up with a Portuguese Army Intelligence operative *(Paulo)* during a one-month deployment to Cape Verde (in support of the NATO exercise – Steadfast Jaguar[33]). Two weeks ahead of the 7500-troop deployment, we were deployed to Praia, the capital and largest city of Cape Verde, situated on Santiago island (as depicted in Figure 2-18[34]).

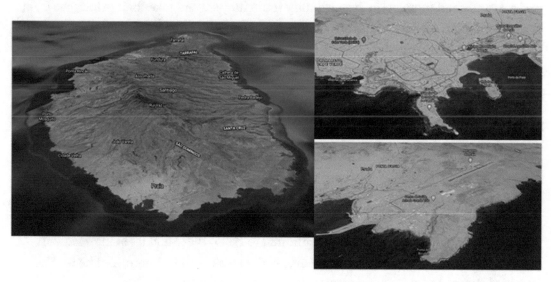

Figure 2-18. *Praia, Cape Verde*

Now, at this point in my RAF Police career, this was the most rewarding and challenging task I had ever been involved in. During the initial 2 weeks, Paulo and I were scoping out the local environment and reaching out to create a comprehensive network of local contacts (e.g., Embassies, Police, Ports, Education, Hotel Managers, NATO Advance Party, etc.). By the time the exercise commenced and the bulk of the NATO teams, and senior officers, had arrived, we had established an extensive intelligence network.

---

[32]https://assets.publishing.service.gov.uk/government/uploads/system/uploads/attachment_data/file/311572/20110830_jdp2_00_ed3_with_change1.pdf

[33]www.af.mil/News/Article-Display/Article/130574/nato-troops-exercise-at-steadfast-jaguar/

[34]https://earth.google.com/web/search/Praia,+Cape+Verde/@14.91710126,-23.48551274,35.22113085a,4471.18142145d,35y,-21.22622233h,59.9114868t,0r/data=Cig iJgokCSn6qjL2BUtAEarDpv2EBUtAGbsqUimJ8vO_IdtKEnNEC_S_

Any intelligence received would be treated like the pieces of a jigsaw puzzle and would be documented in an intelligence report (IntRep) and securely transmitted to the Intelligence Manager, where they would collate these pieces.

As the exercise commenced, we were freely receiving calls from our intelligence network and had become the "go-to" source for local knowledge. In fact, on one occasion, we received a call from the US Ambassador asking whether we could attend the US Embassy to provide the Close Protection teams with a security briefing. Happy to assist, we advised them of the best primary route they should take their principles from the airport and a recommended secondary route *(pointing out the dangerous Red areas they needed to be aware of)*.

The Embassy staff and Close Protection teams were so appreciative of the comprehensive briefing that we provided them that they invited us out for lunch at a local Pizzeria – approximately 15–20 people seated on a long line of tables.

This led to a funny situation. At the start of the deployment, as Paulo and I were getting to know each other, I had informed him that he would likely be caught out by my sense of humor and that by the time he had realized, it would be too late. Well, this was the first occasion.

The party of 15–20 sat down at the table, with Paulo and I sat opposite each other. Now, in the previous 2 weeks, I had mentioned to Paulo that I had been interested in learning a little of the Portuguese language, while I was in Cape Verde, and he had been happy to oblige. This was the opportunity I had been waiting for!

While trying to interpret the menu, I started asking Paulo to clarify certain words. Then I came to the word "Frango":

> I asked, "Paulo, what does this word (Frango) mean?"
>
> Paulo replied, "Argh, that chicken!"
>
> I looked at him with a blank expression and said, "Chicken?"
>
> Paulo asked, "Yes, you know… Chicken?"
>
> I shook my head and replied, with a confused look on my deadpan face, "No!"

Paulo then helpfully went on to try and describe to me what a chicken was, but still I played dumb. That was until, as Paulo's frustration grew, he became louder and more expressive, before standing up and started mimicking and making the sounds of a chicken. At this point, I and the rest of the table had burst out laughing, and Paulo realized what had happened and with a laugh called me (what must have been) expletive words – in Portuguese.

To Paulo's dismay, he was to see me doing the same prank on a Portuguese naval officer *(while wearing his white full-dress uniform)*. To mark the end of Exercise Steadfast Jaguar, the Portuguese Ambassador had invited Paulo and me to accompany him, as his guests, to a formal event being hosted by the Portuguese Navy on one of the frigates. To say I was impressed was an understatement, as the Portuguese Navy had laid out a lavish banquet on their landing deck and hangar aft.

Paulo was on one side of the landing deck and I on the other when the Navy Officer started to explain to me about all the food being traditional Portuguese fair. First, he offered me some Sangria *(not only originating from Spain, as I had thought)* before moving on to explain some of their other delicacies. You've guessed it, he then started to explain a dish called "Duck Rice." Immediately, a glint appeared in my eye, and out of the corner of my other eye, from the other side of the landing deck, I saw Paulo vigorously shaking his head from side to side, before making the dash across the landing deck.

Too late!

By the time Paulo had managed to sprint across, the Navy Officer was happily doing a duck impression.

This established the strong working relationship for the rest of the deployment and formed the basis for our network of contacts knowing that we were approachable and appreciative for any "nuggets" of information they were able to provide to us.

One such "nugget" came through a senior member of the German military communications team. After a long day, Paulo and I would finish with a chat in the hotel bar, accompanied by a shot of the local liqueur (Grogue[35]) and a double espresso coffee. During one of these occasions, we had been having a friendly chat with this senior German communications officer *(having a nonsensitive discussion as to what our roles were)*, who had been frequenting the hotel bar that evening.

Now, our deployed office setup was in the same location as the German communications team. The very next morning, Paulo and I were in the office planning

---

[35]www.capeverdeislands.org/grogue-cape-verdes-alcoholic-beverage/#:~:text=Grogue%
3A%20Cape%20Verde's%20alcoholic%20beverage,an%20alcohol%20rate%20of%2040%25.

for the day's activities when there was a knock at the door, and there was the same German. Something had happened to him the previous afternoon, and he thought it might be of interest to us, in our role.

He went on to tell us of an incident that had happened to him the previous afternoon. While sunbathing at the side of the hotel pool, he had started talking to a local disc jockey (DJ) and his girlfriend. At this point, there was nothing that concerned him. However, shortly after returning to his hotel room from the pool, he had been relaxing on his bed when there was a knock at the door. On opening the door, he was greeted by the DJ's girlfriend, who appeared to be upset.

She came into his room, stood directly in front of him, and stated that her boyfriend needed money to buy some drugs. Next thing before he knew it, she had dropped her loose-fitting dress off her shoulders, revealing her naked body. At which point, she had stated that for the equivalent of $200, she would let him do anything he wanted to her. At this point, he stated that he immediately refused and ushered her out of his room – this was the reason he had been in the bar that night.

That is how we recorded the incident in the IntRep, ensuring that he could see that his details had not been compromised, and he watched the IntRep being securely emailed. He was clearly relieved to have done the right thing; however, I detected that something in his account did not complete. Consequently, after sending the IntRep:

> I asked him, "Okay, what really happened? How did you manage to get her to leave so easily, given that she was in such distress and desperate for money?"

He confessed that he had paid her the equivalent of $100 to leave his room. This was something that he had been embarrassed about and, clearly, did not want to be documented. Consequently, our approach enabled us to gain his trust to record the incident without causing embarrassment – a win-win!

These two incidents demonstrate the importance of threat intelligence, embracing the development of a security culture, proportionality, and a team effort.

After an extremely productive time, we had made a significant impression on the local police constabulary, so much so that they sent a letter of appreciation to our Commanding Officer (as shown in Figure 2-19).

B   V   Q   S

De: B   V   Q   S
Enviado: terça-feira, 27 de Junho de 2006 14:04
Para:
Assunto: Cooperation between PJ Praia and Paulo Ferreira and Jim Seaman

Caro N   S

B   de V   Q   e C   S   respectivamente Inspector Chefe e Inspector da
Polícia Judiciária portuguesa, actualmente colocados em Cabo Verde como assessores do Director Central
da PJ local, vêm de há uns meses a esta parte a ter reuniões informais com o serviço de inteligência da
NATO, com vista a antecipar alguns problemas de segurança no exercício "STEADFAST JAGUAR 2006".
          É na sequência destas reuniões que nos são apresentados o PAULO FERREIRA e o JIM SEAMAN
que vêm desenvolver o seu trabalho nesta ilha de Santiago.
          Aqui e graças ao seu desempenho, lograram granjear o respeito de todos os que com eles tiveram
contacto, porquanto conseguiram trabalhar com todas as entidades de cariz policial e de controlo de
fronteiras, pô-las a trabalhar em conjunto, respeitando sempre as competências de cada um, o que não é
fácil.
          Por isso, esta postura de elevado grau de profissionalismo, para além de pedagógica, poderá ser
exemplarmente seguida na procura da coordenação das várias forças que até hoje não se alcançou, na
perspectiva da segurança que se deseja para Cabo Verde.
          No que diz respeito à Polícia Judiciária portuguesa, esta ligação mostrou-se particularmente positiva,
cujos benefícios esperamos ver contabilizados a breve trecho.
          O aqui exposto vai ser igualmente reportado à Direcção Nacional da Polícia Judiciária Portuguesa.
          Assim, vimos por este meio enaltecer o excelente trabalho desenvolvido pelo PAULO FERREIRA e o
JIM SEAMAN, ao mesmo tempo agradecer-lhe, e a toda a equipa, a disponibilidade e a confiança que
sempre nos dispensaram.

Com os melhores cumprimentos

B   V   Q   e C   S

Figure 2-19. *Letter of appreciation*

The development of an effective "Human" element is often the most difficult and has often been the subject of situation comedies, such as the Maximum Security sketch in *Blackadder Goes Forth*[36] (as depicted in Figure 2-20).

Figure 2-20. *Blackadder Goes Forth*

However, it is equally as important for an effective Protective Security strategy as the implementation of monitoring security tools, which can often be automated to improve efficiency, for example:

- **ExtraHop's Reveal(x)**[37]

    - Asset and vulnerability management

- **Titania's Nipper**[38] and **PAWS**[39]

    - Automated secure configuration management

- **Knogin's CyberEASY**[40]

    - End user and system monitoring

Govern Processes

ISACA[41] defines Governance as being

> *The method by which an enterprise ensures that stakeholder needs, conditions and options are evaluated to determine balanced, agreed-on enterprise objectives are achieved.*
>
> *It involves setting direction through prioritization and decision making; and monitoring performance and compliance against agreed-on direction and objectives.*

NIST[42] defines Data Governance as being

---

[37]www.extrahop.com/products/security/

[38]www.titania.com/products/nipper/

[39]www.titania.com/products/paws/

[40]www.knogin.com/products/

[41]www.isaca.org/resources/glossary#glossg

[42]https://csrc.nist.gov/glossary/term/data_governance

A set of processes that ensures that data assets are formally managed throughout the enterprise.

A data governance model establishes authority and management and decision-making parameters related to the data produced or managed by the enterprise.

In contrast, the Cambridge English Dictionary[43] defines Governance as being

The way that organizations or countries are managed at the highest level, and the systems for doing this.

Consequently, Governance is integral to the **BRIDGES** analogy, knitting everything together, and represents the management and communication of an organization's "good practices."

This is not a case of merely creating a suite of policies and procedures but an integrated approach that supports both "Top-Down" and "Bottom-Up" cohesive cycles of action to ensure the robust protection of the business' essential operations.

To ensure effective Governance, it requires a team effort where everyone understands their responsibilities and roles within Protective Security and is encouraged to play a proactive part.

Within the military, everyone is taught the core skills needed so that they can remain vigilant and received both security refresher training and departmental training. Each department has a "Security Champion," who has the additional responsibilities for championing "good practices," forming part of the security steering committee and required to periodically submit security reports to the Counter Intelligence section for review. These are the unit security officers (USyOs) or branch security officers (BSyOs) whose areas of responsibility will be associated with their primary role *(in the corporate environment, these might often be referred to as Security Champions[44] or Business Information Security Officers (BISOs)[45]).*

However, despite this being a secondary duty and them having to successfully complete a specialist security training (run by the RAF Police), I have experienced situations where apathy has undermined the effective governance.

---

[43]https://dictionary.cambridge.org/dictionary/english/governance

[44]https://adtmag.com/articles/2020/10/22/security-champions-programs-work.aspx

[45]https://gdpr.report/news/2020/09/11/a-new-role-for-the-cybersecurity-industry-the-business-information-security-officer-biso/

Military Example

During my first appointment as a Station Counter Intelligence operative, I became concerned by the actions of one such BSyO. They were frequently absent from the regular security steering committees and would regularly neglect to submit their security checks and after constant reminders would suddenly submit several submissions all at once.

I raised these concerns with the officer commanding the RAF Police Flight (OC Police)/Station security officer (SSyO) and requested authority to carry out a sanity check on the BSyO's security returns.

Now, part of these security checks was to carry out independent integrity checks across a sample of extremely sensitive assets and sign to confirm that everything was all in order. On reviewing their last security return, I discovered that they had signed their monthly return, declaring that they had physically completed the integrity checks and that everything was all in order.

This return had been signed and dated as having been completed in May; however, several assets had been securely destroyed/disposed of in March. Consequently, I was then tasked to carry out a thorough investigation, including a full muster of all the sensitive assets, under their responsibility, and to compare them against the returns.

The investigation confirmed that the BSyO had been cutting and pasting from previous returns and had never actually completed a single return within the past 12 months.

He had been negligent in his responsibilities *(a role that is seen as a delegated role from the Station Commander)* and had merely been "ticking the boxes."

However, an RAF Officer's integrity should always be beyond reproach, and this was regarded as being a serious neglection of their duties. Consequently, toward the end of the security investigation, when all the evidence was presented to the BSyO *(including the fact that they had no access to the secure storage and the asset custodian, responsible for some of these sensitive assets, had never seen the BSyO)*, this officer was left with just two options:

- Be subject to formal disciplinary action (Court Martial)

- Admit their negligence and resign their commission

As you might imagine, with all the evidence against them, they chose to resign their commission, and their career in the RAF ended abruptly.

Evaluate Security Controls

Now that you have established and prioritized your essential assets and processes and evaluated and selected the most appropriate mitigating security controls that the residual risks are within your risk appetite/tolerances,[46] it is essential that these controls be tested to ensure adequacy which can be analyzed against a loss expectancy curve (as depicted in Figure 2-21[47]).

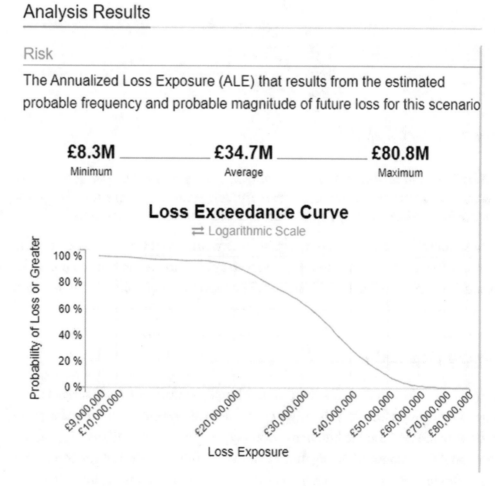

Figure 2-21. *FAIR analysis*

---

[46]www.logicmanager.com/erm-software/knowledge-center/best-practice-articles/
risk-appetite-risk-tolerance-residual-risk/
[47]www.fairinstitute.org/fair-u

Remember that Protective Security is a combination of people, process, and technologies, as described in ISACA's Business Model for Information Security (BMIS),[48] which they describe as (depicted in Figure 2-22)

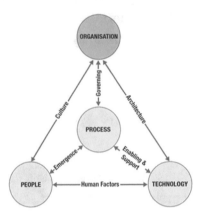

Figure 2-22. *ISACA BMIS*

> *A holistic and business-oriented model that supports enterprise governance and management information security and provides a common language for information security professionals and business management.*

Consequently, it is essential that regular policy/process reviews, independent audits, penetration testing, social engineering, and web application testing be programmed into the annual Protective Security and any result be used to update the risk and resilience profiles.

Military Example

During two appointments on Station Counter Intelligence duties, I was subject to independent reviews (security risk inspection (SRI)) of my proficiency to manage the protection of the RAF establishment's extremely sensitive assets. This would involve a seasoned pair of Counter Intelligence operatives coming onsite and spending a full 5 days evaluating the maturity of my processes, through observations, interviews, and extensive document reviews.

---

[48]www.isaca.org/resources/glossary#glossb

At the end of the evaluation, the Head of the RAF Establishment (Station Commander) and the Station security officer (SSyO) would receive both a verbal debrief and a formal report.

As you might imagine, this was an extremely nerve-racking experience but one that I came to appreciate. However, done correctly, it helps the organization to mature their own processes, based upon peer reviews. For example, during my second SRI *(where I was left with sole responsibility)*, I was confident that I had things in good order and that the SRI would have a positive result. As predicted, the SRI was going well until... They asked the question, "So, what happens if you were to suddenly, without notice, be unavailable to carry out these tasks? Say, you end up in a coma, after being hit by a bus!"

Boom!

I had not documented what I did through standard operating procedures (SOPs), and so all the procedures would be locked in my head. I must say, this is a common mistake that I see today's digital businesses make, where the security and IT Operations team either run light or rely on a handful of "trusted" personnel to carry out their roles. Consequently, when they are not in work, there's no one to cover their roles.

Survive to Operate

Finally, you need to be prepared for when things go wrong or to be ready for things that might be coming. Take, for instance, the increased ransomware threats and the impact that the COVID-19 pandemic has on worldwide businesses.

Security Incident planning, Business Continuity, and Disaster Recovery are essential components. Critical to these are the input of threat intelligence and the development of effective "playbooks" and to validate your business' proficiency to deal with current and potential events that could impact your organization.

Surviving to operate includes the following topic areas:

- **Incident handling**

- Criminals will often seek to gain a clandestine and persistent presence within their target's environment (aka dwell times). Incident handling is heavily reliant on effective anomaly detection processes to enable the timely detection of potential malicious events that could impact your business.

- This is demonstrated in the FireEye 2020 M-Trends report[49] where the average dwell time was reported to be **30 days** for proactive organizations that self-detected their incidents vs. organizations that have learned of their incident through a third party, where the average dwell time is reported to be **141 days**.

    - *How well could they recon your environment, in this time, and how much damage could they potentially do?*

As demonstrated by NIST[50] and CERT,[51] effective incident handling requires defined steps to be efficiently implemented (as depicted in Figure 2-23).

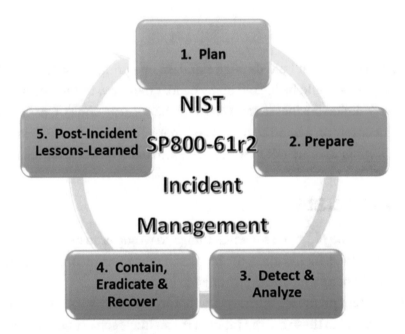

Figure 2-23. *Incident handling steps*

From experience, this should not be seen as a tick box exercise and should be regarded as an important part of a business, with the incident teams being subject to extensive training and practice, so that when "IT HITS THE FAN," your teams are well drilled and not running around like headless chickens. Time wasted in responding to and containing an incident can prove to be extremely detrimental to an organization.

---

[49]www.fireeye.com/current-threats/annual-threat-report/mtrends.html
[50]https://nvlpubs.nist.gov/nistpubs/SpecialPublications/NIST.SP.800-61r2.pdf
[51]https://resources.sei.cmu.edu/asset_files/BookChapter/2016_009_001_514842.pdf

- **Business Continuity Plan**

  This is the lifeline for most businesses and is self-explanatory; how do you plan to continue operations during adverse events?

  Ensuring that critical operations continue to be available and minimizing the impacts to the business, regardless of the type of disruption or incident.

  NIST[52] defines business continuity plan (BCP) as being

  The documentation of a predetermined set of instructions or procedures that describe how an organization's mission/business processes will be sustained during and after a significant disruption.

  In Noggin's guide to developing an effective BCP,[53] they identify the following common elements:

  - A list of relevant company, insurance, and supplier contacts.

  - References. Helpful information might include links to the appropriate state and federal regulator, for example, Emergency Management Australia.

  - Relevant standards with which the plan complies, for example, ISO 22301.

  - Organizing objectives and driving principles. The primary objective of your plan is to ensure maximum possible service levels are maintained.

  - Meanwhile, assessing business risk for probability and impact might also be an important principle to document.

  - The objectives and principles sections might be part of a longer executive summary, a comprehensive overview of the BCP.

---

[52]https://csrc.nist.gov/glossary/term/business_continuity_plan#:~:text=The%20
documentation%20of%20a%20predetermined,NIST%20SP%20800%2D34%20Rev.

[53]www.noggin.io/developing-an-effective-business-continuity-plan

- The contents of a business impact assessment (BIA), including a list of likely threats, that is, building loss, document(s) loss, systems going offline, loss of key staff, and so on.

- Scenario planning for the risks you've identified. Once a risk is listed, the plan will outline the probability and impact of occurrence, likeliest scenario(s) to unfold, business functions affected, actions to take and preventative mitigation strategies, staff responsibilities, as well as operational constraints.

Extensive research, by the Ponemon Institute,[54] into the cost of a data breach revealed that having an effective BCP in place is estimated to save an organization an average of £277,000 ($365,000). Extracts from the latest research are shown in Figures 2-24 to 2-27.

Figure 2-24. *Impact of COVID-19*

---

[54]www.ibm.com/security/digital-assets/cost-data-breach-report/#/

Figure 2-25. *Lifecycle of a data breach*

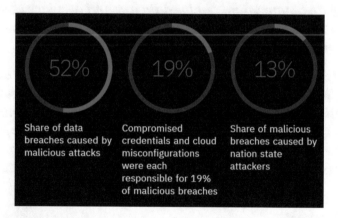

Figure 2-26. *Malicious attacks*

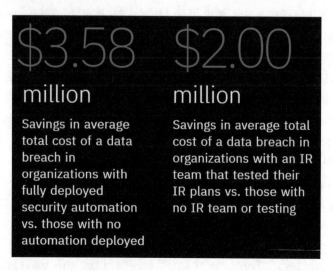

Figure 2-27. *Effective security measures*

- **Disaster Recovery**

  Hopefully, this is something that your business will never need, should everything continue to run effectively. However, there's an old military adage that has a great deal of relevancy here:

  "Failing to plan is planning to fail!"

  TechTarget defines a disaster recovery plan (DRP)[55] as being

  A documented, structured approach that describes how an organization can quickly resume work after an unplanned incident. A DRP is an essential part of a business continuity plan (BCP). It is applied to the aspects of an organization that depend on a functioning IT infrastructure. A DRP aims to help an organization resolve data loss and recover system functionality so that it can perform in the aftermath of an incident, even if it operates at a minimal level.

  The step-by-step plan consists of the precautions to minimize the effects of a disaster so the organization can continue to operate or quickly resume mission-critical functions. Typically, disaster recovery planning involves an analysis of business processes and continuity needs. Before generating a detailed plan, an organization often performs a business impact analysis (BIA) and risk analysis (RA), and it establishes recovery objectives.

Military Example

As you might imagine, during my time in the Royal Air Force Police, I have received extensive training which included preparing us from some extreme scenarios. However, these were all created as the result of the rare events that had happened.

For instance, following my posting to RAF Aldergrove, because of the role that I would be going into, I had to attend a Northern Ireland re-enforcement training (NIRT) course. This consisted of approximately 5 days of specialized training to help adequately prepare us to respond and recover from different scenarios.

The course started with three exceptionally long days of classroom-based theory (aka "Death by Power Point") before going into 2 days of intensive practical training. The practical training would involve extremely realistic incidents (e.g., The Funeral Murders[56]

---

[55]https://searchdisasterrecovery.techtarget.com/definition/disaster-recovery-plan
[56]https://www.thejournal.ie/gibraltar-killings-30-years-3885830-Mar2018/

as depicted in Figure 2-28), where you had to respond to the events as they unfolded.
I recall one of these scenarios involving an attempted terrorist hijack. I and an Army
Private were sent out to drive around a mock rural environment, at night, in a battered
old Fiat Panda, with only the headlights providing anything illumination. Outside of the
headlights, it was just complete darkness as we set off on high alert.

Figure 2-28. *Murder of two British soldiers in Northern Ireland*

We drove along this simulated country lane, just waiting in anticipation for
something to happen, but after having driven for what seemed like half of the night,
nothing happened.

The longer we carried on driving, the more we started to become relaxed. Suddenly,
as we went over a blind summit of a hill in the endless darkness, to our left, this dark van
sped out of a sideline to stop in front of us blocking our path.

Now, as the senior rank in the vehicle, I was deemed to be the vehicle commander,
and the young Private was driving. Well, in the panic of the situation, instead of slamming
his foot on the brake, he jammed his combat boot onto the accelerator pedal – smashing
into the side of the van. However, in the evolving chaos, I was able to instruct the driver to
get out of the vehicle and to get to cover. As I did so, masked and armed with AK47 rifles,
the occupants exited the van, surrounded the front of our vehicle and started shouting
at us. We abandoned and sprinted away from the vehicle, and acting within the rules of
engagement (RoE), and in defense of our lives giving fire toward our enemies.

During this exercise, the adrenaline was pumping, the heart's racing, and everything happens in a complete blur. Afterward, we are debriefed by the instructors and given time to calm down, before moving on to the next scenario.

Now, if I'd thought the last exercise to be realistic, the next urban scenario was terrifying. This time, I was to be the vehicle commander and driver, given the objective of driving through this mock town setup. Imagine the scene; you have an exact representation of a town, which had three main routes through it (as depicted in Figure 2-29).

Figure 2-29. *Urban training area*

As I drove into the urban setting, everything was eerily quiet. We made our way down the main high street, where we were faced with a three-way junction.

- Do we go straight on?

- Do we go left?

- Do we go right?

Not wanting to take the obvious route, I decided to choose the left junction. As we drove along the route, everything was still noticeably quiet, and then, wouldn't you know it, this road was blocked by a barricade. That left us no choice but to reverse backward to take the next right, which returned us to the main high street – straight into a large crowd of protesters!

Now, I know why this Fiat Panda was in such a sorry state. The crowd was made up by the other members of the NIRT course, being instructed to aggressively rock and hammer on the vehicle. Next, I instructed my colleague to be prepared to try and clandestinely get out of the vehicle and try and calmly get away from the crowd. Before I knew it, the crowd's aggression suddenly escalated, and the Private and I got separated. The crowd encircled me, so to save my own life, I needed to draw my weapon and aggressively shout, "Get back!", while getting myself into an open space where I could make my escape.

At the end of the town was a mock Police station, where we had arranged to meet up if we got separated. Upon arrival at the Police station, out of the darkness, I saw the white shining teeth of the private's smile. It turns out that as he had deployed from the passenger side of the vehicle, his pistol had fallen onto the street. This identification of us being members of the military was the reason for the escalation of the crowd's aggression. However, as I was the only person left with a weapon, the entire crowd had focused on me, so while I was drawing them away from the vehicle, the young Private simply picked up his pistol and quietly made his way to the Police station.

These experiences clearly helped me to understand the value of having a well-designed, planned, and practiced incident response (IR) and business continuity plan (BCP).

- Do you have an extensive range of different scenarios, contained within your organization's playbook, and how often do you train and carry out exercises against these scenarios?

- Do you update your scenarios based upon the attackers' known tactics and threat intelligence resources, for example, MITRE ATT&CK (as depicted in Figure 2-30[57])?

---

[57]https://mitre-attack.github.io/attack-navigator/

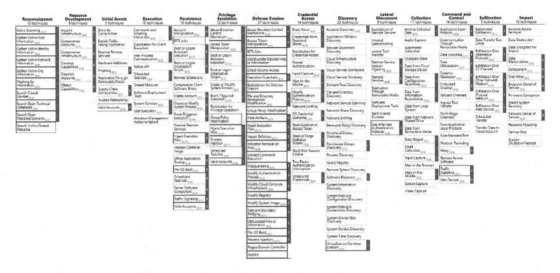

Figure 2-30. *MITRE ATT&CK navigator*

- In the event of a disruptive event happening in your organization, how assured are you that your business is sufficiently capable of responding to and containing the event to minimize the disruption and impact?

- If a valued business asset, function, or process becomes unavailable, as the result of an event, do you understand the potential risk associated with these and what is the organization's level of tolerance for the time length that these assets are not available?

- Are your contingency plans in line with the tolerance levels, or do you need to carry out a risk assessment and create a business case for establishing suitable failover procedures?

Protective Security Ten Key Principles

No two businesses are the same; however, by applying the **BRIDGES** acronym, all organizations should be able to develop a suitable strategy that incorporates the following ten key principles:

1. Business alignment

   Security is a business enabler. It supports the efficient and effective delivery of services.

2. Board-driven risk

   Risk management is key and should be driven from the board level. Assessments will identify potential threats, vulnerabilities, and appropriate controls to reduce the risks to people, information, and infrastructure to an acceptable level. This process will take full account of relevant statutory obligations and protections.

3. Risk ownership

   Accountable authorities own the security risks of their entity and the entity's impact on shared risks.

4. Proportionality

   Security measures applied proportionately protect entities' people, information, and assets in line with their assessed risks.

5. Security culture

   Attitudes and behaviors are fundamental to good security. The right security culture, proper expectations, and effective training are essential.

6. Team effort

   Security is everyone's responsibility. Developing and fostering a positive security culture is critical to security outcomes.

7. Cycles of action

   Cycles of action, evaluation, and learning are evident in response to security incidents.

8. Robust protection

   Protective security should reflect the widest security objectives of the business and ensure that the organization's most sensitive assets are robustly protected.

9. Transparency

Security must be a business enabler and should be framed to support the company's objectives to work transparently and openly and to deliver services efficiently and effectively via digital services wherever appropriate.

10. Policies and procedures

Policies and processes will be in place for reporting, managing, and resolving any security incidents. Where systems have broken down or individuals have acted improperly, the appropriate action will be taken.

Reality Bites

By being focused on only the external digital footprint or on a specific data type, you can miss the bigger picture that can lead to gaps in the internal processes that can be just as (or even more) impactful as a cyber-attack, data breach, or incorrect use, or transmission, of customer/employee personal data.

Protective Security should be looking at the risks to the business' most valued assets and how to protect them.

Look at the impact that an outage has on both the business and the affected customers:

- Citigroup Inc. mistakenly sent out $900 million to a fleet of hedge funds,[58] caused by their decision to upgrade an obscure piece of software, used to manage loan payments.

    - No cyber-attack.

    - No compromised personal data.

    - However, this was a valuable software asset that should have been subject to a risk assessment.

---

[58]www.bnnbloomberg.ca/citi-s-900-million-misfire-happened-in-midst-of-software-switch-1.1484914

Key Takeaways

- The security industry has become focused on the use of "buzzwords/ terms" (e.g., Cyber Security, Information Security, Cyber Resilience, Business Resilience, Compliance, etc.) rather than on implementing effective protective measures to help safeguard those business assets which can cause the most damage if compromised.

- Instead, many businesses are either apathetic to the risks that their critical business assets might be facing daily, try to "tick all the boxes" for everything, or get tunnel vision for a particular industry security controls standard (e.g., ISO/IEC 27001:2013,[59] NIST Cybersecurity Framework (CSF),[60] Center for Internet Security Top 20 Critical Security Controls (CIS 20 CSC),[61] Standards of Good Practice (SoGP),[62] etc.).

Note   The industry security controls should be regarded as reference security controls for the mitigation of identified risks.

- There are many lessons that can be military lessons that can be learned and applied to the benefit of today's Digital Businesses. A common misconception is that the military has bottomless funding and so everything is protected like they were in "Fort Knox." This is far from being the case!

- The military Protective Security principles should not be limited to the safeguarding of National Infrastructures (e.g., UK Government, Australian Government, etc.), and by adopting a similar approach, the digital business can help to ensure that their operations are less vulnerable and susceptible to opportunist attacks and can continue (or rapidly bounce back) in the face of adverse events.

---

[59]www.iso.org/standard/54534.html

[60]www.nist.gov/cyberframework

[61]www.cisecurity.org/controls/cis-controls-list/

[62]www.securityforum.org/tool/the-isf-standard-good-practice-information-security-2018/

- Protective Security is evolving, and businesses and governments are still to realize the wider benefits it brings for the protection of the companies (and the shareholders), the consumers, and a country's economy. Where the primary losses are against the businesses impacted by an opportunist threat actor, there is likely to be a secondary loss to the consumer and the local economy.

- However, much like the evolution of health and safety within the workplace, as these entities start to see the value in effective security and start to become more insistent that effective measures must be in place, I believe you will see an increased volume of affected individuals and governments taking legal action against companies and individuals (e.g., Uber Security Chief,[63] Morrisons Supermarket,[64] Equifax,[65] British Airways,[66] etc.).

---

[63]www.nytimes.com/2020/08/20/technology/joe-sullivan-uber-charged-hack.html

[64]www.burges-salmon.com/news-and-insight/legal-updates/technology-and-communications/uk-supreme-court-sets-november-hearing-date-for-morrisons-data-breach-appeal/

[65]www.equifaxbreachsettlement.com/

[66]www.twobirds.com/en/news/articles/2019/uk/class-action-data-breach-litigation-under-cpr-19-6

Protective Security (PS) in terms of the Legal and Regulatory Considerations for the Digital Business

Every war and conflict that the United States enters has its own RoE [rules of engagement]. Contrary to what most people think, the U.S. military does not have a complete license to kill, even in wartime.

We are not a barbaric state, and we do not enter any war with the intention of unilaterally killing anything in our path. We go out of our way to spare civilian lives, to keep those who are not in the war out of it – sometimes even at the expense of risking our own soldiers' safety.

We do this by creating strict rules to which our soldiers adhere. These rules govern when they can fire, when they cannot; what type of force they can use, what type they cannot; what they can do in particular situations, and what they cannot.

© Jim Seaman 2021

J. Seaman, *Protective Security*, https://doi.org/10.1007/978-1-4842-6908-4_3

*The reason for this is that battles can become very confusing very quickly,
and a common soldier needs simple rules to guide him, to know when he is
or is not allowed to kill – and who is and is not the enemy.*

Second-in-command of the "War on Terror,"[1]

including Operation Iraqi Freedom in Iraq and

Operation Enduring Freedom in Afghanistan

Figure 3-1. *General Michael DeLong*

Introduction

Until recently, businesses have been pretty much lawless and without any regulation.

A law[2] is defined as being

*A body of rules of action or conduct prescribed by a controlling authority,
and having binding legal force. That which must be obeyed and followed
by citizens subject to sanctions or legal consequence is a law.*

A regulation[3] is defined as being

An official rule or the act of controlling something.

However, this is something that is starting to change, and I predict digital businesses
will become increasingly subject to new laws and regulations.[4] Laws are intended to
protect the fundamental rights and liberties of citizens, and, in business, there can often
be a fine line between what can be deemed as legal and illegal and for what basis that
line was even drawn in the first place.

---

[1]www.goodreads.com/book/show/266898.A_General_Speaks_Out

[2]Black's Law Dictionary, 6th ed., s.v. "law."

[3]https://dictionary.cambridge.org/dictionary/english/regulation

[4]www.e-ir.info/2020/03/14/international-law-on-cyber-security-in-the-age-of-
 digital-sovereignty/

As the world continues to move to an increasingly digital environment, I predict
that you will see an increased legal precedent for businesses to ensure that any services
provided to their customers and employees remain suitably protected and available so
that they provide continual operations.

Much like we have laws that regulate the exchange of goods, services, or anything
else of value, and property law that defines the people's rights and duties toward tangible
and intangible possessions, it is extremely likely that such (or equivalent laws) will be
extended to the Digital Business.

We have already seen a shift by global governments to greater protection of people's
personal data, with the updated and new data privacy legislations (as depicted in
Figure 3-2[5]).

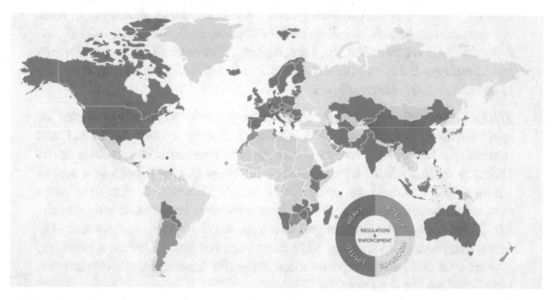

Figure 3-2. *Data protection laws of the world*

Notwithstanding the enhancements to the data privacy laws, additionally, we have
seen new legislations and regulatory attention in regard to resilience and the availability
of services.

---

[5]`www.dlapiperdataprotection.com/index.html?t=world-map&c=ZM`

- **EU network and information systems (NIS Directive)**[6]

The Directive on security of network and information systems (NIS Directive) is the first piece of cybersecurity legislation passed by the European Union (EU). The Directive was adopted on July 6, 2016 and its aim is to achieve a high common standard of network and information security across all EU Member States. The Directive took effect in August 2016, from which point EU Member States have 21 months to integrate its requirements into their own national laws and an additional 6 months to identify the companies which are subject to NIS Directive compliance.

The NIS sets a range of network and information security requirements which apply to operators of essential services and digital service providers (DSPs). The "operators of essential services" referred to in the legislation include enterprises in the energy, transport, banking, financial market infrastructures, health, drinking water supply and distribution, and digital infrastructure sectors. The NIS Directive requires each EU Member State to put together a list of organizations within those sectors who they consider to be essential service providers.

The Directive defines a digital service as "any service normally provided for remuneration, at a distance, by electronic means and at the individual request of a recipient of services." The specific types of DSPs outlines in the Directive include cloud service providers, online marketplaces, and search engines. DSPs should be aware that the NIS Directive also applies to companies based outside of the EU whose services are available within the EU. These companies are obliged to assign an EU-based representative to act on their behalf in ensuring NIS Directive compliance. DSPs are, however, subject to a less stringent framework than the "operators of essential services" outlined in the Directive.[7]

- Failure to comply results in fines that are equivalent to that of the EU General Data Protection Regulation (GDPR), Article 83[8] and 84.[9]

---

[6]https://ec.europa.eu/digital-single-market/en/network-and-information-security-nis-directive

[7]https://digitalguardian.com/blog/what-nis-directive-definition-requirements-penalties-best-practices-compliance-and-more#:~:text=The%20Directive%20on%20security%20of,the%20European%20Union%20(EU).&text=The%20NIS%20sets%20a%20range,digital%20service%20providers%20(DSPs)

[8]https://gdpr-info.eu/art-83-gdpr/

[9]https://gdpr-info.eu/art-84-gdpr/

- **Protective Security Act (2018:585)**[10] **– Sweden**

- **Protective Security Act 2007**[11] **– South Australia**

- **Payment Services Directive 2 (PSD2)**[12]

- **UK Health and Safety**[13]

- **Federal Trade Commission (FTC)'s shift in its approach to cyber security**[14]

Military Example

Despite the high risk to the military operations, they too are not above the law. Consequently, they are subject to extensive training so that they fully understand what are (and what are not) legal ways to carry out their operations.

If an individual steps beyond what might be deemed illegal or acceptable, they will be subject to a criminal investigation, and their actions could result in disciplinary action and even a jail sentence.

One such incident resulted in a change to the rules, and all affected personnel were subjected to extensive and thought-provoking refresher training.

The incident I'm referring to happened in Northern Ireland, in the early 1990s, and involved a Private named Lee Clegg.[15] He had alleged to have been acting in self-defense, and within the rules of engagement (RoE),[16] when he opened fire on an oncoming speeding car which had been approaching a vehicle checkpoint. To this, he opened fire on the said vehicle, killing the occupants inside (as depicted in Figure 3-3).

---

[10]www.sakerhetspolisen.se/en/swedish-security-service/protective-security.html

[11]https://legislation.sa.gov.au/LZ/C/A/PROTECTIVE%20SECURITY%20ACT%202007/CURRENT/2007.25.AUTH.PDF

[12]https://medium.com/savedroid/introducing-psd2-983efa5778ec

[13]www.hse.gov.uk/eci/cyber-security.htm

[14]www.lawfareblog.com/new-decade-and-new-cybersecurity-orders-ftc

[15]https://edm.parliament.uk/early-day-motion/11722/private-clegg-and-the-rules-of-engagement

[16]www.britannica.com/topic/rules-of-engagement-military-directives

Figure 3-3. *Shooting*

The ensuing criminal investigation discovered that the vehicle was not related to any terrorist actions but the actions of some young innocent teenagers. The investigation also deemed that Private Clegg had not acted explicitly in line with the RoE, in place at that time, and was convicted of murder.

However, after a lengthy appeal process, his charge was reduced to that of being found guilty of attempting to wound with intent to cause grievous bodily harm.[17] The appeal had identified that the RoE contained a "gray area" that neither protected the innocent nor the member of the military trying to legally carry out their duties.

Whether this was accurate or not, the military responded through an update of the RoE to ensure that any "gray areas" were eliminated.

In addition to updating the RoE, the military leaders had recognized the importance of providing frontline personnel with both theory and practical situational awareness training. When lives are put at risk, it is not sufficient to just inform personnel that the rules have changed and to "crack on!"

Consequently, we would receive a training session on the theory, followed by a practical element. During the practical session, we would be placed in front of a firearms simulator and be subject to realistic situations, where we would have to decide on whether to open fire or not.

Afterward, depending on the choices made, we would then be subject to a cross-examination by a real-life criminal prosecution barrister. Believe me, this is one of the most nerve-racking experiences that you can ever undergo – knowing that those split second decisions can result in the potential death (or serious injury) to you or your colleagues, to a potential terrorist, or to an innocent bystander.

---

[17]www.theguardian.com/uk/1999/mar/12/johnmullin

The Advantages of a Digital Workplace

Businesses seek to revolutionize their workplace practices through the adoption of digital technologies so that they can profit from the considerable benefits that come with it:

- Increased visibility gained by the digital presence

- New ways of reaching out to customers

- Able to place the customer at the heart of your business

- Improved decision-making

- Improved efficiency and productivity

- Innovation

- Improved communication and teamwork

- Improved working conditions

- Greater flexibility

The recent 2020 COVID-19 pandemic saw a dramatic shift in consumer habits and the business operating model. Many consumers turned to the safety of online purchases (aka ecommerce), and many businesses rapidly changed from their traditional onsite working to majority remote working operations.

In fact, it was reported[18] that consumer shopping saw a **129%** increase in online purchases, across the United Kingdom and Europe, because of COVID-19, and almost one-third of the US workforce and one-half of the "information workers" were able to work from home.[19]

---

[18]https://internetretailing.net/covid-19/covid-19/online-shopping-surges-by-129-across-uk-and-europe-and-ushers-in-new-customer-expectations-of-etail-21286

[19]www.weforum.org/agenda/2020/06/coronavirus-covid19-remote-working-office-employees-employers

Another example is the impact that the digital revolution has made to advertising and marketing. Even the traditional ways of finding a business or service provider have moved to the digital platform, resulting in the killing off of previously successful models:

- Demise of the "Argos" shopping catalogue (a UK stalwart for 48 years[20,21]) or the JCPenney's catalogue in the United States (as depicted in Figure 3-4[22,23])

Figure 3-4. *Argos and JCPenney's catalogues*

- End of the "Yellow Pages" printed directory – Around since 1886[24] (as depicted in Figure 3-5)

Figure 3-5. *Yellow Pages*

---

[20]www.bbc.co.uk/news/business-53592591

[21]https://news.sky.com/story/argos-catalogue-after-48-years-and-1bn-copies-times-up-for-the-laminated-book-of-dreams-12039168

[22]https://news.sky.com/story/argos-catalogue-after-48-years-and-1bn-copies-times-up-for-the-laminated-book-of-dreams-12039168

[23]http://retailhistory.blogspot.com/2009/11/jcpenneys-big-book-catalog-coming-to.html

[24]www.vendasta.com/blog/yellow-pages-evolution/

Clearly, the digital revolution has been extremely powerful and has proved to be very beneficial for business. However, a business should pay heed to the wise advice often attributed to Voltaire[25] or even Spider-Man. However, this originated from a passage that appeared in a collection of decrees, made by the French National Convention,[26] on May 8, 1793 *(long after Voltaire's death in 1778 or long before the creation of Spider-Man (by Stan Lee and Steve Ditko) in 1962)*:

> *They must consider that great responsibility follows inseparably from great power!*

With Great Power Comes Great Responsibility

In 1906, the then statesman Winston Churchill was to use a version of this content in a speech to the House of Commons:[27]

> *Where there is great power there is great responsibility, where there is less power there is less responsibility, and where there is no power there can, I think, be no responsibility.*

Two years later, President Theodore Roosevelt included a version of the same quote from the French Revolution in his letter to Sir George Otto Trevelyan:

> *I believe in a strong executive; I believe in power; but I believe that responsibility should go with power, and that it is not well that the strong executive should be a perpetual executive.*

Both are well-respected and great leaders who recognized the need for a proportionate and balanced approach to the use of power. The adoption of a digitalized business can yield great benefits and can make an organization extremely powerful. However, such business leaders need to be mindful of the dangers that this new found power might bring.

---

[25]www.voltaire.ox.ac.uk/about-voltaire/about-voltaire

[26]https://quoteinvestigator.com/2015/07/23/great-power/

[27]https://quoteinvestigator.com/2015/07/23/great-power/#:~:text=In%201906%20
statesman%20Winston%20Churchill,extended%20instance%20of%20the%20adage%
3A&text=Where%20there%20is%20great%20power,I%20think%2C%20be%20no%20
responsibility

We have recently seen reports of businesses acting in ways that do not reflect their responsibilities for the powers they yield, for example:

- **Cambridge Analytica**[28]

- **Uber former chief security officer**[29]

Note   Both have an association with one of the most successful Digital Businesses in the world (Facebook).

We are seeing a greater distrust from consumers and politicians as to how Digital Businesses are respecting the responsibilities. Consequently, we are increasingly likely to see greater legislations and regulations in the future (as depicted in Figure 3-6[30]).

Figure 3-6. *Facebook CEO testifies in front of congress*

---

[28]www.nytimes.com/2018/04/04/us/politics/cambridge-analytica-scandal-fallout.html

[29]www.nytimes.com/2020/08/20/technology/joe-sullivan-uber-charged-hack.html

[30]www.businessinsider.com/mark-zuckerberg-congress-testimony-how-to-watch-2019-10?r=US&IR=T

Using the infamous words from Benjamin Franklin,[31] it makes good business sense for organizations to employ an effective Protective Security program, to provide essential support of their company's morals and ethics.

It takes many good deeds to build a good reputation, and only one bad one to lose it!

Benjamin Franklin

Embrace the Good: Reputation Is Everything

A business should not be waiting for legislation and regulation to "twist their arms" into having an effective Protective Security program in place.

This just makes good business sense!

Imagine that your business is your home or motor vehicle:

- *Would you leave the doors and windows unlocked or ajar, or leave the locks and hinges poorly maintained, allowing uncontrolled access for anyone?*

- *If you did, would you be surprised to learn that an opportunist threat attacker was to walk off the street and steal, or damage, your valuable and attractive items?*

The difference between your business and your home/motor vehicle is that your business can be considerably larger, and you must be reliant on far more people to keep it safe and secure.

Much like Health and Safety (H&S) was introduced to ensure businesses implement measures to safeguard the individual, I can forecast that the world of protective security will follow similar patterns of development.

---

[31]www.goodreads.com/quotes/66761-it-takes-many-good-deeds-to-build-a-good-reputation

A Health and Safety (H&S) Approach to Protective Security

If you work for an organization that is heavily regulated for H&S, such as manufacturing, you will not need to be reminded of the importance for everyone to respect the H&S rules and to report unsafe practices to ensure everyone **works safely** (as depicted in Figure 3-7).

Figure 3-7. *Work safe*

In fact, in most organizations that are subject to robust H&S regulations, the business leadership are strong supporters of the adherence to safe operating practices and ensure that it is embedded into the organization.

In the United Kingdom, in 1974, the H&S at Work Act[32] was introduced to regulate workplace health, safety, and welfare. Its aim was to protect people from the risk of injury or ill health by

- Ensuring employees' health, safety, and welfare at work

- Protecting non-employees against the health and safety risks arising from work activities

- Controlling the keeping and use of explosive or highly flammable or dangerous substances

- The Health and Safety at Work Act 1974 applies (with a few exceptions) to everyone "at work."

It sets out the obligations for business leaders H&S responsibilities in respect to

- Their employees and members of the public.

- Their employees have to themselves and to each other.

- Certain self-employed individuals have toward themselves and others.

Surely, a business would have understood the importance of protecting their employees, visitors, contractors, and members of the public.

When you look at the basics[33] needed for H&S, it is clear that there are numerous similarities between H&S and Protective Security.

1. **Appoint a competent person.**

Choose who will help you manage health and safety in your business.

- *Appoint a Protective Security (aka Cyber Security, Information Security, Physical Security) specialist.*

- *Appoint a data protection officer (DPO).*

---

[32]www.hse.gov.uk/legislation/hswa.htm#:~:text=The%20Health%20and%20Safety%20
at,and%20members%20of%20the%20public

[33]www.hse.gov.uk/simple-health-safety/index.htm

2. **Prepare a health and safety policy.**

What is a policy and how does it help you manage health and safety?

- *Implement an Information Security policy.*

3. **Risk assessment.**

How to identify hazards and assess risks at work?

- *How to identify anomalies and issues that could impact the confidentiality, integrity, and availability?*

4. **Consult your workers.**

Involve your workers and inform them about health and safety.

- *Create a security steering committee to discuss issues and risks.*

- *Create a business-wide security culture.*

5. **Provide information and training.**

Tell your workers what their health and safety duties are.

- *Create a suite of security policies and procedures.*

- *Develop a security awareness program.*

6. **Have the right workplace facilities.**

Have toilets, washbasins, and other welfare facilities workers need.

- *Ensure that sufficient security tools are in place to allow the efficient detection of anomalies or malicious actions.*

- *Ensure effective defensive measures are in place for the protection of critical business assets.*

7. **First aid in work.**

Advice on your first aid kit, training workers and appointing first aiders.

- *Appoint and train your incident response team.*

8. **Display the law poster.**

You must display the poster or give workers the equivalent leaflet.

- *Complement security awareness training with periodic security campaigns (e.g., emails, posters, etc.), as depicted in Figures 3-8 and 3-9.*

Figure 3-8. *Military security posters*[34]

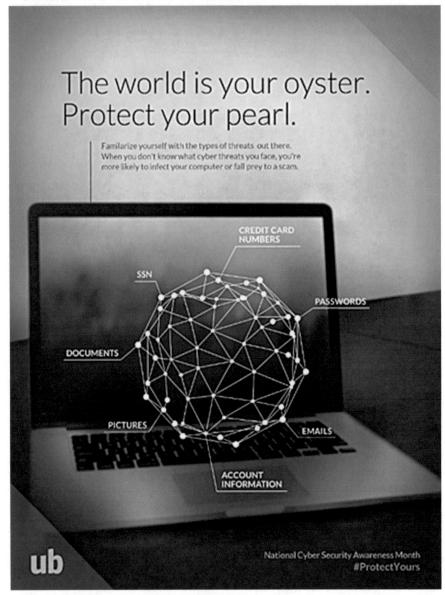

Figure 3-9. *Corporate security posters[35]*

---

[35]www.ubalt.edu/about-ub/offices-and-services/technology-services/security/
cybersec/contest.cfm

- *This can be cost-effectively and professionally achieved through the procurement of the services from a security awareness provider (e.g., KnowBe4[36]).*

9. **Get insurance for your business.**

Find out why you may need employers' liability insurance.

- *Consider the benefits of Cyber Security insurance.*

10. **The law.**

The Health and Safety at Work Act, criminal and civil law

- *Understand the applicable and emerging laws:[37]*

- EU Cybersecurity Act[38]

- Computer Misuse Act 1990[39]

- Data Privacy (e.g., GDPR, PIPEDA, CCPA, POPI, etc.)

11. **Report accidents and illness.**

You must report certain injuries, near misses, and work-related illnesses to Health & Safety Executive (HSE).

- *Provide advice to all workers on how they should respond and report incidents.*

Consequently, if business was to treat Protective Security as seriously as they are legally required to do for H&S, you would see a significant change in direction from the traditional "do the bare minimum" or "tick box" approach and everyone **works securely** (as depicted in Figure 3-10).

---

[36]www.knowbe4.com/

[37]https://iclg.com/practice-areas/cybersecurity-laws-and-regulations/
england-and-wales

[38]https://ec.europa.eu/digital-single-market/en/eu-cybersecurity-act

[39]www.legislation.gov.uk/ukpga/1990/18

Figure 3-10. *Work secure*

Data Privacy and Protection: Setting Your Moral Compass

Most of you will be aware of the data privacy revolution that is impacting the Digital Business' operations. The major contributor to this was the replacement of the 1995 Data Protection Directive with the European Union's General Data Protection Regulation (EU GDPR) on May 25, 2018.[40]

What was the reason for these changes?

The EU believe, quite rightly, that privacy is a universal human right, enshrined in the Universal Declaration of Human Rights (Article 12), the EU convention of Human Rights (Article 8), and the EU Charter of Fundamental Rights (Article 7), whereas this was not seen to be the case regarding data protection.[41]

---

[40]https://edps.europa.eu/data-protection/data-protection/legislation/
history-general-data-protection-regulation_en

[41]"Protecting any information relating to an identified or identifiable natural (living) person."

Following a survey of EU consumers,[42] it became increasingly apparent that consumers were concerned about their privacy and had lost trust in corporations. This, in turn, translated into potential lost opportunities and revenues for companies:

- **81%** of Europeans feel that they do not have complete control over their personal data online.

- A large majority of Europeans (**69%**) would like to give their explicit approval before the collection and processing of their personal data.

- Only **24%** of Europeans have trust in online businesses such as search engines, social networking sites, and email services.

Something needed to be done to encourage businesses to treat consumers' personal data with respect, reduce the opportunity of helping criminals, and rebuild the levels of trust.

Consequently, it was clear that the existing data privacy/data protection legislations were not as effective as they could be and that the supporting legislations needed a considerable overhaul.

This resulted in the introduction of the EU GDPR; further guidance can be gleaned from the supporting *Handbook on European Data Protection Law – 2018 Edition*[43] (as depicted in Figure 3-11).

[42]http://ec.europa.eu/newsroom/just/document.cfm?doc_id=41523

[43]https://fra.europa.eu/en/publication/2018/handbook-european-data-protection-law-2018-edition

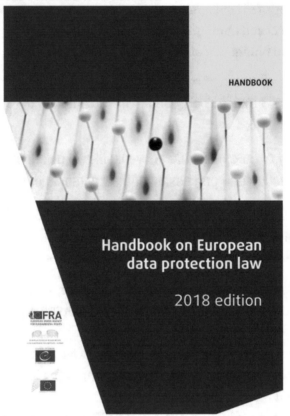

Figure 3-11. *EU Data Protection Law*

Proportionality is a significant concept of both "Protective Security" and the EU Data Protection Law.

Proportionality (n.)[44]

"character or state of being in proportion," 1560s, from French proportion-alité (14c.) or directly from Medieval Latin proportionalitas, from propor-tio "comparative relation, analogy" (see proportion (n.)). The word was used in Middle English (proporcionalite) in mathematics in reference to geometrical ratios (mid-15c.).

---

[44]www.etymonline.com/search?q=proportionality&ref=searchbar_searchhint

The objective is to ensure that the mitigating security controls are **equal to** the perceived threats. To achieve this, you need to have identified the assets and to have valued them. Proportionality is a fundamental element of modern risk management.

In fact, a key term that is used throughout the EU's handbook is "proportionality" *(being used on 31 occasions)*, for example:

- *subject to the principle of proportionality, are necessary.*

- *Proportionality requires that an interference with the rights protected under the ECHR should not go any further than what is needed to fulfil the legitimate aim pursued.*

- *This means that limitations that are so extensive and intrusive so as to devoid a fundamental right of its basic content cannot be justified. If the essence of the right is compromised, the limitation must be considered unlawful, without a need to further assess whether it serves an objective of general interest and satisfies the necessity and proportionality criteria.*

- *Article 52 (1) of the Charter provides that, subject to the principle of proportionality, limitations on the exercise of the fundamental rights and freedoms recognized by the Charter may be made only if they are necessary.*

- *Proportionality means that the advantages resulting from the limitation should outweigh the disadvantages the latter causes on the exercise of the fundamental rights at stake. To reduce disadvantages and risks to the enjoyment of the rights to privacy and data protection, it is important that limitations contain appropriate safeguards.*

- *Example: In Volker und Markus Schecke, the CJEU concluded that by imposing an obligation to publish personal data relating to each natural person who was a beneficiary of aid from certain agricultural funds without drawing a distinction based on relevant criteria, such as the periods during which those persons received such aid, the frequency of such aid or the nature and amount thereof, the Council and the Commission had exceeded the limits imposed by the principle of proportionality.*

The EU GDPR is considered to be one of the most robust data privacy and data protection legislations, currently in place across the globe. However, when you consider the intent and objectives that the EU GDPR tries to achieve, whether you are in scope (as depicted in Figure 3-12[45]) for the EU GDPR or not, as a responsible business, wouldn't it make sense to ensure that your consumers' and employees' personal data is appropriately protected?

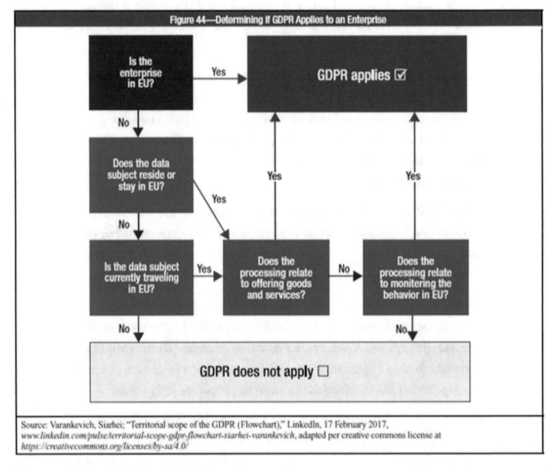

Figure 3-12. *GDPR territorial scope*

---

[45]www.isaca.org/resources/news-and-trends/isaca-now-blog/2018/
   organizations-outside-the-eu-must-not-overlook-gdpr-requirements

Later in the book, I will carry out a deep dive into the subject of Information Security systems protection for both corporate sensitive (aka trade secrets) and personal data.

However, it is important to recognize that the Data Privacy also covers the need to use personal data responsibly, with consideration for any legal requirements, legitimacy, or consent from the individual.

It is extremely important to recognize this distinction between how the data can and must be used and how this data is to be adequately protected.

Frequently, you will see organizations that fall foul of being focused on one and neglecting the other.

For example, have you ever experienced a data protection officer (DPO) who is only interested in the use of the data and has little, or no, interest in understanding the risks that pertain to the supporting assets?

Yet, in 2018, we saw two notices of an intention to apply significant fines (British Airways and Marriott Group), where the information commissioner's office (ICO) had cited:

- *poor security arrangements*[46]

- *failed to undertake sufficient due diligence when it bought Starwood and should also have done more to secure its systems*[47]

Clearly, this shows that the regulators are requiring businesses to protect and appropriately use personal data records in line with their defined lifecycles.

Consequently, where you have a DPO and a cyber/information security manager *(in smaller organizations, this could be one and the same)*, they should be working closely together and with the business reporting the risks and status of any asset involved with the processing, storage, or transmission of personal data.

---

[46]https://ico.org.uk/about-the-ico/news-and-events/news-and-blogs/2019/07/
ico-announces-intention-to-fine-british-airways/#:~:text=Following%20an%20
extensive%20investigation%20the,Data%20Protection%20Regulation%20(GDPR).
&text=Personal%20data%20of%20approximately%20500%2C000,have%20begun%20in%20
June%202018

[47]https://ico.org.uk/about-the-ico/news-and-events/news-and-blogs/2019/07/
statement-intention-to-fine-marriott-international-inc-more-than-99-million-
under-gdpr-for-data-breach/#:~:text=Following%20an%20extensive%20investigation%20
the,by%20Marriott%20in%20November%202018

For instance, in the British Airways security incident, they had vulnerabilities associated to the precluding web pages involved in their customers' flight booking journey. British Airways had handed off the responsibilities for handling the payment card processing to a PCI DSS, so that their customers would input all their payment card information directly into a PCI DSS–compliant (secure) payment service provider's (PSP) interface.

However, the criminals were able to inject malicious code in an earlier web page, within the customers' journeys, to redirect them through a malicious web page (baways. com) – a man-in-the-middle attack (as depicted in Figure 3-13). Consequently, although they thought they had a secure ecommerce operation (fully outsourced) and had this signed off as being PCI DSS compliant, they had omitted to protect the web page that supported the "hand off" to the third-party payment service provider.

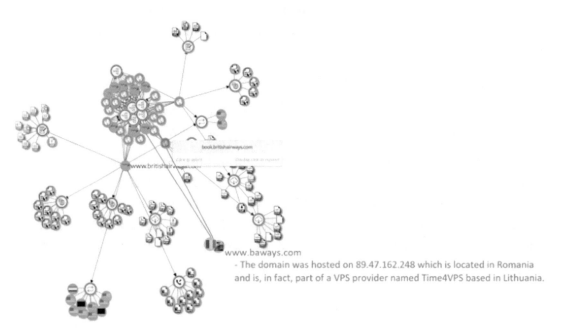

Figure 3-13. *Man-in-the-middle attack*

The online retailer Claire's Accessories[48] were to suffer the same fate, between April 25 and June 13, 2020,[49] when the same criminal group (Magecart[50]) were to apply the very same tactics and redirect Claire's customers through another malicious web page (claires-assets.com).

claires-assets.com

Domain Information	
Domain:	claires-assets.com
Registrar:	NameCheap, Inc.
Registered On:	2020-03-21
Expires On:	2021-03-21
Updated On:	2020-03-21
Status:	clientTransferProhibited
Name Servers:	dns1.registrar-servers.com
	dns2.registrar-servers.com

Figure 3-14. *Domain data*[51]

This involved a skimmer being attached to the submit button of the checkout form. On clicking this button, the full "Demandware Checkout Form" was grabbed, serialized, and base64 encoded.[52] A temporary image was then added to the document object model (DOM) with the preloader identifier. The image was then located on the server, controlled by the attacker. Because all of the customer-submitted data was appended to the image address, the attacker received the full payload.

As a result, every customer making an online purchase into the compromised ecommerce website was to have their sensitive personal and payment card data clandestinely harvested.

Is it reasonable and proportionate for Claire's and the other 2+ million ecommerce websites[53] to continue to ignore the risks from online card skimming?

Only time will tell, once the ICO has completed their investigations into the cyber-attack on the Claire's Accessories ecommerce website.[54]

---

[48]www.claires.com/

[49]https://drmlegal.co.uk/2020/06/18/claires-data-breach/

[50]www.riskiq.com/blog/magecart/

[51]https://whois.domaintools.com/claires-assets.com

[52]www.base64decode.org/

[53]www.bloomberg.com/press-releases/2019-10-04/new-report-shows-magecart-detections-exceed-2-million-and-offers-key-insights-for-e-commerce

[54]https://news.sky.com/story/shopped-with-claires-online-hackers-may-have-stolen-your-card-details-12007303

Focus on the Use of Personal Data

If you were to review the many generally accepted Privacy Principles that are available to businesses, you will see that around **80-90%** of the principles related to how the personal data is used:

- **7 Privacy by Design (PbD) Principles**[55]

1. **Proactive not Reactive; Preventative not Remedial**

   The Privacy by Design approach is characterized by proactive rather than reactive measures. It anticipates and prevents privacy invasive events before they happen.

   PbD does not wait for privacy risks to materialize, nor does it offer remedies for resolving privacy infractions once they have occurred – it aims to prevent them from occurring. In short, Privacy by Design comes before-the-fact, not after.

2. **Privacy as the Default Setting**

   We can all be certain of one thing – the default rules! Privacy by Design seeks to deliver the maximum degree of privacy by ensuring that personal data are automatically protected in any given IT system or business practice. If an individual does nothing, their privacy still remains intact. No action is required on the part of the individual to protect their privacy – it is built into the system, by default.

3. **Privacy Embedded into Design**

   Privacy by Design is embedded into the design and architecture of IT systems and business practices. It is not bolted on as an add-on, after the fact.

   The result is that privacy becomes an essential component of the core functionality being delivered.

   Privacy is integral to the system, without diminishing functionality.

---

[55]https://iapp.org/media/pdf/resource_center/pbd_implement_7found_principles.pdf

4. **Full Functionality – Positive-Sum, not Zero-Sum**

   Privacy by Design seeks to accommodate all legitimate interests and objectives in a positive-sum "win-win" manner, not through a dated, zero-sum approach, where unnecessary trade-offs are made.

   Privacy by Design avoids the pretense of false dichotomies, such as privacy vs. security, demonstrating that it is possible, and far more desirable, to have both.

5. **End-to-End Security – Full Lifecycle Protection**

   Privacy by Design, having been embedded into the system prior to the first element of information being collected, extends securely throughout the entire lifecycle of the data involved — strong security measures are essential to privacy, from start to finish.

   This ensures that all data are securely retained, and then securely destroyed at the end of the process, in a timely fashion. Thus, Privacy by Design ensures cradle to grave, secure lifecycle management of information, end-to-end.

6. **Visibility and Transparency – Keep it Open**

   Privacy by Design seeks to assure all stakeholders that whatever the business practice or technology involved, it is in fact, operating according to the stated promises and objectives, subject to independent verification.

   Its component parts and operations remain visible and transparent, to both users and providers alike.

   Remember, trust but verify!

7. **Respect for User Privacy – Keep it User-Centric**

   Above all, Privacy by Design requires architects and operators to keep the interests of the individual uppermost by offering such measures as strong privacy defaults, appropriate notice, and empowering user-friendly options. Keep it user-centric!

- **Organisation for Economic Co-operation and Development (OECD) Privacy Principles, 2013**[56]

   1. Collection limitation

   2. Data quality

   3. Purpose specification

   4. Use limitation

   5. Security safeguards

   6. Openness

   7. Individual participation

   8. Accountability

- **ISO/IEC 29100:2011 Privacy Principles**[57]

   1. Consent and choice

   2. Purpose legitimacy and specification

   3. Collection limitation

   4. Data minimization

   5. Use, retention, and disclosure limitation

   6. Accuracy and quality

   7. Openness, transparency, and notice

   8. Individual participation and access

   9. Accountability

   10. Information security

   11. Privacy compliance

---

[56]www.oecd.org/sti/ieconomy/privacy-guidelines.htm

[57]www.iso.org/standard/45123.html

- **APEC Privacy Framework**[58]

  1. Preventing harm

  2. Notice

  3. Collection limitations

  4. Uses of personal information

  5. Choice

  6. Integrity of personal information

  7. Security safeguards

  8. Access and correction

  9. Accountability

- **American Institute of Certified Public Accountants (AICPA)/CPA
  Canada (aka AICPA/CICA GAPP)**[59]

  1. Management

  2. Notice

  3. Choice and consent

  4. Collection

  5. Use, retention, and disposal

  6. Access

  7. Disclosure to third parties

  8. Security for privacy

  9. Quality

  10. Monitoring and enforcement

---

[58]https://iapp.org/media/pdf/resource_center/APEC_Privacy_Framework.pdf

[59]www.aicpa.org/content/dam/aicpa/interestareas/informationtechnology/resources/
privacy/downloadabledocuments/10252-346-records-management-pro.pdf

Taking the commonalities of all these different Privacy Principles, ISACA[60] developed 14 overarching Privacy Principles:

1. Choice and consent

2. Legitimate purpose and use limitation

3. Personal information and sensitive information lifecycle

4. Accuracy and quality

5. Openness, transparency, and notice

6. Individual participation

7. Accountability

8. Security safeguards

9. Monitoring, measuring, and reporting

10. Preventing harm

11. Third-party/vendor management

12. Breach management

13. Security and privacy by design

14. Free flow of information and legitimate restriction

As you can see, the common criteria for all these Privacy Principles is having an integrated approach for the safety and security for use of personal data.

Personal data is a highly sought-after commodity by today's criminals as they seek to exploit these data types for financial gain. Consequently, in 2019, we saw several worrying trends,[61] where the criminals are targeting new technologies or poor use of such technologies (either internally or through the Supply Chain):

- Supply chain attacks increased by **78%**, malicious PowerShell scripts up by **1000%**, and Microsoft Office files contributed to **48%** of malicious email attachments.

---

[60]https://isaca.org

[61]https://img03.en25.com/Web/Symantec/%7B984e78e2-c9e5-43b8-a6ee-417a08608b60%7D_
   ISTR_24_2019_April_en.pdf?elqTrackId=136e2f99e16c42e0805cb48597af9016&elqaid=6820
   &elqat=2

- Cybercriminals attack IoT devices an average of **5233 times per month**.

- Formjacking[62] increased by **117%**.

- New account fraud is up by **13%**.

- Account takeovers are up by **79%**.

In addition to these types of attacks, we are also seeing the ingenuity of the attackers' use of the exfiltrated data to turn a profit. This was evident in the identity theft attacks on the Ritz Hotel customers,[63] who received fraudulent calls purporting to be from the Ritz Hotel, and by using the stolen booking data, the attackers convinced the customers to hand over their payment card information.

This information was then used to purchase goods for resale on the black market.

Power to the People

Consequently, much like failures in Health and Safety procedures which can harm or impact others (as depicted in Figure 3-15[64]), if you are handling personal data of your employees or consumers, taking payments via credit/debit cards (in exchange for goods or services), providing services to other businesses, or reliance on IT systems for automated industrial processes (aka manufacturing 4.0), in the event of a compromise of confidentiality, integrity, or availability of sensitive data or the supporting systems or processes, you may well be facing litigation.

---

[62]https://docs.broadcom.com/doc/istr-formjacking-deep-dive-en

[63]www.zdnet.com/article/ritz-london-struck-by-data-breach-fraudsters-pose-as-staff-
in-credit-card-data-scam/

[64]www.poandpo.com/companies/uk-chemical-maker-croda-faces-fine-for-toxic-gas-leak-
in-us-1762019691/#:~:text=The%20British%2Dbased%20chemical%20maker,Atlas%20
Point%20plant%20in%20Delaware.&text=It%20has%20therefore%20recommended%20that%20
Croda%20pays%20a%20%24262%2C548%20fine

UK chemical maker Croda faces fine for toxic gas leak in US

CHRISTIAN FERNSBY ▼ June 17, 2019   **Tweet** **in** Share

The British-based chemical maker, Croda, has been cited by the US Occupational Safety and Health
Administration (OSHA) for 'serious' violations in failing to prevent a toxic gas leak at its Atlas Point plant in
Delaware.

Figure 3-15. *Chemical maker fined*

Unless you are mandated to demonstrate your ability to maintain compliance (e.g., Payment Card Industry Data Security Standard (PCI DSS)[65]), this is where compliance can become a business enabler.

Notwithstanding the legal and regulatory requirements, if an organization is seen to be negligent, we are seeing an increasing volume of legal cases being taken out against businesses:

- **IOOF hit with lawsuit alleging cybersecurity failure**[66]

---

[65]www.apress.com/gp/book/9781484258071

[66]www.afr.com/companies/financial-services/ioof-hit-with-lawsuit-alleging-
 cybersecurity-failure-20200821-p55o27

- **Marriott hit by London lawsuit over one of biggest data breaches in history**[67]

- **Lawsuit by LifeLabs for data breach report disclosure**[68]

- **Blackbaud Hit with Class Action Over Data Breach Stemming from Three-Month Ransomware Attack**[69]

- **The Cybersecurity 202: Zoom sued by consumer group for misrepresenting its encryption protections**[70]

- **Cyberbreach Leads to Legal Malpractice Claim**[71]

- **Epiq Systems faces lawsuit over malware, ransomware attack**[72]

- **Allegheny County Airport Authority sues IT company for alleged cybersecurity failures**[73]

---

[67]www.telegraph.co.uk/technology/2020/08/19/marriott-hit-london-lawsuit-one-biggest-data-breaches-history/

[68]www.cybersecurity-insiders.com/lawsuit-by-lifelabs-for-data-breach-report-disclosure/

[69]www.classaction.org/news/blackbaud-hit-with-class-action-over-data-breach-stemming-from-three-month-ransomware-attack

[70]www.washingtonpost.com/politics/2020/08/11/cybersecurity-202-zoom-sued-by-consumer-group-misrepresenting-its-encryption-protections/

[71]www.americanbar.org/groups/litigation/publications/litigation-news/top-stories/2020/cyberbreach-leads-to-legal-malpractice-claim/

[72]www.bizjournals.com/kansascity/news/2020/07/31/epiq-systems-lawsuit-malware-ransomware.html

[73]https://triblive.com/local/allegheny-county-airport-authority-sues-it-company-for-alleged-cybersecurity-failures/

Reality Bites

It has been evident that the regulators are becoming increasingly committed to ensuring that organizations abide to the rules of privacy and ensuring the confidentiality, integrity, or availability of their valuable business assets.

One such example was seen through the Commodity Futures Trading Commission issue of three orders filing and settling charges against the Bank of Nova Scotia (BNS) (a provisionally registered swap dealer),[74] in resolution of two separate enforcement actions. The combined orders require BNS to pay $127.4 million for spoofing and making false statements, in addition to swap dealer compliance, supervision violations, and additional false statements.

Key Takeaways

We are seeing significant changes to the legal and regulatory landscapes; however, businesses should be preparing for the inevitable additional changes that are to come. Effective Protective Security should automatically result in the adherence to your legal or regulatory obligations while reducing risk.

By looking at protective security in the same manner as you might regard your Health and Safety obligations – so that everyone understands its importance and provides a team effort to help reduce the risk.

Protective Security should not be regarded as something that is bad for business but, rather, as something that will be extremely beneficial to an organization.

As a business, if you are providing services to another organization or individual, you should be embracing Protective Security to help safeguard the operational effectiveness of the supporting assets.

Doing things correctly reflects the organization's "moral compass."

Personal data is just another asset that needs to be appropriately protected. However, this has additional privacy implications to ensure that any personal data is handled correctly.

When approached correctly, compliance can be used as a business enabler.

---

[74]www.cftc.gov/PressRoom/PressReleases/8220-20

CHAPTER 4

The Integration of Compliance with Protective Security (PS)

The day the soldiers stop bringing you their problems is the day you stopped leading them. They have either lost confidence that you can help them or concluded that you do not care. Either case is a failure of leadership!

US Army General[1]
Former Joint Chief of Staff

Figure 4-1. *Colin Powell*

---

[1]www.moaa.org/content/publications-and-media/features-and-columns/moaa-features/ Colin-Powell-Remembers-Desert-Storm-25-years-later/

© Jim Seaman 2021
J. Seaman, *Protective Security*, https://doi.org/10.1007/978-1-4842-6908-4_4

Introduction

The term compliance is something that I have been comfortable with when referenced against security. If you look back at the origins of the word, it infers that adherence is only being done because it has to be done.

> **Compliance (n.)**[2]
>
> 1640s, "act of complying; disposition to yield to others," from comply + -ance. Related: Compliancy.

However, whether I like it or not, the phrase of "being compliant" or "being in compliance" is widely used across business and the security industry.

I could not have explained this better than the former US Army General, Colin Powell. However, I have experienced many occasions where senior management or business leaders were not interested in hearing that their business might have problems.

Consequently, they only want to hear good news and will only seek to support the bare minimum that they are pressed into doing *(being deemed to be compliant)*. The result is that they do not fully embrace the benefits Protective Security measures provide to their business, and, guess what, their most impactful business operations become compromised.

This is where the term "compliance" can get a poor reputation, as businesses can get a false sense of assurance because once a year they are deemed to be secure. Rarely do they make the scope cover the entire organization, and so they limit the scope to an extremely small footprint and then take solace in the fact that they managed to retain their compliance certificate.

I can recall one company that only sought ISO/IEC 27001 compliance because the chief information officer (CIO) did not want to be the only department that were not certified against an industry standard. Consequently, their brief to the head of information security was to choose the easiest scope that they could achieve compliance, and so they limited to a handful of IT Operations personnel, who managed the desktop, and mobile services and support function at a single location.

This was a global business-to-business (B2B), FTSE 250 listed company, operating across 31 countries, that is engaged in the manufacture of raw materials *(over 15 industrial plants)* which they sell *(over 30 sales offices)* and market to other organizations. Consequently, looking at this from a business context, they might have considered other elements as important or even more important:

- Circa 5000 employees accessing and using these desktop and mobile devices and using various business applications *(deemed to be out of scope)*

- A central customer relationship management (CRM) database *(deemed to be out of scope)*

- Numerous business-critical applications *(deemed to be out of scope)*

- Numerous websites *(deemed to be out of scope)*

- Human Resources *(deemed to be out of scope)*

- A global sales team *(deemed to be out of scope)*

- Marketing *(deemed to be out of scope)*

- Cloud services *(deemed to be out of scope)*

- Numerous servers *(deemed to be out of scope)*

- Network components *(deemed to be out of scope)*

However, even though they had limited their compliance to an extremely small scope, they did not communicate this to the key stakeholders and investors (as depicted in Figure 4-2).

> *In line with our established global policies, our information security specialists monitor our IT services and networks, oversee computer and mobile device protection, and provide cyber awareness education globally.*
>
> *Regular penetration testing is undertaken, and we have externally audited ISO 27001 certification for key systems and locations, whilst internal and external auditors review and report on the operation of all cyber and system controls annually.*

Figure 4-2. *Extract from the annual report*

- Do you think that the key stakeholders and investors might have had a different interpretation of what their key systems and location(s) were?

If they were to see what a hacker can see (as depicted in Figure 4-3[3]), they might have a different viewpoint on the assurance they might have gained from being ISO/IEC 27001 compliant.

---

[3]https://securityscorecard.com/

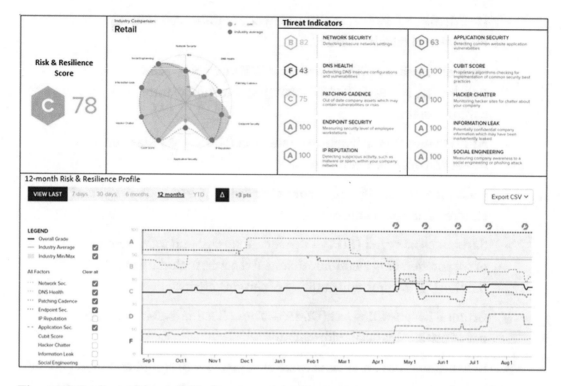

Figure 4-3. *Security scorecard reconnaissance*

Certainly, in the event of a cyber-attack or data breach, they would change their opinion of the value and assurance gained from ISO/IEC 27001 compliance.

It is extremely important to ensure that all identified business valued processes and their supporting assets are risk assessed and suitable controls applied to mitigate these identified risks.

However, these do not necessarily need to be externally validated (certified) for compliance but should be subject to periodic risk and performance metrics reporting (key risk indicators (KRIs) and key performance indicators (KPIs)).

When considering compliance, ensure that the scope is relevant, supports the business objective, and applies the most appropriate industry controls framework,[45] for example:

- **PCI DSS** – Protection of payment card data and supporting systems

- **ISO/IEC 27001** – Protection of sensitive data and supporting systems

---

[4]www.tcdi.com/information-security-compliance-which-regulations/

[5]https://arcticwolf.com/resources/guides/the-financial-industry-cybersecurity-checklist

- **Health Insurance Portability and Accountability Act (HIPAA)** – Protection of health records

- **National Institute of Standards and Technology Special Publication 800:82 (NIST SP800:82)** – Protection of industrial control systems

- **NERC Critical Infrastructure Protection (NERC CIP) Standards** – Protection of critical infrastructure

- **Children's Online Privacy Protection Rule (COPPA)** – Protection of children's personal data online

- **Sarbanes-Oxley Act (SOX)** – The secure storage and management of corporate-facing electronic financial records, including the monitoring, logging, and auditing of certain activity

- **Gramm-Leach-Bliley Act (GLBA)** – The collection, safekeeping, and use of private financial information

Many organizations have often had a bad experience with compliance and find that it can provide little business benefit or help to reduce the risks of a breach. However, this is not created by the industry security standards frameworks but, rather, by the misaligned or poorly applied implementation for compliance and can be extremely beneficial to an organization.

A better term that could be used in place of "compliance" is the term "validation" or "security health check." After all, the objective is to provide independent validation for the effectiveness of the management of a suite of security controls, in support of risk management and assurance of in-house or outsourced business essential operations.

Military Example

When I first trained as a counter intelligence (CI) specialist, I was introduced to the 5 Ts of risk management:

1. **T**reat

2. **T**erminate

3. **T**olerate

4. **T**ransfer

5. **T**ake the opportunity

Later in my career, the fifth T was to be dropped from the RAF's risk management tactics, techniques, and protocols (TTPs). However, before this was to happen, I was able to use compliance as a chance to apply to the fifth T.

Every military airfield is already subject to stringent rules. However, when it comes to the processing of passengers, and especially regarding the nonmilitary aircraft, the rules that must be complied with get even more robust and difficult.

Consequently, in June 2005, when the Royal Ascot event was relocated to York, the local RAF station sought permission to receive nonmilitary aircraft onto their airfield. The initial response was an emphatic **NO**.

I never see risk decisions as a simply linear Yes or No response but rather as a scaled Yes down to a final No (as depicted in Figure 4-4).

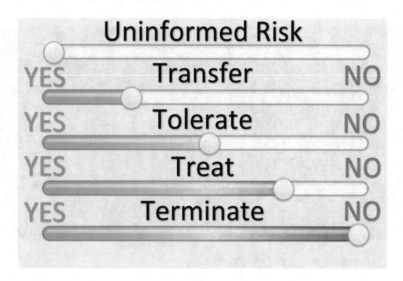

Figure 4-4. *Decision-making risk scales*

Basically, there are many ways to look at a problem and mitigate risks so that they are acceptable to the risk owners. In this case, the risks were above the Station Commander's risk levels, so it was escalated to command. Here, it was deemed to be beyond the levels of comfort for taking such a decision on the risk, and it was then escalated to the UK Government's Department for Transport (DfT[6]).

---

[6]www.gov.uk/transport/aviation

All along this risk decision-making journey, we were being told that it was highly unlikely that the RAF station would be granted approval.

Fortunately, they weren't privy to my knowledge and experience, gained from a couple of years employed on air transport security, during my time in Northern Ireland.

Consequently, within 24 hours, I had managed to plan and establish a suitable passenger processing facility within a hostile environment (Kabul, early 2002), and to establish a department for transport (DfT) and Civil Aviation Authority (CAA[7])-compliant passenger processing facility in RAFO Thumrait, Oman). In addition, to four years' experience of managing the protective security requirements *(including successfully completing an external security review (security risk inspection(SRI)).*

By the time the DfT inspector had arrived, I had formulated a suite of mitigation controls that I could present to him. During a meeting, in my Flight Sergeant's office, I was provided the opportunity to brief the inspector on how I intended to turn this military base into a CAA-compliant facility (as depicted in Figure 4-5).

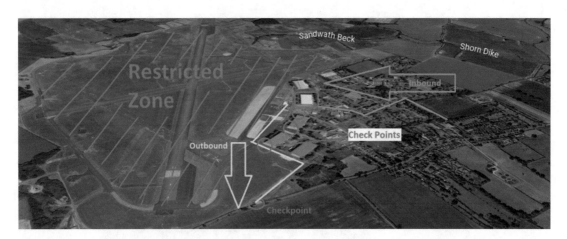

Figure 4-5. *Enhanced security measures*

---

[7]www.caa.co.uk/Commercial-industry/Security/Security-Regulation/

This included

- Creating an isolated restricted zone (*transferring the control of access to the resident guard service*)

- Using the existing physical infrastructures to create a defined boundary between the restricted and uncontrolled areas *(within acceptable tolerances)*

- Restricting inbound and outbound passenger movements, via the conversion of an airside hangar (converted into a passenger terminal), into the restricted zone and creating a controlled flow inbound and outbound, through defined checkpoints *(treating the access control risks)*

- Getting a team of RAF Police personnel civil aviation security trained and certified, hiring metal detectors and X-ray machine

Added to this, the DfT inspector needed to consider the secondary risks and burden to the nearest airport (29 miles (approx. 1-hour drive) away from York racecourse) vs. what impact having the use of the RAF station (12 miles (approx. 30 mins drive) away from York racecourse).

Consequently, given the additional measures that were implemented and the local considerations, the risks were deemed to be within the DfT's risk appetites, and the RAF station was granted temporary DfT accreditation *(covering the Royal Ascot at the York event)*, as depicted in Figure 4-6.[8]

---

[8]www.yorkpress.co.uk/news/7863082.raf-base-becomes-makeshift-airport/

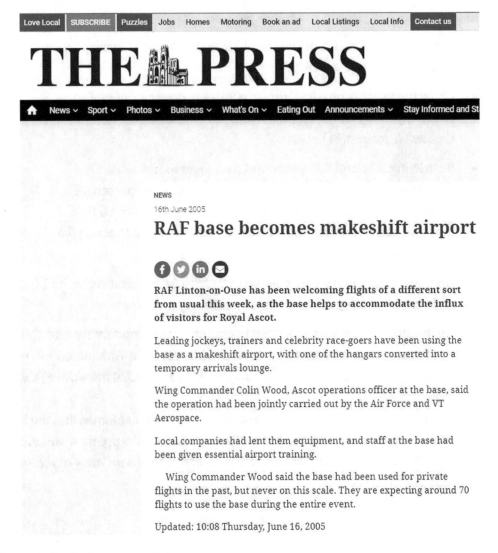

Figure 4-6. *York Press article*

The Value of Standardization

Compliance against a specific standard or suite of standards means that against a defined scope all the processes and systems should be configured to be compatible and work in the same manner (aka standardization), as depicted in Figure 4-7.

Standardization is defined as[9]

---

[9]https://dictionary.cambridge.org/dictionary/english/standardization

- *The process of making things of the same type all have the same basic features.*

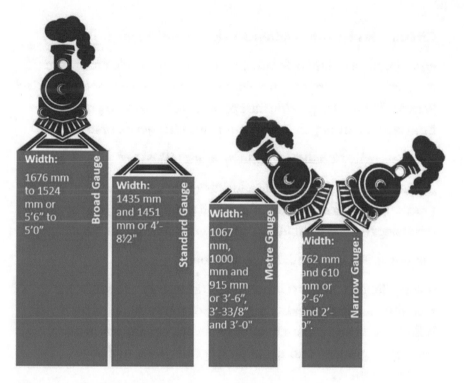

Figure 4-7. *Standardization*

Additionally, this also ensures that the processes have been defined against robust industry security controls, designed, and developed to help mitigate against known risks.

It is important to remember that the different industry security standards have been developed for specific purposes or industries. Consequently, it is important to ensure that you understand what the standards/frameworks were originally designed to do.

However, this does not prevent you from *pick 'n' mixing* the best controls from the available controls frameworks for the enhancement of your risk mitigation efforts.

Industry Security Controls Frameworks

General

- **Criminal Justice Information Services (CJIS) Security Policy**[10]

  A minimum standard of security requirements to help ensure the continuity of information protection. The essential premise of the CJIS Security Policy is to provide the appropriate controls to protect CJI, from creation through dissemination, whether at rest or in transit.

- **Cybersecurity Capability Maturity Model (C2M2)**[11]

  A focus on the implementation and management of cybersecurity practices associated with the information technology (IT) and operations technology (OT) assets and the environments in which they operate.

- **Catalog of Recommendations Revision 7**[12]

  A compilation of practices that various industry bodies have recommended to increase the security of control systems from both physical and cyber-attacks. The recommendations in this catalog are grouped into 19 families, or categories, that have similar emphasis.

- **NIST Special Publication 800-171 Revision 1**[13]

  The standard that all DoD vendors, contractors, and suppliers will be required to be compliant with starting in September 2016.

- **Control Correlation Identifier Specification V2 Release 0.1**[14]

  A decomposition of an IA Control or an IA industry best practice into single, actionable statements. The CCI List is a collection of CCI Items, which express common IA practices or controls.

---

[10]www.fbi.gov/services/cjis/cjis-security-policy-resource-center

[11]www.energy.gov/ceser/activities/cybersecurity-critical-energy-infrastructure/energy-sector-cybersecurity-0

[12]https://us-cert.cisa.gov/sites/default/files/documents/CatalogofRecommendationsVer7.pdf

[13]https://csrc.nist.gov/publications/detail/sp/800-171/rev-1/final

[14]https://public.cyber.mil/stigs/cci/

Chemical, Oil, and Natural Gas

- **CFATS Risk-Based Performance Standards Guide 8-Cyber**[15]

  Risk-based performance standards (RBPSs) for the security of the nation's chemical facilities using a tiered approach

- **INGAA Control Systems Cyber Security Guidelines for the Natural Gas Pipeline Industry**[16]

  A set of guidelines to assist operators of natural gas pipelines in managing their control systems cyber security requirements

Cyber/Information Security

- **Center for Internet Security 20 Critical Security Controls (CIS 20 CSCs)**[17]

  A suite of the controls deemed most critical for the protection of Internet-based business operations.

  This standard consists of a set of 20 controls designed to help organizations safeguard their systems and data from known attack vectors. It can be a helpful guide for companies that do not have a coherent security program.

  The CIS Controls are not a replacement for any existing compliance scheme, but the controls can be mapped against several major compliance frameworks (e.g., the NIST Cybersecurity Framework) and regulations (e.g., PCI DSS and HIPAA). The 20 controls are based on the latest information about common attacks and reflect the combined knowledge of commercial forensics experts, individual penetration testers, and contributors from US Government agencies.

---

[15]www.cisa.gov/rbps-8-cyber

[16]www.aga.org/sites/default/files/legacy-assets/membercenter/gotocommitteepages/ NGS/Documents/INGAAControlSystemsCyberSecurityGuidelines.pdf

[17]www.cisecurity.org/controls/cis-controls-list/

- **ISO/IEC 27001:2013 – Information technology — Security techniques — Information security management systems — Requirements**[18]

    Specifies the requirements for establishing, implementing, maintaining, and continually improving an information security management system within the context of the organization. It also includes requirements for the assessment and treatment of information security risks tailored to the needs of the organization. The requirements set out in ISO/IEC 27001:2013 are generic and are intended to be applicable to all organizations regardless of type, size, or nature.

- **Baseline Cyber Security Controls for Small and Medium Organizations**[19]

    A suite of minimum security controls intended for small and medium organizations in Canada that want recommendations to improve their resiliency via cyber security investments.

Department of Defense Instruction (DoDI) and Committee on National Security Systems (CNSSI)

- **DoD Instruction 8510.01**[20]

    Risk Management Framework (RMF) for DoD Information Technology (IT).

- **CNSSI No. 1253 Baseline V2 March 27, 2014**[21]

---

[18]www.iso.org/standard/54534.html

[19]https://cyber.gc.ca/en/guidance/baseline-cyber-security-controls-small-and-medium-organizations

[20]www.dodea.edu/Offices/PolicyAndLegislation/upload/DoDEA-AI-8510-01-Risk-Management-Framework.pdf

[21]www.dcsa.mil/portals/91/documents/ctp/nao/CNSSI_No1253.pdf

Serves as a companion document to NIST SP 800-53 for organizations that employ national security systems (NSS). It establishes the processes for categorizing NSS and the information they process and for appropriately selecting security controls for NSS from NIST SP 800-53.

Electrical

- **NERC CIP-002 through CIP-014 Revision 6**[22]

    Developed to assist industry stakeholders with bulk electric power systems in North America with constructing and implementing their Cyber Security Plan

- **NISTIR 7628 Guidelines for Smart Grid Cyber Security: Volume 1 Revision 1**[23]

    Intended primarily for individuals and organizations responsible for addressing cyber security for smart grid systems and the constituent subsystems of hardware and software components

Financial

- **Automated Cybersecurity Examination Toolbox (ACET) Maturity Assessment**[24]

    Provides a repeatable, measurable, and transparent process that improves and standardizes our supervision related to cybersecurity in all federally insured credit unions.

- **Payment Card Industry Data Security Standard (PCI DSS)**[25]

    Developed for the protection of payment card data and the supporting systems and processes.

---

[22]https://fas.org/sgp/crs/homesec/R45135.pdf

[23]https://csrc.nist.gov/publications/detail/nistir/7628/rev-1/final

[24]www.ncua.gov/newsroom/ncua-report/2018/
new-tool-will-enhance-ncuas-cybersecurity-assessments-credit-unions

[25]www.pcisecuritystandards.org/document_library

The integration of security and privacy controls into one catalog recognizes the essential relationship between security and privacy objectives.

Health Care

- **Health Insurance Portability and Accountability Act (HIPAA) Security Rule**[26]

  Establishes national standards to protect individuals' medical records and other personal health information and applies to health plans, health-care clearinghouses, and those health-care providers that conduct certain health-care transactions electronically

Information Technology

- **NIST SP800:53 Rev.5 – Security and Privacy Controls for Information Systems and Organizations**[27]

  A comprehensive catalog of technical and nontechnical security and privacy controls. The controls can support a variety of specialty applications including the Risk Management Framework, Cybersecurity Framework, and Systems Engineering Processes used for developing systems, products, components, and services and for protecting organizations, systems, and individuals.

NIST Framework

- **Framework for Improving Critical Infrastructure Cybersecurity 1.1**[28]

  A voluntary risk-based Cybersecurity Framework – a set of industry standards and best practices to help organizations manage cybersecurity risks. The resulting framework, created through collaboration between the government and the private

---

[26]www.hhs.gov/hipaa/for-professionals/security/laws-regulations/index.html
[27]https://csrc.nist.gov/publications/detail/sp/800-53/rev-5/draft
[28]https://nvlpubs.nist.gov/nistpubs/CSWP/NIST.CSWP.04162018.pdf

sector, uses a common language to address and manage cybersecurity risks in a cost-effective way based on business needs without placing additional regulatory requirements on businesses.

Nuclear

- **NEI 08-09 Cyber Security Plan for Nuclear Power Reactors**[29]

  Developed to assist nuclear plant licensees in constructing and implementing their Cyber Security Plan license submittal as required by 10 CFR 73.54.

- **NRC Regulatory Guide 5.71**[30]

  Applies to operating nuclear reactors licensed in accordance with 10 CFR Part 50 and 10 CFR Part 52. Licensees and applicants should consider this guidance in preparing an application for a combined operating license under 10 CFR Part 52. Licensees and applicants bear the sole responsibility for assessing and managing the potential for adverse effects on safety, security, and emergency preparedness (SSEP) to provide high assurance that critical functions are adequately protected from cyber-attacks.

Process Control and Supervisory Control and Data Acquisition (SCADA)

- **NIST Special Publication 800-82 Revision 2**[31]

  Provides guidance for establishing secure industrial control systems (ICS). Many of these controls are based on SP800-53 with minor modifications.

- **American National Standard ISA-62443-4-1-2018 Security for Industrial Automation and Control Systems**[32]

---

[29]www.nrc.gov/docs/ML1011/ML101180437.pdf

[30]www.nrc.gov/docs/ML0903/ML090340159.pdf

[31]https://csrc.nist.gov/publications/detail/sp/800-82/rev-2/final

[32]https://webstore.ansi.org/standards/isa/ansiisa624432018

Part of a multipart standard that addresses the issue of security for industrial automation and control systems (IACS). It has been developed by working group 04, task group 06 of the ISA99 committee in cooperation with IEC TC65/WG10. This document prescribes the activities required to perform security risk assessments on a new or existing IACS and the design activities required to mitigate the risk to tolerable levels.

Supply Chain

- **NIST SP800-161 Supply Chain Risk Management**[33]

Provides guidance to federal agencies on identifying, assessing, and mitigating ICT supply chain risks at all levels of their organizations. The publication integrates ICT supply chain risk management (SCRM) into federal agency risk management activities by applying a multitiered, SCRM-specific approach, including guidance on assessing supply chain risk and applying mitigation activities.

Transportation

- **TSA Pipeline Security Guidelines March 2018**[34]

These guidelines are applicable to operational natural gas and hazardous liquid transmission pipeline systems, natural gas distribution pipeline systems, and liquefied natural gas facility operators. Additionally, they apply to operational pipeline systems that transport materials categorized as toxic inhalation hazards (TIH). TIH materials are gases or liquids that are known or presumed based on tests to be so toxic to humans as to pose a health hazard in the event of a release during transportation.

- **Defining a Security Zone Architecture for Rail Transit and Protecting Critical Zones**[35]

Securing control and communications systems in rail transit environments

---

[33]https://nvlpubs.nist.gov/nistpubs/SpecialPublications/NIST.SP.800-161.pdf
[34]www.hsdl.org/?view&did=809453
[35]https://www.apta.com/research-technical-resources/standards/security/
apta-ss-ccs-rp-002-13/

Building BRIDGES

Whichever industry security standard you are mandated, or choose, to comply with, the **BRIDGES** acronym can assist you achieve your goals.

This acronym (as depicted in Figure 4-8) provides you with a means to identify and evaluate key areas of a Protective Security strategy against a specific topic/subject area.

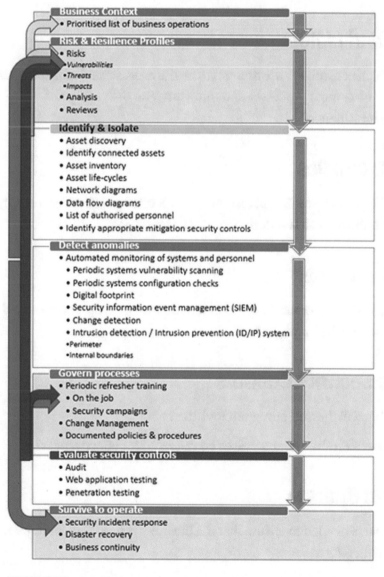

Figure 4-8. *BRIDGES acronym*

Business Context

- What processes are important to the business?

Risk and Resilience Profiles

- What are the risks to these business processes?

Identify and Isolate

- Which control sets are thought to be the most suitable for securing these business processes and mitigating the risks and preserving their resilience?

Detect Anomalies

- What security tools and resources are needed to effectively comply with the chosen standards/control frameworks?

Govern Processes

- How will implementation and maintenance of these standardized processes be managed?

Evaluate Security Controls

- What will the audit program look like?
- How often shall the processes be validated for effectiveness?

Survive to Operate

- What is needed to ensure that the business is prepared for unplanned activities?
- How can these business processes continue to operate in adverse conditions or quickly recover from an incident?

Standardization: A Valuable Lesson from Australian History

If you were to compare your organization's differing essential business processes to the different states and territories in Australia, if they work in isolation to one another, everything is fine.

However, if there is an overlap, where business processes are reliant on one another, you might wish to consider the compatibility between your chosen standards used for compliance.

With Australia being such a vast country, its rail system was developed in isolation from one another. Consequently, there were incompatibilities between states and territories, which resulted in inefficiencies for any longer rail travel that involved cross-state travel.[36]

- **Victoria** – The first railway line in Australia opened between Melbourne's Flinders Street Station and Port Melbourne, then called Sandridge, on September 12, 1854. Operated originally as a **1600 mm** gauge, it has since been converted to a **1435 mm** gauge electric light railway feeding the Melbourne tram system.

- **Queensland** – The first railway in Queensland ran from Ipswich inland to Grandchester using the narrow **1067 mm** gauge. The system was extended further to the Darling Downs before being connected with Brisbane, the capital, in 1875.

- **South Australia** – While South Australia had a horse-drawn railway operating at the mouth of the Murray River in 1854, the first line carrying steam-powered trains opened on April 21, 1856, between Adelaide and Port Adelaide. It was built by the colonial government to the then Australian "standard" gauge of **1600 mm**.

- **Western Australia** – Commencing in 1871, a private timber railway from Lockville to Yoganup, south of Perth, was the first railway to operate in Western Australia. The first government railway opened in 1879 between Geraldton and Northampton. In the nineteenth century, the network in south-western Western Australia was built as **1067 mm** gauge lines,

---

[36]www.infrastructure.gov.au/rail/history.aspx

but in the twentieth century the eastern states were connected to Perth and Esperance with standard (**1435 mm**) gauge lines.

- **Tasmania** – A railway line 72 km long opened between the Northern Tasmanian towns of Launceston and Deloraine in 1868. Built to the **1600 mm** gauge, the operator was the Launceston and Western Railway Company. Subsequently, the Tasmanian Government passed an Act of Parliament incorporating the Tasmanian Main Line Railway Company. This company built the mainline between Launceston and Hobart, the state capital.

- **Northern Territory** – The completion of the Alice Springs to Darwin standard gauge (**1435 mm**) rail link in January 2004 resulted in a national rail network linking all mainland state and territory capital cities. A railway between Darwin and Pine Creek (253 km) became operational on October 1, 1889. The Australian Government took control of the Pine Creek Railway from January 1, 1911. It operated until July 1, 1918, when the line became part of the Commonwealth Railways. The former North Australia Railway linked Darwin with Birdum – a distance of 511 km – by 1929. It was never profitable and has been closed for many years.

- **Australian Capital Territory** – A 10 km standard gauge (**1435 mm**) branch line opened between Queanbeyan, NSW, and Canberra, the Australian capital, in 1914. Passenger operations commenced in 1923.

Supporting Business Health

During my time in the RAF Police, and especially working in Counter Intelligence, the concept of "complying" *(or doing the bare minimum)* was not a concept that I was ever familiar with.

Protective Security was something that was applied to ensure that proportionate defensive measures were applied to ensure that valued assets were provided suitable protection, so that they remained within an individual manager's or department's risk tolerances[37] or within the business' risk appetite.[38]

A department would have defined levels of risk tolerance and would apply the guidance provided by the Defence Manual of Security (Joint Services Publication 440 (JSP 440))[39] to reduce the risks to the essential assets, for which they had responsibility. If after applying mitigation controls, the risks still exceeded their tolerance levels, they would escalate up their reporting chain.

Never did I experience the response:

What is the minimum I need to do to become compliant?

This has been the hardest thing for me to get my head around when starting out in the world of compliance. Many businesses will have critical assets that they are heavily reliant upon, much like the vital organs within the human body.

However, they adopt the mindset of only doing the bare minimum they need to keep these "vital organs" healthy.

Compliance is a business term that is here to stay, so I would recommend that if you are looking to "become compliant," you do so based upon the potential benefits it will bring to the organization.

When considering engaging in a compliance program, ask yourself the following questions:

- Does the scope include the "vital organs" which support essential business operations?

- Will the compliance help to reduce the risks to the "vital organs"?

- Does the proposed compliance program help you to detect abnormal activities that may impact the health of the "vital organs"?

- Does the compliance help promote healthy and effective processes?

---

[37]https://insights.sei.cmu.edu/insider-threat/2017/10/define-your-organizations-risk-tolerance-part-2-of-7-mitigating-risks-of-unsupported-operating-syste.html#:~:text=One%20framework%20is%20CERT%20OCTAVE,if%20the%20threats%20are%20realized.&text=The%20RMF%20enables%20you%20to%20continually%20manage%20your%20operational%20risk

[38]"The amount and type of risk that an organization is prepared to pursue, retain or take." – ISO 31000.

[39]http://wla.1-s.es/uk-mod-jsp-440-2001.pdf

- In the event of an adverse event that can impact the health of the "vital organs," are you able to respond in a timely manner to avoid unnecessary damage to the "vital organs"?

  - First aid

Any compliance program should be regarded by business as being beneficial to the health of the organization and its processes. Think of it like going for a medical/health check or a visit to see a health practitioner (as depicted in Figure 4-9).

Figure 4-9. *Health check*

You may feel like everything is normal or may have self-diagnosed that something is not quite right.

Before your vital organs start to fail, your body will start to provide you with signs and symptoms, long before the organs fail. This allows a person to seek medical intervention, which might help prevent full deterioration of the vital organ.

For example:

- **Liver disease (cirrhosis)**[40]

  - **Early symptoms**

    - Generally feeling unwell and tired all the time

    - Loss of appetite

    - Loss of weight and muscle wasting

    - Feeling sick (nausea) and vomiting

    - Tenderness/pain in the liver area

    - Spider-like small blood capillaries on the skin above waist level (spider angiomas)

    - Blotchy red palms

    - Disturbed sleep patterns

  - **Later symptoms, as the liver is struggling to function**

    - Intensely itchy skin

    - Yellowing of the whites of the eyes and the skin (jaundice)

    - White nails

    - Ends of fingers become wider/thicker (clubbed fingers)

    - Hair loss

    - Swelling of the legs, ankles, feet (edema)

    - Swelling of the abdomen (ascites)

    - Dark urine

    - Pale-colored stools or very dark/black tarry stools

    - Frequent nosebleeds and bleeding gums

    - Easy bruising and difficulty in stopping small bleeds

---

[40]https://britishlivertrust.org.uk/information-and-support/liver-health-2/symptoms-of-liver-disease/

- Vomiting blood

- Frequent muscle cramps

- Right shoulder pain

- In men, enlarged breasts and shrunken testes

- In women, irregular or lack of menstrual periods

- Impotence and loss of sexual desire

- Dizziness and extreme fatigue (anemia)

- Shortness of breath

- Very rapid heartbeat (tachycardia)

- Fevers with high temperature and shivers

- Forgetfulness, memory loss, confusion, and drowsiness

- Subtle change in personality

- Trembling hands

- Writing becomes difficult, spidery, and small

- Staggering gait when walking; tendency to fall

- Increased sensitivity to drugs, both medical and recreational

- Increased sensitivity to alcohol

The same applies to Protective Security and compliance.

By consulting with an external third-party specialist, they might discover something that isn't operating effectively, recommend some lifestyle changes, or confirm that your self-diagnosis is correct.

This is the same with compliance. Your internal audit process should be regarded as being your self-diagnosis, whereas the compliance is the medical/health check of your "vital organs." At the end of a successful compliance audit, you will receive some recommendations (if applicable) and a "certificate of health."

It is important to remember that the "certificate of health" is a stamp in time and only provides a validation that at the time of the medical/health check, an organization was able to provide evidence that they were maintaining good health of their in-scope assets. This is like having an electrocardiogram (ECG), which only confirms that the heart's rhythm and electrical activity was seen to be within acceptable parameters, during the time of the assessment.

- This does not mean that the rest of the body's vital organs are healthy!

Supply Chain Health Checks

As depicted in Figure 4-10, you are only as strong as the weakest link in your chain, and often the supply chain can make up many critical links within your chain.

Figure 4-10. *Managing the supply chain*

It is important for you to treat your outsourced suppliers in the same manner that they would treat your own in-house operations. The use of a third party to deliver services that support the business' "vital organs" is the transference of the responsibilities (perhaps due to resource limitations, specialist services, or budget restraints), but this does not negate the risk or accountability for ensuring that the third party continues to maintain the health of the "vital organs" (or impacting the health of the business' "vital organs").

Consequently, when considering an outsourced service, obtaining evidence of independent health checks can be beneficial, but it is important to remember that this is not the only thing that you should be considering.

Have you considered how the risks to your Supply Chain could impact your organization (as depicted in Figure 4-11[41])?

---

[41]https://nvlpubs.nist.gov/nistpubs/SpecialPublications/NIST.SP.800-161.pdf

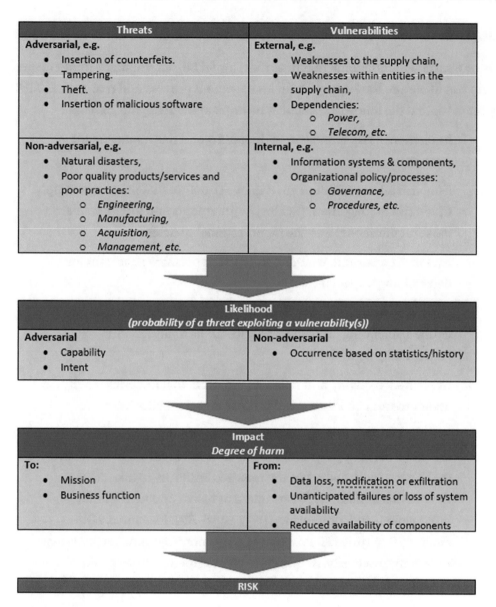

Figure 4-11. *Supply chain risk*

Supplier Chain Management Best Practices

There are several foundational practices that should be incrementally implemented to help you to mature the Supply Chain Management process and reduce risk. NIST[42] recommends that the following practices be implemented as your baseline:

- Implement a risk management hierarchy and risk management process.

- Establish an organization governance structure that integrates Supply Chain risk management (SCRM) requirements and incorporates these requirements into the organizational policies.

- Establish consistent, well-documented, repeatable processes for determining impact levels.

- Use risk assessment processes after the impact level has been defined, including criticality analysis, threat analysis, and vulnerability analysis.

- Implement a quality and reliability program that includes quality assurance and quality control processes and practices.

- Establish a set of roles and responsibilities for SCRM that ensures that the broad set of appropriate stakeholders are involved in decision-making, including who has the required authority to take action, who has accountability for an action or result, and who should be consulted and/or informed (e.g., Legal, Risk Executive, HR, Finance, Enterprise IT, Program Management/Systems Engineering, Information Security, Acquisition/procurement, supply chain logistics, etc.).

- Ensure that adequate resources are allocated to information security and SCRM to ensure proper implementation of guidance and controls.

- Implement consistent, well-documented, repeatable processes for systems engineering, security practices, and acquisition.

---

[42]https://nvlpubs.nist.gov/nistpubs/SpecialPublications/NIST.SP.800-161.pdf

- Implement an appropriate and tailored set of baseline information security controls.

- Establish internal checks and balances to assure compliance with security and quality requirements.

- Establish a supplier management program including guidelines for purchasing directly from qualified original equipment manufacturers (OEMs) or their authorized distributors and resellers.

- Implement a tested and repeatable contingency plan that integrates supply chain risk considerations to ensure the integrity and reliability of the supply chain including during adverse events (e.g., natural disasters such as hurricanes or economic disruptions such as labor strikes).

- Implement a robust incident management program to successfully identify, respond to, and mitigate security incidents. This program should be capable of identifying causes of security incidents, including those originating from the ICT supply chain.

Supplier Selection

Prior to selecting your preferred supplier, evaluate their ability to deliver the service to your business *(being wary of the services that can be supplied but that have not been scoped for)*, based upon what is likely to be included in the legally binding document (contract).

Once you have chosen your preferred supplier, work with your legal teams to ensure that the contract allows for reasonable schedules of "right to audit" and outlines your expected tolerances. Remember that even though this is an outsourced service, this is a service that you are paying for, and so the supplier must have their tolerances documented so that they support your business' risk appetite thresholds. If you have not clearly outlined this for the supplier, it is reasonable to presume that the supplier will align with their own or their other customers' tolerance levels, which may not be aligned to your organization's levels of risk tolerance.

Having chosen your supplier, ensure that you maintain a categorized list of your suppliers so that you can easily see which of your suppliers is providing the most critical services to your business. This should then be used to feed into your risk and resilience profiles.

Next, as part of the ongoing supplier management, based upon the category of the suppliers, create a workable supplier management assurance schedule.

This has four benefits:

1. Build supplier relationship *(this is a partnership)*.

2. Confirm that they are still able to deliver against the contracts.

3. Feed into the risk management process.

4. Provide added security assurance.

During the schedule, should you discover something that causes you concern, then you would need to carry out a risk assessment and add it to your risk register.

Additionally, you may discover external, unplanned, events/incidents that you may wish to implement additional security assurance reviews to the schedule. For example, you receive threat intelligence that threat actors are using specific tactics, techniques, and protocols (TTPs) against suppliers like one of your tier 1 suppliers *(e.g., remote access Trojan (RAT) attacks against cloud service providers)*.

Although you can carry out supplier due diligence activities, as a manual process, using a myriad of documents, spreadsheets, and so on, this is an extremely laborious and time-consuming process. I would highly recommend that you consider the advantages of using third-party provided software solutions.

- **Security Scorecard – ATLAS (as depicted in Figure 4-12[43])**

---

[43]assistance@cyberrescue.co.uk

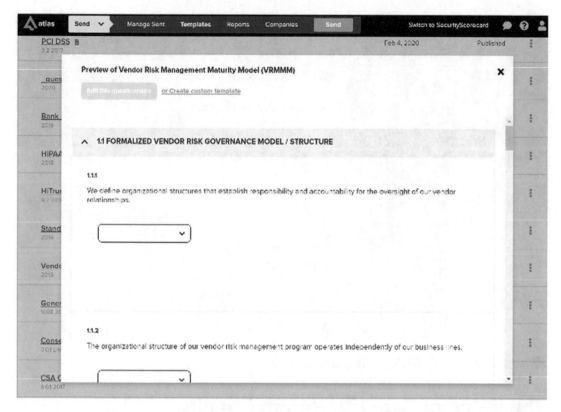

Figure 4-12. *VRMMM questionnaire*

- **Cyber Security Evaluation Tool – CSET (as depicted in Figure 4-13[44])**

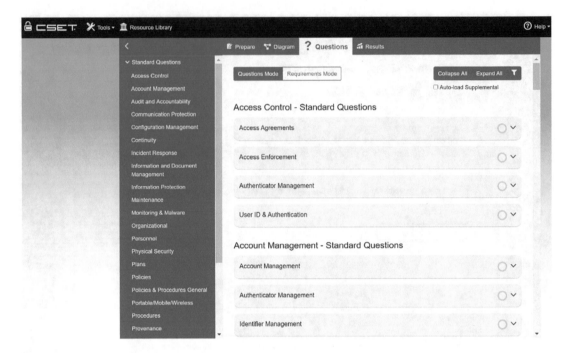

Figure 4-13. *NIST SP800:161 questionnaire*

The Value of Security Health Checks in Forecasting Risk

Whether your essential assets are managed by your in-house teams or you have transferred the responsibility to a third party *(of course, after having done extensive due diligence)*, by seeing the output of independent evaluations, you will be better placed to understand how well your critical assets and processes are being supported.

Let's have a look at an example to see how this might look.

Scenario

ABC Bank *(a well-known and respected bank)* relies on a third party to manage the maintenance of their mainframe computer. The mainframe computer is deemed to be a critical asset, as it is needed for processing enormous volumes of transactions.

The mainframe computer supports the primary operations, which revolves around credit card transactions, ATM withdrawals, and online account updates. Consequently, the mainframe allows the bank to process this data on a scale that commodity servers are unable to cope with.

During a supplier compliance review, it shows signs that the supplier had poor network security, DNS health, and patching cadence (as depicted in Figure 4-14[45]).

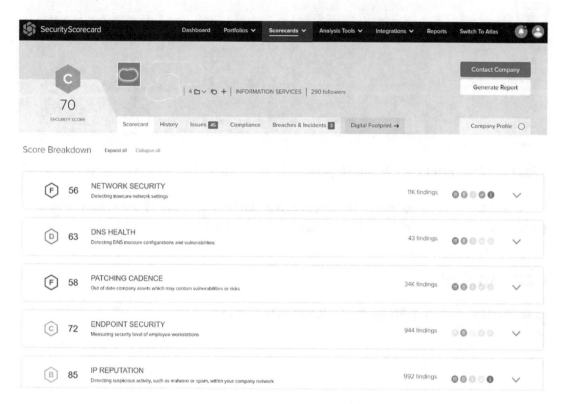

Figure 4-14. *Critical supplier risk and resilience profile*

Within the supplier's risk and resilience profile, although their score had been on the low side, this had been deemed to be within the bank's risk appetite. However, aligned with a change in normal working practices *(caused by a global pandemic)*, the supplier's profile score had seen a marked drop (as depicted in Figure 4-15).

---

[45]assistance@cyberrescue.co.uk

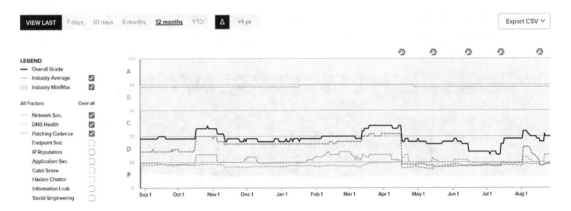

Figure 4-15. *Supplier 12-month profile*

Concerned that degraded patching practices could impact the critical mainframe computer, an analysis of the potential risk was carried out.

Risk Analysis

Loss Event Frequency Analysis (as depicted in Figure 4-16)

Analysis purpose.	To provide a forecast of the quantitative risk from a prolonged outage to the Bank's Mainframe computer.	
Asset.	Third-party managed Mainframe computer.	
Threat Actor.	Critical supplier (patching process).	
Threat Effect.	Availability.	
Threat Event Frequency.	How many times over the next year is the threat event likely to occur? How many times will the asset face a threat action?	
	Minimum	4
	Mostly likely	6
	Maximum	12
	Confidence rating	HIGH
	Rationale	Evidence has highlighted a potential issue with their changed working practices. This could impact their ability to meet their contract obligations.
Vulnerability.	What percentage of threat events are likely to result in loss events?	
	Minimum	50%
	Mostly likely	70%
	Maximum	90%
	Confidence rating	HIGH
	Rational	The Mainframe centrally supports the processing of critical data processes.

Figure 4-16. *LEF*

Loss Magnitude Analysis

- **Primary loss** (as depicted in Figure 4-17)

Primary Loss.	How much money are we likely to lose from each loss event?	
Productivity	Minimum	£68,000
	Mostly likely	£136,000
	Maximum	£204,000
	Confidence rating	HIGH
	Rationale	Based upon the following equation: $C \times H \times A \times N$ C = average hourly employee costs H = the duration of the outage in hours A = employees' productivity during downtime *(the percentage of normal productivity, expressed as a decimal)* N = the number of people affected
Response	Minimum	£8000
	Mostly likely	£15000
	Maximum	£20000
	Confidence rating	Medium
	Rational	The Mainframe centrally supports the processing of critical data processes.
Replacement	Minimum	£190,000
	Mostly likely	£375,000
	Maximum	£563,000
	Confidence rating	HIGH
	Rational	The costs were validated through the supply chain.
Competitive Advantage	Minimum	£10,000
	Mostly likely	£40,000
	Maximum	£100,000
	Confidence rating	Low
	Rationale	The competitive advantage was already established.
Fines & Judgements	Minimum	£1,000,000
	Mostly likely	£3,000,000
	Maximum	£5,000,000
	Confidence rating	HIGH
	Rationale	Based on other outage fines issued by the Regulators.
Reputation	Minimum	£20,900,000
	Mostly likely	£31,350,000
	Maximum	£47,000,000
	Confidence rating	MEDIUM
	Rationale	Based on 10% - 30% reduction in customer retention.

Figure 4-17. *LM – primary*

Secondary Risk Analysis

- **Secondary loss event frequency** (LEF (as depicted in Figure 4-18))

Secondary LEF	What percentage of primary loss events are likely to result in losses from secondary stakeholder reactions?	
	Minimum	60%
	Most Likely	80%
	Maximum	100%
	Confidence	Medium
	Rationale	These outages will be highly likely to impact the customer experience and longer outages could result in the Regulators becoming aware.

Figure 4-18. *Second LEF*

- **Secondary loss magnitude** (as depicted in Figure 4-19)

Secondary LM	How much loss is our organization likely to experience as a result of secondary stakeholders' reactions to the primary loss event?	
Productivity	Minimum	£1,000,000
	Most Likely	£5,000,000
	Maximum	£10,000,000
	Confidence	Medium
	Rationale	The stakeholder will recognize the impact on the customer experience and will look to disassociate their investments.
Replacement	Minimum	£0
	Most Likely	£0
	Maximum	£0
	Confidence	Low
	Rationale	Not applicable.
Replacement	Minimum	£0
	Most Likely	£0
	Maximum	£0
	Confidence	Low
	Rationale	Not applicable.
Competitive Advantage	Minimum	£0
	Most Likely	£0
	Maximum	£0
	Confidence	Low
	Rationale	Not applicable.
Fines & Judgements	Minimum	£0
	Most Likely	£0
	Maximum	£0
	Confidence	Low
	Rationale	Not applicable.
Reputation	Minimum	£0
	Most Likely	£0
	Maximum	£0
	Confidence	Low
	Rationale	Not applicable.

Figure 4-19. *Second LM*

Analysis Results

Risk

Using the FAIR-U tool,[46] I have visualized the forecasted Annualized Loss Exposure (ALE) that results from the estimated probable frequency and probable magnitude of future loss for a mainframe outage, lasting for a period of 7 days (as depicted in Figure 4-20).

---

[46]www.fairinstitute.org/fair-u

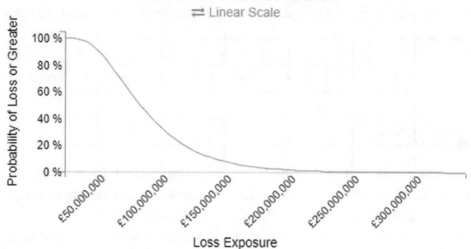

Figure 4-20. *LEC-mainframe 7-day outage*

Summary of Simulation Results

- **Primary**

	Min	Avg	Max
Loss Events/Year	3	5.05	9
Loss Magnitude	£5.1M	£14.0M	£44.3M

- **Secondary**

	Min	Avg	Max
Loss Events/Year	0	4.05	8
Loss Magnitude	£1.1M	£15.1M	£9.9M

- **Vulnerability**

  - **78.72%**

As you can see, the mainframe outage may not necessarily be an external-facing *(Cyber Security)* asset, but can impact the external-facing assets, and may not necessarily be an information *(Information Security)* system, but can impact information systems.

However, the potential impact to the bank from a mainframe outage could be equally or considerably more expensive than a cyber-attack or data breach and needs to be protected against.

It is essential that any compliance efforts are embedded into your Protective Security to ensure that they are an integral part and that they act in support of the overall strategy.

Reality Bites

Despite many ecommerce organizations choosing to reduce their payment card compliance burden by fully outsourcing the responsibility for interacting with any customers' sensitive data, the responsibility still resides with them.

By using an embedded iFrame or redirecting to a third-party, PCI DSS–compliant, payment service providers (PSPs), criminals are continuing to find workarounds. Groups like the Magecart hackers are reported to be infecting different websites every 16 minutes.[47]

The attackers inject malicious code into the unprotected out-of-scope web pages, allowing them to redirect the customers' journeys through their infrastructures. Consequently, they can carry out clandestine harvesting of the customers' personal and payment card data, as the data is input into the third-party PSP's payment card web interface.

There have been some high-profile and notable data breaches using this very same man-in-the-middle (MITM) style attack:

- Claire's Accessories[48]

- Michigan State University[49]

- NutriBullet[50]

---

[47]www.riskiq.com/blog/external-threat-management/inter-skimmer/

[48]https://threatpost.com/claires-customers-magecart-payment-card-skimmer/156552/

[49]https://msutoday.msu.edu/news/2020/msu-confirms-unauthorized-access-to-online-shopping-site/

[50]www.riskiq.com/blog/labs/magecart-nutribullet/

Key Takeaways

- Businesses should avoid the "tick box" or "do the bare minimum" approaches to compliance.

- Compliance programs should be implemented based upon what is important to the business.

- Compliance should use the most relevant industry security standard to be baselined against.

- Organizations should treat compliance as having an independent validation or health check to ensure that internal or outsourced operations remain "fit for purpose."

- It is important to understand the scope of any compliance program to ensure that it covers the company's expectations.

- Should an adverse occurrence be identified, it is important to engage with the internal/external operators to validate the potential impact it may have on your business.

- Business should not become overreliant on the annual compliance certificates and should build working relationships with their critical suppliers and periodically monitor their effectiveness.

- All in-house/outsourced operations should be identified, listed, and categorized based upon their value to the organization.

- Outsourced services are merely the transference of risk, and so all third-party suppliers need to be proportionately managed, ensuring that their risk tolerances are aligned with your levels of risk appetite.

- Any third-party supplier will own the responsibility for the delivered services; however, the accountability for these services remains with you.

CHAPTER 5

Developing a Protective Security Strategy

SEALs...fight in teams, only in teams, each man relying entirely on the others to do exactly the right thing.

That's how we do it, fighting as one in a team of four or maybe even 10 or even 20, but always as one unit, one mind, one strategy.

We are, instinctively, always backing up, always covering, always moving to plug the gap or pave the way.

That's what makes us great.

Figure 5-1. *Marcus Luttrell*

US Navy SEAL[1]

Lone Survivor[2]

---

[1]www.onthisday.com/people/marcus-luttrell

[2]Luttrell, M. and Robinson, P. (2014). Lone survivor: The incredible true story of Navy SEALs under siege. London: Sphere.

© Jim Seaman 2021

J. Seaman, *Protective Security*, https://doi.org/10.1007/978-1-4842-6908-4_5

Introduction

The origins of "strategy" can be traced by to 1810,[3] meaning the "art of a General" and can be causally linked with the Greek strategia "office or command of a general," from strategos "general, commander of an army," and from the title of various civil officials and magistrates, from stratos "multitude, army, expedition, encamped army." This first became a nonmilitary used term from 1887.

The origins of "Protective"[4] *(designed or intended to protect something or someone from harm[5])* can be traced back to the 1660s, and "Security"[6] can be traced back to the mid-1500s, with a meaning of providing a condition of being secure.

Consequently, when you think of strategic planning for effective Protective Security, you will be looking for a command-and-control plan to ensure that your valuable business assets are adequately protected from harm, so that the business achieves that feeling of being secure.

However, in the corporate environments, often Protective Security is associated with agencies, such as the United Kingdom's MI5 or the US Department of Homeland Security, Cybersecurity and Infrastructure Security Agency (CISA), Infrastructure Security Division, or the US Federal Protective Security Service:

- **MI5**[7]

  The provision of protective security is one of MI5's main activities – we work to ensure there is enough protection for the critical parts of the UK's national infrastructure. The Centre for the Protection of National Infrastructure (CPNI) carries out much of this work and is accountable to the Director General of MI5.

  CPNI aims to reduce the vulnerability of the national infrastructure to terrorism and other threats. The national infrastructure consists of key assets – physical and electronic – that are vital to the continued delivery and integrity of essential services such as energy, communications, transport and water.

---

[3] www.etymonline.com/word/strategy#etymonline_v_22152
[4] www.etymonline.com/search?q=protective&ref=searchbar_searchhint
[5] www.collinsdictionary.com/dictionary/english/protective
[6] www.etymonline.com/search?q=security
[7] www.mi5.gov.uk/what-we-do

The national infrastructure faces threats from international and domestic terrorism, espionage and other hostile foreign activity.

To counter these, CPNI provides authoritative expert advice to organisations across the national infrastructure, covering physical and personnel/people protective security. All the advice is informed by access to intelligence and information about the threats. CPNI works closely with the National Cyber Security Centre which provides advice on cyber security.

- **CISA Protective Security Advisors**[8]

The Department of Homeland Security, Cybersecurity and Infrastructure Security Agency (CISA), Infrastructure Security Division operates the Protective Security Advisor (PSA) Program.

PSAs are trained critical infrastructure protection and vulnerability mitigation subject matter experts who facilitate local field activities in coordination with other Department of Homeland Security offices.

They also advise and assist state, local, and private sector officials and critical infrastructure facility owners and operators.

- **Federal Protective Security Service**[9]

To prevent, protect, respond to and recover from terrorism, criminal acts, and other hazards threatening the U.S. Government's critical infrastructure, services, and the people who provide or receive them.

However, just as having an effective strategy for the protection of a country's critical national infrastructure is important to the nation, having an effective strategy in defense of your organization's critical assets and processes is just as important.

Consequently, by applying the concepts from Protective Security strategy development, you will be better placed to create a more effective defensive plan for your digital business.

---

[8]www.cisa.gov/protective-security-advisors
[9]www.dhs.gov/topic/federal-protective-service

Components of an Effective Strategy

Other than helping the reader to appreciate the value and components of an effective strategy, one of the primary drivers for including this chapter was to address some of the security industry misconceptions regarding military defenses.

Having moved into the corporate security environment, I recall working for someone who made a comment *(as a former member of the British Army's Parachute Regiment[10] should have known better)* which demonstrated his naïve understanding of military defensive strategies.

As a Payment Card Industry Qualified Security Assessor (PCI QSA), I had been carrying out a physical security survey of a client's onsite data centers when I had identified a risk and noncompliance finding. All three data centers had been fitted with electronic automated access control systems (EAACS), which required the authorized personnel to present their proximity access cards/fobs and enter their personal identity number (PIN).

On the face of it, for compliance, they were meeting their Payment Card Industry Data Security Standard (PCI DSS) requirements (as depicted in Figure 5-2[11]) and over the past few years had these facility entry controls assessed by other PCI QSAs as being appropriate.

Requirement 9:   Restrict physical access to cardholder data

Any physical access to data or systems that house cardholder data provides the opportunity for individuals to access devices or data and to remove systems or hardcopies, and should be appropriately restricted. For the purposes of Requirement 9, "onsite personnel" refers to full-time and part-time employees, temporary employees, contractors and consultants who are physically present on the entity's premises. A "visitor" refers to a vendor, guest of any onsite personnel, service workers, or anyone who needs to enter the facility for a short duration, usually not more than one day. "Media" refers to all paper and electronic media containing cardholder data.

PCI DSS Requirements	Testing Procedures	Guidance
9.1 Use appropriate facility entry controls to limit and monitor physical access to systems in the cardholder data environment.	**9.1** Verify the existence of physical security controls for each computer room, data center, and other physical areas with systems in the cardholder data environment. • Verify that access is controlled with badge readers or other devices including authorized badges and lock and key. • Observe a system administrator's attempt to log into consoles for randomly selected systems in the cardholder data environment and verify that they are "locked" to prevent unauthorized use.	Without physical access controls, such as badge systems and door controls, unauthorized persons could potentially gain access to the facility to steal, disable, disrupt, or destroy critical systems and cardholder data. Locking console login screens prevents unauthorized persons from gaining access to sensitive information, altering system configurations, introducing vulnerabilities into the network, or destroying records.

Figure 5-2. *PCI DSS physical security – 9.1*

---

[10]www.army.mod.uk/who-we-are/corps-regiments-and-units/infantry/parachute-regiment/

[11]www.pcisecuritystandards.org/documents/PCI_DSS_v3-2-1.pdf?agreement=true&t
ime=1608113745414

Now, during my Protective Security training phase of the RAF Police Counter Intelligence course, I had been taught to evaluate physical security countermeasures through a risk perspective and to look at the evaluation through the eyes of an attacker.

Well, when looking at the fitting of the EAACS locking mechanism, I could see that it had been incorrectly located, on the outer doorframe. As a result, the screws that secured the mechanism were exposed, and any attacker, armed with just a screwdriver, could remove the securing mechanism from the doorframe. This would then allow the door to open, with the entire locking mechanism still attached.

My recommendation was for them to relocate the EAACS onto the inner doorframe (as depicted in Figure 5-3[12]), so that this could truly be considered as being an "appropriate facility entry control."

Figure 5-3. *EAACS locking mechanism*

The client was far from impressed that this had never been picked up through their previous physical security reviews and vocalized their displeasure to my boss, at the time.

This is when he made the statement that completely undermined his credibility to me and became the final "nail in the coffin" to ensure that I did not continue working with this company after the conclusion of my six-month probation.

What could he have said that was so bad?

---

[12]https://getsafeandsound.com/2020/10/components-of-access-control/

Jim, you are being too harsh!

The client does not need military grade defenses, such as 'Gun Emplacements' to meet their PCI DSS obligations!

Despite that my then boss had been ex-military and was now transitioned to work in the corporate security industry, it appeared that he had not heard of the terms "proportionality" and "risk."

If you look at the righthand column of the 9.1 PCI DSS guidance text, the Payment Card Industry Security Standards Council have identified that the threat of attackers gaining unauthorized access (risk) and that the physical access controls need to be appropriate (proportionate) to mitigate this threat.

Additionally, these data centers served as the hub to the client's payment card operations and would have an aggregated value, requiring effective access control measures to be in place and effectively restricted access to only authorized personnel.

As it turned out, my observations were to be fully vindicated when, during an interview with the facilities manager, they told their tale of a previous physical security incident. The incident had involved an authorized member of staff gaining access to one of the data centers (despite them having forgotten their proximity access card) by unscrewing the screws to EAACS locking mechanism.

Consequently, as per the CPNI advice,[13] when formulating your strategy, it needs to be coherent, holistic, risk based, and proportionate, avoiding ad hoc, siloed, and unstructured approaches, which can lead to wasted resources that provide a minimal impact on reducing the identified security risks.

Rather than trying to "boil the ocean" and to try and do everything, here I have itemized my top 6 priorities.

Priority 1: Asset Management

A proactive methodology should always start by identifying, categorizing, and prioritizing the value of the business asset with its associated business process and the identified risks. The objective of an effective Protective Security strategy is to ensure that any defensive measures that are applied are commensurate to (not greater than) the value of the business asset and that the identified risks are reduced to within acceptable parameters *(with which the asset owners and senior management are comfortable with).*

---

[13]www.cpni.gov.uk/developing-security-strategy

Assets[14] are much wider than just being the valuable data and the technologies that support the processing, transmission, and storage of such data assets. However, when dealing with valued electronic/digital data assets, it is important to ensure that they are adequately protected.

Your first consideration is to apply the **KISS** (Keep It Simple Solution) model and to ensure data minimization:

- Avoiding the unnecessary use and retention of data assets, through data obfuscation[15] technologies

  - Data masking[16]

  - Data obfuscation

  - Tokenization[17] (e.g., Zortrex[18])

  - Dual-tone multi-frequency (DTMF) technologies (e.g., GCI Com (aka Nasstar) AgentPay[19])

Think of your electronic/digital data assets the same as you might do for hardcopy data assets. Hardcopy data assets are subject to periodic musters, to ensure unnecessary storage *(requiring space in a physical security container)* is avoided (unlike electronic/digital data assets, hardcopy storage takes up a great deal of space).

When storage is unavoidable for high-value or aggregated value hardcopy data assets, you might consider storing them within a high security container (as depicted in Figure 5-4[20]).

---

[14]https://csrc.nist.gov/glossary/term/asset

[15]www.talend.com/resources/data-obfuscation/

[16]www.techfunnel.com/information-technology/data-masking/

[17]www.techopedia.com/definition/13698/tokenization

[18]www.zortrex.com/

[19]www.gcicom.net/Our-Services/Unified-Communications/GCI-Contact-Centre

[20]www.cpni.gov.uk/cse/apex-%E2%80%98templar%E2%80%99-2-door-6-x-3?ref=ajax

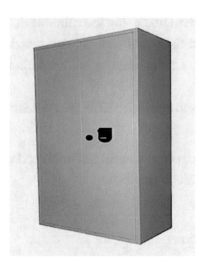

Figure 5-4. *Persistent storage container*

This container would restrict access to only authorized personnel and would be subject to other layers of defense (e.g., in an access-restricted locked room, in an access-restricted locked building, etc.).

Where you need to protect the hardcopy data assets, which need to have mobility, you might consider a suitable storage container that provides the ability to protect the asset in transit *(think Cash in Transit)*. The data asset will be moved from a secured location (point A) to another secured location (point B) while being afforded a suitable level of protection. For example, the hardcopy data asset will be recorded as being deposited in a security document box (as depicted in Figure 5-5) and signed for by the person responsible for moving the hardcopy data asset between the secured locations. During the transit phase, the movement will be tracked, and the security document box will be contained within a secure vehicle. On arrival at the destination point, the hardcopy data asset will be signed for and deposited in a suitable persistent storage container (similar to Figure 5-4).

Figure 5-5. *Security document box*

With electronic/digital data storage and transmission *(where this cannot be avoided)*, you need to ensure that appropriate levels of encryption are applied to ensure that these data assets are suitably protected *(in addition to the existing defensive layers (e.g., network segmentation, secure systems configurations, access controls, monitoring, intrusion detection/prevention, anti-virus, etc.))*.

In the event that the enterprise network *(site)*, segmented network *(building)*, and database *(room)* are compromised, the data assets are still afforded an appropriate level of protection.

The term encryption comes from the verb "encrypt":[21]

- *1968 in telecommunications, a back-formation from encryption (1964), or from en- (1) + crypt (n.) on the notion of "hidden place" (see crypto-).*

  - ***crypto-***[22]

    - *before vowels crypt-, word-forming element meaning "secret" or "hidden, not evident or obvious," used in forming English words at least since 1760 (crypto-Calvinianism), from Latinized form of Greek kryptos "hidden, concealed, secret" (see crypt; the Greek combining form was krypho-).*

NIST[23] defines encryption as being

The cryptographic transformation of data to produce ciphertext.

In essence, by applying encryption to your valuable electronic/digital data assets, you are hiding this data away, under lock and key.

Much in the same way that security containers come in different classes (as depicted in Figure 5-6), so does encryption (as depicted in Figure 5-7[24, 25, 26]).

---

[21]www.etymonline.com/search?q=encrypt

[22]www.etymonline.com/search?q=crypto-&ref=searchbar_searchhint

[23]https://csrc.nist.gov/glossary/term/encryption

[24]www.techopedia.com/dictionary

[25]https://choosetoencrypt.com/tech/twofish-encryption/

[26]www.geeksforgeeks.org/simplified-international-data-encryption-algorithm-idea/

Class 4 containers.

- These are HIGH SECURITY containers which:
- Have a high degree of resistance to an attacker using force and fully equipped with hand and power tools.
- Offers resistance to the prising of doors, drawers or lids to facilitate a fishing or probing attack.

Class 3 containers.

- These are MEDIUM SECURITY containers which:
- Offer a degree of resistance to an attacker using force and having access to a limited range of hand tools.
- Resist flexing, twisting or jolting that will distort the carcass and allow the insertion of probes or devices in order to gain access to the container.

Class 2 containers.

- These are SECURITY containers which are:
- Of substantial design and construction.
- Offer resistance to the casual or opportunist attacker who has not been prepared for the attack and only has use of items that are readily to hand.

Class 1 containers.

- These are GENERAL PURPOSE containers which have no particular security design features but which are lockable and are judged to offer a level of privacy.

Figure 5-6. *Security container classes*

Triple Data Encryption Standard (TripleDES)

- Triple Data Encryption Standard (DES) is a type of computerized cryptography where block cipher algorithms are applied three times to each data block. The key size is increased in Triple DES to ensure additional security through encryption capabilities. Each block contains 64 bits of data. Three keys are referred to as bundle keys with 56 bits per key. There are three keying options in data encryption standards:

1. All keys being independent
2. Key 1 and key 2 being independent keys
3. All three keys being identical.

- Key option #3 is known as triple DES. The triple DES key length contains 168 bits but the key security falls to 112 bits.

Blowfish Encryption Algorithm.

- Blowfish is a license-free cipher-block algorithm that propels a 32-bit, variable-length key to 448 bits. The original design was intended to replace the older and less-advanced data encryption standard (DES) by way of public domain access. Its basic functions utilize S-keys, which are key-dependent.

Twofish Encryption Algorithm

- Twofish is an encryption algorithm designed by Bruce Schneier. It's a symmetric key block cipher with a block size of 128 bits, with keys up to 256 bits. It is related to AES (Advanced Encryption Standard) and an earlier block cipher called Blowfish. Twofish was actually a finalist to become the industry standard for encryption, but was ultimately beaten out by the current AES.

Advanced Encryption Standard (AES).

- The Advanced Encryption Standard (AES) is a symmetric-key block cipher algorithm and U.S. government standard for secure and classified data encryption and decryption.
- In December 2001, the National Institute of Standards (NIST) approved the AES as Federal Information Processing Standards Publication (FIPS PUB) 197, which specifies application of the Rijndael algorithm to all sensitive classified data.
- The Advanced Encryption Standard was originally known as Rijndael.

International data encryption algorithm (IDEA) Encryption Algorithm

- The Simplified International Data Encryption Algorithm (IDEA) is a symmetric key block cypher that:

  - uses a fixed-length plaintext of 16 bits and
  - Encrypts them in 4 chunks of 4 bits each
  - to produce 16 bits ciphertext.
- The length of the key used is 32 bits.
- The key is also divided into 8 blocks of 4 bits each.

Message digest 5 (MD5) Encryption Algorithm

- MD5 is a type of algorithm that is known as a cryptographic hash algorithm. MD5 produces a hash value in a hexadecimal format. This competes with other designs where hash functions take in a certain piece of data, and change it to provide a key or value that can be used in place of the original value.

Hash message authentication code (HMAC) Encryption Algorithm

- A hashed message authentication code (HMAC) is a message authentication code that makes use of a cryptographic key along with a hash function. The actual algorithm behind a hashed message authentication code is complicated, with hashing being performed twice. This helps in resisting some forms of cryptographic analysis. A hashed message authentication code is considered to be more secure than other similar message authentication codes, as the data transmitted and key used in the process are hashed separately.

Ron Rivest, Adi Shamir and Leonard Adleman (RSA) Security

- RSA encryption is a public-key encryption technology developed by RSA Data Security. The RSA algorithm is based on the difficulty in factoring very large numbers. Based on this principle, the RSA encryption algorithm uses prime factorization as the trap door for encryption. Deducing an RSA key, therefore, takes a huge amount of time and processing power. RSA is the standard encryption method for important data, especially data that's transmitted over the Internet.

Figure 5-7. *Encryption classes*

With 256-bit encryption, the AES encryption standard is often referred to as the "military-grade" encryption. Thus, for your most precious data electronic/digital assets, this has become the go-to standard. However, for your lower graded assets, you might want to consider an alternative encryption standard.

If you have data which has been identified as being valuable to the business, their customers, their employees, or to the opportunist attacker, your strategy should include the selection of the most appropriate encryption for the proportionate protection of these data assets *(included any aggregated values)*.

Think of it using the following analogies:

- **Banking**

  - When you go to deposit your hard-earned money into the bank, you would expect that the bank teller/cashier has been trained on how to handle the cash deposits safely and that they will have secure storage facilities (e.g., secure cash drawer, safe, vault, etc. (as the volume of cash aggregates, it is moved from the secure cash drawer to the safe and to the vault).

  - When cash is moved from a bank branch, it is moved under escort, in a secure cash box, into an armored vehicle.

  - When cash is deposited in an automated teller machine (ATM), there are proportionate levels of security afforded to the machine, based upon the perceived aggregated value of that ATM.

- **Jewelry stores**

  - When you walk into a jewelry store, you will expect to see that the most valuable assets will be afforded the more robust layers of protective measures.

    - You would not expect to see the most expensive items left insecure, when on display.

  - When the valuable assets are moved between premises, they are done so using appropriate protective security measures.

Any organization that is not considering the implementation of appropriate encryption, or data protection measures, for their valued data assets is leaving their "crown jewels" on display and not behind a lock and key.

Priority 2: Risk Management

Having identified and prioritized your assets, you need to understand the potential threats to these assets. This can be achieved by familiarizing yourself with the tactics, techniques, and protocols (TTPs) that are known to be leveraged against such assets.

You may wish to consider valuing and prioritizing your business assets based upon the following:

- Potential impact in the event of them being compromised (e.g., denial of service (DoS), ransomware, etc.)

- Their involvement with the processing, transmission, or storage of sensitive data assets (e.g., payment cards, personal information, financial information, intellectual property, etc.)

- Environmental factors (e.g., public facing, connectivity to more valuable assets)

A great resource to start gaining that understanding of the threats is through the familiarization of the MITRE ATT&CK framework (as depicted in Figure 5-8[27]).

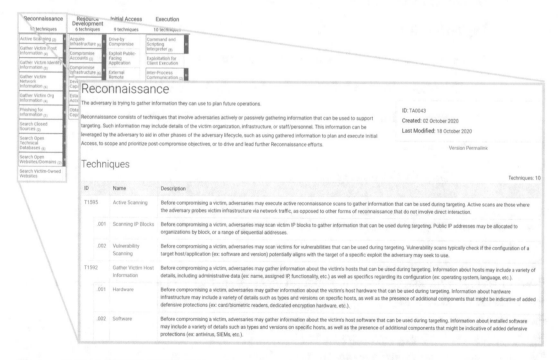

Figure 5-8. *MITRE ATT&CK recon*

---

[27]https://attack.mitre.org/

Further resources that can be used include various threat feeds or the procurement of threat intelligence services to help process information into actionable intelligence relevant to your organization (as depicted in Figure 5-9[28]).

The raw data needs to be analyzed and contextualized to ensure that it remains relevant to your business.

Figure 5-9. *Information processing*

For example:

- OSINT Resources Framework[29]

- OSINT Framework[30]

- Blueliv Threat Compass[31]

- Digital Shadows[32]

- Cyber Information Sharing and Collaboration Program (CISCP)[33]

    - Cybersecurity and Infrastructure Security Agency (CISA) alerts[34]

- Cyber Security Information Sharing Partnership (CiSP)[35]

- Maltiverse[36]

- A10 DDoS Threat Intelligence[37]

---

[28]www.echosec.net/open-source-threat-intelligence
[29]https://osint.link/
[30]https://osintframework.com/
[31]www.blueliv.com/products/prevent-cyber-attacks-with-threat-compass-products-blueliv/
[32]www.digitalshadows.com/
[33]www.cisa.gov/ciscp
[34]https://us-cert.cisa.gov/ncas/alerts
[35]www.ncsc.gov.uk/section/keep-up-to-date/cisp
[36]https://maltiverse.com/collection
[37]www.a10networks.com/products/network-security-services/threat-intelligence-service/

- Recorded Future[38]

- QRadar[39]

- Pktintel[40]

Priority 3: Vulnerability and Impact Management

Having established an understanding of your valued assets and the threats that pertain to them, it is important to effectively manage the existing and emerging vulnerabilities, which could be leveraged against them.

Consequently, it is essential that your assets are securely configured and scanned to ensure that new exploits are not introduced into your environments.

Having satisfied yourself that no existing exploitable vulnerabilities are being introduced into the estate, you then need to establish a formal program for the timely identification and remediation of any emerging vulnerabilities.

This is achieved through periodic and event-driven (threat intelligence) scanning and reviews of your critical business operations and assets. After any emerging vulnerabilities have been identified, it is essential that these vulnerabilities are contextualized based upon the probability of such an event occurring and the potential impact of this asset being compromised.

Bearing in mind that Protective Security incorporates several security industry terms (e.g., Cyber Security, Information Security, Resilience, Network Security, Physical Security, Personnel Security, etc.), your vulnerability intelligence may be sourced from a variety of mediums:

- Exploit Database[41]

- Common Vulnerabilities and Exposures (CVE) data feeds[42]

- US National Vulnerability Database (NVD) data feeds[43]

---

[38]www.recordedfuture.com/about/

[39]www.ibm.com/security/security-intelligence/qradar

[40]https://github.com/SecurityNik/pktIntel

[41]www.exploit-db.com/

[42]https://cve.mitre.org/cve/data_feeds.html

[43]https://nvd.nist.gov/vuln/data-feeds

- Security Content Automation Protocol (SCAP) validated products and modules[44]

- Digital footprint vulnerability scanners[45]

- Physical Security Systems assessments[46]

Whether you are using in-house resources or a procured service, it is essential that the various information feeds are contextualized, so that you understand the risks these threats, vulnerabilities, and potential impacts present to your company.

- This is achieved through an evaluation, using the "Pyramid of Pain" (as depicted in Figure 5-10[47]). This helps you to identify the potential pain that may be felt by attackers once a particular kind of indicator for their attack becomes known. This helps you to better forecast the probability of an attacker leveraging such approaches against your defenses. Not all indicators of compromise are the same. Consequently, the pyramid shows the increasing difficulties that an adversary will face and where you build your defenses to identify and respond to these indicators, this decreases the probability of their success.

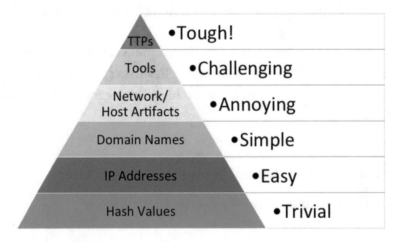

Figure 5-10. *Pyramid of Pain*

---

[44]https://csrc.nist.gov/Projects/scap-validation-program/Validated-Products-and-Modules

[45]https://securityscorecard.com/ (assistance@cyberrescue.co.uk)

[46]www.energy.gov/sites/prod/files/2017/02/f34/PhysicalSecuritySystemsAssessment Guide_Dec2016.pdf

[47]https://detect-respond.blogspot.com/2013/03/the-pyramid-of-pain.html

These three stages should be the foundations of any strategy development, before you do anything else.

Having established the foundations, you can then start to identify your controls and countermeasures that will help you mitigate the identified threats, for your critical assets and business processes.

Here, you can choose from the most appropriate industry security controls/ frameworks to help you build a baseline to proportionately mitigate your identified threats and vulnerabilities, so that they reside within acceptable risk tolerances. The chosen security controls needn't be limited to a single security controls standard/ framework and can easily be an integration of security controls, taken from various standards/frameworks, to help you achieve your objectives:

- To reduce risk to within acceptable tolerance ranges

- To reduce your organization's attack surfaces

- To reduce the attackers' windows of opportunity

Only after you have built your firm foundations and you understand what needs to be protected and the risks can you hope to develop an effective Protective Security strategy.

Much the same as designing and implementing an effective business strategy, you need to ensure that you have incorporated the following:

1. **Develop a true vision of the Protective Security strategy.**

    This is a visionary statement, providing a snapshot into the future, clearly demonstrating the aspirations of what the strategy hopes to achieve. Unlike a mission statement, this will articulate what success will look like.

2. **Define the advantages.**

    How will the strategy deliver a unique value to the internal (e.g., business, key stakeholders, employees, shareholders, etc.) and/or external customers (e.g., regulators, customers, clients, etc.)?

3. **Define your targets.**

    Clear strategic targets provide you with the ability to create an integrated Protective Security approach, identifying where the measures may complement existing defensive efforts.

4. **Focus on systematic development.**

   A thriving Protective Security model is one that embraces the opportunity to strengthen the model, with investment into appropriate new technologies, people, training, and security tools. The strategic plan should identify the aging technologies that could be replaced by newer technologies (e.g., machine learning, artificial intelligence, cloud, etc.), which could be more effective.

5. **Fact-based decision-making.**

   An effective Protective Security strategy thrives on producing visible risk and performance metrics, showing how the integrated solutions are effectively helping to mitigate the known risks. Investments need to produce quantified results, showing the benefits they are providing for the defense of the business.

6. **Long-term thinking.**

   You may not be able to implement everything, all at once, you need for your effective Protective Security strategy. However, knowing and documenting what the long-term strategy looks like will ensure that you can prioritize your wish list into more digestible chunks for the business.

7. **Flexibility.**

   Based upon the fact that the effectiveness of your strategy is driven by the perceived risks, you need to ensure that you can quickly respond and adapt to any event-driven (business or external) changes that might need to be included into this year's strategic plan.

8. **All-inclusiveness.**

   The ability to provide a flexible Protective Security requires the inclusion and contribution from across multiple departments. This will provide greater transparency and "buy-in" from trusted and strategic thinking key stakeholders.

9. **Preparation.**

   If you want the key stakeholders to take your strategy seriously, you need to be adequately prepared so that when you have your strategy meetings, the key stakeholders can see the need and potential value in the propositions you are making.

10. **Measured results.**

    A common mistake that is made with Protective Security is the failure to ensure that any new strategies are measured against clearly defined SMART (Specific, Measurable, Achievable, Realistic, and Time-bound)[48] objectives.

    It is all too easy to get caught up in the vendor's "sales pitch" and the "shiny" user interfaces, but before procuring a new solution/ service/product, have you considered how this integrates into the other elements of your strategy and what type of additional benefits and visibility it will provide to your organization?

    Do you periodically review and measure the effectiveness of the elements that support your Protective Security strategy? At regular periods, you should review the effectiveness of the security assets that support your strategic Protective Security program.

    - The strategic review should identify deficiencies as well as any elements that have failed to meet their objectives or that can be replaced with more cost-effective, or better, offerings.

        - *They shouldn't be wary about replacing an existing security tool, from your toolbox, for a newer, improved, or more cost-effective option.*

        - *They shouldn't hesitate at replacing a costly security solution with an alternative (or selection of alternative options) if their original choice of product has failed to meet their expectations or to provide them with an appropriate return on investment, for example:*

---

[48]www.lifehack.org/853712/write-smart-goals-template

- *Replacing a $475,000, per annum, outsourced network monitoring solution with an artificial intelligence/ machine learning security information and event management (SIEM) and security operations center (SOC) service (e.g., CyberEasy[49])*

Priority 4: Access Management

It is essential that proportionate access control measures are implemented so that only the explicitly authorized personnel can gain access to these business valuable assets.

This should be a harmony between back-end operations (management of the locking mechanism) and the front-end operations (users of the keys). Consequently, both parties need to be made aware of the importance their role plays in preventing unauthorized access to these identified assets, and these individuals need regular reminders and to be subject to periodic, and regular, integrity checks (auditing).

Priority 5: Security Information and Event Management

Having established priorities 1 through 4, an effective monitoring tool and supporting processes are essential to ensure that timely identification of the **ABNORMAL** from the NORMAL can be identified.

It is important to remember that a security information management (SIEM[50]) solution is there to collate together various security information event notifications. These will then need to be investigated to ascertain whether these **ABNORMAL** events should be escalated and treated as a security incident. During the NCSC-Certified Cyber Incident Planning and Response Course, with Cyber Management Alliance,[51] they provided me with an excellent explanation of this concept, through a burglary scenario (as depicted in Figure 5-11).

---

[49]www.knogin.com/products/#Pricing

[50]https://searchsecurity.techtarget.com/definition/security-information-and-event-management-SIEM

[51]www.cm-alliance.com/training/cipr-cyber-incident-planning-response/

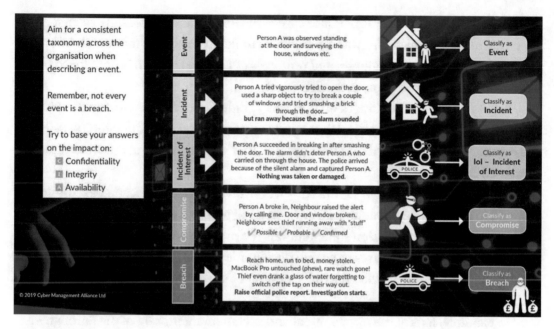

Figure 5-11. *Defining a breach*

Priority 6: Incident Management

Inevitably, things will go wrong, and accordingly it is essential that you have an effective incident management process in place. This will ensure that you can minimize the potential impact of such an event, by quickly identifying, responding to, containing, and recovering from an incident.

As you can see, the development of your effective strategy needs to be flexible and risk driven. Consequently, it is essential that your foundation phases are supported by a suitable platform for providing a centralized view of the risks to your identified, and prioritized, valued business assets.

Military Comparison

As you may imagine, the Royal Air Force is constantly enhancing and evolving its strategies. During my 22-year career, I saw many strategy changes, having occurred because of external influences.

Just look at the adjustments that were made to mitigate against the counter terrorism threat.

In the first decade of my RAF Police career, the focus was on defending against the domestic terrorist threat. This was a completely different "beast" to that which was to come from the tactics, techniques, and protocols (TTPs) that were to be employed by international terrorist groups, such as Al Qaeda.

Despite Ramzi Yousef's attack on the World Trade Center,[52] on February 26, 1993, and various other Al Qaeda terrorist attacks that were carried out during the 1990s,[53] the counter terrorism shifted significantly with their second attack on the World Trade Center on September 11, 2001.

The equipment needed to support the ever-evolving strategies needed to continually respond to the changing operations. However, a big problem with the updating of equipment to fulfill the mission statement was the procurement process.

As you can imagine, the research and development (R&D) time could be quite lengthy, and as a result, by the time that a new piece of equipment came into service, the mission may have changed.

For example, look at the development and procurement process of the Eurofighter Typhoon to replace the aging Harrier, Buccaneer, and Tornado aircraft.

The contract to produce a prototype through the Experimental Aircraft Program (EAP)[54] was first signed in 1983. This was to be the origin of the Typhoon aircraft (as depicted in Figure 5-12[55]).

---

[52]https://moneyweek.com/428236/26-february-1993-world-trade-center-bombing

[53]www.history.com/news/government-terrorist-trackers-before-911-higher-ups-wouldnt-listen

[54]www.baesystems.com/en-uk/feature/eap

[55]www.itv.com/news/westcountry/2015-06-23/
raf-typhoon-fighter-jets-training-in-cornwall

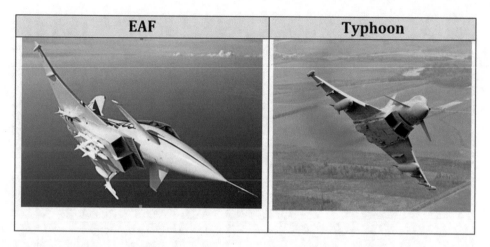

EAF	Typhoon

Figure 5-12. *EAF vs. Typhoon*

At the time, the conflicts (e.g., Cold War, Falkland Islands) meant that the aircraft needed to have a "dogfighting"[56] capability. However, the aircraft did not come into service until 2003,[57] and the last occasion that an RAF aircraft had been required to engage in an aircraft-to-aircraft battle (aka dogfight) was on June 8, 1982, during the Falklands conflict.[58]

The RAF was faced with the problem of having to re-engineer these new aircraft as a fighter-bomber[59] – something distinctly different to that which it had been originally designed and developed for.

The deployments to Iraq and Afghanistan clearly demonstrated to the Ministry of Defence (MoD) that they needed a more rapid and flexible R&D and procurement process, which could be quickly adapted to meet the demands of different environments and mission requirements.

For example, the L85A1 (aka small arms for the 1980s (SA80)[60]) was first introduced to the British military in 1985, but during its use in the "Desert Storm" *(having not been designed for sandy and hot environments)*, it proved to be plagued with problems and needed to be re-engineered by Heckler & Koch,[61] and the L85A2 variant was introduced into service (as depicted in Figure 5-13[62]).

---

[56]https://dictionary.cambridge.org/dictionary/english/dogfight

[57]www.eurofighter.com/about-us

[58]www.dailymail.co.uk/news/article-6816751/Falklands-pilot-71-shot-enemy-plane-combat-meets-former-foes-return-island.html

[59]www.thinkdefence.co.uk/uk-complex-weapons/brimstone/

[60]https://nationalinterest.org/blog/buzz/introducing-sa80-worst-military-rifle-ever-44987

[61]www.forgottenweapons.com/sa80-history-l85-a1-vs-a2-and-the-coming-a3/

[62]www.military-today.com/firearms/l85a2.htm

Figure 5-13. *L85 variants*

During the later operations with Iraq and Afghanistan, the insurgents would rapidly adapt the TTPs, and as a result, the British military needed an R&D and procurement process that could meet these demands.

As a result, in my final overseas deployments, I observed some significant changes to the types of training and equipment provided in support of the overseas engagements.

Building BRIDGES

As I have mentioned, your Protective Security strategy needs to be integrated, proportionate, and be driven by the risks to the business. Consequently, I am going to demonstrate the development of an effective strategy, for a large enterprise, centralized around a risk management platform that I have used in the past (Acuity STREAM[63]).

---

[63]https://acuityrm.com/platform

This will be presented using the **BRIDGES** acronym (as depicted in Figure 5-14).

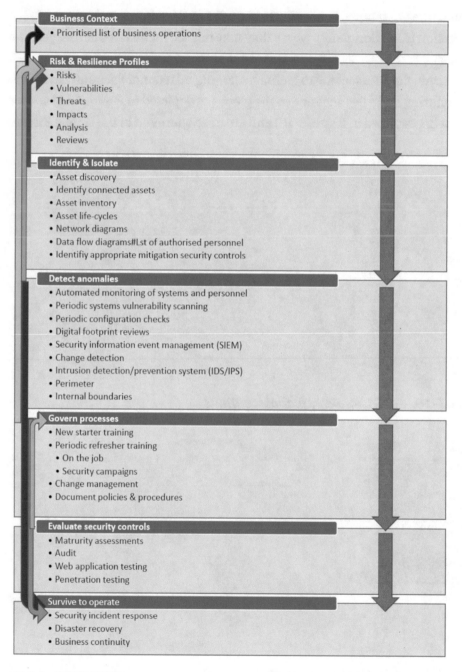

Figure 5-14. *BRIDGES acronym*

Business Context

For this strategy example, I am going to choose a large manufacturing type of organization (ABC Company), where they may not see themselves as a target for today's criminals.

However, they are seeking to embrace new digital technologies and have a mixture of manufacturing and sales sites across the globe (as depicted in Figure 5-15) and a digital footprint (as depicted in Figure 5-16) and are headquartered in the United Kingdom.

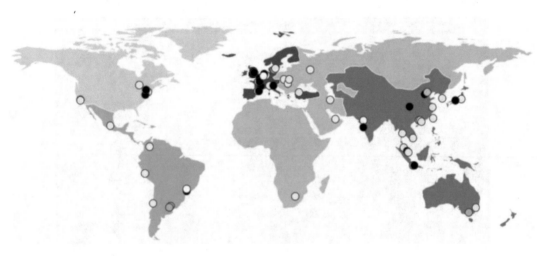

Figure 5-15. *ABC Company global locations*

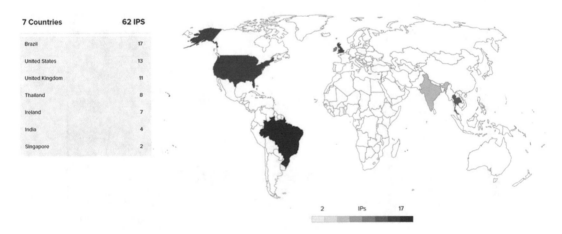

Figure 5-16. *ABC Company digital footprint*

In addition to their primary digital footprint, ABC Company also has numerous supplementary digital footprint profiles (as depicted in Figure 5-17), and the supporting IT infrastructure consists of a third-party managed wide area network, connecting several local area networks.

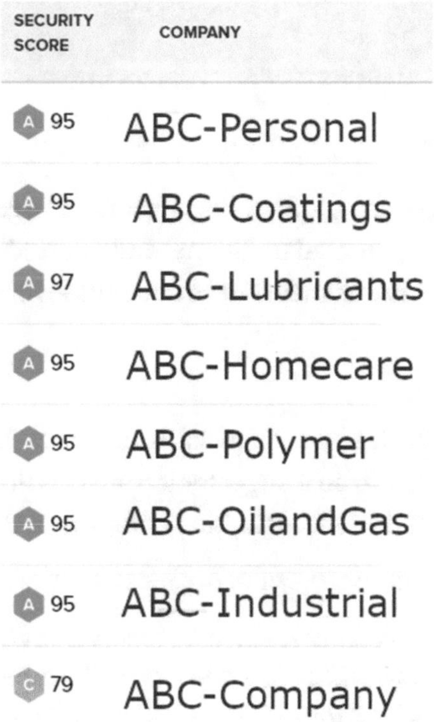

SECURITY SCORE	COMPANY
Ⓐ 95	ABC-Personal
Ⓐ 95	ABC-Coatings
Ⓐ 97	ABC-Lubricants
Ⓐ 95	ABC-Homecare
Ⓐ 95	ABC-Polymer
Ⓐ 95	ABC-OilandGas
Ⓐ 95	ABC-Industrial
Ⓒ 79	ABC-Company

Figure 5-17. *Supplementary profile scores*

As a business-to-business (B2B) manufacturing organization, their focus is on protecting the following:

- Brand name (reputation)

- As a publicly listed UK company, adherence to the Cadbury Rules[64]

- Compliance with data privacy regulations

- Customer lists

- Account/payment data

---

[64]https://thebusinessprofessor.com/lesson/cadbury-rules-definition/

- Intellectual property
  - Chemical recipes
- Sales functions
- Manufacturing plant IT systems
- Employee data

Risk and Resilience

By using the Terrorism, Espionage, Subversion, Sabotage, Organized Crime (**TESSOC**[65]) abbreviation to evaluate the potential traditional and nontraditional threats, we can quickly evaluate how these threats may be a consideration for the ABC Company.

Terrorism[66]

As a manufacturer of chemicals and a Financial Times Stock Exchange (FTSE) 100[67] listed company, they are likely to be a target for terrorist, as they seek opportunities to carry out acts that align with the legal definition of terrorism:[68]

Terrorism means the use or threat of action where;

a) *It involves serious violence against a person, involves serious damage to property, endangers a person's life (other than that of the person committing the action), creates a serious risk to health and safety of the public, or a section of the public, or is designed seriously to interfere with or seriously disrupt an electronic system;*

b) *It is designed to influence government, or an international government organization, or to intimidate the public or a section of the public;*

and;

c) *Is made for the purpose of advancing a political, religious, radical or ideological cause.*

---

[65]www.abbreviations.com/term/2042215

[66]www.etymonline.com/search?q=terrorism&ref=searchbar_searchhint

[67]www.londonstockexchange.com/indices/ftse-100

[68]Staniforth, A. and Police National Legal Database (2009). Blackstone's counter-terrorism handbook by Andrew Staniforth. Oxford: Oxford University Press.

Consequently, a large chemical plant could easily become a target, especially if, in response to the recent pandemic, they were to change their role to help with the challenges faced in the mass manufacture of the materials needed for the COVID-19 vaccine.[69]

- Has the terrorist threat been evaluated (or reevaluated because of the changed role)?

- Are there sufficient and effective physical security controls in place to align with the UK Government's counter terrorism (CONTEST) strategy?[70]

Espionage[71]

Being that ABC Company is a FTSE 100 listed company, they are constantly seeking new profitable ventures and innovative ideas, which makes them a target for industrial or insider espionage, as well as from hostile nation states.

The value of espionage to a rival competitor is that they can steal and use any intellectual property, without having to pay for the initial development costs. Additionally, they could approach a key member of the sales team and offer them a lucrative position in their organization, and this individual might have a desire to make a good first impression by bringing a customer list with them.

This can provide them with a considerable advantage in the marketplace.

- Are there sufficient defensive measures in place, or are the only defenses those built on trust?

- Are they able to detect unauthorized or unexpected exports of sensitive data?

---

[69]https://bgr.com/2020/12/04/coronavirus-vaccine-pfizer-supply-2020/
[70]www.gov.uk/government/publications/counter-terrorism-strategy-contest
[71]www.etymonline.com/search?q=espionage&ref=searchbar_searchhint

Sabotage[72]

All it takes is for a "trusted" employee to become disillusioned with the business or to be blackmailed or to be paid by a hostile entity for them to carry out a malicious action that could severely impact a critical business function.

It is important to remember that sabotage could originate from outside of the business, where a country uprising could damage your business or prevent your employees from being able to get into work.

- Has the ABC Company evaluated the roles that could present a greater risk from sabotage?

- What contingencies are in place?

- Is this with acceptable risk tolerances?

Subversion[73]

In the digital era, subversion is becoming more of a threat as social media becomes an extremely effective platform to spread subversive messages.

This is especially the case regarding the manufacturing and chemical industries, where they could be the target of the attention of Global Warming or Animal Rights protests.

- Has the risk of subversive activities been risk assessed?

- Is this with acceptable risk tolerances?

Organized Crime[74]

ABC Company has a great number of valuable and attractive (V&A) assets that could be of interest to thieves, while cybercriminals would be targeting financial data assets or the opportunity to carry out a ransomware attack (increased by 156%[75]). In such

---

[72]www.etymonline.com/search?q=sabotage&ref=searchbar_searchhint

[73]www.etymonline.com/search?q=subversion&ref=searchbar_searchhint

[74]www.britannica.com/topic/organized-crime

[75]www.plantservices.com/industrynews/2020/
manufacturing-ransomware-attacks-increased-156/

an attack, the ABC Company would be expected to pay the attackers a fee *(often the attackers know the net worth of their targets)* to unlock the valuable data and processing systems.

- Has ABC Company evaluated the threats from Organized Crime fraternities, who are consistently looking for opportunities to exploit businesses, such as the ABC Company?

- Have such scenarios been developed and risk assessed against?

- How quickly can a malicious activity be identified, responded to, and contained to enable a quick recovery to normal operations?

- In the event of a ransomware attack, what are the capabilities to quickly recover and what are the contingency plans?

- Does the ABC Company have sufficient backups of all the essential data assets that are needed to keep the business operational?

- Are these within the organization's risk tolerances?

Other Nontraditional Threats

Your nontraditional threats are focused on such things as

- Those nonmalicious accidental actions of one of your employees

    - Inappropriate use of personal data

    - Careless response to malicious communications

        - Phishing[76]

        - Spear phishing[77]

        - Whaling[78]

---

[76]www.collinsdictionary.com/dictionary/english/phishing
[77]https://digitalguardian.com/blog/
 what-is-spear-phishing-defining-and-differentiating-spear-phishing-and-phishing
[78]www.lifewire.com/what-is-whaling-2483605

- Smishing[79]

- Vishing (aka voice phishing)[80]

- The actions of the "lone wolf" hackers/script kiddies

- Natural disasters

  - Earthquake

  - Fire

  - Flooding

  - Pandemic

- Theft of V&A business assets

  - Mobile IT

  - Precious metals

An Example Evaluation of the Canadian Sales Office

Using the MITRE ATT&CK framework, you can identify further threats which could present a risk to your business. For example, within ABC Company's Canadian Sales office, you can identify risk pertaining to numerous attack surfaces – *highlighted in blue* (as depicted in Figure 5-18[81]).

---

[79]https://cybersecurity.att.com/blogs/security-essentials/
sms-phishing-explained-what-is-smishing

[80]www.computerhope.com/jargon/v/vishing.htm

[81]https://mitre-attack.github.io/attack-navigator/#layerURL=https%
3A%2F%2Fraw.githubusercontent.com%2Fcenter-for-threat-informed-
defense%2Fattack-control-framework-mappings%2Fmaster%2Fframeworks%2Fn
ist800-53-r5%2Flayers%2Fnist800-53-r5-overview

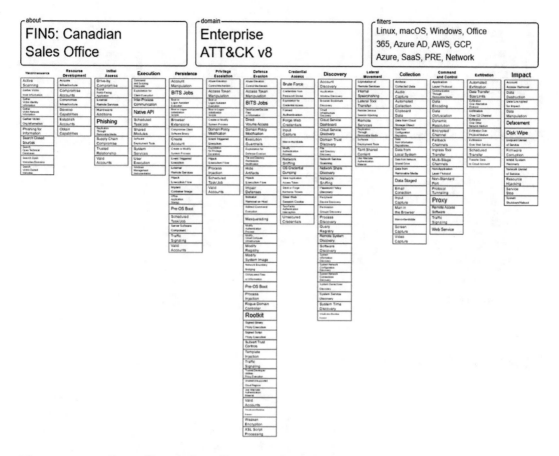

Figure 5-18. *Canadian Sales office attack surfaces*

The output of the business context and risk and resilience profiles would then be entered into the STREAM platform, providing a consolidated view (as depicted in Figures 5-19 to 5-35[82]).

---

[82]https://acuityrm.com/

Figure 5-19. *Enterprise tree structure*

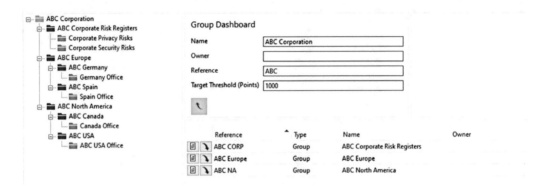

Figure 5-20. *Enterprise tree hierarchy*

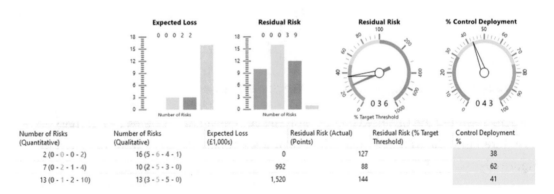

Number of Risks (Quantitative)	Number of Risks (Qualitative)	Expected Loss (£1,000s)	Residual Risk (Actual) (Points)	Residual Risk (% Target Threshold)	Control Deployment %
2 (0 - 0 - 0 - 2)	16 (5 - 6 - 4 - 1)	0	127		38
7 (0 - 2 - 1 - 4)	10 (2 - 5 - 3 - 0)	992	88		62
13 (0 - 1 - 2 - 10)	13 (3 - 5 - 5 - 0)	1,520	144		41

Figure 5-21. *Enterprise tree risks*

Figure 5-22. *North America view*

Figure 5-23. *North America tree hierarchy*

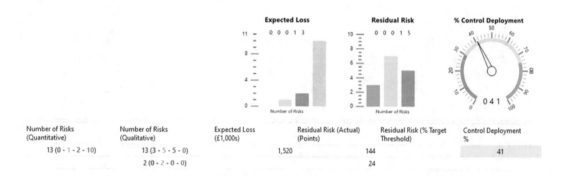

Figure 5-24. *North America risk view*

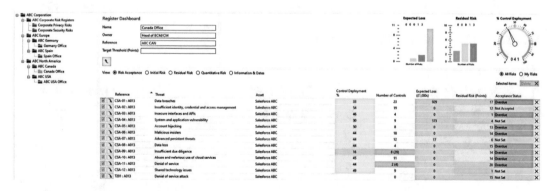

Figure 5-25. *Canada Office overview*

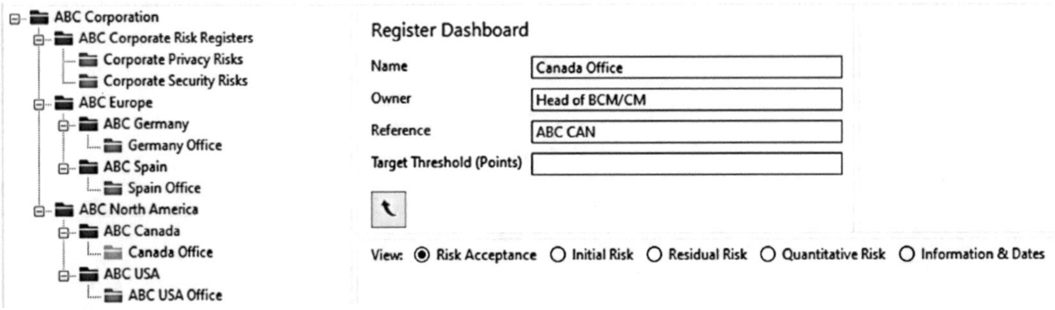

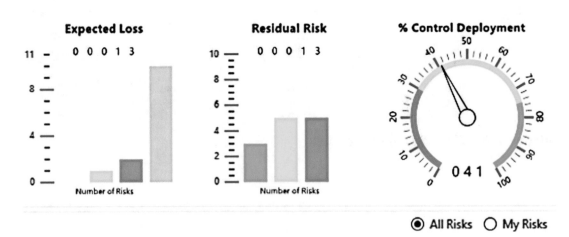

Figure 5-26. *Canada Office hierarchy*

	Reference	Threat	Asset
	CSA-01 : A013	Data breaches	Salesforce ABC
	CSA-02 : A013	Insufficient identity, credential and access management	Salesforce ABC
	CSA-03 : A013	Insecure interfaces and APIs	Salesforce ABC
	CSA-04 : A013	System and application vulnerability	Salesforce ABC
	CSA-05 : A013	Account hijacking	Salesforce ABC
	CSA-06 : A013	Malicious insiders	Salesforce ABC
	CSA-07 : A013	Advanced persistent threats	Salesforce ABC
	CSA-08 : A013	Data loss	Salesforce ABC
	CSA-09 : A013	Insufficient due diligence	Salesforce ABC
	CSA-10 : A013	Abuse and nefarious use of cloud services	Salesforce ABC
	CSA-11 : A013	Denial of service	Salesforce ABC
	CSA-12 : A013	Shared technology issues	Salesforce ABC
	T201 : A013	Denial of service attack	Salesforce ABC

Figure 5-27. *Canada Office threats*

Figure 5-28. *Canada Office risks dashboard*

33	23	929	17	Overdue	×
54	19	0	12	Not Accepted	×
46	4	0	1	Overdue	×
30	9	573	4	Not Set	×
50	8	0	13	Overdue	×
44	18	0	14	Overdue	×
44	12	17	6	Not Set	×
44	4	0	15	Overdue	×
16	8 (29)	0	14	Overdue	×
45	11	0	14	Overdue	×
44	2 (4)	0	20	Overdue	×
10	0	0	1	Not Set	∨

Figure 5-29. *Canada Office controls assessments record*

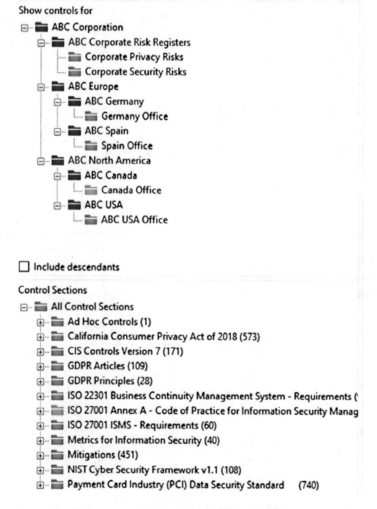

Control Assessment Screen

Show controls for
- 📁 ABC Corporation
  - 📁 ABC Corporate Risk Registers
    - 📁 Corporate Privacy Risks
    - 📁 Corporate Security Risks
  - 📁 ABC Europe
    - 📁 ABC Germany
      - 📁 Germany Office
    - 📁 ABC Spain
      - 📁 Spain Office
  - 📁 ABC North America
    - 📁 ABC Canada
      - 📁 Canada Office
    - 📁 ABC USA
      - 📁 ABC USA Office

☐ Include descendants

Control Sections
- 📁 All Control Sections
  - 📁 Ad Hoc Controls (1)
  - 📁 California Consumer Privacy Act of 2018 (573)
  - 📁 CIS Controls Version 7 (171)
  - 📁 GDPR Articles (109)
  - 📁 GDPR Principles (28)
  - 📁 ISO 22301 Business Continuity Management System - Requirements ('
  - 📁 ISO 27001 Annex A - Code of Practice for Information Security Manag
  - 📁 ISO 27001 ISMS - Requirements (60)
  - 📁 Metrics for Information Security (40)
  - 📁 Mitigations (451)
  - 📁 NIST Cyber Security Framework v1.1 (108)
  - 📁 Payment Card Industry (PCI) Data Security Standard   (740)

Figure 5-30. *Canada Office controls assessment selection*

	Next Assessment			Control Deployment			
	0	0	0	114	41	52	21	0

ISO 27001 Annex A - Code of Practice for Information Security Management

○ My Owned ○ My Assessments My Approvals ● All

	Reference	Owner	Control	Asset	Last Update	Last Assess	Next Assess	Deployment (%)
	A.05.01.01 : ISO 27001	STREAM	Policies for information security	ABC ISO 27K Assessment		01/11/2019		50
	A.05.01.02 : ISO 27001	STREAM	Review of the policies for information security	ABC ISO 27K Assessment		01/11/2019		100
	A.06.01.01 : ISO 27001	STREAM	Information security roles and responsibilities	ABC ISO 27K Assessment		01/11/2019		23
	A.06.01.02 : ISO 27001	STREAM	Segregation of duties	ABC ISO 27K Assessment		01/11/2019		67
	A.06.01.03 : ISO 27001	STREAM	Contact with authorities	ABC ISO 27K Assessment		01/11/2019		30
	A.06.01.04 : ISO 27001	STREAM	Contact with special interest groups	ABC ISO 27K Assessment		01/11/2019		75
	A.06.01.05 : ISO 27001	STREAM	Information security in project management	ABC ISO 27K Assessment		01/11/2019		62
	A.06.02.01 : ISO 27001	STREAM	Mobile device policy	ABC ISO 27K Assessment		01/11/2019		16
	A.06.02.02 : ISO 27001	STREAM	Teleworking	ABC ISO 27K Assessment		01/11/2019		21
	A.07.01.01 : ISO 27001	STREAM	Screening	ABC ISO 27K Assessment		01/11/2019		50
	A.07.01.02 : ISO 27001	STREAM	Terms and conditions of employment	ABC ISO 27K Assessment		01/11/2019		82
	A.07.02.01 : ISO 27001	STREAM	Management responsibilities	ABC ISO 27K Assessment		01/11/2019		25
	A.07.02.02 : ISO 27001	STREAM	Information security awareness, education and training	ABC ISO 27K Assessment		19/03/2020		100
	A.07.02.03 : ISO 27001	STREAM	Disciplinary process	ABC ISO 27K Assessment		01/11/2019		45
	A.07.03.01 : ISO 27001	STREAM	Termination or change of employment responsibilities	ABC ISO 27K Assessment		01/11/2019		25
	A.08.01.01 : ISO 27001	STREAM	Inventory of assets	ABC ISO 27K Assessment		01/11/2019		57
	A.08.01.02 : ISO 27001	STREAM	Ownership of assets	ABC ISO 27K Assessment		01/11/2019		75
	A.08.01.03 : ISO 27001	STREAM	Acceptable use of assets	ABC ISO 27K Assessment		01/11/2019		50
	A.08.01.04 : ISO 27001	STREAM	Return of assets	ABC ISO 27K Assessment		01/11/2019		19
	A.08.02.01 : ISO 27001	STREAM	Classification of information	ABC ISO 27K Assessment		01/11/2019		41
	A.08.02.02 : ISO 27001	STREAM	Labelling of information	ABC ISO 27K Assessment		01/11/2019		75
	A.08.02.03 : ISO 27001	STREAM	Handling of assets	ABC ISO 27K Assessment		01/11/2019		100
	A.08.03.01 : ISO 27001	STREAM	Management of removable media	ABC ISO 27K Assessment		01/11/2019		88
	A.08.03.02 : ISO 27001	STREAM	Disposal of media	ABC ISO 27K Assessment		01/11/2019		75
	A.08.03.03 : ISO 27001	STREAM	Physical media transfer	ABC ISO 27K Assessment		01/11/2019		100

Figure 5-31. *Canada Office controls assessment overview*

ISO 27001 Annex A - Code of Practice for Information Security Management

	Reference	Owner ▲	Control
	A.05.01.01 : A030	STREAM	Policies for information security
	A.05.01.02 : A030	STREAM	Review of the policies for information security
	A.06.01.01 : A030	STREAM	Information security roles and responsibilities
	A.06.01.02 : A030	STREAM	Segregation of duties
	A.06.01.03 : A030	STREAM	Contact with authorities
	A.06.01.04 : A030	STREAM	Contact with special interest groups
	A.06.01.05 : A030	STREAM	Information security in project management
	A.06.02.01 : A030	STREAM	Mobile device policy
	A.06.02.02 : A030	STREAM	Teleworking
	A.07.01.01 : A030	STREAM	Screening
	A.07.01.02 : A030	STREAM	Terms and conditions of employment
	A.07.02.01 : A030	STREAM	Management responsibilities
	A.07.02.02 : A030	STREAM	Information security awareness, education and training
	A.07.02.03 : A030	STREAM	Disciplinary process
	A.07.03.01 : A030	STREAM	Termination or change of employment responsibilities
	A.08.01.01 : A030	STREAM	Inventory of assets
	A.08.01.02 : A030	STREAM	Ownership of assets
	A.08.01.03 : A030	STREAM	Acceptable use of assets
	A.08.01.04 : A030	STREAM	Return of assets

Figure 5-32. *Canada Office controls status (left side)*

	Next Assessment			Control Deployment			
	0	0	0	114	15	49	50	0

○ My Owned   ○ My Assessments   ○ My Approvals   ⦿ All

Asset	Last Assess	Next Assess	Deployment (%)
Canada Office ISO 27001 Assessment	12/11/2020		40
Canada Office ISO 27001 Assessment	12/11/2020		0
Canada Office ISO 27001 Assessment	12/11/2020		38
Canada Office ISO 27001 Assessment	12/11/2020		40
Canada Office ISO 27001 Assessment	12/11/2020		50
Canada Office ISO 27001 Assessment	12/11/2020		42
Canada Office ISO 27001 Assessment	12/11/2020		20
Canada Office ISO 27001 Assessment	12/11/2020		0
Canada Office ISO 27001 Assessment	12/11/2020		0
Canada Office ISO 27001 Assessment	12/11/2020		100
Canada Office ISO 27001 Assessment	12/11/2020		44
Canada Office ISO 27001 Assessment	12/11/2020		50
Canada Office ISO 27001 Assessment	12/11/2020		22
Canada Office ISO 27001 Assessment	12/11/2020		75
Canada Office ISO 27001 Assessment	12/11/2020		38
Canada Office ISO 27001 Assessment	12/11/2020		85
Canada Office ISO 27001 Assessment	12/11/2020		50
Canada Office ISO 27001 Assessment	12/11/2020		25
Canada Office ISO 27001 Assessment	12/11/2020		25

Figure 5-33. *Canada Office controls status (right side)*

Risk: CSA-01 : A013

Reference:	CSA-01 : A013
Threat:	Data breaches
Asset:	Sales Platform ABC

Assignment:	⊟ ☐ ABC Spain
	 └─ ☐ Spain Office
	 ⊟ ☐ ABC North America
	   ⊟ ☐ ABC Canada
	     └─ ☑ Canada Office

Description:	A data breach is an incident in which sensitive, protected or confidential information is released, viewed, stolen or used by an individual who is not authorized to do so. A data breach may be the primary objective of a targeted attack or may simply be the result of human error, application vulnerabilities or poor security practices. A data breach may involve any kind of information that was not intended for public release including, but not limited to, personal health information, financial information, personally identifiable information (PII), trade secrets and intellectual property. An organization's cloud-based data may have value to different parties for different reasons. For example, organized crime often seeks financial, health and personal information to carry out a range of fraudulent activities. Competitors and foreign nationals may be keenly interested in proprietary information, intellectual property and trade secrets. Activists may want to expose information that can cause damage or embarrassment. Unauthorized insiders obtaining data within the cloud are a major concern for organizations.
Risk Category:	CSA Cloud Threats
Owner:	STREAM
Next Assessment Date:	27 December 2019
Next Acceptance Date:	31 May 2020
Origin	☑ Deliberate ☐ Accidental ☑ Environmental
[i]Threat Actor	☑ Hacker, cracker ☐ Computer criminal ☑ Terrorist ☐ Industrial espionage (intelligence companies, foreign governments, other government interests) ☐ Insiders (poorly trained, disgruntled, malicious, negligent, dishonest, or terminated employees)

Figure 5-34.   *Canada Office risk view (left side)*

Figure 5-35. *Canada Office risk view (right side)*

Identify and Isolate

With a greater understanding of the threats and risks that pertain to your type of business, you then need to identify and categorize your assets, based upon the value/importance to your business.

Another important area is to understand how the assets are integrated and connected and which of your third-party suppliers deliver the greatest concern/risk to your business.

Having identified and evaluated your assets, you are then able to document them and plot the risks against them (as depicted in Figure 5-36).

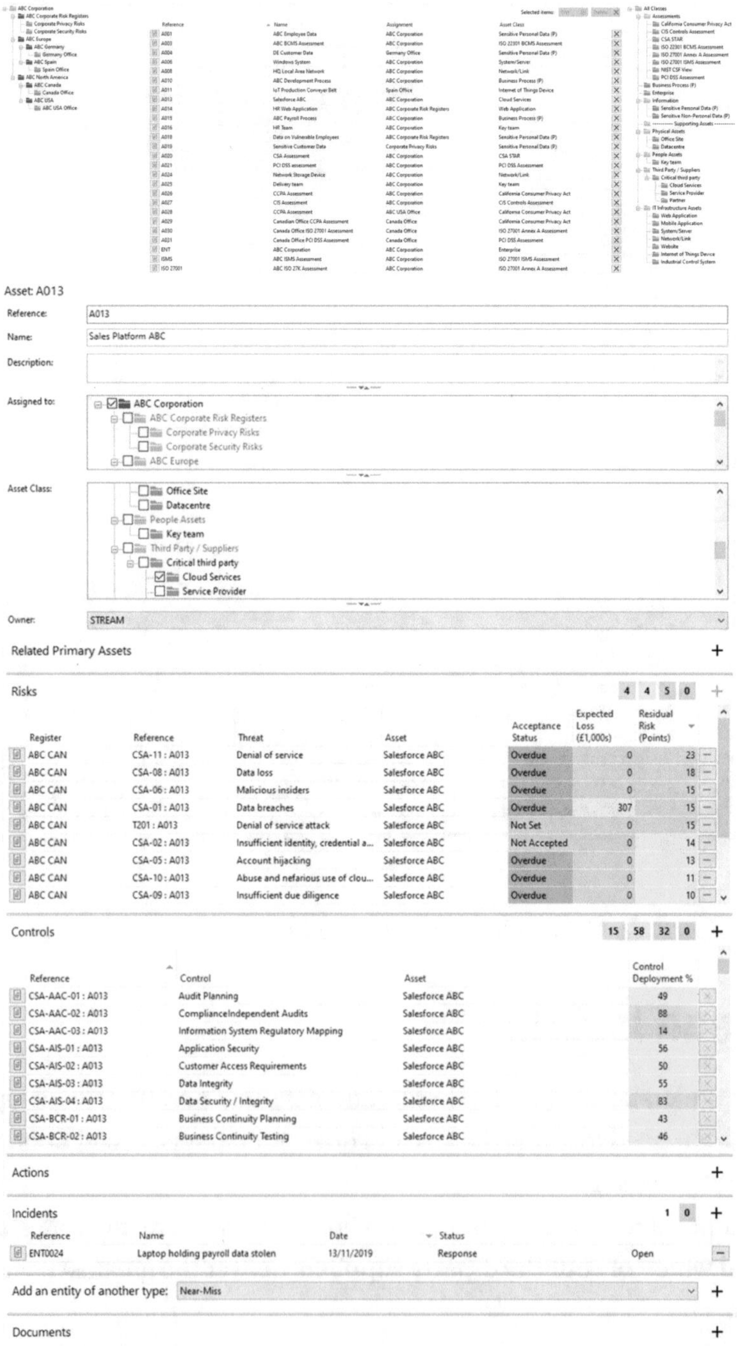

Figure 5-36. Asset risk views

After having identified the assets and their associated risks, for any risks that reside above your levels of tolerance, you will be needing to select some mitigation controls that can be applied to reduce these risks to a range with which you are comfortable with.

The selection of mitigation controls needn't be restricted to a single control framework and could be a "mix and match" from various industry security control standards/frameworks (as depicted in Figure 5-37[83]).

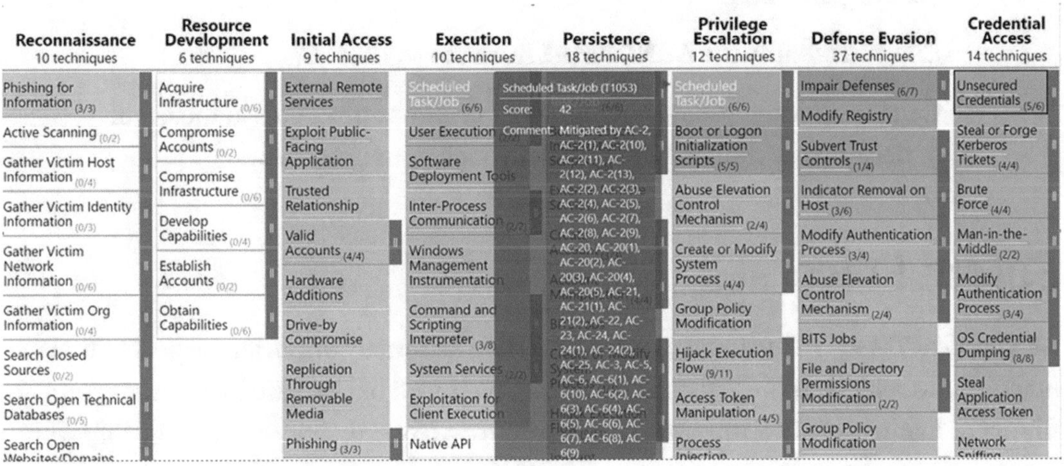

Figure 5-37. *NIST SP800-53 Security Controls*

When evaluating your mitigation controls, you need to start looking at your estate through the eyes of an attacker. For example, you should be asking yourself questions such as

- If your perimeter is breached, how easily can an attacker navigate through your estate?

- Are they provided free lateral movement[84] across your estate?

- Are the risks within acceptable tolerances?

- Do you need additional mitigation security controls?

[83]https://mitre-attack.github.io/attack-navigator/#layerURL=https%3A%2F%2Fraw.
githubusercontent.com%2Fcenter-for-threat-informed-defense%2Fattack-control-
framework-mappings%2Fmaster%2Fframeworks%2Fnist800-53-r5%2Flayers%2Fby_
family%2FAC%2FAC-overview.json

[84]www.exabeam.com/information-security/protecting-your-network-from-lateral-
movement/

Detect Anomalies

After establishing what needs to be protected, their value, their associated risks, and your chosen mitigation controls, you now need to be able to identify those **ABNORMAL** activities.

- Can you easily and quickly identify those activities that could harm your organization?

- Can you identify the **ABNORMAL** from the NORMAL?

- Can you quickly initiate your incident response protocols in the event of detection of unusual or potentially malicious activities?

Govern Processes

As a publicly listed UK business, governance is an extremely important aspect of their business model. The term "Governance"[85] can be traced back to the 14th century and is the act or manner of governing, and the Institute on Governance provides the following working definition for the term Governance:[86]

> *Governance is how society or groups within it, organize to make decisions.*

This definition reflects the following three dimensions:

1. Authority

2. Decision-making

3. Accountability

Consequently, for effective governance to be implemented and managed, it is essential that there is an established command and control[87] structure.

---

[85]www.etymonline.com/search?q=governance
[86]https://iog.ca/what-is-governance/
[87]https://military.wikia.org/wiki/Command_and_control

The US *Department of Defense Dictionary of Military and Associated Terms* defines command and control[88] as

> *The exercise of authority and direction by a properly designated commander over assigned and attached forces in the accomplishment of the mission. Also called C2.*

In essence, this is setting the "tone at the top," supported by a defined hierarchical structure where commands and instructions are cascaded down the "chain of roles and responsibilities" and with business intelligence being communicated up the "chain of command" (as depicted in Figure 5-38[89]) to ensure that timely and informed decision-making can be established.

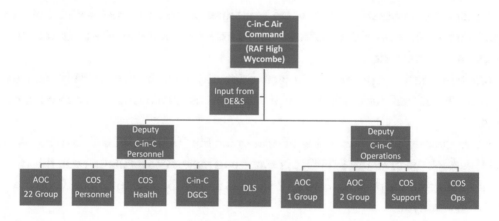

Figure 5-38. *RAF command and control structure*

Everyone within ABC Company's Protective Security command and control structure needs to understand their rules of conduct (provided through policies and procedures and regular security awareness training) and their roles and responsibilities and how important they are for the protection of the business.

- Are senior leadership supportive of the Protective Security strategy?

- Does senior leadership set an effective "tone at the top"?

- Are the rules of conduct cascaded down from senior leadership?

---

[88]www.jcs.mil/Portals/36/Documents/Doctrine/pubs/dictionary.pdf

[89]www.armedforces.co.uk/Europeandefence/edcountries/countryuk.html

- Does the business hierarchy have established department management roles, with Protective Security responsibilities?

- Are there effective two-way (downward and upward) communication channels in place?

Evaluate Security Controls

An effective Protective Security strategy needs to be treated as a business-as-usual (BAU) activity and become an integrated part of your organization's routine activities (as natural as breathing).

Protective Security should be treated as another business process, with the aim of supporting the defense of the business' valued assets and reducing the risks to within acceptable risk tolerances.

Much like business processes, Protective Security needs to be effectively managed to ensure that it continues to deliver qualitative results and continues to be a business benefit.

Consequently, many businesses have adopted the "Deming Wheel" (aka PDCA Cycle (as depicted in Figure 5-39[90])) approach as a means of articulating that this is a continually rotating process. However, this has already been incorporated into the BRIDGES acronym.

---

[90]https://betterprocesssolutions.com/2020/04/13/what-is-pdca/

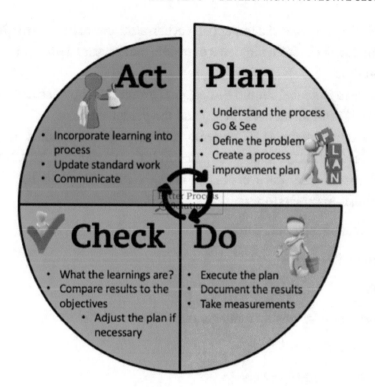

Figure 5-39. *Deming Cycle*

Within the "Deming Wheel," the requirement to evaluate the effectiveness of the selected mitigation controls resides within the "Check" segment. Consequently, a proportionate formal program should be established to evaluate the effectiveness of the security controls in helping to appropriately mitigate the identified risks.

These evaluations should be independent, open, and unbiased to ensure that the results provide an objective view of the risks, and the outcome of these reviews should be documented and cascaded up the "command chain."

Where a chosen control is identified as no longer effectively mitigating the identified risks, or where the threat landscape has changed, this needs to be made subject to another risk assessment so that the key stakeholders are fully informed of the situation so that they can make an informed decision as to their best course of actions to take.

Survive to Operate

Even the most robust Protective Security strategies need to include preparations for when, or if, things go wrong. The strategy must include planning in response to events and incidents. This should be designed and developed to ensure that the organization is able to minimize the potential impact of a cyber-attack or to be able to quickly and efficiently "bounce back" from incidents or events that present a disruption to valued business operations.

The "Survive to Operate" should be designed around the business context (what the organization feels is important to protect) and the perceived risks.

Using the example of the ABC Company, they may wish to consider developing incident response (e.g., NIST SP800-61[91]), Business Continuity (e.g., ISO/IEC 22301:2019[92]), and Disaster Recovery (e.g., FEMA,[93] NIST SP 1190GB-16,[94] etc.) plans for the following business assets/operations:

- Manufacturing operations

- Human Resources

- Sales

- Customer relationship management (CRM) role-based access

- Marketing

- Senior executive/leadership

- Intellectual property

To Certify or Not to Certify – That Is the Question?

A question you may be thinking is

- Should I consider the inclusion of an independent certification into my Protective Security strategy?

Well, the answer is "That all depends!"
This is all down to the following considerations:

- What is the business context?

- How important it is for you to protect your assets?

---

[91]https://nvlpubs.nist.gov/nistpubs/SpecialPublications/NIST.SP.800-61r2.pdf
[92]www.iso.org/standard/75106.html
[93]www.fema.gov/sites/default/files/2020-06/national_disaster_recovery_framework_2nd.pdf
[94]https://nvlpubs.nist.gov/nistpubs/SpecialPublications/NIST.SP.1190GB-16.pdf

- What type of assets are you trying to protect?

- What are the threats to these assets?

- What is the objective of certification?

All too often, I see businesses taking the wrong approach to certification, by either treating it as

- A reluctant "compliance" obligation

- A "badge of honor"

Another mistake is to choose a scope that does not align with or provide value to the business' objectives.

I'm not a big fan of the term "compliance" when referring to Protective Security, Information Security, Data Privacy, Cyber Security, and so on. If you investigate the 1640s origins[95] of the term:

The act of complying; disposition to yield to others.

It is an amalgamation of the term "comply"[96] with "-ance"[97] to form an abstract noun of process or fact or of state or quality.

- Is this something that your business should be proud of?

A better way of looking at the decision to certify an element of your business' Protective Security strategy is by what additional assurance of quality and security it may bring to your organization.

- **Assurance (late 14th century)**[98]

  "A formal or solemn pledge, promise," also "certainty, full confidence," from Old French asseurance "assurance, promise; truce; certainty, safety, security" (11c., Modern French assurance), from asseurer "to reassure, to render sure".

---

[95]www.etymonline.com/word/compliance#etymonline_v_28480

[96]www.etymonline.com/word/comply?ref=etymonline_crossreference

[97]www.etymonline.com/word/-ance?ref=etymonline_crossreference

[98]www.etymonline.com/search?q=assurance

- **Quality (13th century)**[99]

  "Temperament, character, disposition," from Old French qualite "quality, nature, characteristic" (12c., Modern French qualité), from Latin qualitatem (nominative qualitas).

  "A quality, property; nature, state, condition" (said [Tucker, etc.] to have been coined by Cicero to translate Greek poiotes), from qualis "what kind of a," from PIE root *kwo-, stem of relative and interrogative pronouns. Meaning "degree of goodness".

- **Security (mid-15th century)**[100]

  "Condition of being secure," from Latin securitas, from securus "free from care" (see secure). Replacing sikerte (early 15c.), from an earlier borrowing from Latin; earlier in the sense "security" was sikerhede (early 13c.); sikernesse (c. 1200).

  Meaning "something which secures" is from 1580s; "safety of a state, person, etc." is from 1941. Legal sense of "property in bonds" is from mid-15c.; that of "document held by a creditor" is from 1680s. Phrase security blanket in figurative sense is attested from 1966, in reference to the crib blanket carried by the character Linus in the "Peanuts" comic strip (1956).

Not all certification schemes are the same, and each will bring different gains to your company. For example, a certification against the Payment Card Industry Data Security Standard (PCI DSS) will provide an added layer of reassurance that your business' payment card data operations are aligned to help mitigate the risks to the payment card data. However, the level of assurance gained is heavily dependent on the quality and independence of the reviews.

If you are an organization that needs to adhere to the enhanced data privacy regulations, such as the European Union's General Data Protection Regulation (EU GDPR),[101] you may benefit from the certification against an appropriate standard from the International Organization for Standardization (ISO),[102] for example:

---

[99]www.etymonline.com/search?q=quality
[100]www.etymonline.com/search?q=security
[101]https://gdpr-info.eu/
[102]www.iso.org/home.html

- **ISO/IEC 27001:2013** – Information Security Management[103]

- **ISO/IEC 27007:2020** – Information security, cybersecurity, and privacy protection; guidelines for information security management systems auditing[104]

- **ISO/IEC 22316:2017(en)** – Security and resilience, organizational resilience, principles and attributes[105]

- **ISO 22301:2019** – Security and resilience, business continuity management systems, requirements[106]

- **ISO/IEC 28001:2007(en)** – Security management systems for the supply chain; best practices for implementing supply chain security, assessments, and plans; requirements and guidance[107]

- **ISO/IEC 9001:2015** – Quality management systems, requirements[108]

Although the ISO is not widely embraced or used within countries like North America or Canada, this global standard incorporates a unique approach of delivering assurance through a management system (as depicted in Figures 5-40 and 5-41).

---

[103]www.iso.org/isoiec-27001-information-security.html

[104]www.iso.org/standard/77802.html

[105]www.iso.org/obp/ui/#iso:std:iso:22316:ed-1:v1:en

[106]www.iso.org/standard/75106.html

[107]www.iso.org/obp/ui/#iso:std:iso:28001:ed-1:v1:en

[108]www.iso.org/standard/62085.html

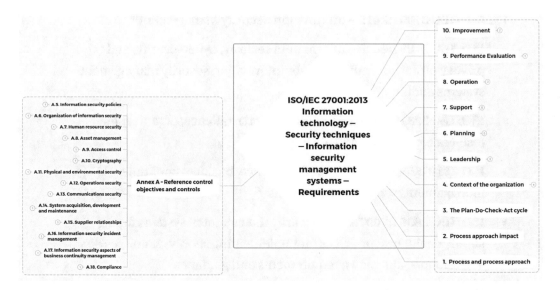

Figure 5-40. *ISO/IEC 27001 Management Systems*

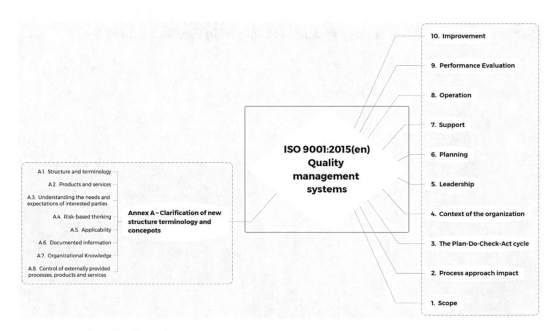

Figure 5-41. *ISO/IEC 9001*

Article 42 of the EU GDPR[109] "encourages the establishment of data protection certification mechanisms and of data protection seals and marks, for the purpose of demonstrating compliance with this Regulation of processing operations by controllers and processors."

Consequently, should an organization seek greater assurance for the quality, security, and resilience of their personal data processing operations, they could choose to implement the ISO/IEC 27001:2013 or the ISO/IEC 27007:2020 management systems, along with the applicable mitigation controls, and have this independently certified.

Alternatively, an organization that has a PCI DSS obligation may choose to implement the Management System from the ISO/IEC 27001:2013 or ISO/IEC 27007:2020 standards but replace the Annex A controls from the PCI DSS control framework.

This could then be independently certified for both PCI DSS and ISO/IEC 27001.

Having considered the value of certification, with ISO/IEC, an added value can be gained through certification by an accredited body.[110]

When correctly understood and implemented, certification can provide exceptional benefits to an organization's Protective Security strategy. However, if your business is investigating the certification avenue, ensure that you get some mentoring from a suitable experienced and knowledgeable specialist, to help ensure that you get the maximum benefits from your endeavors.

Remember that done properly and embraced by your business, certification (such as ISO/IEC) can provide far more benefit than being that "badge of honor," which you might get framed and hung on your office wall.

But don't take my word for it; listen to the words of a fellow industry professional (Sandy Domingos-Shipley, CQP, MCQI[111]), who has helped many businesses like yours to appreciate the true business value of ISO/IEC certification and to improve the alignment of the implementation of an effective management system, so that your organization gains a greater feeling of assurance and security:

> *The problem is too many businesses focus on the certification element – the bit of paper that says you've ticked all the boxes.*

---

[109]https://gdpr-info.eu/art-42-gdpr/

[110]www.ukas.com/sectors/security/

[111]www.linkedin.com/in/sandy-domingos-shipley/

- ***But that's all it is – a bit of paper!***

  The real value comes from utilizing the framework. And notice I say utilizing, not just implementing. Because what's the point of having a fantastic framework if you're not going to maximize the potential?

  Source: **Not another boring ISO guide…**[112]
  The Systems Link[113]

Reality Bites

In 2020, we saw reports of some of the best-known and reputable security companies (SolarWinds[114] and FireEye[115]) that fell victim to alleged state-sponsored cyber-attacks. In the SolarWinds incident, the attackers appear to have been able to bypass the Duo Multifactor Authentication (Duo-sid)[116] measures.[117]

Few would argue that such organizations would have had a "Cyber Security" or "Information Security" strategy in place, but was this based upon protecting those assets that were most valuable to the business or those that could be the most impactful if compromised?

This is where a "Protective Security" type of strategic approach can be a game changer for safeguarding businesses from the opportunist attackers.

Today's cybercriminals are like burglars, constantly looking for those insecure doors or windows or the negligence of authorized persons, which allows them to gain unauthorized access to the inner confines of your organization.

Consequently, it is essential that organizations start to change how they look at their defensive efforts and start looking at their environment from the perspective of a cybercriminal.

---

[112]www.thesystemslink.co.uk/wp-content/uploads/2020/08/Not-Another-Boring-ISO-Guide_E-Book.pdf

[113]www.thesystemslink.co.uk/

[114]www.bbc.co.uk/news/technology-55318815

[115]www.theguardian.com/technology/2020/dec/08/fireeye-hack-cybersecurity-theft

[116]https://duo.com/product/multi-factor-authentication-mfa

[117]www.schneier.com/blog/archives/2020/12/how-the-solarwinds-hackers-bypassed-duo-multi-factor-authentication.html

There are many accounts from history where a determined enough enemy has managed to breach even the most fortified of defenses, for example:

- **Siege of Troy** (as depicted in Figure 5-42)[118] – After 10 years of continual assault, the defenses held firm. However, the city was compromised, after the occupants wheeled through a wooden horse. Once the horse was inside the inner confines of the city, the malicious payload (hidden inside the wooden horse) could attack the city from within.

  - This was to become the origin of the term "Trojan malware."

Figure 5-42. *City of Troy*

- **Siege of Constantinople** (as depicted in Figure 5-43)[119] – It is believed that the fate of Constantinople was caused by someone failing to resecure a perimeter gate after returning from seeing off an attacking enemy.

  - Demonstrates the importance of strict change controls and secure configuration checks of your firewalls.

---

[118]www.britannica.com/event/Siege-of-Troy-1250-BCE

[119]www.britannica.com/event/Siege-of-Constantinople-1422

Figure 5-43. *City of Constantinople*

Consequently, no matter the size and type of business that you are, it is essential that you appreciate that there are "enemies at the gates" of your organization and that you need to ensure that your assets are suitably fortified and that you are able to rapidly detect and respond to potentially dangerous or malicious activities.

Additionally, everyone within the organization should understand that they are part of these defensive measures.

Key Takeaways

- Protective Security is an all-encompassing term for the protection of a business' valued assets.

- The defense of your organization should never, ever, be regarded as something that is the responsibility of a single department (e.g., IT Operations) or an individual (Information Security Manager).

  - *Every role within an organization should include security responsibilities.*

  - *An effective security strategy should be a "team effort."*

- Any strategy should be treated as a BAU activity and be designed and developed to support the continued protection of the business.

- It is essential that the business understand what assets are important to them and their customers.

- The key stakeholders should be involved in understanding the risks and threats.

- The key stakeholders need to be comfortable with the level of risks that pertain to these assets.

- The defenses should be proportionate to the risks.

- The strategy should be regularly reviewed and include input from the key stakeholders of the business.

- The strategy should provide a holistic and flexible approach to ensure that all aspects for Protective Security act in harmony while allowing for rapid adjustments (based upon new impactful influences).

- The effectiveness of the risk mitigation controls should be evaluated and reported on to provide additional reassurances.

- Any certification scope should cover those assets that require additional reassurances.

- The protective defenses should never be treated as a "check box" or "tick box" exercise.

- The threat is ever present, and the attackers come in various guises, with a variety of skillsets and capabilities.

- No business is exempt from being a victim of an opportunist cyber-attack.

CHAPTER 6

Cyber Security and the Digital Business

In the afternoon we were on patrol when I experienced the first really serious result of the Squadron's losses and lack of leadership.

There were several small formations of 109s (as depicted in Figure 6-1[1]) high above us over the south coast and every now and then one or two of them would start to dive towards us but I always turned to meet them head-on and they would break off their attack.

For some reason the German pilots seemed to loathe head-on attacks and would invariably break always if one turned and flew straight at them – later on in the way, they overcame this and carried out some very daring head-on attacks, particularly against the American bomber formations.

On this occasion, after a number of these abortive passes had been made, I found that several of my pilots had broken formation and were heading for home. It was clearly a case of what was called 'one-oh-nine-it is' and it was apparent that these pilots had lost all confidence in their ability to cope with the German fighters. I knew that this confidence had to be restored as rapidly as possible and the place to do it was in a combat area and not when on a so-called rest.

When we returned to our airfield I had all the pilots in and gave them a good talking to and announced that if I had any more people breaking away – and by so doing exposing not only themselves to attack but the rest of the squadron – I would not wait for the Germans to shoot down the offender but would do it myself.

---

[1]www.wildfire3.com/the-enemy.html

© Jim Seaman 2021
J. Seaman, *Protective Security*, https://doi.org/10.1007/978-1-4842-6908-4_6

They all looked a bit glum and there was little doubt that they loathed my guts – I didn't care as I felt that they needed a bit of straight talking.

Although they obviously disliked me, they were beginning to appreciate the fact that I was, after all, the first Commanding Officer they had had who was more experienced in war than they were.

Writing on his Command of 92 Squadron,[2] WWII

From *One of the Few*,[3] 1971

Figure 6-1. *Messerschmitt Me 109*

Figure 6-2. *Group Captain Johnny A Kent*

---

[2]https://cambridgemilitaryhistory.com/tag/second-world-war/
[3]www.thehistorypress.co.uk/publication/one-of-the-few/9780750993401/

214

One of her sister aircraft, MK1 Supermarine Spitfire P9372. An early photo of a No. 92 Squadron Spitfire Mk1, The GR codes date it to the Spring of 1940 and the lack of an armour plated windscreen dates it to before the evacuation of Dunkirk. P9372 was shot down over Rye in September 1940. The wreck was recovered and much of the aeroplane is on display at Biggin Hill Heritage Hangar. Unknown Photographer.

Figure 6-3. *92 Squadron, Royal Air Force*

Figure 6-4. *One of the Few*

Introduction

It is important to remember to differentiate that Cyber Security (a now popular term, earliest recorded use of the term in 1989[4]) is only one of the domains for Protective Security, with the focus being on the protection of business valuable assets that are externally facing and that are the target of attacks originating from outside an organization.

Once the perimeter has been compromised, other terms (e.g., Information Security, IT Security, Network Security, etc.) would be more appropriate.

The term Cyber Security *(sometimes written as Cybersecurity)* frequently gets confused with other terms, such as Information Security, Network Security, IT Security, or Cyber Resilience. Even more confusing is that there is not a common definition for this term and that these definitions are very closely worded to the other terms.

Cyber Security Definitions

Cambridge Dictionary

Things that are done to protect a person, organization, or country and their computer information against crime or attacks carried out using the internet.

NIST[5]

Prevention of damage to, protection of, and restoration of computers, electronic communications systems, electronic communications services, wire communication, and electronic communication, including information contained therein, to ensure its availability, integrity, authentication, confidentiality, and nonrepudiation.

TechTarget[6]

Cybersecurity is the protection of internet-connected systems such as hardware, software and data from cyber-threats. The practice is used by individuals and enterprises to protect against unauthorized access to data centers and other computerized systems.

---

[4]https://io9.gizmodo.com/today-cyber-means-war-but-back-in-the-1990s-it-mean-1325671487

[5]https://csrc.nist.gov/glossary/term/cybersecurity

[6]https://searchsecurity.techtarget.com/definition/cybersecurity

NCSC[7]

Cyber security is how individuals and organizations reduce the risk of cyber-attack.

Cyber security's core function is to protect the devices we all use (smartphones, laptops, tablets, and computers), and the services we access – both online and at work – from theft or damage.

It's also about preventing unauthorized access to the vast amounts of personal information we store on these devices, and online.

Cybrary[8]

Cyber Security are the processes employed to safeguard and secure assets used to carry information of an organization from being stolen or attacked.

It requires extensive knowledge of the possible threats such as Virus or such other malicious objects. Identity management, risk management and incident management form the crux of cyber security strategies of an organization.

CISCO[9]

Cybersecurity is the practice of protecting systems, networks, and programs from digital attacks. These cyberattacks are usually aimed at accessing, changing, or destroying sensitive information; extorting money from users; or interrupting normal business processes.

Digital Guardian[10]

Cyber security refers to the body of technologies, processes, and practices designed to protect networks, devices, programs, and data from attack, damage, or unauthorized access. Cyber security may also be referred to as information technology security.

---

[7]www.ncsc.gov.uk/section/about-ncsc/what-is-cyber-security

[8]www.cybrary.it/glossary/c-the-glossary/cyber-security/

[9]www.cisco.com/c/en/us/products/security/what-is-cybersecurity.html

[10]https://digitalguardian.com/blog/what-cyber-security

Information Security Definitions

NIST[11]

> *The protection of information and information systems from unauthorized access, use, disclosure, disruption, modification, or destruction in order to provide confidentiality, integrity, and availability.*

TechTarget[12]

> *Information security (infosec) is a set of strategies for managing the processes, tools and policies necessary to prevent, detect, document and counter threats to digital and non-digital information.*

> *Infosec responsibilities include establishing a set of business processes that will protect information assets regardless of how the information is formatted or whether it is in transit, is being processed or is at rest in storage.*

IT Security Definitions

NIST[13]

> *Technological discipline concerned with ensuring that IT systems perform as expected and do nothing more; that information is provided adequate protection for confidentiality; that system, data and software integrity is maintained; and that information and system resources are protected against unplanned disruptions of processing that could seriously impact mission accomplishment.*

> *Synonymous with Automated Information System Security, Computer Security and Information Systems Security.*

TechTarget[14]

> *Security, in information technology (IT), is the defense of digital information and IT assets against internal and external, malicious and accidental threats. This defense includes detection, prevention and response to threats through the use of security policies, software tools and IT services.*

---

[11]https://csrc.nist.gov/glossary/term/information_security

[12]https://searchsecurity.techtarget.com/definition/information-security-infosec

[13]https://csrc.nist.gov/glossary/term/IT_security

[14]https://searchsecurity.techtarget.com/definition/security#:~:text=Security%2C%20 in%20information%20technology%20(IT,software%20tools%20and%20IT%20services)

CISCO[15]

IT security is a set of cybersecurity strategies that prevents unauthorized access to organizational assets such as computers, networks, and data. It maintains the integrity and confidentiality of sensitive information, blocking the access of sophisticated hackers.

Cyber Resilience Definitions

NIST[16]

The ability to anticipate, withstand, recover from, and adapt to adverse conditions, stresses, attacks, or compromises on systems that use or are enabled by cyber resources.

TechTarget[17]

Cyber resilience is the ability of a computing system to recover quickly should it experience adverse conditions.

It requires continuous effort and touches on many aspects of information security (infosec), including disaster recovery (DR), business continuity (BC) and computer forensics.

Digital Guardian[18]

In simple terms, cyber resilience is a measure of how well an enterprise can manage a cyberattack or data breach while continuing to operate its business effectively.

IT security infrastructures likely use policy-based security to defend against attacks or to raise a flag when a threat is detected. However, can critical business processes such as accounting, customer service, and order fulfillment be carried out during a security breach?

---

[15]www.cisco.com/c/en/us/products/security/what-is-it-security.html

[16]https://csrc.nist.gov/glossary/term/cyber_resiliency

[17]https://whatis.techtarget.com/definition/cyber-resilience#:~:text=Cyber%20 resilience%20is%20the%20ability,(BC)%20and%20computer%20forensics

[18]https://digitalguardian.com/blog/what-cyber-resilience

This is where cyber resilience can help. The aim of cyber resilience is to ensure that business operations are safeguarded, and a threat or breach does not demobilize the entire business. Threats may either be intentional (malicious hacker) or unintentional (failed software upload).

These differing viewpoints on the differing security terms create confusion and blur the lines within business. If an organization advertises for a Cyber Security specialist, does this mean that they are only focused on the external-facing assets and external threat actors?

Consequently, when I look at the domain of Cyber Security, I believe it is important to understand the backstory to the two words that make up this term.

Definition of Cyber

TechTarget[19]

A prefix used to describe a person, thing, or idea as part of the computer and information age.

Taken from kybernetes, Greek for "steersman" or "governor," it was first used in cybernetics, a word coined by Norbert Wiener and his colleagues (first coined in 1992).

Definition of Security

NIST[20]

A condition that results from the establishment and maintenance of protective measures that enable an organization to perform its mission or critical functions despite risks posed by threats to its use of systems.

Protective measures may involve a combination of deterrence, avoidance, prevention, detection, recovery, and correction that should form part of the organization's risk management approach.

---

[19]https://whatis.techtarget.com/definition/cyber
[20]https://csrc.nist.gov/glossary/term/security

Consequently, I regard Cyber Security as a domain with protective security where you identify all your Internet-facing assets and ensure that they are adequately protected from the external threat actors.

The other terms are then complementary terms, within Protective Security, to ensure that the valuable internal assets are adequately protected from the internal threat actors. *(Once an attacker has breached your perimeter and gained a persistent presence within your environment, are they still an external threat actor? Especially, when you consider that the average dwell times[21] are now reported to be around 56-days of undetected presence.)*

Considering Gartner's[22] definition of the Digital Business:

> *The creation of new business designs by blurring the digital and physical worlds.*

Defending your perimeter will become increasingly important for any business seeking to embrace the digital revolution.

Much like Great Britain's protective measures used in World War 2 (WWII), against the Germans (as depicted in Figures 6-5[23] and 6-6[24]), if you think of your business as being like an island (as depicted in Figure 6-7[25]), Cyber Security can be likened to defending against hostile and malicious activities originating externally from the island.

In WWII, the British used air, land, and sea power to defend against incoming attacks *(Cyber Security)* and still had a resident Home Guard *(Information Security)* to act in defense of their island.

---

[21]https://content.fireeye.com/m-trends/rpt-m-trends-2020

[22]www.gartner.com/en/information-technology/glossary/digital-business

[23]https://249squadron.wordpress.com/category/battle-of-britain/page/2/

[24]www.forces-war-records.co.uk/blog/2017/09/12/was-your-relative-serving-in-the-top-secret-home-guard-auxiliary-units-in-the-second-world-war

[25]www.brooksart.com/bobmap.jpg

Figure 6-5. *Air power*

Figure 6-6. *Home Guard*

Figure 6-7. *RAF Fighter Command map*

It is essential that your protective measures can distinguish between these differing terms and environments, but integrate and complement each other, in the defense of your realm.

In doing so, your business will truly be able to create an effective defense-in-depth[26] model.

---

[26]https://searchsecurity.techtarget.com/definition/defense-in-depth

Military Comparison

One role, during my 22 years in the RAF Police, stands out for me as something that is comparable to the term "Cyber Security."

With just a 2-week notice, in 2005, I was notified that after an eight-year absence from active dog patrol duties, I was to be returning to this role. However, it was not going to be based in the United Kingdom but in an overseas hostile environment.

To be adequately prepared for this, I needed to undergo a 2-week predeployment training, with the RAF Regiment at RAF Honington, before flying out to RAF Akrotiri to complete a 2-week reteam with my patrol dog (aka 42-toothed furry Exocet) called "Snap" – a Belgian Malinois (as depicted in Figure 6-8).

Figure 6-8. *Patrol dog Snap*

This was a real step-up in pressure and responsibilities from my last overseas deployment to RAFO Thumrait, Oman, and I can confess that I was extremely apprehensive and nervous for such an impending deployment. Consequently, my focus, in the following 2 weeks, was on completing the intensive predeployment training.

This training would include a familiarization of the local environment, learning about the insurgent tactics, techniques, and protocols (TTPs) and how to defend ourselves against them.

- Lots of classroom-based theory learning

- Many hours of practical exercises to test our capability to effectively react and respond to known insurgent activities

On conclusion of the training on Thursday evening, I had to drive 3 hours to my home so that I could unpack my "Green Kit" and pack my "Desert Kit" to drive 4 hours to RAF Brize Norton, to fly out to Cyprus.

Before starting my predeployment training, I took the opportunity to telephone the Sergeant who oversaw the RAF Akrotiri RAF Police Dog Section. When I inquired about "Snap" and why the typical 5-day reteam had been extended to 2 weeks, I was told that "Snap" was an absolute "Fighting Machine" and to read the press coverage in the UK Press (as depicted in Figure 6-9[27]).

The reason for the extended time frame for the reteam was to allow additional time for Snap and me to bond as a unit, prior to being sent on to the deployed operating base (DOB) Basra as an operational defensive asset.

Armed with pockets full of dog biscuits and treats, on my first day of the reteam, I set about starting to build a strong working partnership with "Snap."

I can honestly say that this was truly an awesome machine and 100% protective of me. I could not have wanted for a more effective weapon for my role in defending the military's deployed critical assets.

This dog could instantly pick up on any air of fear or nervousness, and, boy oh boy, he would respond with the utmost aggression to help elevate this fear level even more.

Believe me when I say that I was less fearful for my life when accompanied by "Snap" than even when patrolling as part of a six-vehicle Force Protection patrol.

"Snap" could react to dangers long before I was ever aware of them, and any enemy would certainly think twice about their actions when faced with this seemingly possessed patrol dog, baring the full extent of his sharp teeth, as he strongly lunged to the full extent of the restraining lead – just waiting to be unleashed or for the leash to break.

---

[27]www.mirror.co.uk/news/uk-news/the-hound-of-basraville-561573

Figure 6-9. *Media article – Snap*

On arrival at DOB Basra, I discovered that working as part of a two-team shift, I would be primarily responsible for providing protection to the airfield side perimeter (as depicted in Figure 6-10[28]).

Figure 6-10. *DOB Basra*

The patrol area consisted of an unlit fenced-off area, with two locked airfield gates allowing authorized access/egress. Between each of the airfield gates was a single road, stretching for approximately 10 km. To the right of this road was a single chain link perimeter fence *(segregating the airbase from the "Badlands"),* and to the left of the road was a six-foot steep embankment that took the landscape to a lower terrain.

This was to be our primary responsibility during the night shifts.

The shifts consisted of working a shift patrol of two night shifts, with one night off for rest (during the recovery period, the dog team had to provide a high-profile patrol, during the daytime, covering a 6-hour period).

During the hours of darkness, two dog teams would be deployed (one on foot and one in mobile support) to help defend, detect, delay, disrupt, or detain intruders seeking to gain unauthorized access through the airfield perimeter. Given the nature

---

[28]https://earth.google.com/web/search/Basrah+International+Airport,+Basrah,+Iraq/@3
0.80886314,48.03869051,3.11487804a,1277850.28659371d,35y,0h,0t,0r/data=CpUBGmsSZQ
olMHgzZmM0YTZkZThkNGY5MGE3OjB4N2M5ZjEzYjcxNWJmMzg0NRnxcPGmEc8-QCE8FXDP8wRIQCoqQmF
zcmFoIEludGVybmF0aW9uYWwgQWlycG9ydCwgQmFzcmFoLCBJcmFxGAIgASImCiQJm9GQ43DqPkARLFwq
o2V0PkAZTP3lY_9NSEAhR_DpQcXTR0A

and high-risk environment, the mobile support vehicle would need to drive covertly *(without lights and avoiding applying the foot brake (illuminating the rear brake lights))* so that we did not become an easy target for the opportunist attacker.

When changing over between the on foot and mobile support, in complete darkness, the driver would need to negotiate their way down the numerous slipways into the lower terrain. Using the cover of the steep embankment, the changeovers could safely take place.

During the foot patrols, the dog handler would need to make use of the dog's exceptional ability to detect scent on the air and their advanced vision and hearing to help in the early detection of insurgents. If the dog were to show an interest, outside the perimeter (once taking cover), we had the ability to temporarily illuminate the area using "Para-Flares" (as depicted in Figure 6-11[29]).

Figure 6-11. *Para-Flares*

In the event that either of the dog teams were to be engaged by hostile fire, we were to follow the rules of engagement, radio for armed support from the Force Protection's RAF Regiment Quick Reaction Force (QRF), and try to stay alive until their arrival *(approximately 10 minutes – 8km)*.

The objective of these patrols was to protect the perimeter and to rapidly identify any potential incursions into the dog patrol area, so that we could stop any hostile or malicious threat actors' activities before they were able to gain unauthorized access to the protected zone, to impact mission-critical assets, or to cause serious injury or take the lives of service personnel living within.

During one of these night shifts, "Snap" and I were on foot patrol with my only communications being a personal management radio (PMR) between myself and my shift colleague (Phil and his patrol dog "Hero" *(another Malinois)*), providing mobile support. Suddenly, there was a flash across the sky followed by a loud whoosh! Next, Phil was on the radio, urgently instructing me to get myself quickly back to the dog vehicle. A short sprint later, I was back at the dog vehicle, where Phil informed me that we had been recalled back to the Command Center.

After putting "Snap" safely into the back of the dog vehicle, we sped back to the Command Center, where we received a briefing from the Officer Commanding the Force Protection Wing. The base had suffered an indirect 107 mm rocket (as depicted in Figure 6-12[30]) attack.

Figure 6-12. *107 mm rocket attack*

---

[30]www.talos-iraq.com/rocket-strike-in-makmour-4-august/

The RAF Regiment's covert observation team had identified and challenged the "rocketeer," but he had gone to ground.[31] Both Phil and I were to deploy with an RAF Regiment patrol to try and locate and flush out this "rocketeer." However, we needed to travel "outside the wire" in our soft-skinned converted Chevrolet Suburban dog vehicle and without any electronic countermeasures (ECM).[32] Consequently, to minimize this risk, we would be squeezed into the middle of the patrol convoy so that our vehicle would be protected by the ECMs from the RAF Regiment's 51 Sqn vehicles in front and the vehicles behind us.

Before we knew it, we were patrolling in potentially hostile, unknown terrain, accompanied by an RAF Regiment fire team to the rear. Phil and "Hero" took one flank, and "Snap" and I took the other. After hours of negotiating undulating terrain and numerous irrigation ditches, in complete ditches, we had managed to flush out the "rocketeer," who had taken cover in a local house. It was decided to recall the main patrol and to keep observations on the house until first light, the next morning. At first light, Phil and "Hero" accompanied by a fresh RAF Regiment patrol returned to make the arrest (as shown in the *RAF News* press clippings, depicted in Figure 6-13).

---

[31]http://news.bbc.co.uk/1/hi/scotland/4780296.stm

[32]www.britannica.com/technology/electronic-countermeasure

Figure 6-13. *Press clippings*

During the day patrols, the assigned dog teams would be required to deliver high-profile foot patrols, within the Protected Zone, or to accompany the RAF Regiment Force Protection on "outside the wire" patrols.

I recall a couple of incidents where "Snap" demonstrated why he was such an effective defensive weapon – the first being while I was at the main access point to DOB Basra (as depicted in Figure 6-14[33]).

---

[33]www.rafpa.com/RAFP%20100%206%20Page%20Story.pdf

Figure 6-14. *RAF Police – Basra*

I had been standing adjacent to one of my RAF Police colleagues when a local national had suddenly stepped out of the processing queue to our left. Before either of us had realized, "Snap" had reacted and had launched himself, with full aggression, toward the incoming potential threat. The next thing I saw was this local national furiously flailing his arms and legs, trying to sidestep away (almost breakdancing) from "Snap."

My final tale from my time at DOB Basra involved an incident that occurred while on a daytime patrol of the domestic area. However, before I get into the detail, it is important that I explain a characteristic that may be unique to people who have served in the military and especially those who have deployed into hostile environments. During predeployment training and during deployment, you forge some extraordinarily strong connections, but soon after the deployment ends, the connections are severed. However, should you ever meet up with these people again, in the future, these strong connections are immediately reestablished.

During my predeployment training, during the various simulation exercises, I had commanded teams of non-RAF Police personnel, which in turn had created these strong connections. While on foot patrol with "Snap," I had been patrolling past the Expeditionary Forces Institutes' (EFI) welfare facility *(wearing full patrol rig (circa 15 kgs) in approximately 36C heat)* when one of the personnel from predeployment had been sitting outside, at a large wooden table/bench, had called me over, and offered to buy me a cold can of soft drink. This would be a most welcomed opportunity to take a short respite from the foot patrol.

Wary that I was with "Snap," I sat to the left ("socially distanced") distanced from this colleague. Now, patrol dogs are extremely perceptive at detecting whether someone is a threat or not, and after around 10 minutes or so, "Snap" had become extremely relaxed and, realizing that this colleague did not represent any threats, allowed himself to be stroked. Before long, "Snap" had climbed up onto this colleague, placing his front paws on his lap and his head onto the colleague's shoulder.

However, although "Snap" appeared to be relaxed and enjoying this attention, he had never switched off. Suddenly, "Snap" had angrily reacted and explosively launched himself (as depicted in Figure 6-15[34]) over the shoulders of my colleague toward an oncoming stranger.

The stranger had thought that he could just come up and give "Snap" a friendly stroke. However, "Snap" was clearly the one who was going to decide who could approach him, and this would only ever be on his terms.

Consequently, the stranger had turned ghostly white and was frozen to the spot, while my colleague had virtually stopped breathing and had become statue like.

Figure 6-15. *Malinois launch*

---

[34]https://youtu.be/myO3K3vJQbO

Those of you who have experienced the awesome agility or faced a full-on attack (as depicted in Figure 6-16[35]) will be fully appreciative of the value of such an effective defensive security measure that the working RAF Police dog provides.

Figure 6-16. *A proactive "Mally"*

For those who have not been so fortunate, I hope these images help you to gain an improved admiration for these assets, and if you were ever faced with such a foe, you wouldn't be the first, neither the last, to be frozen with fear.

Snap was one of an assortment of defensive measures that were introduced because of the ever-present and emerging threats. In fact, the threat from indirect fire attacks was to become so prevalent that DOB Basra was to have enhanced defensive capabilities, with the repurposed use of the C-RAM batteries (Counter Rocket, Artillery, and Mortar) battery gun – aka Phalanx (as depicted in Figure 6-17[36]).

---

[35]www.military.com/undertheradar/2015/02/the-9-biggest-myths-about-military-working-dogs
[36]www.forces.net/services/tri-service/frightening-footage-phalanx-battery-emerges

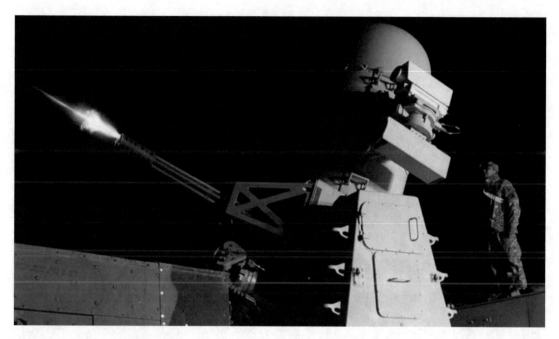

Figure 6-17. *Phalanx*

Unfortunately, even the most impressive defenses are not 100% effective all the time, and even with the automated capabilities of the awesome Phalanx, some rockets would still manage to get through.

This was clear when three Royal Air Force personnel were killed after DOB Basra had been the target of a sustained rocket attack.[37]

Building BRIDGES

When looking at an organization's ecommerce or digital operation, once again the BRIDGES acronym provides a useful basis upon which to develop an effective strategy.

---

[37]www.theguardian.com/uk/2007/jul/21/iraq.world#:~:text=On%20Thursday%20three%20 RAF%20personnel,Bury%20St%20Edmunds%20in%20Suffolk

Business Context

When Sir Tim Berners-Lee invented the World Wide Web (www), I doubt that he could ever have imagined that it would have grown in the beast that it has now become (as depicted in Figure 6-18[38]), and, hence, he has unveiled plans to save the Internet.[39]

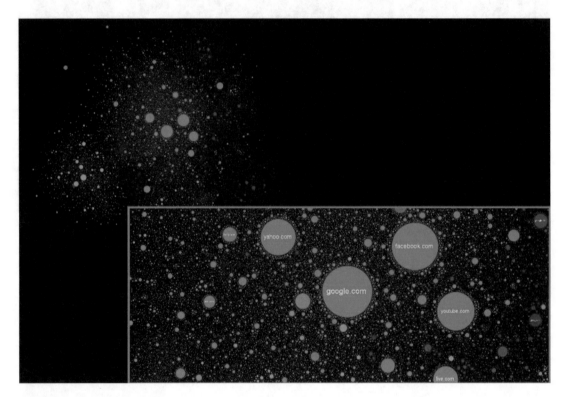

Figure 6-18. *Internet map*

This growing Internet and companies with increasing public-facing digital footprints (whether that be through a growing number of websites or Internet-connected devices) make this an extremely attractive and rewarding battleground for the digital enemy.

This growth can lead to numerous plates needing to be spun, when it is more important to prioritize and categorize your importance based upon the value to the business.

---

[38]https://internet-map.net/

[39]www.dw.com/en/web-inventor-tim-berners-lee-unveils-plan-to-save-the-internet/a-51395985

Remember that you can't protect what you don't know and that the protection needs to be proportionate based upon its value to your business. Consequently, you should be mirroring the tactics, techniques, and protocols (TTPs) employed by the attackers (as depicted in Figures 6-19[40] and 6-20[41]).

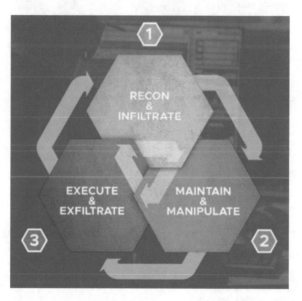

Figure 6-19. *Carbon Black Cognitive Attack Loop*

---

[40]www.carbonblack.com/blog/introducing-the-cognitive-attack-loop-and-the-3-phases-of-cybercriminal-behavior/

[41]www.lockheedmartin.com/en-us/capabilities/cyber/cyber-kill-chain.html

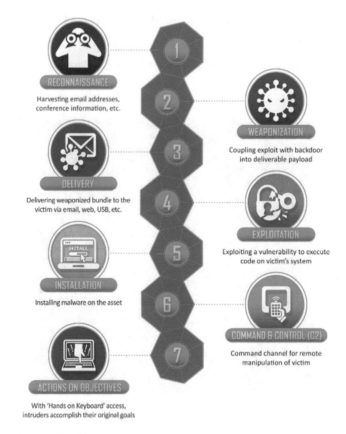

Figure 6-20. *Cyber Kill Chain*

Much like the criminal will identify and map your public-facing assets and categorize their finding (based upon value), you should understand which business processes are publicly facing and which are valued to both the business and to the criminal.

Consequently *(remembering that a "customer" can be internal (e.g., employee) as well as external)*, it can be extremely helpful for both the business and Protective Security to have a visualization of the "Customer Journeys" (aka Customer Journey Map[42]).

For example, the marketing team may use this to enhance the customer's journey, whereas in Protective Security this could be extremely helpful in identifying potential attack surfaces.

Figure 6-21 shows an example Customer Journey Map.[43]

---

[42]https://digitalagencynetwork.com/12-steps-of-creating-an-effective-customer-journey-map/

[43]https://uxpressia.com/w/vZSOm

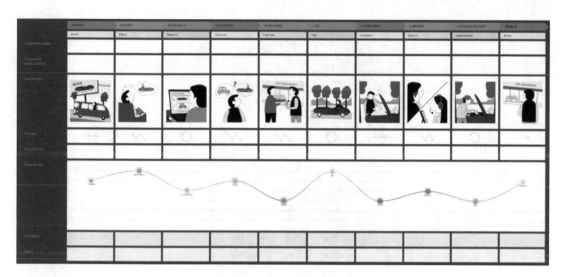

Figure 6-21. *Auto ecommerce*

To gain a greater understanding of Cyber Security and the digital risks, it is beneficial to appreciate how the seven layers of the open systems interconnection (OSI) model enable the communication functions of telecommunications or computer systems.

A useful example is to follow the journey of an email through the OSI model (as depicted in Figure 6-22[44]).

---

[44]www.rebeladmin.com/2014/06/osi-in-action/

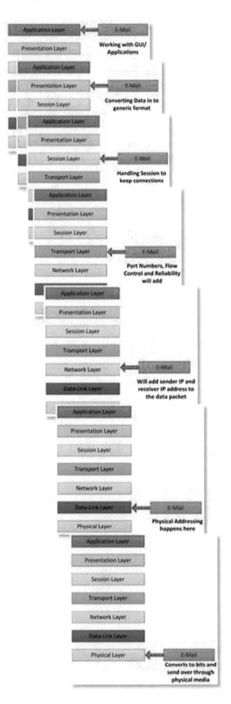

Figure 6-22. *Email – OSI model*

Consequently, phishing[45] attacks have become so favorable to today's cybercriminals as a means of exploiting vulnerabilities in the User layers of the OSI model (as depicted in Figure 6-23) to breach the perimeter defenses.

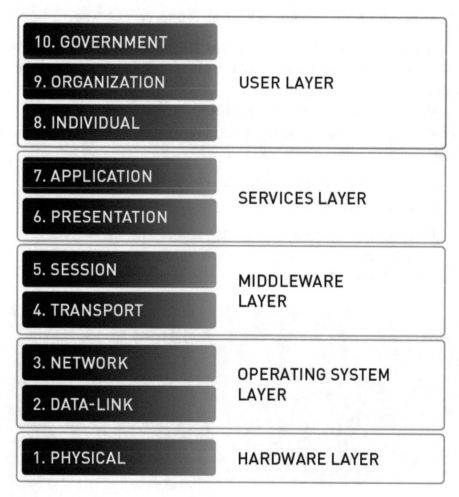

Figure 6-23. *User layers*

The output from the business context reviews can then be used to provide input into the risk and resilience profiling.

---

[45]www.itproportal.com/features/ten-types-of-phishing-attacks-and-phishing-scams/

Risk and Resilience

Which of these public-facing business operations are known to be at risk? Remember that a risk relates to the following:

Asset value X Vulnerabilities X Threat X Impact

Consequently, an essential part of identifying the potential risk is to engage with your business stake to identify the initial risks and to ascertain whether these are within risk tolerances.

To be able to understand the risks to your business, you need to be able to understand your potential attack surfaces and the tactics, techniques, and protocols that the attackers could use against your business.

- At what layer of your network (as depicted in Figure 6-24[46]) are you most vulnerable to compromise?

- Based upon the OSI model,[47] will the attackers compromise your firewalls (Layer 3) or through the human-computer interaction layer (Layer 7) or both?

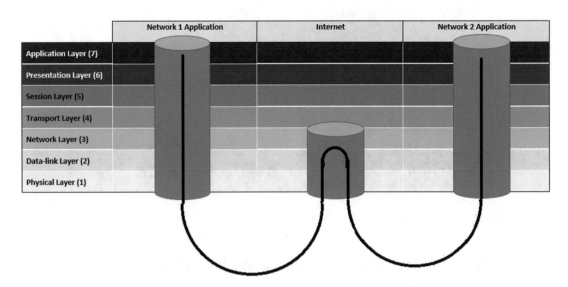

Figure 6-24. *Seven-layer OSI model*

---

[46]https://nostarch.com/hacking2.htm

[47]www.imperva.com/learn/application-security/osi-model/

- Do you understand the threats your organization faces against each of these various layers?[48]

- Have you created suitable attack trees[49] (examples in Figures 6-25, 6-26,[50] and 6-27[51]) to help with your threat modeling?

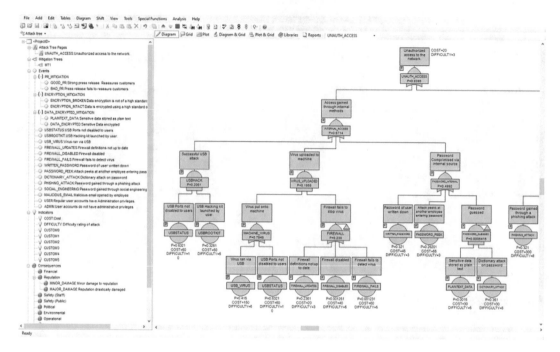

Figure 6-25. *Isograph*

[48]https://training.nhlearninggroup.com/blog/7-layers-of-cybersecurity-threats-in-the-iso-osi-model

[49]www.isograph.com/software/attacktree/

[50]www.isograph.com/software/attacktree/creating-an-attack-tree/

[51]www.slideshare.net/marco_morana/owasp-app-seceu2011version1

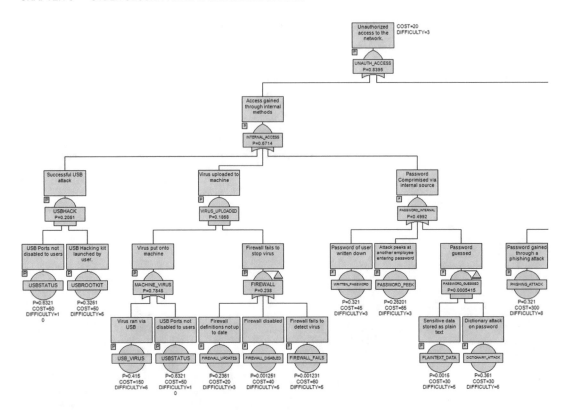

Figure 6-26. *Isograph extract*

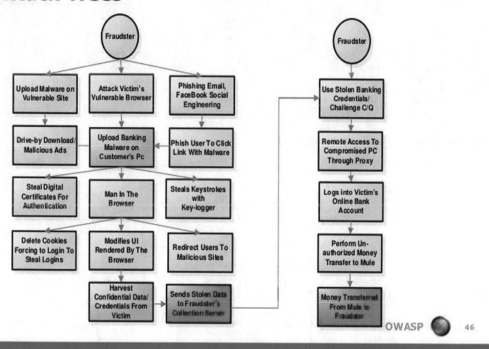

Figure 6-27. *OWASP*

- Have you threat modeled your ecommerce and digital business operations (examples depicted in Figures 6-28,[52] 6-29,[53] and 6-30[54])?

---

[52]https://martinfowler.com/articles/agile-threat-modelling.html

[53]https://online.visual-paradigm.com/diagrams/templates/threat-model-diagram/stride-threat-model/

[54]www.microsoft.com/en-us/securityengineering/sdl/threatmodeling

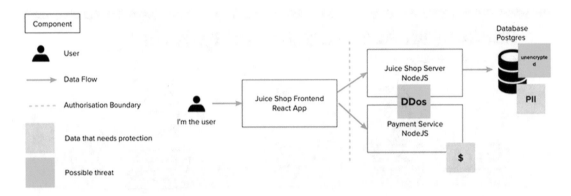

Figure 6-28. *DDoS threat model*

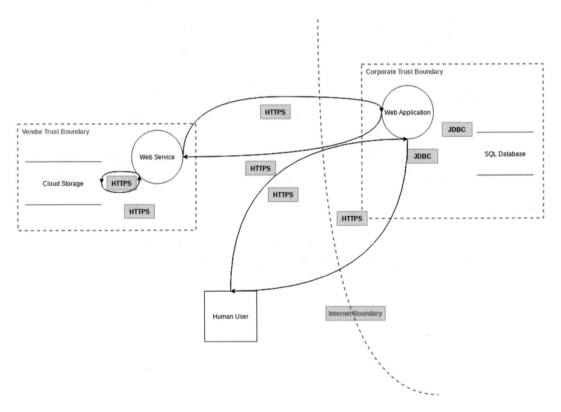

Figure 6-29. *STRIDE threat model*

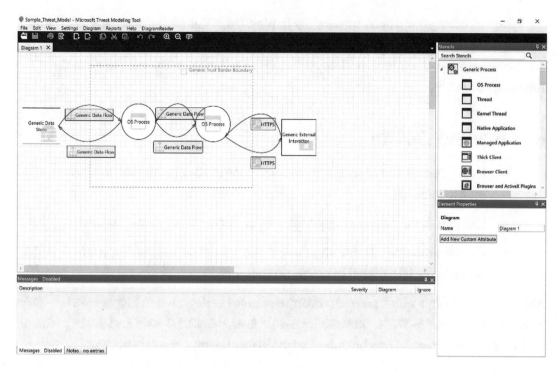

Figure 6-30. *Microsoft threat modeling tool*

When looking at your ecommerce and digital business operations, you need to be answering the following four questions:

1. What are the existing/planned Internet-facing business operations?

2. What could go wrong?

3. What could we do better?

4. Are we comfortable with the current state?

Take each business operation as a separate process and break down the analysis into the following four stages:

1. Decompose the application or infrastructure.

2. Determine the threats.

3. Determine countermeasures and mitigations.

4. Rank the threats.

247

When creating your threat models, the Exploit DB,[55] Vulnerabilities database,[56] and MITRE ATT&CK[57] are extremely useful resources.

As you can see, the threat modeling has a close reliance on the next stage in the BRIDGES acronym.

Identify and Isolate

- How often do you carry out reconnaissance of your public-facing infrastructures?

- Can you rapidly detect rogue websites or network-connected assets?

- Do you understand what should and should not be supporting your ecommerce and digital business operations?

As you can see from a quick piece of reconnaissance (as depicted in Figures 6-31–6-33,[58] 6-34,[59] 6-35,[60] 6-36,[61] 6-37,[62] 6-38,[63] 6-39,[64] 6-40,[65] 6-41,[66] 6-42,[67] 6-43,[68] and 6-44[69]), what is visible to the wider world can be quite insightful for the opportunist attacker.

---

[55]www.exploit-db.com/

[56]https://nvd.nist.gov/vuln/search

[57]https://attack.mitre.org/

[58]www.shodan.io/

[59]https://securitytrails.com/list/apex_domain/www.umaine.edu

[60]https://dnsdumpster.com/

[61]www.visualsitemapper.com/map/www.umaine.edu

[62]www.virustotal.com/graph/www.umaine.edu

[63]https://securityheaders.com/?q=www.umaine.edu&followRedirects=on

[64]https://builtwith.com/umaine.edu

[65]https://securityheaders.com/

[66]www.ssllabs.com/ssltest/analyze.html?d=umaine.edu

[67]https://gf.dev/hsts-test

[68]www.zaproxy.org/

[69]https://portswigger.net/burp

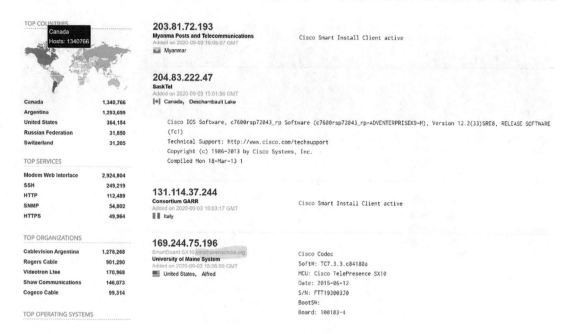

Figure 6-31. *Cisco devices*

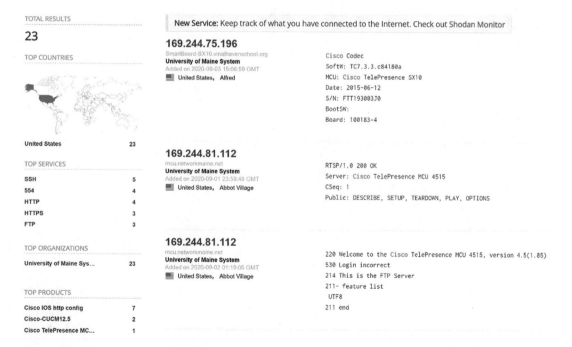

Figure 6-32. *Cisco – University of Maine*

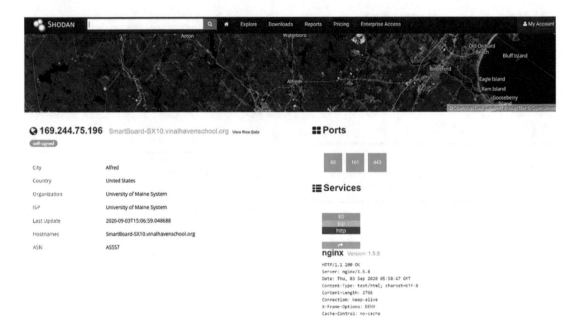

Figure 6-33. *University of Maine System*

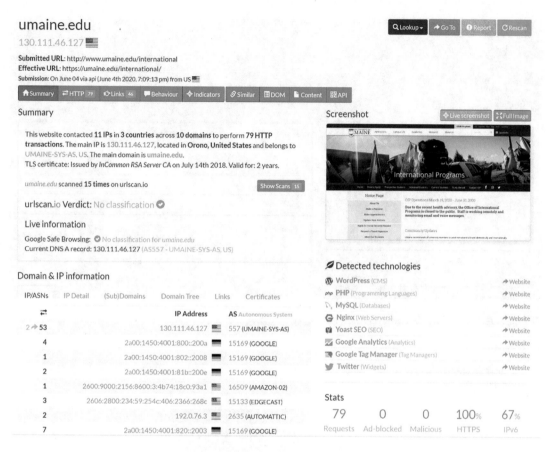

Figure 6-34. *University of Maine overview*

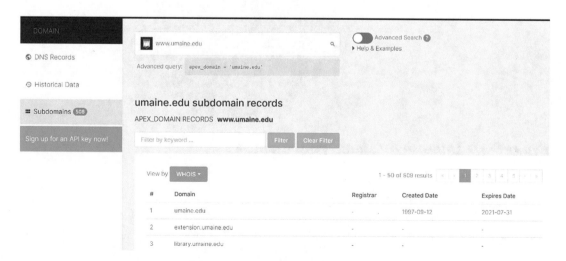

Figure 6-35. *University of Maine Subdomains list*

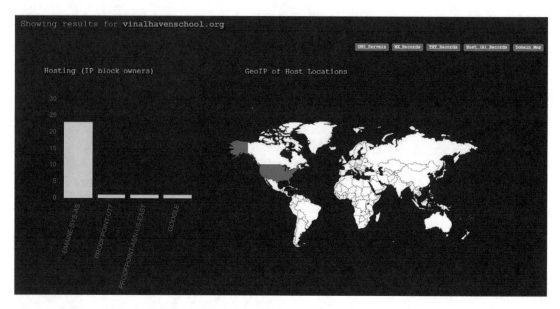

Figure 6-36. *Vinalhaven School, Maine, devices*

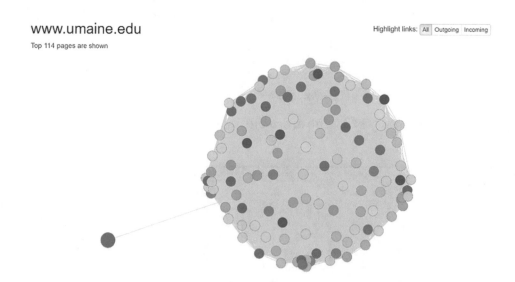

Figure 6-37. *University of Maine website topology*

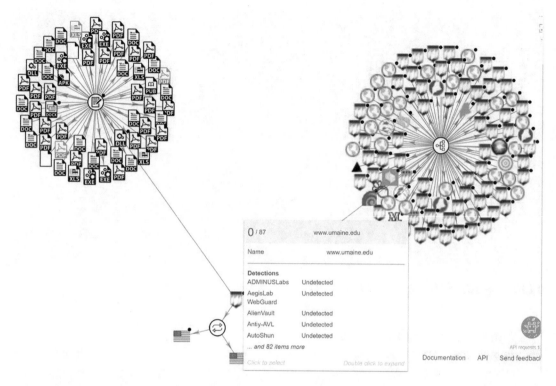

Figure 6-38. *VirusTotal Graph*

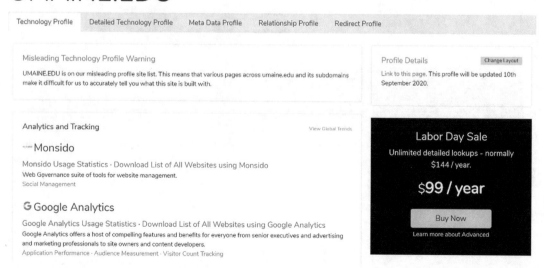

Figure 6-39. *BuiltWith*

Figure 6-40. *Security Headers*

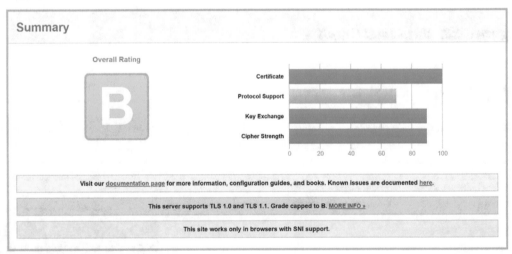

Figure 6-41. *SSL Report*

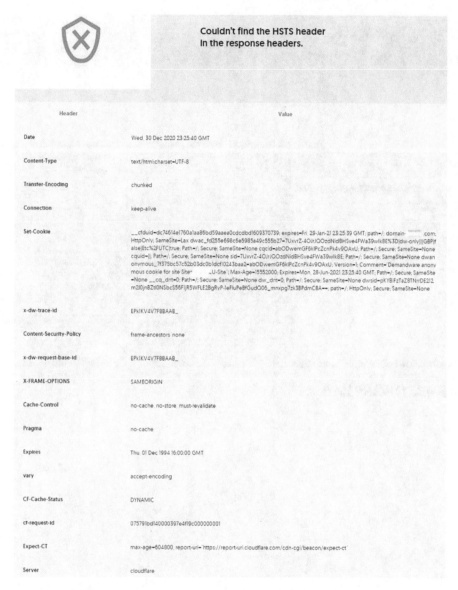

Figure 6-42. *Geekflare*

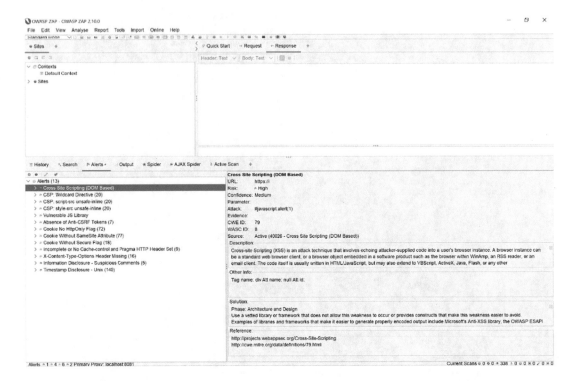

Figure 6-43. *OWASP ZAP*

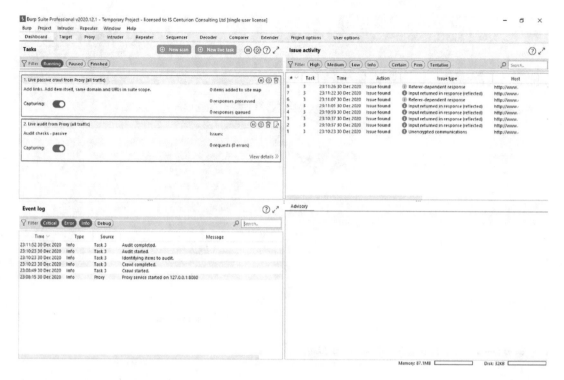

Figure 6-44. *Burp Suite*

All this information is available to both your organization and to the opportunist criminal. Unfortunately, whereas the criminal has got a great deal more time available to them (or they have written a clever program to automate things), this is rarely a luxury that the modern ecommerce or digital business has available to them.

However, there is a way to help try and level up the playing field. Consider the benefits of using a vendor service that automates the process, so that all you need to do is review a single dashboard (as depicted in Figures 6-45 to 6-47[70]).

---

[70]assistance@cyberrescue.co.uk

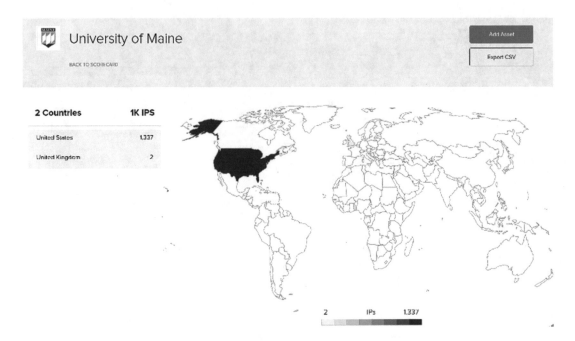

Figure 6-45. *University of Maine Digital Footprint*

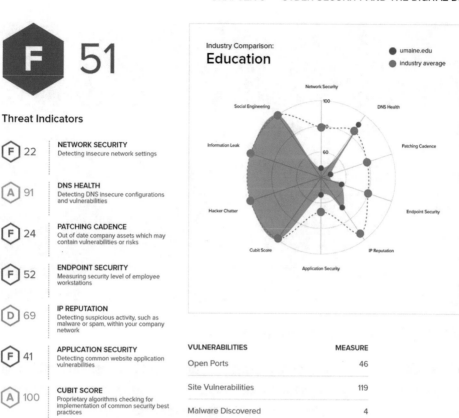

Threat Indicators

F 22 NETWORK SECURITY
Detecting insecure network settings

A 91 DNS HEALTH
Detecting DNS insecure configurations
and vulnerabilities

F 24 PATCHING CADENCE
Out of date company assets which may
contain vulnerabilities or risks

F 52 ENDPOINT SECURITY
Measuring security level of employee
workstations

D 69 IP REPUTATION
Detecting suspicious activity, such as
malware or spam, within your company
network

F 41 APPLICATION SECURITY
Detecting common website application
vulnerabilities

A 100 CUBIT SCORE
Proprietary algorithms checking for
implementation of common security best
practices

A 100 HACKER CHATTER
Monitoring hacker sites for chatter about
your company

A 100 INFORMATION LEAK
Potentially confidential company
information which may have been
inadvertently leaked

A 100 SOCIAL ENGINEERING
Measuring company awareness to a
social engineering or phishing attack

VULNERABILITIES	MEASURE
Open Ports	46
Site Vulnerabilities	119
Malware Discovered	4
Leaked Information	0

Security-related analyses, including ratings, and statements in the Content of this document are
statements of opinion of relative future security risks of entities as of the date they are expressed,
and not statements of current or historical fact as to safety of transacting with any entity,
recommendations regarding decision to do business with any entity, endorsements of the accuracy
of any of the data or conclusions or attempts to independently assess or vouch for the security
measures of any entity. SECURITYSCORECARD PARTIES DISCLAIM ANY AND ALL EXPRESS OR
IMPLIED WARRANTIES, INCLUDING, BUT NOT LIMITED TO, (1) ANY WARRANTIES OF
MERCHANTABILITY OR FITNESS FOR A PARTICULAR PURPOSE OR USE, (2) ACCURACY,
RESULTS, TIMELINESS AND COMPLETENESS, (3) FREEDOM FROM BUGS, SOFTWARE ERRORS
AND DEFECTS, (4) THAT THE CONTENT'S FUNCTIONING WILL BE UNINTERRUPTED AND (5)
THAT THE CONTENT WILL OPERATE WITH ANY SOFTWARE OR HARDWARE CONFIGURATION.

Figure 6-46. *Risk and resilience summary*

Figure 6-47. *Risk and resilience profile*

All this information is important for ensuring that there is an established baseline (initial risk), from which you can then start to identify and apply appropriate mitigation controls, to ensure that the risks remain with risk tolerances.

Once you have achieved the baseline, you will be better placed to be able to detect the **ABNORMAL** from the NORMAL. These anomalies could be an indicator of negligent/accidental actions by authorized personnel or the actions of a malicious actor.

Detect Anomalies

Having established what the most valuable business operations are, what assets are necessary to support them, where they reside (and their interconnections), and who is approved to have access (based upon legitimate business needs), you will be better placed to identify the **ABNORMAL**.

Can you recognize the validated business activities and approved data and network traffic flows?

Remember that your employees will be creatures of habit and will establish routines, whereas intruders will not be familiar with the environment and will try to establish an undetected persistent presence within, to allow them to carry out the clandestine reconnaissance needed for a successful attack.

Frequently, organizations do not fully understand their topologies, as they relate to their business operations, and as a result are reliant on the concept of

Security through Obscurity!

It is the obscurity and lack of an understanding of the business operations and its supporting infrastructure that provides the criminal with the edge that they need.

Once they have breached the perimeter *(note that this could be through your Supply Chain)*, they are often allowed unfettered access to move laterally across the internal network.[71]

- How easily can you detect malicious or unauthorized activities within your network?

- Can you quickly detect an attacker carrying out internal reconnaissance and attack planning before they compromise your valuable assets?

As identified by IBM,[72] it's not about having more security tools but more about integrating your security toolsets to ensure that you can detect an intruder within your estate (as depicted in Figure 6-48[73]).

---

[71]www.stackrox.com/post/2020/09/protecting-against-kubernetes-threats-chapter-8-lateral-movement/

[72]www.ibm.com/blogs/nordic-msp/cybersecurity-doesnt-need-more-tools-it-needs-new-rules/

[73]https://github.com/cisagov/cset/releases/download/v10.0.1/CSETStandAlone.exe

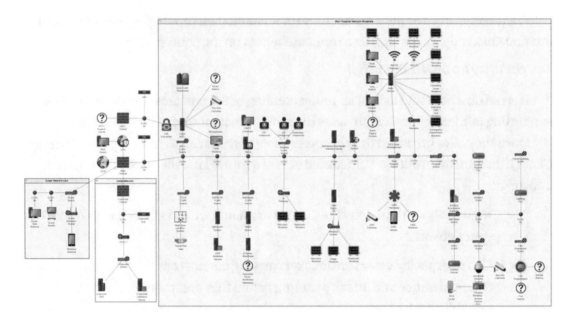

Figure 6-48. *Example medical network*

Govern Processes

With human error being cited as being the greatest cause of Cyber Security–related incidents, the effective governance of the internal processes (both in-house and outsourced) is critical for ensuring that your external-facing business operations and systems remain effective.

- **95%** of Cyber Security breaches are due to human error.[74]

- **90%** of UK data breaches are due to human error in 2019.[75]

- A massive **83%** of reported breaches could be simple human error or lack of GDPR awareness.[76]

---

[74]www.cybintsolutions.com/cyber-security-facts-stats/#:~:text=95%25%20of%20 cybersecurity%20breaches%20are,never%20in%20the%20IT%20departmente,never%20in%20 the%20IT%20department

[75]www.infosecurity-magazine.com/news/90-data-breaches-human-error/

[76]https://thedefenceworks.com/blog/human-error-could-be-behind-gdpr-breaches/

- More than **70%** of data center and service outages are caused by human error.

- Human error is the chief cause of downtime, a new study finds.[77]

- Human error is the #1 cause of IT outages in the United States and Canada.[78]

The 1992 report on the Financial Aspects of Corporate Governance[79] (aka the Cadbury Report) defines governance as being

The system by which companies are directed and controlled.

Contained within this report are a set of rules, and although adherence to the Cadbury Rules is not required to do business in Great Britain, any publicly traded companies are expected to follow the Cadbury Rules, and if they don't adhere to them, they will need to answer to their shareholders.

It has never been more important to embed good practices as an integral and essential part of business-as-usual activities. Consequently, there needs to be a formal suite of policies and procedures, supported by a formal employee awareness program.

The program needs to be tailored against the identified risks for the entire business, as well as for each high-risk business department or operation. This should incorporate the use of an overarching enterprise-wide program, supported by enhanced training tailored to the receiving business unit. This could well be delivered through the department managers, who, after receiving relevant cyber security training, could be delegated the responsibility for delivering periodic on-the-job awareness training and carrying out periodic reviews. The results of which would then be reported to the Cyber Security lead.

All too often, there is a lack of delegation for security awareness, and there is a false belief that a small security department can deliver effective training that is tailored and relevant to all departments and roles.

---

[77]www.networkworld.com/article/3444762/the-biggest-risk-to-uptime-your-staff.html
[78]www.apmdigest.com/leading-causes-of-it-outages-and-how-to-prevent-them
[79]https://ecgi.global/sites/default//files//codes/documents/cadbury.pdf

Of course, the overall business-wide training can benefit from the procurement of security awareness software, managed by a third-party vendor (e.g., KnowBe4,[80] Phishing T@ckle,[81] etc.)

Further validation would then require the output from the various security testing; vulnerability management programs would then be incorporated into periodic performance measurement[82] reports.

For example:

- New or upgraded information systems that are not configured with required information security settings and patches would be an indication of poor configuration management habits.

- Information system and information security architectures that render information systems vulnerable would be a sign of deficient security architecture practices.

The results would then feed into the risk and resilience profiles and would then be augmented by a suitable audit program.

Evaluate Security Controls

I am often perplexed by senior leadership's apparent apathy when it comes to evaluating the effectiveness of those mitigation controls that have been introduced to help protect their business.

- Is it that they don't want to hear that there are problems?

- Is it complacency in the reliance on annual compliance program?

- Do they only do this because they are told that they must do it?

- Is it that the department managers don't want to be embarrassed or criticized?

- Is it regarded as wasted resources?

---

[80]www.knowbe4.com/

[81]www.phishingtackle.com/

[82]https://nvlpubs.nist.gov/nistpubs/Legacy/SP/nistspecialpublication800-55r1.pdf

The leadership of countries recognize the need for rules and laws and that these need to be policed. Why should this be any different in the business world?

Would you rather have an evaluation identify ineffective controls (or recommendations to enhance and reduce risk) or wait for a cyber-attack to identify an exploitable vulnerability, which allows them the opportunity for clandestine infiltration and exfiltration of sensitive data?

When you compare the potential cost of having a well-designed and planned evaluation (aka audit) program vs. the cost of a data breach, suddenly the evaluation program becomes more appealing.

The evaluation program should be designed so that it is proportionate to the risks and that the findings feed into the risk and resilience profiling, as well as the governance program.

NIST's draft NISTIR 8183, Rev 1[83]: Cyber security Framework v1.1 – Manufacturing Profile (as depicted in Figure 6-49) demonstrates how they have prioritized the manufacturing profile, based upon their potential impact.

Function	Category	Subcategory	Manufacturing Profile		Reference
IDENTIFY	Asset Management (ID.AM)	ID.AM-1	**Low**		62443-2-1:2009 4.2.3.4 62443-3-3:2013 SR 7.8 CM-8
			Document an inventory of manufacturing system components that reflects the current system.		
			Manufacturing system components include for example PLCs, sensors, actuators, robots, machine tools, firmware, network switches, routers, power supplies, and other networked components or devices. System component inventory is reviewed and updated as defined by the organization.		
			Information deemed necessary for effective accountability of manufacturing system components includes, for example, hardware inventory specifications, component owners, networked components or devices, machine names and network addresses. Inventory specifications include, for example, manufacturer, device type, model, serial number, and physical location.		
			Moderate		
			Identify individuals who are both responsible and accountable for administering manufacturing system components.		
			High		CM-8 (1)(4)(5) CM-8 (2)(3)
			Identify where automated mechanisms are safe to implement for detecting the presence of unauthorized hardware and firmware components within the manufacturing system.		
		ID.AM-2	**Low**		62443-2-1:2009 4.2.3.4 62443-3-3:2013 SR 7.8 CM-8
			Document an inventory of manufacturing system software components that reflects the current system.		
			Manufacturing system software components include for example software license information, software version numbers, HMI and other ICS component applications, software, operating systems. System software inventory is reviewed and updated as defined by the organization.		
			Moderate		
			Update the inventory of manufacturing system software as an integral part of component installations, removals, and system updates. Identify individuals who are both responsible and accountable for administering manufacturing system software.		CM-8 (1)(4)(5)
			High		CM-8 (2)(3)
			Identify where automated mechanisms are safe and feasible to implement for detecting the presence of unauthorized software within the manufacturing system.		

Figure 6-49. *Extract from NISTIR 8183r1*

---

[83]https://nvlpubs.nist.gov/nistpubs/ir/2020/NIST.IR.8183r1-draft.pdf

As identified in the Cadbury Report, a formal evaluation program is a recommended best practice.

Survive to Operate

The world of cyber security is extremely dynamic and is ever changing. Consequently, it is essential that you plan and train for when things go wrong, and so having effective playbooks that represent a wide range of possible cyber security–related events is pivotal to the protection of your business.

For example, have you considered developing and practicing your response to events, such as the following types of attacks (provided by MITRE ATT&CK[84] (as depicted in Figure 6-50))?

Figure 6-50. *MITRE ATT&CK matrix*

---

[84]https://attack.mitre.org/

- **Initial access**

  - Drive-by compromise[85]

  - Exploit public-facing application[86]

  - External remote services[87]

  - Phishing[88]

  - Replication through removable media[89]

  - Supply chain compromise[90]

  - Trusted relationship[91]

- Can you effectively respond to *(aka Crisis and Incident Management)*, continue business operations *(aka Business Continuity)*, and recover *(aka Disaster Recovery)* in the event of an attack originating from outside your organization (e.g., a ransomware attack[92])?

- How well can you limit the damage caused by such an incident?

Reality Bites

A cyber-attack on the Baltimore city government's computer systems, involving the use of RobbinHood ransomware malware.[93] During this attack, on May 7, the attackers managed to breach the city's servers, blocking government email accounts and disabling their online payment systems.

---

[85]https://attack.mitre.org/techniques/T1189/
[86]https://attack.mitre.org/techniques/T1190/
[87]https://attack.mitre.org/techniques/T1133/
[88]https://attack.mitre.org/techniques/T1566/
[89]https://attack.mitre.org/techniques/T1091/
[90]https://attack.mitre.org/techniques/T1195/
[91]https://attack.mitre.org/techniques/T1199/
[92]www.nccoe.nist.gov/projects/building-blocks/data-integrity/recover
[93]www.carbonblack.com/blog/cb-tau-threat-intelligence-notification-robbinhood-ransomware-stops-181-windows-services-before-encryption/

This was the city's second ransomware attack,[94] in as many years, and on this occasion the demand was for $100,000 worth of Bitcoins, and their systems were unavailable for a period of 2 weeks. The root cause of the attack is believed to have been via hacked remote desktop protocols (RDP) services.

It is estimated that this attack will cost them **$18 million** and has led to the CIO being heavily scrutinized into his handling of this attack and has now, subsequently, been terminated from his appointment.[95]

Key Takeaways

- It is important that businesses do not get confused by the term Cyber Security and to regard this as providing proportionate protection from the external attacks.

- This is protecting your business' external-facing digital footprint from opportunist attackers.

- Cyber Security is an integral part of a Protective Security strategy and is complemented and supported by other defensive programs (e.g., IT Security, Information Security, Resilience, Compliance, etc.).

- It is essential that the design and development of the supporting network provides a secure basis, with easily identifiable perimeter layers (both hardware and software).

- An effective Protective Security strategy incorporates a focus on the perimeter assets, almost like a "front line" but supported by the other defensive lines. This is a commonly seen defensive strategy used and perfected over many centuries, as seen in the Battle of Gaugamela[96] (as depicted in Figure 6-51[97]).

---

[94]www.vox.com/recode/2019/5/21/18634505/
baltimore-ransom-robbinhood-mayor-jack-young-hackers
[95]https://statescoop.com/baltimore-cio-frank-johnson-no-longer-with-city-ransomware/
[96]www.britannica.com/event/Battle-of-Gaugamela
[97]https://commons.wikimedia.org/wiki/File:Battle_of_Gaugamela,_331_BC_-_Opening_
movements.png

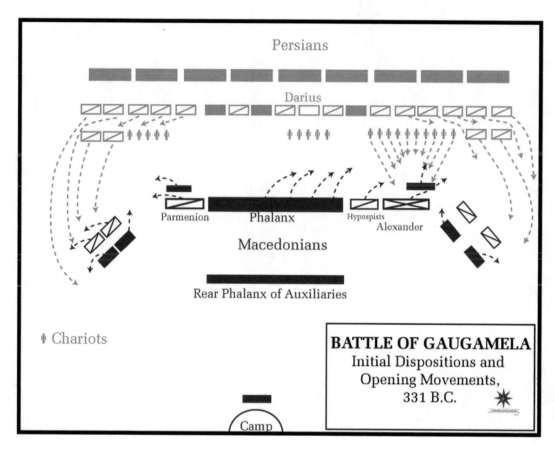

Figure 6-51. *Defensive lines*

CHAPTER 7

Network/IT Security in Protective Security (PS)

The German occupation of Crete in May 1941, after a rain of destruction from the air, provoked British Prime Minister Sir Winston Churchill to shoot a hotly worded memo to his secretary of state for air and to the chief of the air staff.

Churchill (as depicted in Figure 7-1[1]) demanded that

> *"All airmen ought to be armed with something – a rifle, a tommy-gun, a pistol, a pike, or a mace" and trained "to fight and die in defence of their airfields; … every airfield should be a stronghold of fighting air-ground men, and not the abode of uniformed civilians in the prime of life protected by detachments of soldiers."*

In response to Churchill's demand, the Royal Air Force Regiment, at its height 85,000 officers and men, was formed in February 1942.

Air base ground defense: The training controversy (Hoover 1991)[2]

---

[1]www.bbc.co.uk/history/worldwars/wwtwo/churchill_defender_01.shtml

[2]Hoover, K., 1991. Air Base Ground Defense. [Randolph Air Force Base, Tex.]: Headquarters Air Training Command, History and Research Office.

© Jim Seaman 2021
J. Seaman, *Protective Security*, https://doi.org/10.1007/978-1-4842-6908-4_7

Figure 7-1. *Winston Churchill*

Introduction

It is often the case that business will design and develop their network architecture with the sole purpose of supporting business operations, by providing inter-business connectivity, data storage, and internal/external customer interfaces.

The issue then arises that the convenience of having an interconnected network provides opportunities for attackers to exploit. Once the attackers manage to breach the perimeter, they are often given unfettered access to the inner connections of the corporate network architecture.

They will often seek to gain a persistent presence within your environment, using clandestine actions to avoid detection. Consequently, by the time most organizations are aware of the intruder, they have already carried out their reconnaissance to plan their attack, and when they are detected, it is often too late to prevent any harm.

Now, if you were to treat your supporting architecture in the same manner that the military treat the development of their bases, you will be incorporating security into the design and development of the architecture.

All military bases must be engineered to meet minimum security standards,[3] which provides military guidance for the exercise of authority by combatant commanders and other joint force commanders; prescribes doctrine and selected tactics, techniques, and procedures for joint operations and training; and provides military guidance for use by the Armed Forces in preparing their appropriate plans.

In order to successfully implement an effective model, it is important to ensure that the fundamentals of base defense are understood (as depicted in Figure 7-2).

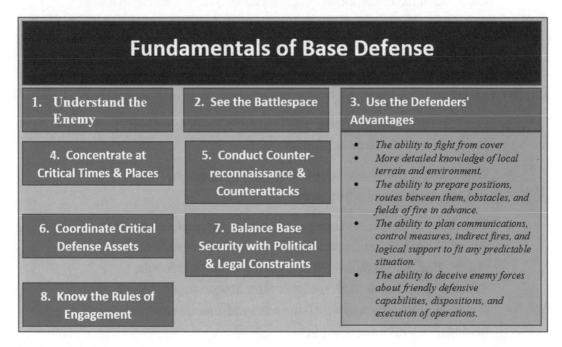

Figure 7-2. *Fundamentals of base defense*

The principles are to support the following capabilities:

- **Detection** – The ability to detect any enemy attempts to reconnoiter or attack the base, or to interfere with the performance of the base functions, at the earliest stage possible.

- **Warn** – The base must be warned that an attack is imminent or under way.

---

[3]www.hsdl.org/?abstract&did=3755

- **Deny** – Defense forces must prevent the enemy from accessing the base and from downgrading the base's primary function.

- **Destroy** – If possible, defense forces must eliminate the attacking enemy's capability to threaten the base.

- **Delay** – If base forces lack the combat power to defeat the attacking enemy, defense forces must disrupt the attack and attempt to create the conditions for response forces or tactical combat forces to react and destroy the enemy force or to remove or deny base resources to the enemy.

Another essential element is that there are effective and established intelligence functions in place:

1. Provision of information and intelligence to the defense force and maintaining current threat databases.

2. Establishment of intelligence liaison with applicable area, subarea, higher, and adjacent commands.

3. Direction of the reconnaissance and observation effort of the base defense force and arrangement for reconnaissance and observation, to be conducted by commands supporting the base defense force. Deconfliction of these intelligence collection efforts is an ongoing process in which the base commander and the intelligence staff must take part.

4. Collection of target information and the dissemination of this information to the base cluster or other higher headquarters and any units providing fire support to the base.

5. Procurement of nonstandard maps, charts, and imagery.

6. Development and implementation of local counter intelligence (CI) measures.

7. Request for augmentation or support by intelligence specialists.

8. Establishment and maintenance of contact with local home nation police and intelligence agencies.

Additionally, it is an expectation that the base commanders will develop effective defense plans, including

a) **Forces in base defense areas** – Successful defense depends on integrated aggressive, all-around, in-depth measures.

   - **Areas of operations** – Areas within the base should be assigned to cover all likely avenues of approach and other key terrain.

   - **Defense in depth**

   - A security area from the defense force's primary defense positions outward to the limits of the base area of operations (AO) may contain observation posts (OPs), listening posts (LPs), and mounted and dismounted patrols.

   - Boundary areas of various base defense forces must be clearly defined, and information must be disseminated to defending forces.

   - Defense forces in the base's primary defense positions must be prepared to prevent hostile forces from penetrating the base and interfering with its primary mission.

   - Some forces *(augmentees and selectively armed personnel)* may be directed to secure areas or facilities within the base vital to performance of the base's mission.

   - Relationship with other joint rear area (JRA) defense forces.

   - When a tactical combat force (TCF) is committed, the situation is serious enough to assign to the TCF commander an AO that encompasses a large portion of the rear area.

b) **Mobile reserve** – The base's mobile reserve may be used to reinforce threatened areas of the base perimeter, to block enemy penetrations of primary defense positions, or to counterattack to regain lost defense positions or destroy the hostile attacking force.

c) **Anti-armor weapons** – Rear area forces generally have few organic anti-armor weapons. Anti-armor weapons, including tanks, available to base defense forces will be positioned to cover the most likely high-speed avenues of enemy vehicular approach in mutually supporting positions.

d) **Indirect fire systems** – The fires of mortars, field artillery, and naval guns can support the base defense effort.

- Fire support planning

- Fire support coordination measures

- Observers

- Aviation fire support

e) **Other aviation support**

f) **Obstacles and mines** – Careful consideration should be given to the use of anti-tank and antipersonnel mines in the rear area.

g) **Communications countermeasures**

h) **Security measures**

i) **Work priorities** – The commander must set priorities for the many tasks involved in base defense.

j) **Counterattack plans** – The base mobile reserve normally conducts counterattacks with the objective of sealing a penetration or regaining positions lost to the attacker.

k) **Area damage control measures** – Area damage control (ADC) includes the measures taken before, during, and after hostile actions or natural or accidental disasters to reduce the probability of damage and minimize its effects.

l) **Air and missile defense measures** – Air and missile defenses nullify or reduce the effectiveness of attack or surveillance by hostile aircraft or attack by missiles after they are airborne.

m) **NBC defense measures**

n) **Threat response contingency plan** – The threat response contingency plan outlines specific duties and responsibilities to combat terrorism.

o) **Physical facilities** – Commanders must stress continuous
   upgrading for base physical security.

   - **Intrusion detection** – Defenders can place sensors on likely
     avenues of approach, locating them at the limits of the AO or
     outside the AO if coordinated with adjacent commands.

   - **Observation** – To improve observation, defenders should clear
     the ground to the front of positions and from near perimeter
     fences by cutting foliage or applying defoliant.

   - **Communications** – Defenders should install a reliable, secure,
     and redundant communications system at all guard locations.

   - **Entrances** – The base should have as few entrances as possible.

   - **Working and living areas** – Buildings housing personnel and
     sensitive equipment should be out of grenade throwing range
     from exterior fences.

   - **Internal and external territories** – Defenders must retain or
     deny terrain, facilities, and activities and preserve forces essential
     to base functions while minimizing the impact of security efforts
     on the local population.

   - **Medical facilities** – Medical facilities should be well marked if
     the tactical commander so directs and placed away from possible
     lucrative targets.

Many of these principles should be applied when designing and developing a secure
corporate network architecture. That way, you can continue to operate the business
efficiently (supporting the business objectives), while maintaining an effective defensive
program, through well-designed and modeled network architecture that integrates
security considerations into the design.

Consequently, you will be better placed to identify and respond effectively to
possible incursions, to prevent or limit the harm that can be done once the perimeter
has been breached.

Military Comparison

A good example is when the military enhanced Kandahar Airport to make it suitable for the support of the Southern Afghanistan Air operations.

- Making it the fortified Kandahar Airfield (KAF) base (as depicted in Figure 7-3[4])

Figure 7-3. *KAF – not your typical airport*

---

[4]https://foreignpolicy.com/2015/12/09/at-least-37-dead-in-taliban-attack-on-kandahar-airfield-indian-opposition-stalls-parliament-over-court-case-pakistan-china-hold-joint-military-exercise/

II Squadron can look back with a great deal of pride on all they have accomplished.

Against a backdrop of a 200 per cent increase in the number of rocket attacks against KAF, the deliberate IED targeting of their personnel and the most intense period of insurgent activity around KAF since 2001, II Squadron has undoubtedly disrupted insurgent efforts and made KAF a safer and more secure place for its 26,000 personnel.

Figure 7-4. *Kandahar base commander, 2010*

Air Commodore Gordon Moulds (Figure 7-4[5])
Kandahar Airfield (KAF), Afghanistan[6]
September 2010

My deployment to KAF was my very first time that I had been attached to provide a counter intelligence field team (CIFT) component for the resident Force Protection Wing (as shown in Figure 7-5).

---

[5]www.secret-bases.co.uk/wiki/Gordon_Moulds

[6]www.gov.uk/government/news/two-raf-squadrons-work-together-to-protect-kandahar

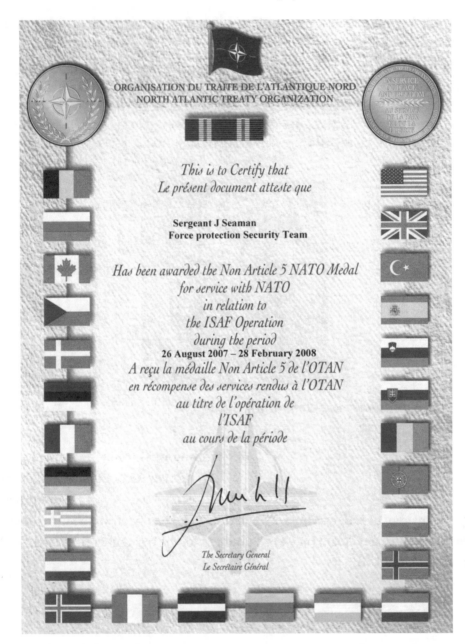

Figure 7-5. *NATO award (KAF)*

Working in civilian clothing (as depicted in Figure 7-6), while on base, and uniform when attached to an off-base patrol, the CIFT (as depicted in Figure 7-7[7]) was responsible for piecing together the pieces of information and building an intelligence picture.

Figure 7-6. *KAF CIFT*

This was achieved through numerous interactions with personnel residing within the confines of KAF, as well as from interactions with local nationals residing beyond KAF's perimeter.

---

[7]https://assets.publishing.service.gov.uk/government/uploads/system/uploads/
attachment_data/file/311572/20110830_jdp2_00_ed3_with_change1.pdf

Counter-Intelligence Activities in Afghanistan

In Helmand Province in Afghanistan during October 2010, an RAF Police Counter-Intelligence Field Team (CIFT) was operating from Camp Bastion providing support to the force protection operation. While conducting screening of locally employed personnel, information was received about a firm of civilian contractors who were in possession of unauthorised automatic weapons. A counter-intelligence investigation was commenced. Liaison with base staff and the Afghan authorities established that the contractors were not entitled to posses firearms nor were they permitted to carry those firearms in Afghanistan. Intelligence was collected about the contractor and this identified the names of the individuals who had control of the weapons and where the weapons were being stored. Further liaison identified that the same contractor was also operating at Kandahar Airfield and the intelligence collected was shared with the

Weapons and ammunition seized by the RAF Police Counter-Intelligence Field Team Kandahar Airfield, October 2010

Kandahar RAF Police CIFT. Intelligence collected at Kandahar identified that the contractor had a large compound on the base. The weapons were held contrary to Afghan Law and there was a risk that they could be stolen or used against Coalition forces. Briefed by the RAF Police team leaders, both base commanders agreed an intervention plan.

Simultaneous searches were co-ordinated at both bases and resulted in the seizure of a number of uncontrolled automatic weapons and ammunition for exploitation by TECHINT and FABINT. It also provided intelligence about the supply of black-market weapons.

Figure 7-7. *Extract from Joint Doctrine Publication 2-00*

Now, I do not mind admitting that this was a significant change from my previous deployments. In preparation for the CIFT role, I had commenced a training package that should have spanned a 10-week period *(a substantial increase on the previous predeployment training)* and was to include the following training:

- Team medic

- Off-road driving

- Field radio

- Close-quarters battle

- Field exercises

- Intelligence source handling

- Counter terrorism

- Interpreter familiarization

- Combat photography

- Weapon qualification live firing

This was an extremely intensive period of training which was both physically and mentally demanding and which was made even more traumatic when my then wife stated, just 5 days before I was due to deploy, that she was ending the 10-year marriage – not exactly the best frame of mind in which to deploy to such a high-pressure role.

Consequently, I deployed to KAF, not knowing exactly what conditions were going to be like going out there and what dangers I would be facing or what I might be returning to. However, on returning to the United Kingdom (after my first 3 months deployed on the CIFT role) for a 2-week period of rest and recuperation (R&R), the 3 months of interviewing and investigating several incidents had tuned my ability to read body language and to pick up when things didn't feel right. This led to my discovering male items *(that were not mine)* and Christmas presents addressed to another unknown male.

I returned to KAF to complete the remaining 3 months, knowing that my ex-wife had already replaced me with another and, I suspected, had been having an affair while I had been training for my high-risk deployment.

Fortunately, the high-pressure/high tempo CIFT role made for a welcome distraction, providing me little time to dwell on what might (or might not) be happening back home.

Added to this (picture the scene), we are all waiting in the departure lounge at RAF Brize Norton when on the Air Terminal lounge TV, the BBC News announced the sad news that SAC Bridge, RAF Regiment, had been killed when the vehicle he had been traveling in hit an improvised explosive device (IED).[8]

He had been part of the resident Force Protection Wing that we were flying out to replace.

---

[8]http://news.bbc.co.uk/1/hi/uk/6972896.stm

If it had seemed a little surreal beforehand, this was certainly something that changed things for everyone sat in there in that Air Terminal that morning.

Quickly, the mood became very somber!

Now, imagine that KAF was your typical civilian airfield with standard passenger airlines arriving and departing and being parked up overnight. The defenses that were in place would have been suitable for its role then but nowhere near adequate as a deployed military airbase. Consequently, the perimeter was enhanced with heavy fortification measures (as depicted in Figure 7-8[9]), an extended demilitarized zone (DMZ), in addition to several observation towers strategically placed along the perimeter.

Figure 7-8. *KAF perimeter*

The internal architecture (as depicted in Figure 7-9[10]) was also subject to extensive enhancements, creating a maze of internal segmented areas that could provide an additional layer of defense from indirect fire and provide additional layers of access control and barriers, to help prevent free lateral movement into mission-critical areas. Just because an individual had gained access within the perimeter did not automatically give them access to any place within the confines.

---

[9]www.forces.net/forces-tv/warzone-behind-scenes-kandahar
[10]www.forces.net/forces-tv/warzone-behind-scenes-kandahar

Figure 7-9. *KAF architecture*

Additionally, within the inner architecture, where assets were deemed to be high value or mission critical, they would be housed in their own secure citadel – almost like a separate base within a base (as depicted in Figure 7-10).

Figure 7-10. *Secure internal enclosure*

As part of the CIFT team, my role was to respond to and investigate all events and incidents while also creating an internal and external network of sources that could provide timely information, which we could then analyze and turn into useful intelligence. All information received, no matter how small or trivial it would appear, would be entered into an i2 database (as depicted in Figure 7-11[11]) to help create easily interpreted link diagrams.

---

[11]https://jimgarrityonline.com/2011/07/25/employers-scouring-internet-for-employee-information/

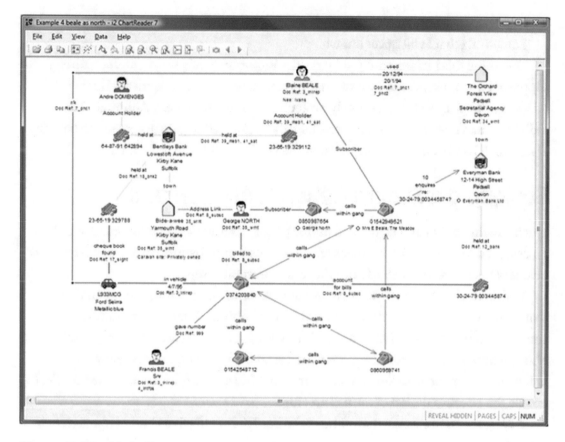

Figure 7-11. *Link diagram*

This proved to be an invaluable resource when it came to being able to understand the complex environment of KAF. On one occasion, it proved its value when the internal intelligence cells were looking for a person of interest and needed to ensure that this individual did not have access to anywhere within KAF.

All the other agencies were reporting that they had no records of this individual being linked to KAF. However, when we reviewed the CIFT intelligence database, we confirmed that he was not one of the local nationals who were granted access to KAF for regular work assignments.

However, we did have a reference to an incident that had previously occurred in the Saturday morning bazaar, where someone fitting this description had been allowed access as a stall owner. This turned out to be the very same person of interest and who had been casually gaining access to the on-base bazaar, every Saturday morning.

Strangely though, this individual never returned to the KAF bazaar after we had confirmed that he had been a previous frequent visitor to the Saturday bazaars.

Perhaps, the insurgents' intelligence operations were just as effective as ours. Something that I will never know!

One thing this incident did prove was the importance of a secure architecture, supported by robust access controls and proactive defenses to ensure that the mission-critical areas are adequately protected and restrict access. Although this individual had been a person of interest, he had managed to gain access to the bazaar area, which had been located adjacent to the DMZ, outside the main areas of KAF.

Designing a Secure Network Architecture

Much like the design and layout of a military base, your network architecture should be designed to support the business requirements while ensuring that the most valued business assets are isolated off from the less important assets.

Within the NIST SP 1800-5: IT Asset Management,[12] one of the greatest challenges that security engineers faced was being able to identify and track the status and configurations (including hardware and software) of IT assets across an organization. This is where a well-designed and managed secure architecture can be extremely beneficial, as you need to know what your valuable assets are, and where they reside, to enable the effective design of the architecture.

NIST goes on to suggest that some of the benefits of effective IT asset management are as follows:

- Faster responses to security alerts, through the identification of the location, configuration, and owner of a device.

- Increased cybersecurity resilience: you can focus attention on the most valuable assets.

- Provision of detailed system information to auditors.

- Provide a determination how many software licenses are actually used in relation to how many have been paid for.

- Reduced help desk response times: staff will know what is installed and the latest pertinent errors and alerts.

- Reduced device attack surfaces, by ensuring that software is correctly updated.

---

[12]https://csrc.nist.gov/publications/detail/sp/1800-5/final

Consequently, if you already have a corporate network in place, there will be a few phases that you will want to achieve (as depicted in Figure 7-12).

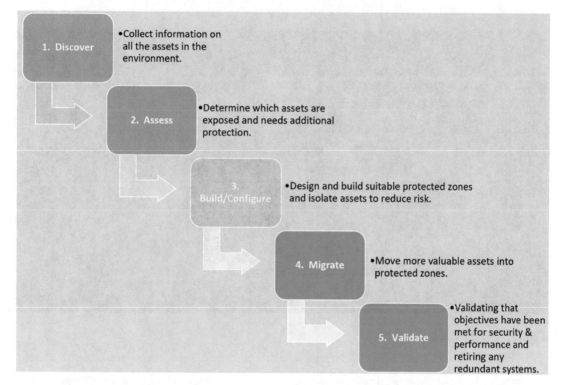

Figure 7-12. Preparatory phases

Phase 1 can be achieved as a manual process, semi-manual, or fully automated:

- **Manual** – Inventory existing systems utilizing CMDBs, spreadsheets, and management consoles

- **Semi-manual** – Validating the manual process, with some asset discovery scanning (Tenable.io,[13] Qualys,[14] Open-AudIT,[15] Nmap,[16] etc.)

---

[13]www.youtube.com/watch?v=0uzBMKOoEtA

[14]https://vimeo.com/214559373

[15]www.open-audit.org/

[16]https://nmap.org/

- **Fully automated** – Using a suitable solution (e.g., ExtraHop Reveal(x) (as depicted in Figure 7-13) to automatically identify and classify the network-connected IT assets and their connected systems.

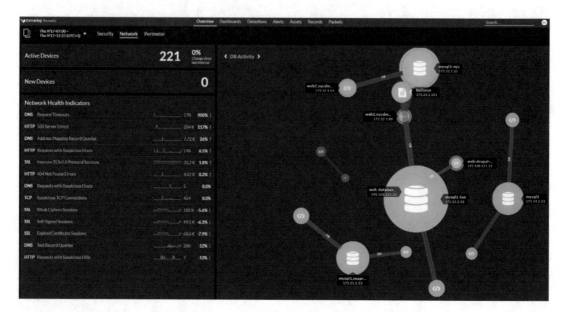

Figure 7-13. *Reveal(x)*

Much like the military stipulates the design components for their bases, the same can be implemented within a corporate network design. There are several design models[17] to choose from, for example:

- **Bell-LaPadula**[18] **(as depicted in Figure 7-14**[19]**)** – This state machine model was introduced to enforce access control in government and military applications. This model is primarily focused on the confidentiality of data and controlled access to classified information.

---

[17]www.cs.utexas.edu/~byoung/cs361/slides2-policy-4up.pdf

[18]https://computerms.net/what-is-bell-lapadula-security-model/#:~:text=The%20
Bell%2DLapadula%20(BLP),a%20discretionary%20access%20control%20policy.&text=A%20
set%20of%20subjects%2C%20a,and%20an%20access%20control%20matrix.

[19]www.chegg.com/homework-help/questions-and-answers/bell-lapadula-multilevel-
security-model-please-use-example-shown-re-draw-figure-demonstrat-q43015320

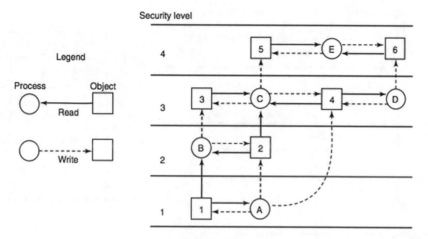

Figure 7-14. *Bell-LaPadula*

- **Biba Model[20] (as depicted in Figure 7-15[21])** – This lattice-based
  model was developed to focus on integrity of data. Data and subjects
  are grouped into ordered levels of integrity. The model is designed so
  that subjects may not write to objects in a higher level.

---

[20]www.coursehero.com/file/p65b232t/The-goal-of-the-model-is-to-prevent-the-
contamination-of-clean-high-level/

[21]https://pdfs.semanticscholar.org/9416/81c9210b334b9b4abe011f260179ddb82401.
pdf?_ga=2.167036734.1000684186.1600353495-142072036.1600353495

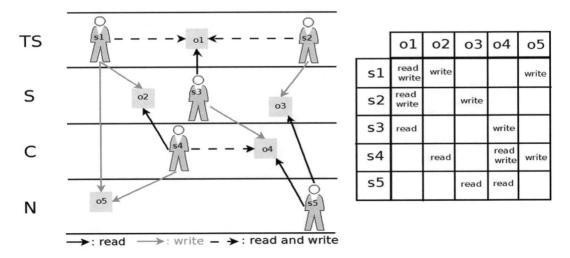

Figure 7-15. *Biba Model*

- **Clark-Wilson model[22] (as depicted in Figure 7-16[23])** – This model
  was developed to address integrity for commercial activities
  (whereas the previous two models were developed for government
  and military applications). The model uses a system of a three-part
  relationship known as a triple, consisting of a subject, a program,
  and an object. Within this relationship, a subject can only access an
  object through a program.

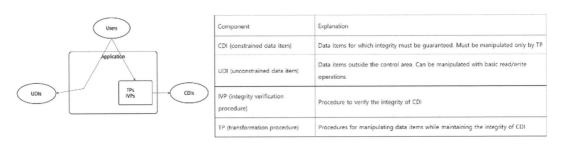

Figure 7-16. *Clark-Wilson model*

---

[22]www.studynotesandtheory.com/single-post/The-Clark-Wilson-Model
[23]https://devage.tistory.com/68

- **Lattice-based model**[24] **(as depicted in Figure 7-17**[25]**)** – This mandatory access control (MAC)–based model employs a lattice approach to define the levels of security for subjects and objects. A subject can only access objects that have a security level equal to or lower than their own security level.

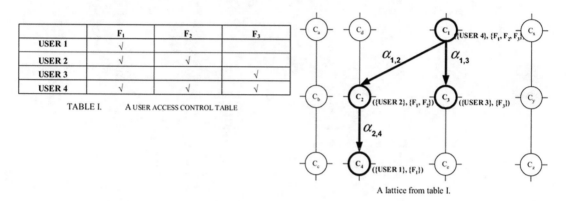

	F_1	F_2	F_3
USER 1	√		
USER 2	√	√	
USER 3			√
USER 4	√	√	√

TABLE I.   A USER ACCESS CONTROL TABLE

A lattice from table I.

Figure 7-17. *Lattice-based model*

- **Cisco SAFE**[26] **(as depicted in Figure 7-18**[27]**)** – This provides a method for analyzing threats, risks, and policies across an organization and implementing controls. It considers that all organizations are not the same by providing a modular structure that can be customized for any type and size of organization.

---

[24]https://oracle-patches.com/en/security/4147-security-models-review-cisco-safe-bell%E2%80%93lapadula-biba#:~:text=Lattice%2DBased%20Model%3A%20This%20mandatory,than%20its%20own%20security%20level

[25]www.semanticscholar.org/paper/Design-of-a-lattice-based-access-control-scheme-Chiang-Bayrak/f4f7a5d1e38abf4f49229be0fd2ecf917eba689b#extracted

[26]www.cisco.com/c/en/us/solutions/enterprise/design-zone-security/landing_safe.html

[27]www.cisco.com/c/dam/en/us/solutions/collateral/enterprise/design-zone-security/safe-secure-branch-architecture-guide.pdf

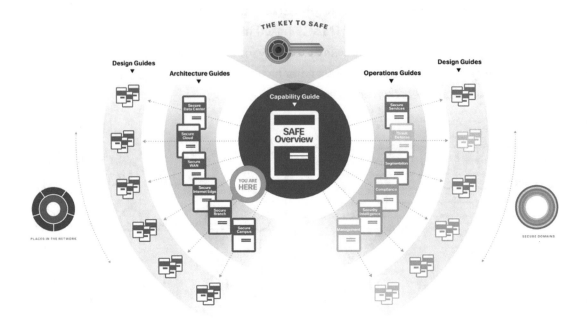

Figure 7-18. *SAFE guidance hierarchy*

- **Zero Trust**[28] **(as depicted in Figure 7-19**[29]**)** – Instead of assuming everything behind the corporate firewall is safe, the Zero Trust model assumes breach and verifies each request as though it originates from an open network.

Regardless of where the request originates or what resource it accesses, Zero Trust teaches us to "never trust, always verify."

Every access request is fully authenticated, authorized, and encrypted before granting access. Microsegmentation and least privileged access principles are applied to minimize lateral movement. Rich intelligence and analytics are utilized to detect and respond to anomalies in real time.

---

[28]www.microsoft.com/en-gb/security/business/zero-trust
[29]https://www.zdnet.com/article/identity-management-101-how-digital-identity-works/

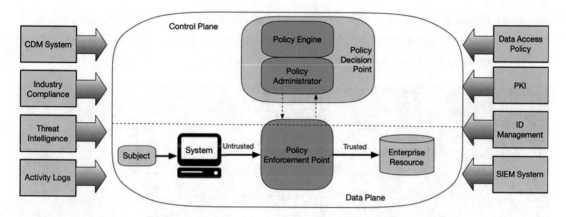

Figure 7-19. *Core Zero Trust logical components*

A common factor of all of these secure network modeling is the restriction of free flow access across the architecture. Does your network architecture prevent lateral movement (as depicted in Figure 7-20[30])?

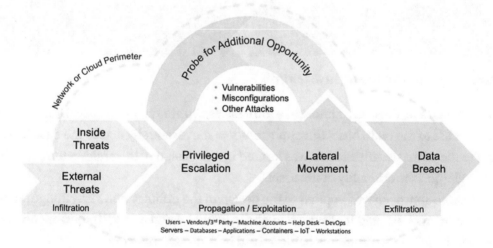

Figure 7-20. *Cyber-attack chain*

Much the same as on a military base, just because someone has gained access to within the perimeter (either legitimately or not), this does not automatically give them access to the more sensitive, mission-critical, or valuable areas of the base. The internal

---

[30]www.beyondtrust.com/blog/entry/cybersecurity-strategies-to-stop-lateral-movement-attacks-leave-your-adversaries-marooned

defenses are proportionally applied to ensure that the most valuable assets are protected by increasing layers of defense, and access is strictly limited to those personnel who have a legitimate need to access (as depicted in Figure 7-21[31]).

Figure 7-21. *Secure silo infrastructure*

As you can see, these are almost like mini bases, within the main base. By just having gained access to the main base, the opportunity to move laterally across the base to gain access to the more sensitive assets was limited by the design of the architecture, which was based upon the criticality of the assets.

The same approach was applied to the design of the military network configurations, with the network designed for secret and above being treated as a **RED** network and the lower classification requirements being served by a **BLACK** network.

---

[31]https://earth.google.com/web/search/RAF+Honington/@52.34384053,0.75586775,53.7462
1347a,420.55267309d,35y,21.72928771h,60.0003454t,0r/data=CigiJgokCZkls98GiD9AEXpE
ZjSOdz9AGUfQ4ChrfFBAIZOZ_ScRclBA

During my routine role, I would routinely operate on the **BLACK** network. However, on the occasions when I needed to work on more sensitive items, using a secure keyboard, video, and mouse (KVM) (as depicted in Figure 7-22[32]), I would transfer across to the more secure **RED** network. Consequently, the network was used to support the strict delineation of roles and strict access control.

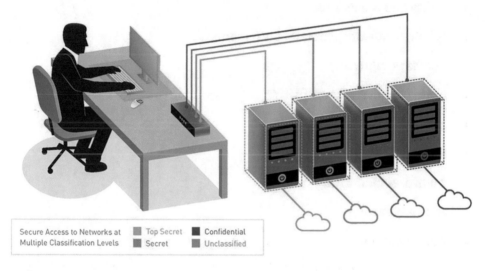

Figure 7-22. *Segregation of networks*

This process shows a clear delineation between the less sensitive and more sensitive networks. Consequently, if the less sensitive network was to be compromised (say as the result of a phishing email, malware delivery, etc.), the risk of this compromise being able to impact the more sensitive network is minimized to within tolerances or even terminated.

Remember that the defenses need to be commensurate with the perceived value and risk to the assets/business operations.

---

[32]www.kvm-switches-online.com/secure-kvm-guide.html

Wireless Networks

Whether your network is wired or wireless, the principles are the same; they must be against a defined standard (e.g., IEEE 802.11,[33, 34] Cisco,[35] Zero Trust,[36] etc.) and enforce a suite of technical security control requirements:[37]

- Policy and procedures

- Wireless network general requirements

- Access points (APs)

- Authentication servers (ASs)

- Enterprise network

- Partner users

- Audit and monitoring

- Access control

- Administration

- Incident management

If you think of your wired and wireless networks, they need to be able to support business communications while ensuring that only approved transports can travel and are allowed access to sensitive areas.

Just because the network is functioning correctly does not mean that it is safely filtering the network traffic based upon strict business needs.

---

[33]www.techstreet.com/standards/ieee-802-11-2016?product_id=1867583#full

[34]www.giac.org/paper/gsec/4214/wireless-security-ieee-80211-standards/106760

[35]www.cisco.com/c/en/us/td/docs/solutions/Enterprise/Mobility/emob41dg/emob41dg-wrapper/ch4_Secu.html

[36]www.digitalairwireless.com/articles/blog/wi-fi-zero-trust-architecture

[37]https://assets.publishing.service.gov.uk/government/uploads/system/uploads/attachment_data/file/882775/dwp-ss019-security-standard-wireless-network-v1.1.pdf

Building BRIDGES

When applying the BRIDGES acronym to the secure network architecture, the potential importance this element provides in support of Protective Security becomes increasingly relevant.

Business Context

At the forefront of any secure network design should embrace the concept of making any essential or valuable business processes secure by design/default. Therefore, it is important that the network engineers and the key stakeholders (alongside the protective security staff) identify what is important to the business, so that they can be designed with security in mind.

For example, take the Eurofighter Typhoon (as depicted in Figure 7-23[38]). This was developed to address the "dogfighting" capability requirement, following the lessons learned from the 1982 Falkland Islands conflict. Consequently, the design of the new fighter aircraft needed to have agility incorporated into it. To enable this, the design of the aircraft became heavily reliant on the onboard computer to enable this agility.

Figure 7-23. *Typhoon aircraft*

---

[38]https://ukdefencejournal.org.uk/typhoon-jets-scrambled-in-response-to-unresponsive-aircraft/

However, by making sensitive elements of the onboard computer system removable, it made it easier to secure these elements when deployed away from the confines of its parent base.

Ironically, the Falklands conflict was the last time that an RAF aircraft was required to be involved in a "dogfight" situation, and, as a result, the Typhoon needed to be repurposed as a "fighter/bomber" aircraft.

Risk and Resilience

Having identified what business processes are important or valued, it is extremely important to start building a picture of how these processes might impact the organization if they are compromised or become unavailable.

An essential part of this process is to stay current with any emerging or persistent threats that could affect these business processes.

For example:

- Where an essential business process has an associated function requiring the use of email, have you considered the potential risks from phishing attacks?

- Where you have an essential and expensive IT systems (e.g., a mainframe *(circa $75,000)*), have you considered the potential impact and contingencies for when this item is no longer supported by the vendor?

Identify and Isolate

Now that you understand what is important to the business, do you understand how the supporting systems interact/connect (as depicted in Figures 7-24–7-26[39])?

---

[39]https://security-demo.extrahop.com/

Figure 7-24. *Asset inventory*

Figure 7-25. *Web database-01*

Figure 7-26. *Peer connections*

- Are there any connected assets that could be used to impact the more valuable assets?

- Can you isolate off the assets that support the most valued assets from the less valuable/critical systems on the network?

- Are your assets that support your most valuable business processes residing on a "flat network"?

- How has authorized access to these network-connected assets been established?

- Has access been strictly limited based upon a strict need-to-know basis?

- If your perimeter were to be breached, or an unauthorized user, could they gain access to the assets that support the valuable business operations?

It is important that each network-connected asset is identified, categorized (based upon their importance), and assigned to an asset group. These should then be maintained in an inventory and visualized through effective network and data flow diagrams, to show the connectivity and to identify the systems that directly interact with sensitive data.

Just like the complex workings of a motor vehicle (as depicted in Figure 7-27[40]), with some components being more critical than others (as depicted in Figure 7-28[41]), the modern corporate network can be extremely complex, with many component parts – some being more valuable than others for the maintenance of safe and secure operations.

Figure 7-27. *Complex motor vehicle construction*

---

[40]www.autoblog.com/2019/03/07/2020-porsche-911-deep-dive-internals-technology/#slide-1290672

[41]www.autoblog.com/2019/03/07/2020-porsche-911-deep-dive-internals-technology/#slide-1290662

Figure 7-28. *Front strut assembly*

Detect Anomalies

The architectural design of the network is an essential component for helping to assure that your security tools and testing are applied in the most effective manner.

Much like the design of a military base, it is important that your suite of detection measures are suitably placed to detect unauthorized and malicious activities, or vulnerabilities, that could impact your most sensitive and valuable assets that support your key business processes.

For example, at KAF, the perimeter was protected by robust access control and a myriad of well-placed observation towers (as depicted in Figure 7-29[42]).

---

[42]www.dvidshub.net/news/98810/usaces-military-construction-program-southern-afghanistan-winds-down

Figure 7-29. *KAF perimeter defenses*

In the network-enabled environment, your perimeter can be very extensive and difficult to monitor, with several mobile network–connected devices and end users providing extended attack surfaces for the criminals to try and exploit.

Consequently, every endpoint (e.g., servers, desktops, laptops, mobile phones, tablet PCs, etc.) needs to be afforded a proportionate level of protective measures.

Endpoint Protection[43]

- Mobile device management (MDM)[44]

- Email protection[45]

---

[43]www.datto.com/library/what-is-endpoint-protection#:~:text=Endpoint%20 protection%20(also%20referred%20to,a%20threat%20path%20becomes%20possible.

[44]www.techradar.com/uk/best/best-mdm-solutions

[45]www.comparitech.com/net-admin/best-email-protection-solutions/

- Frequently updated anti-virus protection[46]

- Secure system configurations

  - Titania Nipper[47]

  - Nipper PAWS[48]

  - CIS configuration assessment tool (CAT)[49]

- Configuration management database (CMDB)[50]

- Host-based intrusion detection (HIDS)[51]/host-based intrusion prevention (HIPS)[52]

- File integrity checker (FIC)[53]

- Host-based network firewall[54]

- Web browser firewall[55]

- Address space layout randomization (ASLR)[56]

- Data execution prevention (DEP)[57]

- Containerization, Virtualization and Sandboxing[58].

---

[46]www.tomsguide.com/uk/us/best-antivirus,review-2588.html

[47]www.titania.com/products/nipper/

[48]www.titania.com/products/paws/

[49]https://learn.cisecurity.org/cis-cat-lite

[50]www.atlassian.com/itsm/it-asset-management/cmdb

[51]www.pcwdld.com/host-based-intrusion-detection-systems-hids-tools-and-software#:~:text=A%20Host%2Dbased%20Intrusion%20Detection,possible%20break%2Dins%20and%20thieves

[52]https://support.eset.com/en/enable-host-based-intrusion-prevention-system-hips-in-eset-windows-home-products#:~:text=The%20Host%2Dbased%20Intrusion%20Prevention,to%20negatively%20affect%20your%20computer.&text=HIPS%20is%20separate%20from%20Real,running%20within%20the%20operating%20system

[53]www.raymond.cc/blog/7-tools-verify-file-integrity-using-md5-sha1-hashes/

[54]www.juniper.net/documentation/en_US/contrail20/topics/topic-map/host-based-firewalls.html

[55]www.zonealarm.com/software/web-secure-free

[56]www.ibm.com/support/knowledgecenter/SSLTBW_2.4.0/com.ibm.zos.v2r4.ieae100/aslr.htm

[57]www.systemconf.com/2020/05/21/what-is-depdata-execution-prevention-and-how-is-it-used/

[58]https://systemadminspro.com/overview-of-container-sandbox-technologies/

- Digital certificate monitoring[59]

  - Authentication

  - Code signing

  - Certification revocation list (CRL)

Network Protection

- Firewalls

  - Network firewall[60]

    - Perimeter

    - Internal

  - Web application firewall[61]

  - Database firewall[62]

- Network intrusion prevention system (NIPS)[63]

- Malware prevention system (MPS)[64]

- Email security[65]

- Internet proxy[66]

---

[59]www.globalsign.com/en/lp/certificate-inventory-tool-sign-up

[60]www.gartner.com/reviews/market/network-firewalls

[61]www.gartner.com/reviews/market/web-application-firewalls

[62]www.oracle.com/uk/database/technologies/security/audit-vault-firewall.html

[63]www.vmware.com/topics/glossary/content/intrusion-prevention-system

[64]www.fireeye.com/products/endpoint-security.html?utm_source=google&utm_
medium=cpc&utm_content=paid-search&gclid=CjwKCAjw2Jb7BRBHEiwAXTR4jYOTQURr4TuqsICp
VbzeoxL-pOiz7sf5HovG51UcMEVuIusjvrIYAxoCNogQAvD_BwE&gclsrc=aw.ds

[65]www.gartner.com/reviews/market/email-security

[66]www.techradar.com/best/proxies

- Privileged access workstation or jump server[67]

- An effective update program[68] or automated update solution[69]

Now, I'm not saying that you should go out and buy all these security tools. However, these are your alerting systems to help you detect unauthorized or malicious activities that need timely investigation and intervention, to help prevent excessive impact to the business.

Consequently, well-configured and appropriately located security tools can help to detect that unwanted presence within your network, long before they are able to gain a clandestine persistent presence needed to launch a successful attack.

Once you have established what assets are important, where they reside, and the most appropriate tools (correctly sited within your network), you can then seek to develop an effective detection program.

At KAF, the defensive measures would feed into a centralized Command and Control Center, augmented by regular internal/external security patrols and checks (as depicted in Figures 7-30[70] and 7-31).

---

[67]https://securityboulevard.com/2020/02/
privileged-access-workstation-vs-jump-server/

[68]https://searchenterprisedesktop.techtarget.com/definition/patch-management

[69]www.dnsstuff.com/patch-management-software

[70]www.defense.gov/observe/photo-gallery/igphoto/2001337036/

Figure 7-30. *KAF internal security patrol*

Figure 7-31. *External perimeter security patrol*

Think of your alerting, vulnerability scanning, and security information and event management (SIEM) as being part of your detection capabilities.

In addition, all network activity should be considered for monitoring and analysis, using solutions such as

- Domain Name Server (DNS) monitoring[71]

- Data loss prevention[72]

- Anonymizer network monitoring[73]

- Honeypots[74]

---

[71]www.dnsstuff.com/dns-monitoring-software

[72]https://geekflare.com/data-loss-prevention-solutions/

[73]www.dnsstuff.com/free-network-monitoring-software

[74]https://securitytrails.com/blog/top-20-honeypots

Effective vulnerability management[75] is extremely important, as long-standing unremediated vulnerabilities allow the attacker's additional opportunities to compromise network-connected systems and data assets.

Think of your vulnerability management process as being like the external and internal security patrols, seeking to identify and report any new or long-standing vulnerabilities. Each identified vulnerability should then be risk assessed *(based upon the perceived value of the affected asset)* and timely remediation activities actioned.

Additionally, it is essential that the vulnerability management program incorporate the validation that any updates have been successfully applied. This is especially relevant if you are using automated updates software, where the automated rollout of the updates fails to be successfully implemented, against a high-value/critical asset. As a consequence, you may gain a false sense of security and end up with long-term vulnerabilities residing on these high-value/critical assets, which then are able to be exploited by the attackers.

An essential bolt-on to your vulnerability management process should be the inclusion of critical patch reporting, for example:

- Qualys Patch Report[76]

- Tenable Outstanding Patch Tracking[77]

It has been reported that the criminals have identified the advantages of machine learning to help them create highly advanced threats,[78] so you should consider how machine learning could help you better identify the NORMAL from the **ABNORMAL**.

Remember that an advantage of machine learning is that it is extremely effective at recognizing repeating patterns. At present, your employees have human traits and, as such, will be creatures of habit (e.g., logging in/off at a certain time, from a certain device, in a specific location and carrying and establishing set patterns of work).

---

[75]www.sans.org/reading-room/whitepapers/threats/paper/34180

[76]https://qualysguard.qualys.com/qwebhelp/fo_portal/reports/patch_reports/win_patch_report_template.htm

[77]https://docs.tenable.com/tenableio/vulnerabilitymanagement/Content/Reports/ReportTemplates.htm#OutstandingPatchTracking

[78]www.trendmicro.com/vinfo/gb/security/news/cybercrime-and-digital-threats/foreseeing-a-new-era-cybercriminals-using-machine-learning-to-create-highly-advanced-threats

Whereas an attacker or malicious insider may not be as familiar with the internal environment and to a machine learning algorithm, these **ABNORMAL** actions will easily be differentiated from the NORMAL work patterns.

There are several security tools that have started to embrace the machine learning capabilities and have enabled the integration with other security solutions/tools, for example:

- **CyberEasy** (as depicted in Figure 7-32[79])

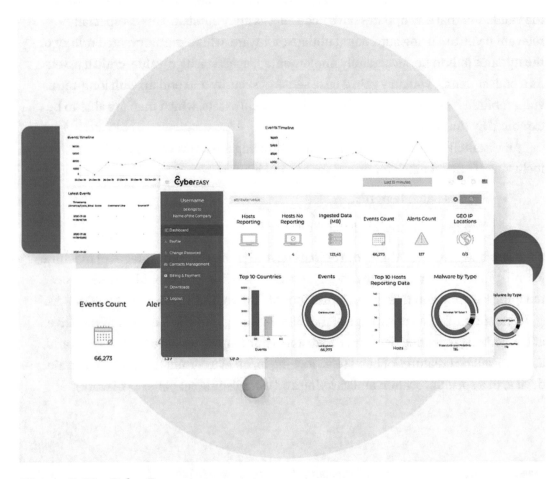

Figure 7-32. *CyberEasy*

---

[79]https://knogin.com/products/#Pricing

- **ExtraHop Reveal(x)** (as depicted in Figure 7-33[80])

Figure 7-33. *Reveal(x)*

- **Faraday Security** (as depicted in Figure 7-34[81])

---

[80]www.extrahop.com/

[81]https://faradaysec.com/vulnerability-management/

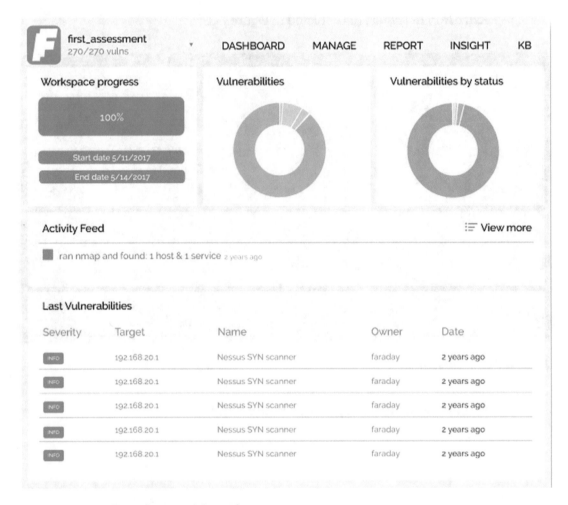

Figure 7-34. *Faraday Dashboard*

Govern Processes

Your network architecture is extremely dynamic by its very nature and, therefore, needs to be strictly controlled, and all personnel involved in using, or supporting, the network-connected devices understand the rules *(policies)* and procedures to keep these systems safe and secure.

Consequently, personnel should be regularly trained and reminded of the rules and procedures, and the reasons for these rules. Any accidental failures to follow this guidance should result in a period of reeducation, and perhaps even some close monitoring, while the personnel should be in no doubt that any deliberate actions will result in disciplinary action.

The governance process should incorporate a "Top-Down" (senior management support) and a "Bottom-Up" approach (personnel are able to voice any incompatibilities between the formal rules and procedures and the needs of their role).

Evaluate Security Controls

One of the advantages of being deployed to hostile, high tempo, environments was that there was an extremely limited requirement to test the effectiveness of the embedded security controls.

Why was this, I hear you ask?

Quite simply, this was something that the insurgents would happily do for us, and these frequent attacks provided all the reminders anyone needed that this threat was an EVER-PRESENT and REAL thing!

The commonality between physical insurgent attacks and attacks against a corporate network architecture is the high ratio that the "human error" plays in such attacks. Both types of threat actors rely on opportunity, and (as reported by IBM[82]) 95% of cyber security breaches are created by "human error."

Surprisingly, I would say that 90–95% of the successful insurgent attacks, at KAF, were as the result of "human error," where the insurgents pounced on the opportunities created by "human error." However, the difference is that everyone had a minimum level of training and could effectively respond and help mitigate the potential impact/damage caused.

Testing the effectiveness of the security controls becomes increasingly important to act as a reminder that this is a REAL thing and to help identify any poor habits, dangerous procedural shortcuts, or outdated rules and procedures that may be developing.

Consequently, it is extremely important to develop an effective audit program, and if you don't happen to have your own insurgents to help you with your own testing, you can always hire a reputable third-party vendor to act as your insurgents, for example:

---

[82]https://blog.usecure.io/the-role-of-human-error-in-successful-cyber-security-breaches#:~:text=According%20to%20a%20study%20by,have%20taken%20place%20at%20all!

- **Northramp**[83]

- **OnSecurity**[84]

- **Pen Test Partners**[85]

When considering your penetration testing engagements, it is important to consider what valuable business operations (and their supporting systems) you want to test and to evaluate the associated risks that come with the scope of the engagement.

Remember that you don't want to be paying for simulated insurgent attacks that will merely report on the things that should have been identified by your internal/external security patrols (vulnerability scans). Penetration testing should be regarded as an enhancement to your vulnerability management procedures.

Why not evaluate the maturity of your penetration testing process using CREST's simple maturity assessment tool (as depicted in Figures 7-35, 7-36, 7-37 and 7-38[86])?

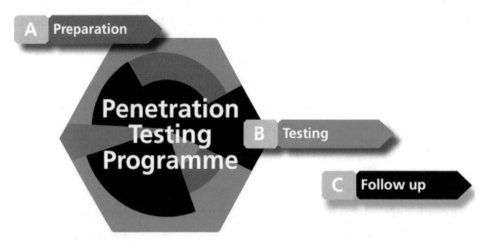

Figure 7-35. *Key steps in the penetration testing management process*

---

[83]www.northramp.com/contact

[84]www.onsecurity.co.uk/our-services/

[85]www.pentestpartners.com/penetration-testing-services/

[86]www.crest-approved.org/knowledge-sharing/maturity-assessment-tools/index.html

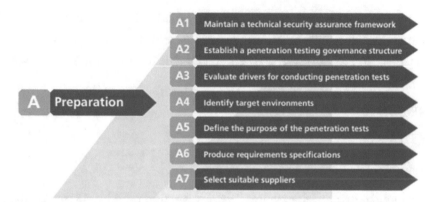

Figure 7-36. *Stage 1 – preparation*

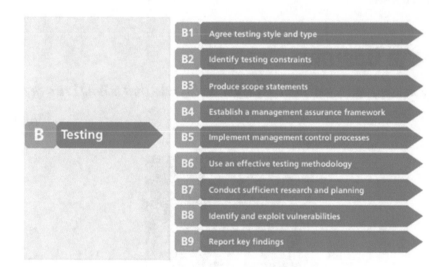

Figure 7-37. *Stage 2 – testing*

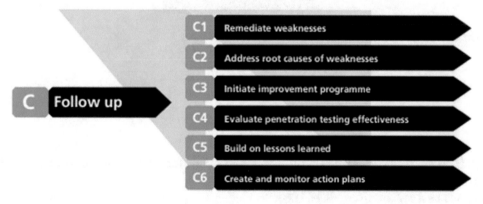

Figure 7-38. *Stage 3 – follow up*

Remember that your security testers need to be skilled, experienced, and sufficiently insured to effectively test your business operations, without putting these services under unnecessary risk. Consequently, the type of test needs to be commensurate with the risk, for example:[87]

- Black Box
- Gray Box
- White Box

It is extremely important to develop the mindset that people will make mistakes and that to continue to operate effectively and minimize the impact, you must be prepared to "Survive to Operate."

Survive to Operate

So, if you stay ready, you ain't gotta get ready, and that is how I run my life! [88]

Actor quote[89]

Figure 7-39. *Will Smith*

---

[87]https://resources.infosecinstitute.com/what-are-black-box-grey-box-and-white-box-penetration-testing/

[88]www.youtube.com/watch?v=_8WuMnJ1X5k

[89]www.caa.com/caaspeakers/will-smith

Never has such a statement been so relevant, as for an organization being prepared for when things go wrong and as well as the deliberate actions, your employees are human, and they will make mistakes.

It is essential that your personnel are well prepared and can identify and efficiently respond to impactful events or incidents.

In the military, we are introduced to the 5 (6) Ps mantra:

*Prior Planning Prevents (**P********) Poor Performance!*

I have extensive firsthand experience of the value of being well drilled on how to effectively handle events and incidents. Even with a degree of rehearsal training, when something happens, people react in different ways:

- Fight

- Flight

- Freeze

By using the latest threat intelligence, you can develop a suite of realistic network architecture–related playbooks, and through extensive rehearsals, you will be better prepared to effectively handle these events.

However, it is important to remember that there is a need for a degree of flexibility, as some events or incidents may happen that have not been included in your playbooks.

Reality Bites

In the United Kingdom, during the COVID-19 pandemic, businesses were faced with the fact that their office workers could no longer work in the offices, and, as a result, the supporting network architecture had to be safely and securely reconfigured to enable their employees to quickly adopt the practice of working from home.

It was reported that due to the coronavirus (COVID-19) pandemic, **46.6%** of employees were working from home, and a whopping **86.0%** of these were doing so directly because of the pandemic.[90]

Many of these UK businesses were ill-prepared[91] for the required changes needed to survive to operate because of the pandemic:

- **25%** have no crisis plan in place.

- **58%** are offering home-working options.

- **41%** have no such policy.

The additional business losses associated with being ill-prepared for more flexible remote working practices (as the result of the pandemic lockdown), which prevented all, but essential workers, from being able to go into their places of work.

Given that prior warnings were evident, with numerous countries going into lockdown, in their attempts to deal with the pandemic:

- **Wuhan City (center of the outbreak)** – January 23, 2020[92]

- **Italy** – *The lockdown is extended nationwide (9172 cases)* – March 9, 2020[93]

- **Australia** – March 12, 2020[94]

- **United Kingdom** – March 16, 2020[95]

- **Canada** – March 17, 2020[96]

---

[90]www.ons.gov.uk/employmentandlabourmarket/peopleinwork/employmentandemployeetypes/bulletins/coronavirusandhomeworkingintheuk/april2020

[91]www.businessleader.co.uk/uk-firms-among-the-worlds-least-prepared-for-home-working-amid-coronavirus-shutdown/80778/

[92]www.express.co.uk/travel/articles/1257717/china-lockdown-how-long-was-china-lockdown-timeframe-wuhan

[93]www.axios.com/italy-coronavirus-timeline-lockdown-deaths-cases-2adb0fc7-6ab5-4b7c-9a55-bc6897494dc6.html

[94]www.theguardian.com/world/2020/may/02/australias-coronavirus-lockdown-the-first-50-days

[95]https://fullfact.org/health/coronavirus-lockdown-hancock-claim/

[96]www.manitoulin.com/updated-canada-goes-on-covid-19-lockdown/

- **United States of America** – *Phased state-by-state lockdown with* Georgia being one of the last states to go into lockdown – April 3, 2020[97]

How could so many businesses have been so ill-prepared?

Key Takeaways

- Understanding the value of any network-connected assets is essential in helping to ensure an adequate network architecture design.

- The network should be designed and developed to minimize the potential impact following a compromise of the network perimeter.

- The network should be designed and developed with security considerations at the forefront of any considerations.

- Effective security architectural model concepts should be incorporated into the design and development.

- Essential/valued business assets and operations should be proportionately protected to ensure that they are adequately protected.

- Supporting network-connected assets need to be securely configured, isolated, and monitored to minimize the attack surfaces and opportunities for an attacker.

- Access to the business valuable assets/processes should be strictly restricted to those with a legitimate need to have access. The network should be designed and developed to enforce this strict access control.

- It is essential that an effective governance strategy is developed and implemented to ensure the continued maintenance of the secure network architecture.

- It's not about using more security testing and monitoring tools/ solutions, but it is more important to use these tools effectively.

---

[97]www.bbc.co.uk/news/world-us-canada-52757150

- Machine learning and automation of the security tools and solutions can help to significantly improve your detection and response capabilities.

- Businesses should be prepared for when things go wrong.

CHAPTER 8

Information Systems Security

I am used to thinking three or four months in advance about what I must do, and I calculate on the worst.

In war nothing is achieved, except by calculation. Everything that is not soundly planned in its details yields no result. If I take so many precautions it is because it is my custom to leave nothing to chance.

Napoleon Bonaparte[1]

Figure 8-1. *Emperor Napoleon*

---

[1]Journal of the US Army War College, Volume 15, Issue 2.

© Jim Seaman 2021
J. Seaman, *Protective Security*, https://doi.org/10.1007/978-1-4842-6908-4_8

Introduction

You may well wonder why I have quoted Napoleon when introducing the subject of "Information Systems Security." Napoleon was a well-renowned tactician and leader, but at the heart of his success was the reliance on his "Information System" *(aka his brain)* to allow him to carry out successful analysis and calculations.

Today, businesses rely on an increasing number of Information Systems. However, many organizations do not know what an Information System relates to.

Much of the focus will be on protecting the information assets that have a legal or regulatory obligation (e.g., PCI DSS, GDPR, PIPEDA, CCPA, etc.) and having an apparent disregard for the potential value and impact the other information systems provide to the business.

Unfortunately, many companies only discover the true value of these systems once they become unavailable or compromised, such as the result of a denial of service, ransomware attack, or human error.

Consequently, when investigating the business context, it is important to identify those other information systems (e.g., not processing personal data), which could impact the business. However, to achieve this, we need to understand and appreciate what constitutes an Information System.

What Is an Information System?

In NIST's SP 800-128[2]: Guide for Security-Focused Configuration Management of Information Systems, they define an information system as being

> *A discrete set of information resources organized for the collection, processing, maintenance, use, sharing, dissemination, or disposition of information.*

Note   *Information systems also include specialized systems such as industrial/ process controls systems, telephone switching and private branch exchange (PBX) systems, and environmental control systems.*

---

[2]https://nvlpubs.nist.gov/nistpubs/SpecialPublications/NIST.SP.800-128.pdf

Let's have a look at a specific scenario, based around a Contact Center, receiving a high volume of customer calls, which includes taking telephone-based payments.

The business decides to remove the PCI DSS compliance burden and to reduce the risk to the processing of their customers' payment card data through the implementation of a PCI DSS–compliant dual-tone multi-frequency (DTMF) solution (such as GCI Com's(aka Nasstar) IVR Contact Center solution[3]).

As a result, they transfer the risk to the third party and remove their need for any systems or personnel to interact with any of their customers' payment card information.

However, the customers still have a need to speak with the call agents, and, consequently, the Voice over Internet Protocol (VoIP) telephone system remains a critical system for the organization.

Perhaps, choosing to baseline themselves against the NIST SP800-58: Voice Over IP Security guidelines[4] to help safeguard themselves against known risks, threats, and vulnerabilities:

- Confidentiality and privacy

- Integrity issues

- Availability and denial of service (DoS)

Imagine the potential impact on this Contact Center; should the VoIP system become unavailable to the call agents for a prolonged period?

The VoIP system becomes increasingly more important and valuable for the business. Therefore, the need to ensure that this valuable business information system is proportionately protected, suddenly, becomes a worthwhile investment.

Military Comparison

In the Summer of 2008, I was posted to RAF Leeming to take up a Computer Security (CompSy) role, which involved the following responsibilities:

- Registering and the accreditation of all computer systems and the compilation of records.

- Arranging for the production and monitoring of all security operating procedures (SyOps).

---

[3]www.gcicom.net/Our-Services/Unified-Communications/GCI-Contact-Centre
[4]https://nvlpubs.nist.gov/nistpubs/Legacy/SP/nistspecialpublication800-58.pdf

325

- Providing advice and guidance on all aspects of CompSy to the unit security officers (USyOs) and installation managers.

- Providing advice for TEMPEST[5] threat assessments for computer systems processing protectively marked (PM) information graded **CONFIDENTIAL** or above and monitoring the recommendations made by the reports.

- Arranging for regular production of CompSy education and its dissemination.

- Coordinating with IT Operations on the issue of maintaining anti-virus (AV) up to the limit of the establishment's license and managing the update of the AV software, as required.

- Conduct CompSy investigations as detailed by the officer commanding RAF Police Flight (OC Police), or their deputy, and follow up on CompSy actions as identified by specialist police wing surveys.

- Acting as the CompSy representative at Information Technology Coordination Committee (ITCC) meetings.

- Conducting security surveys of proposed computer installations.

- Maintaining records and controlling the removal of the establishment's laptop systems.

- Maintaining a close liaison with IT Operations regarding the installation and introduction of computers on the establishment.

- Organizing and monitoring computer installation manager (CIM) courses.

- Ensuring that all the establishment's communications systems comply with their regulations.

- Actioning recommendations highlighted by the technical security reports and maintaining a close liaison with the Headquarters, Strike Command, and InfoSy (RAF).

---

[5]www.sans.org/reading-room/whitepapers/privacy/introduction-tempest-981

In order to complete this role, I had to attend the RAF Police Computer Security level 1 and level 2 courses (as depicted in Figures 8-2 and 8-3).

Figure 8-2. *RAF Police CompSy 1*

Figure 8-3. *RAF Police CompSy 2*

Just six months later was to be my first experience of being heavily involved in a CompSy incident that was going to put me under a great deal of pressure, as the Station started to appreciate their reliance on their IT systems, and the longer it took to return the normal operations, the greater the pressure that was applied to myself and the IT Operations department.

In an earlier chapter, I provided an outline of how the military network architecture was segregated into two separate environments (**RED** (mission critical); **BLACK** (standard operations)) and how I needed to use a KVM switch to move between environments.

Well, in January 2009, the entire RAF **BLACK** network became infected with the Conficker[6] virus.[7] The Conficker virus[8] was a fast-spreading worm that targeted a vulnerability (MS08-067) in Windows operating systems (as depicted in Figure 8-4[9]).

---

[6]www.sans.org/security-resources/malwarefaq/conficker-worm

[7]www.theregister.com/2009/01/20/mod_malware_still_going_strong/

[8]https://whatis.techtarget.com/definition/Conficker#:~:text=Conficker%20is%20a%20
fast%2Dspreading,the%20infrastructure%20for%20a%20botnet

[9]www.exploit-db.com/search?text=MS08-067

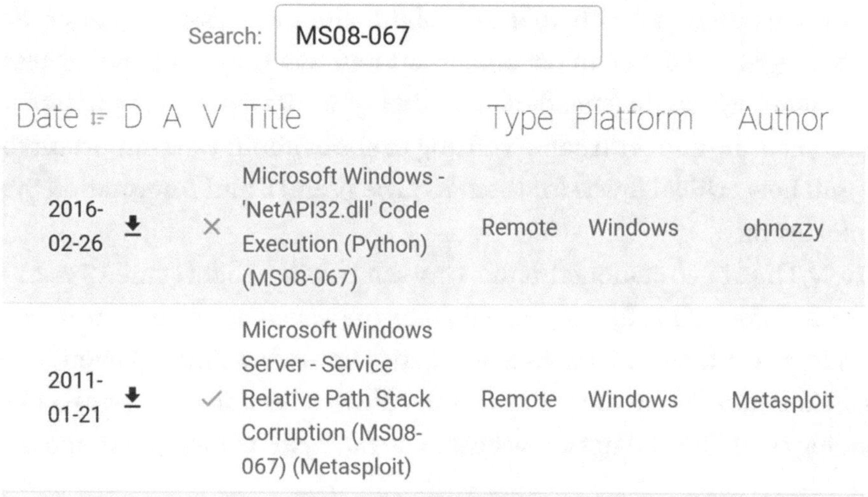

Search: MS08-067

Date ⇄	D	A	V	Title	Type	Platform	Author
2016-02-26	↓		×	Microsoft Windows - 'NetAPl32.dll' Code Execution (Python) (MS08-067)	Remote	Windows	ohnozzy
2011-01-21	↓		✓	Microsoft Windows Server - Service Relative Path Stack Corruption (MS08-067) (Metasploit)	Remote	Windows	Metasploit

Figure 8-4. MS08-067 details – Exploit DB

The only way of dealing with this worm was to disconnect every station network from all other stations and then disconnect every network-connected device from the local area network (LAN). Only then could we start the methodical, time-consuming, and manual process of cleaning each individual system, starting with the core systems. Not until we were able to confirm that every device had been cleaned and could be safely reconnected to the LAN could the Station return to normal operations.

It was not until the systems were unavailable that people started to realize their value and the impact their unavailability had on routine operations.

For example:

- The network-enabled electronic automated access control (EAAC) system which allowed 24-hour (7 days per week) access to the gymnasium, via proximity telemetry cards *(electronically logging everyone accessing the facility)*, was put out of action. Consequently, for Fire and Health and Safety reasons, access to this facility had to be restricted to only normal working hours (0800 hrs to 1800 hrs, Mon to Fri).

- Even several of the IP-connected closed-circuit television (CCTV) cameras were made inoperable, resulting in an increased risk and requiring additional security checks to be carried out on the areas that could no longer be remotely monitored.

Initially, the personnel were tolerable of this situation. However, after the first day or two, they soon started to become frustrated that they could not access their desktop systems, which they needed to do their jobs. It was not long before people started complaining and with some starting to shout about how important their role was and how critical it was for them to have their IT and Information Systems operational again.

Bizarrely, I had been stationed at this very same Police Flight some 12 years earlier, when the only Information Systems that the personnel had access to were a limited number of basic word processors. As a recall, they had either Blue or Green screen interfaces. Consequently, in these 12 years, people had become increasingly reliant on the technology that they did not know how to do their jobs without their Information Systems.

However, we had to be methodical and needed to prioritize the remediation efforts to minimize the potential impact to the organization. Without careful management and strict control of the sequence of remediation, this could go horribly wrong.

Fortunately, I had an incredibly supportive OC Police who helped us to refine the prioritized order for remediation, acted as a buffer from the demands, and provided a team of resources to ensure that, after one week of extremely long days, we had cleaned up the network and was back up and running normally.

This was not the case for other larger establishments, where it was a far bigger beast to try and manage. One of these had spent 2 weeks remediating against the Conficker worm when a senior officer had returned from a period of absence and, without authority, reconnected his desktop system (which had been scheduled to be cleaned) and reinfected every cleaned device that had been reconnected to the LAN.

The result was that they needed to restart the remediation process all over again.

Now, you must be thinking that things have moved on since 2009 and that businesses will never make that same mistake today. I know that this was a valuable lesson learned for the Royal Air Force, but unless you have been through such an experience, viruses are often seen as a bit of an enigma and that the AV will stop this.

Well, Conficker is still a reality, with manufacturing now being the target for the delivery of this worm:

The Conficker worm was the single most commonly detected variant of malware (11% of all detections) in Manufacturing, suggesting that these organizations have outdated or unpatched systems and weak passwords, leaving them vulnerable to infections or other malware variants.

NTT 2020 Global Threat Intelligence Report[10]

How can such a threat vector remain an ever-present risk when it should have been consigned to the dustbin of history? However, in Palo Alto's "Unit 42 IoT Threat[11]" and ZDNet's "Cybersecurity in an IoT and mobile world[12]" reports, they have seen a resurgence in Conficker infections – with around half a million infections having been recorded.

The manufacturing industry is extremely dependent on manufacturing information systems (MIS), which, by their very definition,[13] should be something that should be regarded as being an asset that should be valued:

A computing system that gives a company's managers information about the production process.

Other business types might have different types of information systems that need to be adequately protected to ensure that your organization is not adversely impacted by an event/incident that affects these assets.

- What about a management information system (MgtIS)?[14] Is this something that should be regarded as a valuable business system?

A computer system that provides an organization's employees, especially its managers, with useful information for their work.

---

[10]https://hello.global.ntt/en-us/insights/2020-global-threat-intelligence-report

[11]https://start.paloaltonetworks.com/unit-42-iot-threat-report

[12]www.techrepublic.com/resource-library/whitepapers/special-report-cybersecurity-in-an-iot-and-mobile-world-free-pdf/?ftag=CMG-01-10aaa1b

[13]https://dictionary.cambridge.org/dictionary/english/manufacturing-information-system

[14]https://dictionary.cambridge.org/dictionary/english/management-information-system

- How about a strategic information system (SIS)?[15]

  A computer system used by organizations to examine market and competitor information to help them plan how to make their business more successful.

- What about your executive information system (EIS)[16]?

  A type of computer management information system intended to help important managers of a company or organization to make decisions.

- Perhaps, your organization relies on a geographic information system (GIS)?[17]

  A computer system for storing, organizing, and studying data that relates to the position, area, or size of things.

With these information systems being so important to today's businesses, it has never been more important to ensure that they are adequately protected, and they do not become compromised, as the result of a cyber-attack, rogue device, or human error.

Your information systems are only as robust as the last virus update, the last successful system update, and the integrity of the systems that they are connected to.

Security of Network and Information Systems

On July 6, 2018, the European Parliament adopted a Directive on the security of network and information systems (the NIS Directive[18]), which entered into force in August 2016 and was transposed into national laws on May 9, 2018, and with all operators of essential services having been identified by November 9, 2018.

The NIS Directive applies to all European Union organizations and is intended to address the threats posed to network and information systems, therefore improving the functioning of the digital economy.[19]

---

[15]https://dictionary.cambridge.org/dictionary/english/strategic-information-system

[16]https://dictionary.cambridge.org/dictionary/english/executive-information-system

[17]https://dictionary.cambridge.org/dictionary/english/gis

[18]http://eur-lex.europa.eu/legal-content/EN/TXT/?uri=uriserv:OJ.L_.2016.194.01.0001.01.ENG&toc=OJ:L:2016:194:TOC

[19]https://ico.org.uk/media/for-organisations/the-guide-to-nis-1-0.pdf#page19

The primary purpose of this Directive is to help reduce the disruptive impact of an "incident" and to improve "cybersecurity." Although the fines are like those seen under the EU General Data Protection Regulation[20] (EU GDPR), the NIS Directive is focused on a loss of service rather than a loss of data *(covered by the EU GDPR)*:

Organizations who fail to implement effective cyber security measures, as outlined by the NIS Directive, they could be fined as much as £17 million plus be caught up in a 'double jeopardy' rule, in that if the incident also relates to a breach of personal, then also fined under the GDPR (up to 4 per cent of their global turnover or £20 million, whichever is greater).

If you are one of the Digital Service Provider businesses that are deemed to be applicable for the legislation, there are several security requirements that you must adhere to:

- To take appropriate and proportionate technical and organizational measures to manage the risks to your systems. These measures must ensure a level of security appropriate to the risk posed.

- Measures must be implemented that cover the security of your systems and facilities; incident handling; business continuity management; monitoring, auditing, and testing; and compliance with international standards.

- Many of these requirements align with the security provisions of the GDPR. In cases where you are a data controller, GDPR will apply.

- Documented evidence of the implemented measures must be maintained, which also aligns with the accountability principle of the GDPR and its provisions on documentation.

- In the event of an incident, the regulators may request to see such records during any investigation or inspection.

---

[20]www.raconteur.net/technology/nis-securing-future/what-is-the-nis-directive-and-what-are-the-ramifications#:~:text=Organisations%20who%20fail%20to%20implement,4%20per%20cent%20of%20their

However, even if you are not an organization that needs to comply with this directive, it makes excellent business sense to apply their high-level security principles[21] (as depicted in Figure 8-5 and Table 8-1).

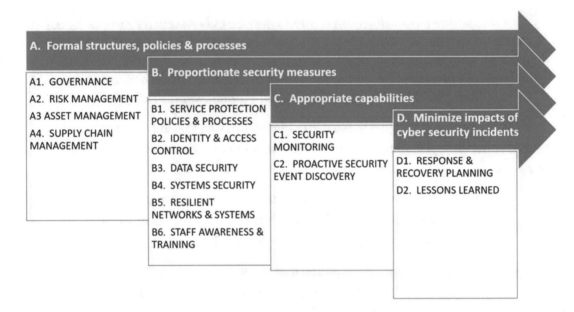

Figure 8-5. *NIS Directive – high-level security principles*

Table 8-1. *NIS Directive – High-Level Security Principles Detail*

A) Appropriate organizational structures, policies, and processes in place to understand, assess, and systematically manage security risks to the network and information systems supporting essential services.	
A.1. GOVERNANCE	The organization has appropriate management policies and processes in place to govern its approach to the security of network and information systems.

(*continued*)

---

[21]https://assets.publishing.service.gov.uk/government/uploads/system/uploads/attachment_data/file/677065/NIS_Consultation_Response_-_Government_Policy_Response.pdf

Table 8-1. (*continued*)

A.2. RISK MANAGEMENT	The organization has appropriate management policies and processes in place to govern its approach to the security of network and information systems.
A.3. ASSET MANAGEMENT	Everything required to deliver, maintain, or support networks and information systems for essential services is determined and understood. This includes data, people, and systems, as well as any supporting infrastructure (such as power or cooling).
A.4. SUPPLY CHAIN MANAGEMENT	The organization understands and manages security risks to the network and information systems supporting the delivery of essential services that arise because of dependencies on external suppliers. This includes ensuring that appropriate measures are employed where third-party services are used.

Explanation

Governance:

- *Effective security of network and information systems should be driven by organizational management and corresponding policies and practices.*
- *There should be clear governance structures in place with well-defined lines of responsibility and accountability for the security of network and information systems.*
- *Senior management should clearly articulate unacceptable impacts to the business (often called risk appetite), which should take into account the organization's role in the delivery of essential services, so decision-makers at all levels can make informed decisions about risks without constantly referring decisions up the governance chain.*
- *There should be an individual(s) who holds overall responsibility and is accountable for security. This individual is empowered and accountable for decisions regarding how services are protected.*
- *For small organizations, the governance structure can be quite simple.*

(*continued*)

Table 8-1. (*continued*)

Risk Management:

- *There is no single blueprint for cyber security, and therefore organizations need to take steps to determine security risks that could affect the delivery of essential services and take measures to appropriately manage those risks.*
- *Threats can come from many sources, in and outside the organization. A good understanding of the threat landscape and the vulnerabilities that may be exploited is essential to effectively identify and manage risks. Such information may come from sources including NCSC, information exchanges relevant to the organization's sector, and reputable government, commercial, and open sources, all of which can inform the organization's own risk assessment process.*
- *Organizations may contribute to the understanding of threats and vulnerabilities in their sector by participating in relevant information exchanges and liaising with authorities as appropriate.*
- *There should be a systematic process in place to ensure that identified risks are managed and the organization has confidence mitigations are working effectively.*
- *Confidence can be gained through, for example, product assurance, monitoring, vulnerability testing, auditing, and supply chain security.*

Asset Management:

- *To manage security risks to the network and information systems of essential service organizations requires a clear understanding of service dependencies.*
- *This might include physical assets, software, data, essential staff, and utilities.*
- *These should all be clearly identified and recorded so that it is possible to understand what things are important to the delivery of the essential service and why.*

Supply Chain:

- *If an organization relies on third parties (such as outsourced or cloud-based technology services), it remains accountable for the protection of any essential service.*
- *This means that there should be confidence that all relevant security requirements are met regardless of whether the organization or a third party delivers the service.*
- *For many organizations, it will make good sense to use third-party technology services.*
- *Where these are used, it is important that contractual agreements provide provisions for the protection of things upon which the essential service depends.*

(*continued*)

Table 8-1. (*continued*)

B) Proportionate security measures in place to protect essential services and systems from cyber-attacks or system failures.	
B.1. SERVICE PROTECTION POLICIES AND PROCESSES	The organization defines, implements, communicates, and enforces appropriate policies and processes that direct its overall approach to securing systems and data that support delivery of essential services.
B.2. IDENTITY AND ACCESS CONTROL	The organization understands, documents, and manages access to systems and functions supporting the delivery of essential services.
	Users (or automated functions) who can access data or services are appropriately verified, authenticated, and authorized.
B.3. DATA SECURITY	Data stored or transmitted electronically is protected from actions such as unauthorized access, modification, or deletion that may cause disruption to essential services.
	Such protection extends to how authorized users, devices, and systems access critical data necessary for the delivery of essential services.
	It also covers information that would assist an attacker, such as design details of networks and information systems.
B.4. SYSTEMS SECURITY	Network and information systems and technology critical for the delivery of essential services are protected from cyber-attacks.
	An organizational understanding of risks to essential services informs the use of robust and reliable protective security measures to effectively limit opportunities for attackers to compromise networks and systems.
B.5. RESILIENT NETWORKS AND SYSTEMS	The organization builds resilience against cyber-attacks and system failures into the design, implementation, operation, and management of systems that support the delivery of essential services.
B.6. STAFF AWARENESS AND TRAINING	Staff have appropriate awareness, knowledge, and skills to carry out their organizational roles effectively in relation to the security of network and information systems supporting the delivery of essential services.

(*continued*)

Table 8-1. (*continued*)

Explanation

Service Protection Policies and Processes:

- *The organization's approach to securing network and information systems that support essential services should be defined in a set of comprehensive security policies with associated processes.*
- *It is essential that these policies and processes are more than just a paper exercise, and steps must be taken to ensure that the policies and processes are well described, communicated, and effectively implemented.*
- *Policies and processes should be written with the intended recipient community in mind.*
- *For example, the message or direction communicated to IT staff will be different from that communicated to senior managers. There should be mechanisms in place to validate the implementation and effectiveness of policies and processes where these are relied upon for the security of the essential service. Such mechanisms should also support an organizational ability to enforce compliance with policies and processes when necessary.*
- *To be effective, service protection policies and processes need to be realistic, i.e., based on a clear understanding of the way people act and make decisions in the workplace, particularly in relation to security. If they are developed without this understanding, there is a significant risk that service protection policies and processes will be routinely circumvented as people use workarounds and shortcuts to achieve their work objectives.*

Identity and Access Control:

- *It is important that the organization is clear about who (or what in the case of automated functions) has authorization to interact with the network and information system of an essential service in any way or access associated sensitive data.*
- *Rights granted should be carefully controlled, especially where those rights provide an ability to materially affect the delivery of the essential service.*
- *Rights granted should be periodically reviewed and technically removed when no longer required such as when an individual changes role or perhaps leaves the organization.*
- *Users, devices, and systems should be appropriately verified, authenticated, and authorized before access to data or services is granted. Verification of a user's identity (they are who they say they are) is a prerequisite for issuing credentials, authentication, and access management.*
- *For highly privileged access, it might be appropriate to include approaches such as two-factor or hardware authentication.*
- *Unauthorized individuals should be prevented from accessing data or services at all points within the system. This includes system users without the appropriate permissions, unauthorized individuals attempting to interact with any online service presentation, or individuals with unauthorized access to user devices (e.g., if a user device were lost or stolen).*

(continued)

Table 8-1. (*continued*)

Data Security:

- *The protection in place for data that supports the delivery of essential services must be matched to the risks associated with that data.*
- *As a minimum, unauthorized access to sensitive information should be prevented (protecting data confidentiality). This may mean, for example, protecting data stored on mobile devices which could be lost or stolen.*
- *Data protection may also need to include measures such as the sanitization of data storage devices and/or media before sending for maintenance or disposal.*
- *Protect data in accordance with the risks to essential services posed by compromises of data integrity and/or availability. In addition to effective data access control measures, other relevant security measures might include maintaining up-to-date backup copies of data, combined with the ability to detect data integrity failures where necessary.*
- *Software and/or hardware used to access critical data may also require protection.*
- *It is important to ensure that data supporting the delivery of essential services is protected in transit. This could be by physically protecting the network infrastructure or using cryptographic means to ensure data is not inappropriately viewed or interfered with.*
- *Duplicating network infrastructure to prevent data flows being easily blocked provides data availability.*
- *Some types of information managed by an OES would, if acquired by an attacker, significantly assist in the planning and execution of a disruptive attack. Such information could be, for example, detailed network and system designs, security measures, or certain staff details. These should be identified and appropriately protected.*

(Note: Data supporting the delivery of essential services must be identified in accordance with Principle A.3 Asset Management).

System Security:

- *There is a range of protective security measures that an organization can use to minimize the opportunities for an attacker to compromise the security of networks and information systems supporting the delivery of essential services.*
- *Not all such measures will necessarily be applicable in all circumstances – each organization should determine and implement the protective security measures that are most effective in limiting those opportunities for attackers associated with the greatest risks to essential services.*

(continued)

Table 8-1. *(continued)*

- *Opportunities for attackers to compromise networks and information systems, also known as vulnerabilities, arise through flaws, features, and user errors.*
- *Organizations should ensure that all three types of vulnerability are considered when selecting and implementing protective security measures.*
- *Organizations should protect networks and information systems from attacks that seek to exploit software vulnerabilities (flaws in software). For example, software should be supported and up to date with security patches applied. Where this is not possible, other security measures should be in place to fully mitigate the software vulnerability risk.*
- *Limiting functionality (e.g., disabling services that are not required) and careful configuration will contribute to managing potential vulnerabilities arising from features in hardware and software.*
- *Some common user errors, such as leaving an organization-issued laptop unattended in a public place, inadvertently revealing security-related information to an attacker (possibly because of social engineering), etc., can provide opportunities for attackers.*
- *Staff training and awareness on cyber security should be designed to minimize such occurrences (see B.6 Staff Awareness and Training).*

Resilient Networks and Systems:

- *The services delivered by an organization should be resilient to cyber-attacks.*
- *Building upon B.4 (the technical protection of systems), organizations should ensure that not only is technology well built and maintained, but consideration is also given to how delivery of the essential service can continue in the event of technology failure or compromise.*
- *In addition to technical means, this might include additional contingency capability such as manual processes to ensure services can continue.*
- *Organizations should ensure that systems are well maintained and administered through life. The devices and interfaces that are used for administration are frequently targeted and so should be well protected.*
- *Spear phishing remains a common method used to compromise management accounts.*
- *Preventing the use of management accounts for routine activities such as email and web browsing significantly limits the ability for a hacker to compromise such accounts.*

(continued)

Table 8-1. (*continued*)

Staff Awareness and Training:

- *Staff are central to any organization's ability to operate securely. Therefore, operators of essential services should ensure that their employees have the information, knowledge, and skills they need to support the security of networks and information systems.*
- *To be effective, any security awareness and training program needs to recognize and be tailored to reflect the way people really work with security in an organization, as part of creating a positive security culture.*

C) **Appropriate capabilities to ensure network and information system security defenses remain effective and to detect cyber security events affecting, or with the potential to affect, essential services.**

C.1. SECURITY MONITORING	The organization monitors the security status of the networks and systems supporting the delivery of essential services to detect potential security problems and to track the ongoing effectiveness of protective security measures.
C.2. PROACTIVE SECURITY EVENT DISCOVERY	The organization detects, within networks and information systems, the malicious activity affecting, or with the potential to affect, the delivery of essential services even when the activity evades standard signature-based security prevent/detect solutions (or when standard solutions are not deployed).

Explanation

Security Monitoring:

- *An effective monitoring strategy is required so that actual or attempted security breaches are discovered, and there are appropriate processes in place to respond.*
- *Good monitoring is more than simply the collection of logs. It is also the use of appropriate tools and skilled analysis to identify indicators of compromise in a timely manner so that corrective action can be taken.*
- *This principle also indicates the need to provide effective and ongoing operational security.*

(*continued*)

Table 8-1. (*continued*)

- *As time goes on, new vulnerabilities are discovered, support arrangements for software and services change, and functional needs and uses for technology change.*
- *Security is a continuous activity, and the effectiveness of the security measures in place should be reviewed and maintained throughout the delivery and operational lifecycle of a system or service.*

Anomaly Detection:

- *Some cyber-attackers will go to great lengths to avoid detection via standard security monitoring tools such as anti-virus software, or signature-based intrusion detection systems, which give a direct indication of compromise.*
- *Other, less direct, security event indicators may provide additional opportunities for detecting attacks that could result in disruption to essential services.*

Examples of less direct indicators could include the following:

- o *Deviations from normal interaction with systems (e.g., user activity outside normal working hours).*
- o *Unusual patterns of network traffic (e.g., unexpectedly high traffic volumes, or traffic of an unexpected type, etc.).*
- o *"Tell-tale" signs of attack, such as attempts to laterally move across networks, or running privilege escalation software.*
- *It is not possible to give a generic list of suitable indicators since their usefulness in detecting a malicious activity will vary considerably, depending on how a typical attacker's actions might reveal themselves in relation to the normal operation of an organization's networks and information systems.*
- *Opportunities for exploiting these less direct security event indicators to improve network and information system security should be proactively investigated, assessed, and implemented when feasible, e.g., technically possible, cost effective, etc.*
- *Successful attack detection by means of less direct security event indicators may depend on identifying combinations of network events that match likely attacker behavior and will therefore require an analysis and assessment capability to determine the security significance of detected events.*
- *Wherever possible, network and information systems supporting the delivery of essential services should be designed with proactive security event discovery in mind.*

(*continued*)

Table 8-1. (*continued*)

D) **Capabilities to minimize the impacts of a cyber security incident on the delivery of essential services including the restoration of those services where necessary.**

D.1. RESPONSE AND RECOVERY PLANNING	There are well-defined and tested incident management processes in place that aim to ensure continuity of essential services in the event of system or service failure. Mitigation activities designed to contain or limit the impact of compromise are also in place.
D.2. LESSONS LEARNED	When an incident occurs, steps must be taken to understand its root causes and ensure appropriate remediating action is taken.

Explanation

Response and Recovery Planning:

- *Incidents will invariably happen. When they do, organizations should be prepared to deal with them and, as far as possible, have mechanisms in place that minimize the impact on the essential service.*
- *The mechanisms required should be determined as part of the organization's overall risk management approach.*
- *Examples might include things such as DDoS protection, protected power supply, critical system redundancy, rate-limiting access to data or service commands, critical data backup, or manual failover processes.*

Improvements:

- *If an incident does occur, it is important the organization learns lessons as to why it happened and where appropriate takes steps to prevent the same issue from recurring.*
- *The aim should be to address the root cause or seek to identify systemic problems rather than solely fix a very narrow issue.*
- *For example, to address the organization's overall patch management process rather than to just apply a specific missing patch.*

Building BRIDGES

Once again, the BRIDGES acronym can be successfully applied to help enhance the protective security measures. However, this time using it for the protection of important business information systems.

Business Context

In the move to more digital business operating models, it is increasingly common for businesses to look at the opportunity for enhancing their business through the analysis of masses of information. The result is that the companies are seeking to identify trends or ways to improve internal business processes.

For instance, let's look at a large retailer that is seeking to better understand the habits and trends of their customers. Through an improved appreciation of their customers' habits, needs, and expectations, they can seek to refine their internal processes to help enhance the customer experience. Additionally, they may identify opportunities to entice their customers into making purchases that they may never have discovered without this type of intervention (*e.g., that product placed at most of the customers' eye levels or that end-of-aisle promotion*).

Embracing the digital revolution, many of these retailers will seek to utilize robotic process automation (RPA) or machine learning (ML) to help enhance the data sorting, rationalization, and analysis of these mass amounts of data.

These individual data sets are like pieces of a jigsaw puzzle and, once pieced together, provide the company with an extremely helpful picture of their customer trends.

As a result, the supporting information systems become extremely valuable business assets. However, this value is often not appreciated or understood until the information systems become compromised or unavailable.

Think about the potential impact on the retailer's marketing team if the information systems compromise the quality and integrity of the data contained within:

- **Inconsistent data inside = Poor quality data outside!**[22]

---

[22]www.hicxsolutions.com/bad-data-common-data-quality-mistakes/

Suddenly, these poorly protected *(but valued)* information systems start to have an impact on the capabilities of the marketing team, and this then starts to have an impact on the business.

Consequently, it is essential that you reach out to each of the business departments to find out which information systems are essential for them to do their normal business operations.

Risk and Resilience

Now that you have a greater understanding on what Information Systems that the business is reliant upon, do you understand the potential impact on the business should that Information System be subject to a compromise of confidentiality, integrity, or availability?

- Have you analyzed the potential risk implications associated with each Information System?

- What would be the potential impact of the following being unavailable to a retail organization?

  - An inventory management solution (IMS)

  - Customer relationship management (CRM) platform

  - Accounting information system (AIS)

Identify and Isolate

As before, this is a case of identifying all the assets that are involved with each Information System[23] (remembering that an Information System is an integrated set of components for collecting, storing, and processing data and for providing information, knowledge, and digital products[24]) and identifying the security controls that can help to mitigate any risks and to minimize any unnecessary connectivity and access.

---

[23]https://bus206.pressbooks.com/chapter/chapter-1/
[24]www.britannica.com/topic/information-system

Detect Anomalies

For a Contact Center that is heavily reliant on their VoIP telephone–based Information Systems, have you considered what detection security considerations[25] are needed to help reduce the risks to these Information Systems to address known VoIP risks, threats, and vulnerabilities?

- **Confidentiality and privacy**
    - **Vulnerabilities**
        - Switch default password vulnerability
        - Classical wiretap vulnerability
        - Address resolution protocol (ARP) cache poisoning and ARP floods
        - Web server interfaces
        - IP phone netmask vulnerability
        - Extension to IP address mapping vulnerability
- **Integrity**
    - **Threat vectors**
        - **Intrusion** – An intruder may masquerade as a legitimate user and access an operations port of the switch.
        - **Insecure state** – At certain times, the switch may be vulnerable since it is not in a secure state.
    - **Attack vectors**
        - Dynamic host configuration protocol (DHCP) server insertion attack
        - Trivial file transfer protocol (TFTP) server insertion attack

---

[25]https://nvlpubs.nist.gov/nistpubs/Legacy/SP/nistspecialpublication800-58.pdf

- **Availability and denial of service**

  - **Attack vectors**

    - CPU resource consumption attack without any account information

    - Default password vulnerability

    - Exploitable software flaws

    - Account lockout vulnerability

Govern Processes

If you think of your business as being like a complex road system, you will have numerous different drivers, driving different modes of transport. To reduce the risk, each driver of these different modes of transport needs to understand the rules and procedures for the safe operation of their vehicles.

Consequently, much like the UK Government and their Department for Transport stipulate the rules, each driver needs to understand these rules and follow appropriate procedures to drive safely on the UK roads.

To ensure that everyone is legally driving on the UK roads, they need to have demonstrated their proficiency (passed the theory and practical driving tests) and to be familiar with the "Highway Code"[26] (as depicted in Figures 8-6 and 8-7).

- **Rules for pedestrians (1 to 35)**

  Rules for pedestrians, including general guidance, crossing the road, crossings, and situations needing extra care

  - **Rule 19**

    - **Zebra crossings**

---

[26]www.gov.uk/guidance/the-highway-code

Give traffic plenty of time to see you and to stop before you start to cross. Vehicles will need more time when the road is slippery. Wait until traffic has stopped from both directions and the road is clear before crossing. Remember that traffic does not have to stop until someone has moved on to the crossing. Keep looking both ways, and listening, in case a driver or rider has not seen you and attempts to overtake a vehicle that has stopped.

Figure 8-6. *Rule 19 – zebra crossings have flashing beacons*

Using the road (159 to 203)

Rules for using the road, including general rules, overtaking, road junctions, roundabouts, pedestrian crossings, and reversing

- **Roundabouts (rules 184 to 190)**

- **Rule 184**

  On approaching a roundabout, take notice and act on all the information available to you, including traffic signs, traffic lights, and lane markings which direct you into the correct lane. You should

  - Use mirrors – signal – maneuver at all stages.

  - Decide as early as possible which exit you need to take

- Give an appropriate signal. Time your signals so as not to confuse other road users.

- Get into the correct lane.

- Adjust your speed and position to fit in with traffic conditions.

- Be aware of the speed and position of all the road users around you.

- **Rule 185**

    When reaching the roundabout, you should

    - Give priority to traffic approaching from your right, unless directed otherwise by signs, road markings, or traffic lights.

    - Check whether road markings allow you to enter the roundabout without giving way. If so, proceed, but still look to the right before joining.

    - Watch out for all other road users already on the roundabout; be aware they may not be signaling correctly or at all.

    - Look forward before moving off to make sure traffic in front has moved off.

Figure 8-7 *Rule 185 – correct procedure at roundabouts*

If an organization fails to document, communicate, and educate their personnel on the rules and procedures for driving, it is reasonable to expect that crashes will happen, be that because of a deliberate reckless or accidental action.

Evaluate Security Controls

Remembering that the protective security measures that are implemented need to be proportionate to the perceived risk, it is also important to ensure that a suitable audit program is established to ensure that the Information Security systems remain appropriately protected.

This need not be as robust a regime as for a system involved with more sensitive, higher-priority systems or those assets associated with compliance programs, but, nevertheless, these measures need to be assessed to ensure that they remain effective to help mitigate the risks and to provide resilience.

Survive to Operate

Although not deemed to be "mission critical," what Information Systems could impact your business' standard operations and, consequently, adversely affect your business and how are you ensuring that they can "Survive to Operate"?

Have you considered how your business might be impacted if an important business Information System is compromised or becomes unavailable?

Are your teams proficiently prepared for when things go wrong, as, undoubtedly, they will do?

How quickly can your teams identify and react to events that might impact these Information Systems to help minimize the disruption and impact?

For an older or obsolete Information System, have you considered the contingency plans for if a component part becomes unserviceable?

Do you know where to go to get these replacement parts? Are these components still freely available?

What are your contingency plans to ensure minimal disruption to business plans if things go wrong?

For aging or obsolete Information Systems, have you carried out a risk assessment and informed senior management of your findings and the potential mitigation options?

In the event of a disaster, such as the COVID-19 pandemic, can your personnel still get access to these Information Systems?

What alternative measures have you considered to provide continued business operations when these Information Systems are no longer accessible or operational?

Are the identified risks associated with any contingency/disaster recovery measures documented, communicated to senior management, and still within the organization's risk appetite levels?

Reality Bites

On September 23, 2020, the Tesla motor company suffered an outage[27] to one of their Information Systems which resulted in the Tesla owners being locked out of their vehicles and the accompanying mobile application for around one hour.

All this chaos was caused by a defective application programming interface (API). The affected API is an important part of the Information System that supports the Tesla mobile application, which is critical for giving the Tesla owners control over numerous functions on their vehicle.

Often, the importance of components, such as APIs, is underappreciated, and as a result, they are not afforded the same protective security as an organization might afford to a supporting hardware (e.g., secure configurations[28]) or software applications (e.g., OWASP Top 10 Web Application Security Risks[29]). However, much like the hardware and software applications, APIs need to be managed and have their own vulnerabilities tested and mitigated.[30]

---

[27]https://techcrunch.com/2020/09/23/tesla-experienced-an-hour-long-network-outage-early-wednesday/

[28]www.cisecurity.org/cis-benchmarks/

[29]https://owasp.org/www-project-top-ten/

[30]https://owasp.org/www-project-api-security/

API Security Top 10 2019

1. **Broken object level authorization**

   APIs tend to expose endpoints that handle object identifiers, creating a wide attack surface level access control issue. Object level authorization checks should be considered in every function that accesses a data source using an input from the user.

2. **Broken user authentication**

   Authentication mechanisms are often implemented incorrectly, allowing attackers to compromise authentication tokens or to exploit implementation flaws to assume other users' identities temporarily or permanently. Compromising system's ability to identify the client/user, compromises API security overall.

3. **Excessive data exposure**

   Looking forward to generic implementations, developers tend to expose all object properties without considering their individual sensitivity, relying on clients to perform the data filtering before displaying it to the user.

4. **Lack of resources and rate limiting**

   Quite often, APIs do not impose any restrictions on the size or number of resources that can be requested by the client/user. Not only can this impact the API server performance, leading to denial of service (DoS), but also leaves the door open to authentication flaws such as brute force.

5. **Broken function level authorization**

   Complex access control policies with different hierarchies, groups, and roles, and an unclear separation between administrative and regular functions, tend to lead to authorization flaws. By exploiting these issues, attackers gain access to other users' resources and/or administrative functions.

6. **Mass assignment**

   Binding client-provided data (e.g., JSON) to data models, without proper properties filtering based on a whitelist, usually leads to mass assignment. Either guessing object properties, exploring other API endpoints, reading the documentation, or providing additional object properties in request payloads allows attackers to modify object properties they are not supposed to.

7. **Security misconfiguration**

   Security misconfiguration is commonly a result of unsecure default configurations, incomplete or ad hoc configurations, open cloud storage, misconfigured HTTP headers, unnecessary HTTP methods, permissive cross-origin resource sharing (CORS), and verbose error messages containing sensitive information.

8. **Injection**

   Injection flaws, such as SQL, NoSQL, Command Injection, and so on, occur when untrusted data is sent to an interpreter as part of a command or query. The attacker's malicious data can trick the interpreter into executing unintended commands or accessing data without proper authorization.

9. **Improper assets management**

   APIs tend to expose more endpoints than traditional web applications, making proper and updated documentation incredibly important. Proper hosts and deployed API versions inventory also play an important role to mitigate issues such as deprecated API versions and exposed debug endpoints.

10. **Insufficient logging and monitoring**

    Insufficient logging and monitoring, coupled with missing or ineffective integration with incident response, allows attackers to further attack systems, maintain persistence, pivot to more systems to tamper with, extract, or destroy data. Most breach studies demonstrate the time to detect a breach is over 200 days, typically detected by external parties rather than internal processes or monitoring.

Key Takeaways

- Protective Security measures should not be limited to just critical data assets (e.g., compliance) but should be extended to help safeguard any Information Systems that could impact the business.

- An Information System is an integrated set of components for collecting, storing, and processing data and for providing information, knowledge, and digital products.

- Increasingly, as businesses are adopting the digital revolution, there is an ever-growing reliance on Information Systems to help support efficient business operations.

- It is common for an organization to not understand or appreciate the value of its business information systems. For example, in a Contact Center, a VoIP telephone–based system is frequently seen as only being a telephone system used to communicate with their customers. However, it is not until this IP-connected system goes wrong that they understand its importance in the business.

- Information are like pieces in a jigsaw puzzle. The Information Systems are like the jigsaw puzzle box, and much like a jigsaw puzzle, some are more complex (with more pieces than others), and the different pieces are more important than others in helping to piece together the true picture.

- Criminals will seek any opportunity to steal pieces from the jigsaw puzzle box. Think of how many pieces of the jigsaw may be contained in an employee's email inbox.

- It is essential that the business understands what their important business systems are and what the potential impact might be for them being compromised or not being available.

- There need to be defined and documented rules for the use and maintenance of a business' Information Systems.[31]

- Based upon the perceived importance of these Information Systems, it is essential that proportionate protective measures are applied and audited to ensure that they are adequately safeguarded.

- You need to be prepared for when things happen or go wrong with these Information Systems to ensure that minimal disruption and impact occurs.

---

[31]www.helsinki.fi/en/it/rules-for-the-maintenance-of-information-systems

CHAPTER 9

Physical Security

If we do not wish to fight, we can prevent the enemy from engaging us even though the lines of our encampment be merely traced out on the ground.

All we need do is to throw something odd and unaccountable in his way!

The Art of War[1]

Figure 9-1. *Sun Tzu*

Introduction

There is often a misconception within the industry as to what constitutes an effective Physical Security strategy, and individuals may perceive effective Physical Security as being likened to that of a prison (with the high thick walls marking the perimeter). However, as you can see from Sun Tzu's[2] 512 BC quote, the opposite provides effective Physical Security defensive measures.

---

[1]Sunzi (2014). The art of war. New York: Black & White Classics.
[2]www.history.com/topics/ancient-china/sun-tzu

© Jim Seaman 2021
J. Seaman, *Protective Security*, https://doi.org/10.1007/978-1-4842-6908-4_9

You are looking to build consequential layers, which need to be individually peeled back *(like peeling through the layers of an onion)* to get to the asset. These layers will get proportionately thicker the closer you get to the asset needing to be protected, to provide the 5 Ds of defense (as depicted in Figure 9-2[3]).

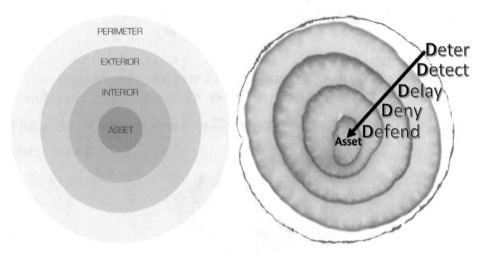

Figure 9-2. 5 Ds of defense in depth

- **Defense in depth[4] (as depicted in Figure 9-3)**

  Physical measures represent only one aspect of protective security, and they need to be supported by sound personnel, document handling, communications, and computer security.

  Sensible management of security risks involves finding the most effective (and cost effective) ways of countering the given threats by a combination of measures from each of these areas. Good physical protection, preferably built into any site or building from the beginning, is of fundamental importance.

---

[3]www.charter-global.com/common-physical-security-threats/

[4]Extract from the Defence Manual of Security (JSP 440) (http://wla.1-s.es/uk-mod-jsp-440-2001.pdf).

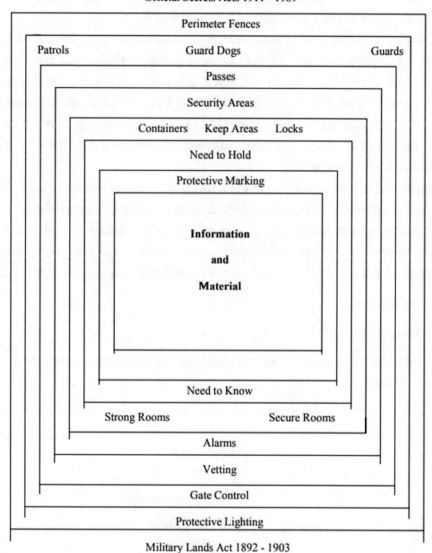

· Official Secrets Acts 1911 - 1989

Perimeter Fences

Patrols   Guard Dogs   Guards

Passes

Security Areas

Containers   Keep Areas   Locks

Need to Hold

Protective Marking

Information

and

Material

Need to Know

Strong Rooms   Secure Rooms

Alarms

Vetting

Gate Control

Protective Lighting

Military Lands Act 1892 - 1903

Figure 9-3. *Military defense in depth*

Each defensive layer should act in isolation but be complementary to the subsequent layers, meaning that things get progressively more robust as an opportunist attacker makes their way inward.

If you were to construct your defenses in the manner of a prison, you will be advertising to your attackers that there is something of value inside. Remember that the purpose of a prison is to defend against breakouts – the opposite for the Physical Security goals in Protective Security.

You should evaluate the integrity and effectiveness of each individual layer to proportionately protect your most valued business assets.

If an attacker is unable to gain unauthorized access to your valuable/critical business assets from cyberspace, they will also seek to socially engineer[5] their way into your physical environment to try and identify potential opportunities to gain unauthorized access.

Not everyone of your threat actor is seeking to infiltrate your physical environment, to steal data or compromise your IT systems. In many cases, the impact of a successful incursion may result in data loss or asset compromise; however, that may not have been the threat actors' direct intentions.

It is important to remember that many important business assets are intrinsically valuable and attractive (V&A) to an opportunist thief, and an effective defense-in-depth Physical Security approach will help to reduce their opportunities to steel a V&A item.

Another threat that your Physical Security measures should be designed to mitigate against are natural disasters. Consequently, your threats can be categorized into two types:

- **Traditional**

- **Nontraditional**

In the military, we would use the **TESSOC** acronym to identify these threat vectors (as depicted in Table 9-1).

TESSOC	
Traditional	**Nontraditional**
Terrorism	Other
Espionage	• Investigative journalist
Sabotage	• Insider: accidental
Subversion	• Natural disaster
	Crime
	• Organized crime
	• Theft
	• Hacker
	• Insider: malicious

---

[5]Watson, G., Mason, A.G. and Ackroyd, R. (2014). Social engineering penetration testing : executing social engineering pen tests, assessments and defense. Amsterdam ; Boston: Syngress, An Imprint Of Elsevier.

By measuring the defensive layers against their capability to mitigate these threats vs. the impact on the business operations, you will be better placed to ensure that your Physical Security measures remain effective.

However, the greatest threat to the effectiveness of the Physical Security measures remains with the authorized personnel, who have the responsibility to use or maintain such measures.

Remember, if it is convenient to your personnel, it will be convenient for your attacker. Do not assume that just because a Physical Security measure is in place, it will continue to remain effective unless these measures are policed.

A propped open security door has no intrinsic security value!

The Military Matrix Model

In the RAF Police, Physical Security is an integral part of Protective Security and is one of the responsibilities of an RAF station Counter Intelligence operative (as shown in Figure 9-4).

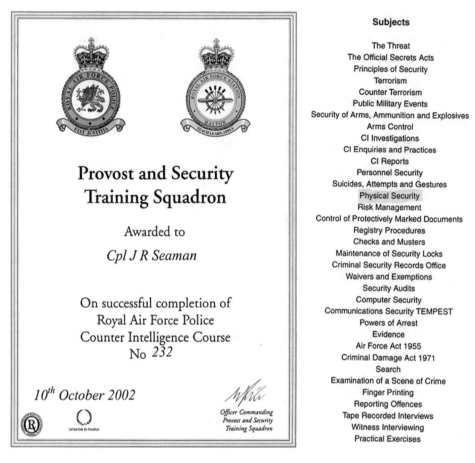

Subjects

The Threat
The Official Secrets Acts
Principles of Security
Terrorism
Counter Terrorism
Public Military Events
Security of Arms, Ammunition and Explosives
Arms Control
CI Investigations
CI Enquiries and Practices
CI Reports
Personnel Security
Suicides, Attempts and Gestures
Physical Security
Risk Management
Control of Protectively Marked Documents
Registry Procedures
Checks and Musters
Maintenance of Security Locks
Criminal Security Records Office
Waivers and Exemptions
Security Audits
Computer Security
Communications Security TEMPEST
Powers of Arrest
Evidence
Air Force Act 1955
Criminal Damage Act 1971
Search
Examination of a Scene of Crime
Finger Printing
Reporting Offences
Tape Recorded Interviews
Witness Interviewing
Practical Exercises

Figure 9-4. RAF Police Counter Intelligence

Unfortunately, the Physical Security section of the Counter Intelligence course was interrupted for me, following the sudden death of my father, meaning that I missed one week of this training. However, I had incredibly supportive course colleagues and instructors, who gave up their spare time to enable me to catch up on the missing week.

The part I did manage to complete included carrying out Physical Security assessment, using the minimum baseline measures matrix (MBMM) (as depicted in Figure 9-5), and our visit to the Police Scientific Development Branch (PSDB) *(later to be renamed the Home Office Scientific Development Branch (HOSDB) and then renamed the Centre for Applied Science and Technology (CAST[6]) and now the Defence Science and Technology Laboratory*

---

[6]https://assets.publishing.service.gov.uk/government/uploads/system/uploads/
attachment_data/file/204674/intro-to-cast-may13.pdf

(Dstl[7])), to see how each piece of security equipment was tested and scored for entry into the security equipment approved product (SEAP) catalogue (similar to the Centre for the Protection of National Infrastructure (CPNI)'s Catalogue of Security Equipment[8]).

**MINIMUM BASELINE MEASURES MATRIX FOR
LARGE ITEMS OF EQUIPMENT KEPT INSIDE
SPECIAL-TO-TYPE BUILDINGS**

TOP SECRET	L	M	S	H	VH
Mandatory - Section 1	1	1	1	1	1
Mandatory - Section 3	2	2	2	2	2
Mandatory - Sections 4 plus 5 **	6	6	7	7	7
Additional - Any sections #	9	11	11	14	18
Total	18	20	21	24	28
SECRET	**L**	**M**	**S**	**H**	**VH**
Mandatory - Section 1	1	1	1	1	1
Mandatory - Section 3	2	2	2	2	2
Mandatory - Sections 4 plus 5 *	4	4	5	5	6
Additional - Any sections #	7	9	9	12	15
Total	14	16	17	20	24
CONFIDENTIAL	**L**	**M**	**S**	**H**	**VH**
Mandatory - Section 1	1	1	1	1	1
Mandatory - Section 3	2	2	2	2	2
Mandatory - Sections 4 plus 5	3	3	3	3	3
Additional - Any sections #	4	5	7	9	13
Total	10	11	13	15	19
RESTRICTED	**L**	**M**	**S**	**H**	**VH**
Mandatory - Section 1	1	1	1	1	1
Mandatory - Section 3	1	1	1	1	1
Additional - Any sections #	-	-	1	2	3
Total	2	2	3	4	5

Figure 9-5. *MBMM scoring matrix*

Now, you always get at least one character on a military training course – my Counter Intelligence course was no different. For our day visit to the PSDB, the entire course was driven there, by the Physical Security instructor (aka Ned Flanders), in a white minibus.

On arrival at the PSDB, Ned had asked to watch out of the back window of the minibus, while he reversed it into a parking bay. Well, as he carefully reversed into the parking bay, the bus fell into complete silence.

---

[7]www.gov.uk/government/organisations/defence-science-and-technology-laboratory
[8]www.cpni.gov.uk/cse-categories

When, suddenly, "Yakka" (the student comedian) shouted out…

Woah……!

Ned immediately slammed on the brakes, and everyone's hearts started racing. The next thing we knew, Yakka continued by singing…

I'm going to Barbados![9]

Everyone *(except for Ned)* on the minibus immediately cracked up laughing.
That was to set up the tone for a very enjoyable and informative visit.

We discovered that each of the items were graded and scored based upon their resistance to brute-force attacks, with some items having a reliance on others (e.g., a secure room'sscore being dependent on the effectiveness of the walls, ceiling, floor, doorframe, door, and locking system). If the room were fitted with an inferior or unserviceable lock, the room's score would be impacted by this (as depicted in Figure 9-6).

---

[9]`https://youtu.be/TIWoUmqLGjw`

Measure			Loading	Remarks
Section 1 – Container/casing				
1.	**Container/casing:**			
	a.	Class 4	4	
	b.	Class 3	3	
	c.	Class 2	2	
	d.	Class 1	1	
Sub-score (ss1) = a, b, c or d				
2.	**Lock**			
	a.	Class 4	4	
	b.	Class 3	3	
	c.	Class 2	2	
	d.	Class 1	1	
Sub-score (ss2) = a, b, c or d				

Section score (S1) = ss1 x ss2	NB. Multiply	

Measure			Loading	
Section 2 – Room				
3.	**Room:**			
	a.	Strong Room	4	
	b.	Strong Room	3	
	c.	Secure Room	1	
	d.	Locked Room	0	
Sub-score (ss3) = a, b, c or d				
4.	**Lock**			
	a.	Class 4	4	
	b.	Class 4	3	
	c.	Class 3	2	
	d.	Class 2	1	
	e	Class 1	0	
Sub-score (ss4) = a, b, c, d or e				

Figure 9-6. *MBMM – room grading*

When you think about this concept, it makes a great deal of sense. Which is the most effective?

A Class 2 fence[10] within an unlit environment?

or

Security lighting[11] providing a 10-meter-wide stretch of floodlit land?

As an example, let's look at ABC Company's data center.

1. **Section 1 – Container**

    At the core of their estate, they have chosen to securely house their servers in a Class 2 security cage,[12] fitted with a Class 3 lock (as depicted in Figure 9-7[13]).

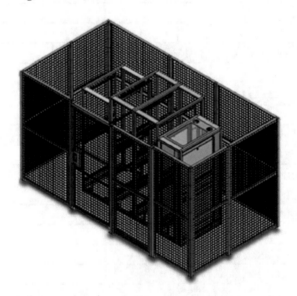

Figure 9-7. *Class 2 cage*

---

[10]A Class 2 fence is an anti-intruder fence which offers a degree of resistance to climbing and breaching by an opportunist intruder not having particular skills and using material and breaching items that are readily to hand.

[11]Security lighting can offer a high degree of deterrence to a potential intruder in addition to providing the illumination necessary for effective surveillance either directly by the guards or indirectly through a CCTV system. The standard of lighting is to meet the minimum requirement and its installation be appropriate to the site conditions.

[12]These are SECURITY containers which are

    (1) Of substantial design and construction

    (2) Offer resistance to the casual or opportunist attacker who has not been prepared for the attack and only has use of items that are readily to hand

[13]www.swdp.com/datacenter-cages.html

- (ss1) Class 2 container = 2 points

- (ss2) Class 2 lock = 2 points

- **Section 1 Total = 4 points (ss1 x ss2)**

2. **Section 2 – Room**

   The cage is housed in a standard Type A Secure Room,[14] fitted
   with a Class 3 lock.[15]

   - (ss3) Secure Room = 1 point

   - (ss4) Class 3 lock = 2 points

   - **Section 2 Total = 2 points (ss3 x ss4)**

3. **Section 3 – Building**

The secure room located with a Class 3 building.[16]

   - **Section 3 Total = 3 points**

---

[14]There should be only one entrance in Type A Secure Room, but if emergency exits are necessary,
they must be fitted with approved doors and emergency exit devices and be wired into any
installed intrusion detection system.

Windows are not permitted. Air vents and ducts must be fitted with steel grilles or bar sets. Protectively
marked material may be held on open racking or in non-SEAP approved containers in a Type A Secure
Room. A lightweight version of the Type A Secure Room is available for use when the standard structure
is too heavy for the building.

Specification:

a. **Walls** – 150mm (min) reinforced concrete or in existing buildings, 340mm solid brick, cement
rendered on both sides

b. **Floor and roof** – 150mm solid reinforced concrete

c. **Door** – Oxford or Cambridge door

d. **Lock** – Medway Locking unit or Fraser Bar, for emergency exits

[15]These are **MEDIUM SECURITY** locks which have a high degree of resistance to expert and
professional attack using skills and resources that are available commercially to a professional
locksmith.

[16]A building which

(1) Offers a degree of resistance to a forced attack

(2) Is of solid construction, normally brick or block, on cavity wall principles

(3) Has windows and doors of a standard equal to that of the building in its resistance to a forced
attack

Modern building techniques of precast or fabricated panels or steel frame and glass may also rate
Class 3.

4. **Section 4 – Control of entry**

Entry to the building is protected by Class 1 control of entry[17] and escorted visitor control.[18]

- (ss6) Class 1 control of entry = 1 point

- (ss7) Escorted access = 3 points

- **Section 4 Total = 4 points (ss6 + ss7)**

By just applying these basic physical building infrastructure security measures, from Sections 1 to 4 *(if these measures remain effective)*, the ABC Company data center has already achieved **13 points**.

This can then be easily supplemented with the ancillary external measures from Sections 5 and 6 to help bolster the remaining elements of the 5 Ds.

5. **Section 5 – Guards and IDS**

The ABC Company employs infrequent internal patrols and alarm systems.

- (ss8) Infrequent internal patrols[19] = 4 points

- (ss9) Class 2 intrusion detection system[20] = 3 points

- **Section 5 Total = 7 points (ss8 + ss9)**

---

[17]A Class 1 entry control system is one based on a locked door with access allowed by either
  (1) A mechanical or stand-alone electronic push-button code lock (PBCL)
  (2) The issue of keys to "authorized key holders"

[18]Visitors who are required to be escorted within a protected area are always accompanied by an appointed escort or by personnel they are visiting. If they need to visit several different departments or other members of staff, they are to be formally handed over from one escort to the next with, if required, the visitor's pass being annotated accordingly.

[19]Internal random patrols at intervals not exceeding 6 hours allow for two or three patrols during the night and periodic security checks during a weekend or holiday period. The first patrol is to normally take place soon after cease work and is to be concerned with checking that the site or building is properly secure. Patrol routes are to be varied so that the timing and location of the guard cannot be predicted.

[20]A Class 2 alarm system is one which
  (1) Is used in premises where the security risks of a sophisticated attack are not high.
  (2) Intruders are expected to have a limited knowledge of alarm systems and have available only basic tools and portable instruments.

6. **Section 6 – Secure silo**

    The data center building is sited within an internally segmented area.

    - (ss10) Class 2 fence[21] = 2 points

    - (ss11) Entry control = 1 point

    - (ss12) No random entry +/or exit searches = 0 points

    - (ss13) Perimeter intrusion detection system (PIDS) = 2 points

    - (ss14) Appropriate standard closed-circuit television (CCTV) = 2 points

    - (ss15) Appropriate security lighting = 2 points

    - **Section 6 Total = <u>8 points</u> ((ss10 x ss11) + ss12 + ss13 + ss14 + ss15)**

7. **Section 7 – Outer perimeter**

    The ABC Company does not wish to draw attention to the fact that they have valuable assets onsite and so has minimized the outer perimeter defenses.

    - (ss16) Class 1 fence = 1 point

    - (ss17) No entry control = 0 points

    - (ss18) No entry/exit searches = 0 points

    - (ss19) No PIDS = 0 points

    - (ss20) No CCTV = 0 points

    - (ss21) No appropriate security lighting = 0 points

    - **Section 7 Total = <u>0 points</u> ((ss16 x ss17) + ss18 + ss19 + ss20 + ss21) – as depicted in Table 9-1**

Defend, Deny, Delay, Detect, and Deter

---

[21]A Class 2 fence is an anti-intruder fence which offers a degree of resistance to climbing and breaching by an opportunist intruder not having particular skills and using material and breaching items that are readily to hand.

Table 9-1. *Scoring Results*

Mandatory	Score	Secret Asset	Substantial Threat
Sections 1 +/or 2, plus 3	**9 points**	**8 points**	
Sections 4 plus 5 **	**11 points**	**5 points**	
Additional			
Any sections	**8 points**	**4 points**	
Total	**28 points**	**17 points**	

As you can see from this exercise, the ABC Company data center score exceeds the requirements needed for the protection of an asset graded at the **SECRET**[22] level and with a threat level of substantial.

It is important that your Physical Security measures need to be proportionate to the perceived value of the business asset, and, although you may not have **SECRET** assets, you are likely to have an equivalent value to your organization (*e.g., the compromise of this information or material would be likely to cause serious damage to the operational effectiveness of essential business operations (such as industrial control systems)*).

Additionally, you may have information systems and data stores that relate to personal or financial data, which you may consider as being deemed the equivalent of **CONFIDENTIAL.**[23]

---

[22]The compromise of **SECRET** information or material would be likely to raise international tension; to damage seriously relations with friendly governments; to threaten life directly, or seriously prejudice public order, or individual security or liberty; to cause serious damage to the operational effectiveness or security of UK or allied forces or the continuing effectiveness of highly valuable security or intelligence operations; to cause substantial material damage to national finances or economic and commercial interests.

(Source: http://wla.1-s.es/uk-mod-jsp-440-2001.pdf)

[23]The compromise of **CONFIDENTIAL** information or material would be likely to materially damage diplomatic relations (i.e., cause formal protest or other sanction); to prejudice individual security or liberty; to cause damage to the operational effectiveness or security of UK or allied forces or the effectiveness of valuable security or intelligence operations; to work substantially against national finances or economic and commercial interests; substantially to undermine the financial viability of major organizations; to impede the investigation or facilitate the commission of serious crime; to impede seriously the development or operation of major government policies; and to shut down or otherwise substantially disrupt significant national operations.

(Source: http://wla.1-s.es/uk-mod-jsp-440-2001.pdf)

When you are considering the introduction of any new, or additional, Physical Security measures, it is extremely important for you to have completed any Operational Requirements.[24] This will ensure that when you go out to the vendors for quotes, you will receive comparable solutions that meet your Physical Security needs.

Operational Requirements

Not all Physical Security solutions are the same. Consequently, when tendering for these defensive solutions, it is essential to ensure that these effectively meet your needs.

By providing each of your prospective vendors with a detailed level 1 and level 2 Operational Requirements (ORs[25]), you are providing the vendors with explicit and detailed descriptions of the risks you are trying to mitigate against and the specification requirements you are wanting.

Consequently, a well-defined OR becomes an essential tool for ensuring that the vendors provide like for like solutions that meet your specific needs.

For instance, with a CCTV installation, there are numerous factors[26] that need to be considered and factored into the CCTV solution:

- Do you need to identify facial features?

- Do you need low-light performance capabilities?

- What about identifying colors at night?

- What are your image retention requirements?

- Do you need to be able to read vehicle registration numbers?

During our visit to the PSDB facility, we were introduced to "ROTAKIN" (as depicted in Figure 9-8[27]) and how it was used during a CCTV capability assessment.[28]

However, since then, CCTV technology has moved on, and "ROTAKIN" has been replaced with "NORMAN" (National Operational Requirement Mannequin) (as depicted in Figure 9-9[29]).

---

[24]www.cpni.gov.uk/operational-requirements

[25]www.cpni.gov.uk/system/files/documents/2c/cc/Operational_Requirements.pdf

[26]www.globalmsc.net/wp-content/uploads/2016/01/operational-requirements.pdf

[27]www.ifsecglobal.com/installers/cctv-guide-setting-objectives-requirements/
attachment/rotakin/

[28]http://rotatest.com/

[29]https://silo.tips/download/tavcom-training-courses-part-of-the

Figure 9-8. ROTAKIN

Figure 9-9. NORMAN

OR CCTV Template

To ensure that all your potential suppliers provide you with estimates that meet your exact specifications and needs, the Operational Requirements template proves to be an exceptional resource that you can utilize.

This will enable you to produce a clear, considered, and high-level statement of your security needs based on the risks you face.

Further reading:

- **Operational Requirements Guidance**[30]

  - Principles of assessing and implementing effective protective security

Level 1 OR

Statement of Problem	Stakeholders	Risk Assessment	Success Criteria	
Define the Problem	Location	Activity	Purpose of Observation	Target Speed
Operational Issues	Who Monitors?	When Monitored?	Where Monitored?	Response
System Requirements	Alert Functions	Displays	Recording	Export/ Archive
Management Issues	Constraints	Legal Issues	Maintenance	Resources

Level 2 OR

Level 2 ORs are a continuation of the level 1 OR but focus in more detail on each area of concern and its possible solution.

The level 2 ORs investigate each of the suggested solutions and expand upon the level 1 OR. In addition, they consider the function(s) of the possible solution, concerns, operator interfaces, risk analyses, and performance requirements.

A flow chart of the entire system for producing ORs is in Figure 9-10.[31]

---

[30]www.cpni.gov.uk/system/files/documents/2c/cc/Operational_Requirements.pdf
[31]www.frontierpitts.com/wp-content/uploads/Documents/Guide-to-producing-operational-requirements-for-security-measures.pdf

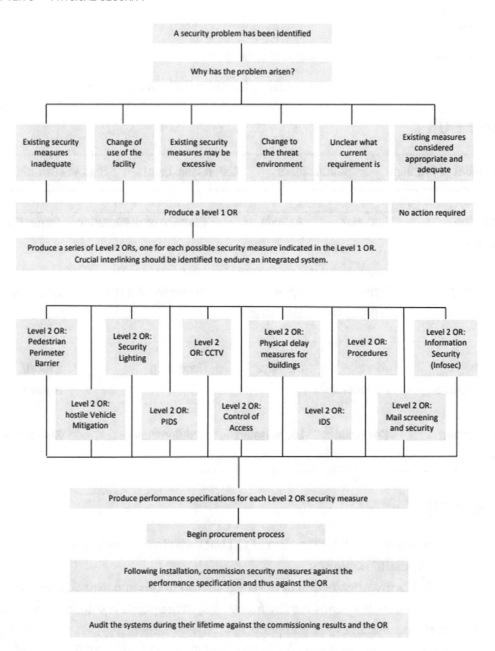

Figure 9-10. *OR flow chart*

Military Comparison
Perimeter Fence Line Survey

During my appointment as RAF Leeming's[32] Counter Intelligence operative, I was tasked by the Station Commander to carry out a review of the perimeter fence.

The Station Commander was concerned that the perimeter fence was no longer sufficient for the changed role of the station. RAF Leeming had been established in 1939 and had previously been an operational Tornado F.3 airhead[33] (as depicted in Figure 9-11[34]), and the Physical Security infrastructure had not appeared to have changed since I had been there, on dog handling duties (1995 to 1997).

Tremblers' Farewell - the end of the Tornado F.3 - RAF Leeming - 18/06/2007 ◊ Karl Drage - globalaviationresource.com
Image 29 of 59   CLOSE ✕

Figure 9-11. *RAF Leeming Tornado F3*

---

[32]www.raf.mod.uk/our-organisation/stations/raf-leeming/
[33]A designated location in an operational area used as a base for supply and evacuation by air.
[34]www.globalaviationresource.com/reports/2011/f3retirement.php

Although a dog patrol was deemed to be an extremely effective Physical Security measure (scoring 8 points), starting with the UK Government's "Options for Change"[35] and the various "Strategic Defense Reviews,"[36] the role of RAF Leeming changed and the RAF Police Dog Section was disbanded.

Consequently (as depicted in Figure 9-12), RAF Leeming had minimal scores from Section 5 onward. However, the role of the station was to change again, taking on the role of telecommunications in support of deployed operations.

---

[35]www.rafpa.com/history.htm
[36]http://researchbriefings.files.parliament.uk/documents/RP98-91/RP98-91.pdf

Measure	Loading	Remarks
Section 5 – Guards and IDS		
8. **Guards:**		
a. Point Guard	10	
b. Dog Patrol	8	
c. Frequent Internal Patrols	5	
d. Infrequent Internal Patrols	4	*4*
e. External Patrols	3	
f. Resident/Site Guard	2	
g. Visiting Guard	1	
h. None	0	
Sub-score (ss8) = [(a, b, c or d)* + (e or f)*] or g* or h		*4*
* = if applicable. Resident/site guard will only score if there has been no other score for other guards or patrols		
9. **IDS:**		
a. Class 4	5	
b. Class 3	4	
c. Class 2	3	
d. Class 1	1	
e. None	0	
Sub-score (ss9) = a, b, or c		*0*
Section score (S5) = ss8 + ss9	NB. Add	*4*

Measure	Loading	Remarks
Section 6 – Immediate dispersal/ parking/storage area		
10. **Fence:**		
a. Class 4	4	
b. Class 3	3	
c. Class 2	2	
d. Class 1	1	
e. None	0	
Sub-score (ss10) = a, b, c, d or e		*0*
11. **Entry control:**		
a. Yes	1	
b. No	0	
Sub-score (ss11) = a or b		*0*

Scoring:
Sections 5 to 7
4 + 3 = 7

Measure	Loading	Remarks
12. Random entry and/or exit searches:		
a. Yes	1	
b. No	0	*0*
Sub-score (ss12) = a or b		*0*
13. **PIDS:**		
a. Yes	2	
b. No	0	*0*
Sub-score (ss13) = a or b		*0*
14. **CCTV (to appropriate standards):**		
a. Yes	2	
b. No	0	*0*
Sub-score (ss14) = a or b		*0*
15. **Lighting (to appropriate standards):**		
a. Yes	2	
b. No	0	*0*
Sub-score (ss15) = a or b		*0*
Section score (S6) = (ss10 x ss11) + ss12 + ss13 + ss14 + ss15		*0*

Measure	Loading	Remarks
Section 7 – Outer Perimeter		
16. **Fence:**		
a. Class 4	4	
b. Class 3	3	
c. Class 2	2	
d. Class 1	1	*1*
e. None	0	
Sub-score (ss16) = a, b, c, d or e		*1*
17. **Entry control:**		
a. Yes	1	*1*
b. No	0	
Sub-score (ss17) = a or b		*1*
18. Random entry and/or exit searches:		
a. Yes	1	
b. No	0	*1*
Sub-score (ss18) = a or b		*1*
19. **PIDS:**		
a. Yes	2	
b. No	0	
Sub-score (ss19) = a or b		*0*
20. **CCTV (to appropriate standards):**		
a. Yes	2	
b. No	0	*0*
Sub-score (ss20) = a or b		*0*
21. **Lighting (to appropriate standards):**		
a. Yes	2	
b. No	0	*0*
Sub-score (ss21) = a or b		*0*
Section score (S7) = (ss16 x ss17) + ss18 + ss19 + ss20 + ss21		*3*
TOTAL SCORE is the sum of SECTIONS 1 to 7		

Figure 9-12. *MBMM – Sections 5–7*

Quite rightly, the Station Commander was worried and wanted to invest in improving the Physical Security measures.

As you can see the outer Deter, Detect, and Delay layers were extremely weak, and the station needed to rely on the Physical Security measures provided by the building infrastructures.

Consequently, the Station Commander requested that I carry out a Physical Security survey of the entire perimeter fence, in order to identify what would be required to upgrade the existing perimeter fence to the equivalent of a Class 2 style fence (as depicted in Figure 9-13[37]) and to then provide him with a report for his consideration.

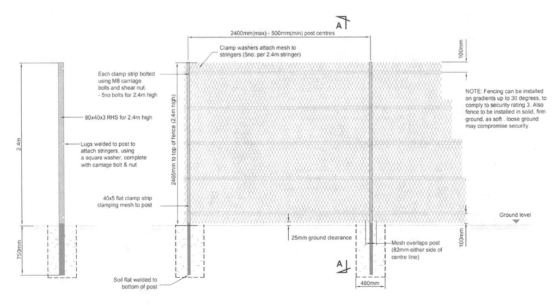

Figure 9-13. *Class 2 fence schematics*

Despite my thinking that there were far better ways to invest in improving the Physical Security measures, I agreed to carry out the survey of the entire perimeter fence.

Accompanied with an RAF Police colleague (Karl), we set about surveying the entire perimeter of the base. This involved GPS plotting and categorizing different elements of the fence line:

- **GREEN** = Close match to a Class 2 fence

- **AMBER** = Class 1 delineation

- **RED** = No security value

---

[37]http://exmeshsecurity.co.uk/wp-content/uploads/2019/10/Exmesh-Security-Data-Sheets-Class-2-v1.1.pdf

It is important to remember that the perimeter fence had many stretches of the fence line that were in good order (as depicted in Figures 9-14[38] and 9-15).

Figure 9-14. *Class 2 grade fence line (notice how the anti-climb component faces outward)*

Figure 9-15. *Class 2 grade fence line (in the background)*

---

[38]By The joy of all things – Own work, CC BY-SA 4.0, https://commons.wikimedia.org/w/index.php?curid=57363538

However, in areas that were less accessible, the fence line had not been maintained and had completely collapsed or had been overgrown (as depicted in Figures 9-16 and 9-17).

Where nature had compromised the effectiveness of the fence line to act as a barrier, this could only be graded as being Class 1 *(a boundary delineation)*, as an intruder could be completely covered from view, as they cut through the fencing, or could use the tree as a means of climbing over the fence line (as depicted in Figure 9-18).

Figure 9-16. *Nature-compromised perimeter fence (1)*

Figure 9-17. *Nature-compromised perimeter fence (2)*

Figure 9-18. *Tree-compromised fence line*

By the end of the survey, we had identified all the areas of the perimeter fence line that would need improvement or replacement, with a predicted cost of between £1 million and £1.5 million.

Additionally, when evaluating the return on investment and proportionality for these improvements, the perceived additional 10-minute delay for an intruder (just 1 additional point on the MBMM), the Station Commander agreed that there were far better ways of investing in Physical Security improvements.

Consequently, it was decided that the investment would be better placed to investigate the additional measures that could be applied to create secured areas within the RAF base (as depicted in Figure 9-19).

Figure 9-19. *Internal secure area*

It is extremely important that you do not assume that the construction teams will understand the security requirements, so it is vital that you are involved in the planning stages of any build that has a Physical Security element.

A particularly good example of this was when I was providing the Physical Security oversight for the construction of a secure room. The construction team had been told to build the room using the thickness of a breeze block for the walls. However, as you can see from Figures 9-20 and 9-21, there are different interpretations for this.

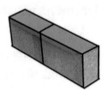

Figure 9-20. *Breeze block layout 1*

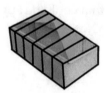

Figure 9-21. *Breeze block layout 2*

Okay, so the builders started the construction, applying layout no. 1, and having constructed the walls up to around 3 feet in height, they came across a significant problem:

- How was this wall ever going to support the weight of the high security door and frame (as depicted in Figure 9-22[39])?

Figure 9-22. *Class 3 style high security door*

The only options available to them were to either

- **Option 1**

  Undue all the work they had already done and start again.

- **Option 2**

  Create a second outer breeze block wall to create the desired thickness of the wall, for this to be deemed to be a secure room.

Although both options available came at additional cost and wasted time, option 2 was chosen as the better approach.

A point to note is that you should not assume that the engineers understand how the infrastructure should be correctly constructed or implemented. This was clear during the review of the perimeter fence line, when we observed such an error at a neighboring haulage yard (as depicted in Figure 9-23).

---

[39]www.securitydoorsdirect.co.uk/lps-1175-level-3/#iLightbox[product-gallery]/1

Figure 9-23. *Haulage yard*

- Are the fence posts facing in the right direction?

- Is the anti-climb protection (encircled in yellow) designed to deter an intruder breaking in or to deter an intruder from breaking out of the haulage yard?

- Does the wooden fence assist an intruder and, thus, reduce the effectiveness of their perimeter fence?

CCTV Security Survey

Another example from my time on Counter Intelligence operations happened during my appointment at RAF Linton On Ouse. At the time, we had the Protective Security oversight responsibilities for an auxiliary RAF station – RAF Church Fenton[40] (as depicted in Figures 9-24 and 9-25).

---

[40]www.rafchurchfenton.com/

Figure 9-24. *RAF Church Fenton main gate*

Figure 9-25. *RAF Church Fenton*

The OC RAF Police/Station security officer (SSyO) had become concerned that the aging CCTV system was not fit for purpose and may not even meet the legal requirements of the Data Protection Act 1998[41] (replaced by the EU GDPR, on May 25, 2018[42]).

---

[41]www.ic2cctv.com/pdfs/iC2-ico-compliance-guide.pdf

[42]https://ico.org.uk/for-organisations/guide-to-data-protection-1998/encryption/ scenarios/cctv/

My predecessor in the Counter Intelligence role had already carried out a Physical Security review of the CCTV system and had estimated the improvement work to be in the region of between £20,000 and £30,000.

However, on reviewing this survey work, there was no record of any OR 1 and 2 having been completed, and, therefore, the three supplier quotations appeared to have been "finger in the air" estimates.

I was left with no other option than to start the process all over again and started by reaching out to the key stakeholders to complete the initial OR 1 (as depicted in Figure 9-26[43]).

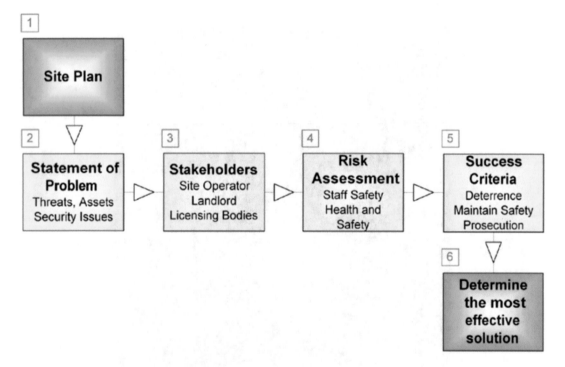

Figure 9-26. *Level 1 OR checklist*

---

[43]www.globalmsc.net/wp-content/uploads/2016/01/operational-requirements.pdf

Having completed OR 1, I was then better placed to complete OR 2 (as depicted in Figure 9-27[44]), and having completed these supporting documents and received key stakeholder approval that these were the requirements being needed to be addressed, I was well placed to reach out to the UK Government's Security Services Group (SSG[45]).

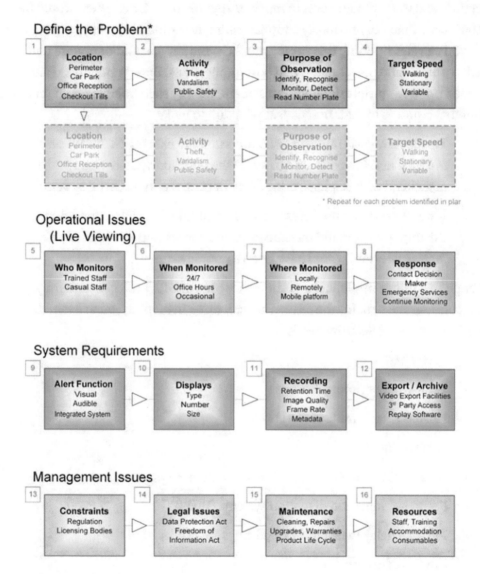

Figure 9-27. *Level 2 OR checklist*

[44]https://assets.publishing.service.gov.uk/government/uploads/system/uploads/attachment_data/file/378443/28_09_CCTV_OR_Manual2835.pdf

[45]www.gov.uk/government/groups/security-services-group

The next stage was for a representative from SSG to visit RAF Church Fenton to carry out a full security survey of the CCTV system.[46]

Following this CCTV site survey, the SSG report confirmed my suspicions. The CCTV was completely inappropriate and did not meet the legal requirements for data protection, and the estimated cost to replace/upgrade the CCTV system would be £100,000 more than the previously supplied estimate (around £120,000 to £130,000).

As you can see, by doing this survey properly, the key stakeholders were better placed to understand the situation and cost implications. Based upon this review, and based upon the proportionality assessment, the key stakeholders could make an informed decision as to their best causes of action to make.

- The decision was made to decommission the existing CCTV *(meeting the legal requirements)* and to avoid the unproportionate costs associated with implementing a "fit for purpose" new CCTV system.

- It was agreed that the investment of £20,000 to £30,000 to upgrade the existing system would have been inappropriate *(neither legal nor fit for purpose)* and would have been a poor investment.

I hope that this example helps to show the value of ORs, and, consequently, you should consider the benefits the OR format can bring in helping you to evaluate other areas of your Physical Security needs:[47]

- Flow chart

- Pedestrian perimeter barrier

- Hostile vehicle mitigation (HVM)

- Security lighting

- Closed-circuit television (CCTV) surveillance systems

- Perimeter intrusion detection systems (PIDS)

- Physical delay measures for buildings

- Control of access

---

[46]It is important to note that, at this point, I still had not engaged with any potential suppliers.

[47]www.frontierpitts.com/wp-content/uploads/Documents/Guide-to-producing-operational-requirements-for-security-measures.pdf

- Intrusion detection systems (IDS)

- Information Security (INFOSEC)

- Mail screening and security

- Procedures

- Guard hut

Telecommunications Electronics Materials Protected from Emanating Spurious Transmissions (TEMPEST)

Another area where the outer perimeter Physical Security controls become important is when you are processing highly sensitive information through an IT system and where this information is displayed on a CRT (cathode ray tube) or LCD (liquid crystal display).

With basic equipment, an opportunist attacker could intercept these electromagnetic emissions.[48] In the military, this threat was termed the TEMPEST threat,[49] but it also goes by the term Van Eck phreaking[50] (named after Wim van Eck's original technical analysis of the security risks of emanations from computer monitors), which was detailed in a University of Cambridge Technical Report[51] in 2003.

With this style of attack, the aggressor does not even need to gain access to layers 1–4 to steal this sensitive data. Depicted in Figure 9-28 is an example of the image that was intercepted by Cambridge University, at 3 meters away from the monitor.

---

[48]https://medium.com/knowledge-stew/a-computer-spying-method-youve-probably-never-heard-of-7e7008c72be6

[49]www.ncsc.gov.uk/information/tempest-and-electromagnetic-security

[50]https://searchsecurity.techtarget.com/definition/van-Eck-phreaking

[51]www.cl.cam.ac.uk/techreports/UCAM-CL-TR-577.pdf

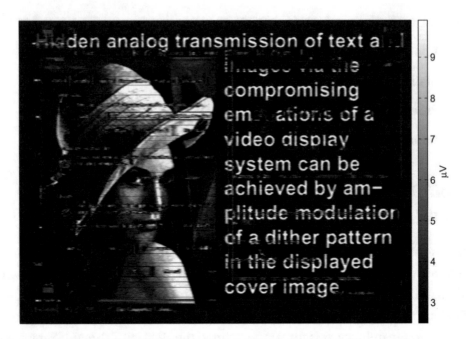

Figure 9-28. *Captured image*

Consequently, when an extremely sensitive briefing was to be carried out, part of the planning for this was to identify the measures that could be implemented to help prevent the leakage of such information.

Should this information have gotten into the wrong hands, it could have had grave consequences, and even though the likelihood of this happening was deemed to be extremely low, the potential impact was too great.

Consequently, where technical countermeasures[52] were not available for use, we would temporarily increase the Physical Security measures at levels 5–7. This would involve measures such as

- Prohibiting mobile electronic devices within the building and room

- Random entry/exit searches

- Carrying out the briefings within a secure internal compound

- Additional internal patrols

- Additional external patrols

---

[52]https://hollandshielding.com/Faraday-cages-EMI-RFI-shielded-tents-rooms-and-shielded-enclosures

All these measures were for the sole purpose of enhancing the 5 Ds of defense and helping to prevent unauthorized leakages of this extremely sensitive information.

Building BRIDGES

The BRIDGES acronym would have been extremely useful during the cost-saving decision-making process, following the acquisition of a large UK bank by another large UK bank.

Business Context

As a major competitor UK bank, they are requirements to ensure that any operations (which involve the processing of sensitive customer data) are proportionately protected from known threats.

However, the decision was made to save money by removing the Physical Security measures at layers 5–7 and to solely rely on a streamlined suite of countermeasures, at layers 1–4, for some of their most sensitive data processing facilities.

- Was this really a well-informed, risk-based, decision or one that was primarily driven by the potential cost savings?

Risk and Resilience

It is well known that banks are a valuable and attractive target for criminals, with the attackers being known for trying to gain unauthorized access to a bank's premises (e.g., in 2013, an organized criminal gang attempts to infiltrate the Banks of Barclays and Santander, to place a rogue device (KVM switch) to gain unauthorized access to the banking systems, to steal around £1.25 million[53]).

Additionally, this facility was in an area that had high crime rates for burglary, theft, and drugs (as depicted in Figure 9-29[54]).

---

[53]www.standard.co.uk/news/crime/cyber-gang-who-stole-125m-from-banks-guilty-of-fraud-9190978.html

[54]www.ukcrimestats.com/

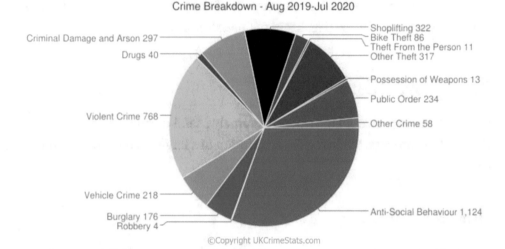

Figure 9-29. *Crime statistics*

Consequently, the Physical Security measures need to be proportionate enough to defend against the following types of physical security threats:[55,56]

- Terrorism

- Rogue employees

- Casual attitudes

- Unattended assets and areas

- Clandestine technical eavesdropping

- Social engineering

- Unauthorized use of a lost/stolen proximity card

- Forced entry

- Theft and burglary

- Use of a cloned proximity card[57]

- Vandalism

- Sabotage

---

[55]www.getkisi.com/blog/types-of-physical-security-threats
[56]www.charter-global.com/common-physical-security-threats/
[57]www.getkisi.com/blog/copy-clone-prox-hid-id-card

Identify and Isolate

The sensitive data processing facilities were housed in a multiple-occupancy compound (as depicted in Figure 9-30), in a large building, housing multiple internal business departments.

Figure 9-30. *UK banking HQ facility*

The location of this building had resided within its own complex, with two manned, barrier-controlled, points of access/egress where random entry searches were carried out.

Within the complex were a through road and several parking locations, which were monitored by CCTV, subject to frequent internal patrols, and a main building with two main points of access/egress (only one with a manned reception).

Access to this building was restricted to authorized personnel only using electronic automated access control (EAACS), via proximity card readers. Internal areas were restricted based upon individual access control rules, and in areas deemed to be more sensitive, the use of an additional personal identification number (PIN) was required.

Detect Anomalies

With the reduced number of Physical Security measures, the bank had an increasing reliance on the honesty and alerting capability of its employees to detect the presence of unauthorized access and rogue devices.

It is natural for employees to be trusting of others or feel comfortable with challenging others, and therefore "social engineering" has become such a lucrative attack surface for criminals.

People become overcomplacent when working within the relative security of the business premises, having gone through the various physical access control barriers. This creates the illusion that anything happening inside must be authorized.

Govern Processes

As part of this cost-cutting venture, the business decided that they no longer needed the senior Physical Security personnel responsible for the following responsibilities:

- Physical security management
- Strategy
- Tactical delivery
- Project management
- System management
- Team development
- Incident management and exercising
- Engagement with law enforcement and the National Counter Terrorism Security Office (NaCTSO[58])
- Delivering training and awareness for all colleagues and the security teams
- Physical Security audits and assessments
- Operational delivery

---

[58]www.gov.uk/government/organisations/national-counter-terrorism-security-office

- Supplier management

- Acting as the employees' first point of contact

- Threat and risk analysis and assessments

- Out-of-hours incident response

Evaluate Security Controls

Looking at the roles and responsibilities that were seen as being surplus to requirements, the organization had clearly disregarded the importance of ensuring that the range of Physical Security measures remained effective.

- **Who was going to "Police the Police"?**

  If a member of the security team decided to change or disable the configuration of a Physical Security system (e.g., disabling or changing the weight limit on a "mantrap" (depicted in Figure 9-31[59]), so that this no longer prevented two persons from entering the facility with just a single proximity card).

Figure 9-31. Mantrap

---

[59]www.cpni.gov.uk/cse/meesons-fpj140-2sx-semi-circular-portal?ref=ajax

Survive to Operate

One of the roles that was terminated during this review happened to be the individual who implemented and oversaw the Physical Security incident response and disaster recovery exercises.

I know from personal experience the inherent value of having personnel who are well trained in dealing with Physical Security incidents. Without effective training, an organization increases their risks associated with whom their employees will respond to a Physical Security incident. This is also known as the 4 Fs responses:[60]

- **Fight**

  To become aggressive

- **Flight**

  Running or fleeing the situation

- **Freeze**

  To literally become incapable of moving or making a choice

- **Fawn**

  Immediately moving to try to please a person to avoid any conflict

When "It Hits the Fan!", how confident are they that their employees will respond effectively?

Reality Bites

In March 2014, a malicious employee (a senior IT auditor) of the Morrisons[61] UK Supermarket had used a rogue USB stick to carry out the unauthorized downloading of the personal data details of almost 100,000 supermarket employees.[62]

---

[60]www.psychologytoday.com/gb/blog/addiction-and-recovery/202008/understanding-fight-flight-freeze-and-the-fawn-response#:~:text=Flight%20includes%20running%20or%20fleeing,person%20to%20avoid%20any%20conflict

[61]www.morrisons.com

[62]www.securityprivacybytes.com/2020/04/morrisons-data-breach-revisiting-the-rogue-employee-question/

Rogue employees of South Africa's Postbank stole the master encryption key,[63] leading to around $3.2 million in *(in excess of 25,000)* fraudulent transactions and a cost to the bank, of approximately $58 million, to replace around 12 million of its customers' payment cards.

Although I am not aware of the specific Physical Security measures that these organizations had in place, at the time of the incidents, there are Physical Security measures that could have provided additional defensive benefits.

For example, could the actions of these rogue employees have been deterred, defended, or detected, through the monitoring of the employees' access, supplemented with additional Physical Security measures, such as

- Random exit/entry searches (especially in areas of higher value/ sensitivity)

No doubt that the cost of managing and ensuring that these measures are effectively implemented is likely to be considerably less than the potential impact felt by these organizations.

It is important to remember that opportunist thieves may see a piece of technology by its "black market" resale value and not by the value of the data contained within the device.

As identified in the Ponemon Institute's investigation into the "Cost of a Stolen Laptop"[64] (as depicted in Figure 9-32[65]), the business value of the device could be considerably greater than the cost of the device itself.

---

[63]www.fintechfutures.com/2020/06/postbank-replaces-12m-cards-after-employees-steal-master-key/

[64]www.intel.com.au/content/dam/doc/white-paper/enterprise-security-the-cost-of-a-lost-laptop-paper.pdf

[65]https://visual.ly/community/Infographics/technology/cost-stolen-laptops-tablets-and-smartphones

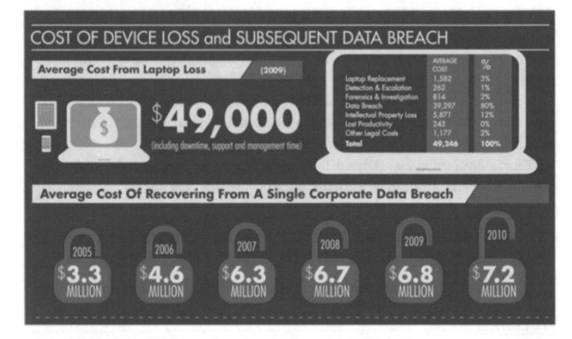

Figure 9-32.   *Cost of device loss*

If you were a business that is looking at implementing cost-saving measures and that might be thinking that streamlining your Physical Security operations might be an easy way to do this, I would recommend that you consider carrying out a BRIDGES assessment before doing so.

You might be surprised at what you discover from this.

Key Takeaways

- Physical Security is an essential component of an effective Protective Security strategy.

- Your approach needs to embrace the application of layered defensive layers that support the 5 Ds of defense.

  - **D**efend

  - **D**eny

  - **D**elay

- **D**etect

- **D**eter

- An effective Protective Security strategy will help your organization to mitigate and reduce the risks associated with both the traditional and nontraditional threat vectors.

- The defensive layers need to provide an appropriate level of defense proportionate to the perceived value of the business asset being protected.

- These defensive layers need to act in isolation and should become progressively more robust the closer you get to the valued asset.

- The MBMM type of format enables for a concise and consistent evaluation of the defensive layers that are in place.

- Operational Requirements ensure that any vendor's tender for work is based upon defined needs and, thus, removes the potential for the "finger in the air" quotations. Each vendor will be provided with the same specifications to quote for.

- An Operational Requirement reduces the potential for misguided Physical Security investments, where a procured solution proves to be unsuitable.

- Where a determined attacker is unable to compromise your systems through cyberspace, they will seek opportunities to exploit vulnerabilities in the physical environment.

- As businesses increasingly seek to embrace the digital revolution of the internal processes, there will be an increasing reliance on new technologies. These new technologies have an intrinsic value and become increasingly attractive to opportunist thieves, who may not be interested in the data that they contain but only concerned with the potential "black market" resale value.

- The theft of a laptop/mobile device has a far greater value than the mere costs associated with purchasing a replacement device.

CHAPTER 10

Industrial Systems Protective Security

Now, everybody, friends, and enemies alike, admit that the Red Army proved equal to its tremendous task. But this was not the case six years ago, in the period before the war.

As we know, prominent foreign journalists, and many recognized authorities on military affairs abroad, repeatedly stated that the condition of the Red Army roused grave doubts, that the Red Army was poorly armed and lacked a proper commanding staff, that its morale was beneath criticism, that while it might be fit for defense, it was useless for attack, and that, if struck by the German troops, the Red Army would collapse like "a colossus with feet of clay."

Such statements were made not only in Germany, but also in France, Great Britain, and America. Now we can say that the war refuted all these statements and proved them to have been groundless and ridiculous.

The war proved that the Red Army is not "a colossus with feet of clay," but a first-class modern army, equipped with the most up-to-date armaments, led by most experienced commanders, and possessing high morale and fighting qualities.[1]

Joseph Stalin (Figure 10-1[2])

---

[1]"Speech Delivered by Stalin at a Meeting of Voters of the Stalin Electoral District, Moscow," February 09, 1946, History and Public Policy Program Digital Archive, Gospolitizdat, Moscow, 1946. http://digitalarchive.wilsoncenter.org/document/116179

[2]www.military-history.org/articles/stalin-facts-10-little-known-facts.htm

© Jim Seaman 2021
J. Seaman, *Protective Security*, https://doi.org/10.1007/978-1-4842-6908-4_10

Figure 10-1. *Joseph Stalin*

Introduction

In Joseph Stalin's address to the Voters of the Stalin Electoral District meeting, he acknowledged the importance being equipped with the most up-to-date armaments played in their success during World War 2.

The supporting manufacturing deemed to be a critical process in their war efforts. The same applies in the modern business. If you are reliant on third-party suppliers to provide goods and services that are essential to your continued business operations, then your manufacturing suppliers, by their very nature, become one of your critical suppliers.

Consequently, you should be periodically engaging with those suppliers to ascertain how they ensure that the systems are adequately managed to protect them from harm and to ensure that they remain resilient.

For example, think about a large manufacturing company, such as Croda International PLC,[3] that are seeking to embrace digital transformation,[4] if this includes their manufacturing operations, providing the ingredients to the personal care industry:[5]

- How is this being managed with security and resilience in mind?

- How might this impact their business-to-business (B2B) customers?[6]

---

[3]www.croda.com/en-gb

[4]www.technologymagazine.com/brochure/croda-internationals-customer-focused-digital-transformation-through-strategic-partnerships

[5]www.crodapersonalcare.com/en-gb?utm_campaign=Industry%20News%20%22In-Cosmetics%20%20Roundtable%22%20Re-marketing%201&utm_source=blog&utm_medium=Industry%20News%20Incosmetic%20Roundtable%201&utm_term=Croda%20website&utm_content=external

[6]https://chemberry.com/company/croda?utm_campaign=Industry%20News%20%22In-Cosmetics%20%20Roundtable%22%20Re-marketing%201&utm_source=blog&utm_medium=IndustryNews%20Incosmetic%20Roundtable%201&utm_term=Croda%20landing%20page&utm_content=internal

- What impact will this have on their B2B clients, if the manufacturing IT systems were to be compromised?

  - **Integrity breach** – Incorrect manufacture of ingredients

  - **Availability** – Inability to deliver the ordered ingredients

This is something that you may not have considered, but in addition to being a Health and Safety[7] concern, because the manufacturing industry provides essential services to a large number of other businesses (a key link in the Supply Chain (as depicted in Figure 10-2)), they are increasingly becoming viable targets[8] for state-sponsored[9] or organized criminal groups (e.g., ransomware[10]).

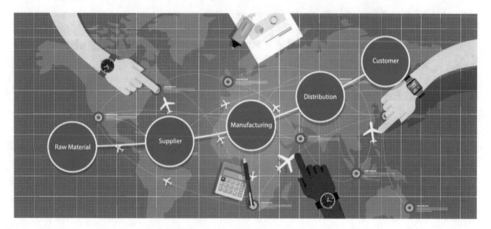

Figure 10-2. *Manufacturing Supply Chain*

As a result, it is essential for both the manufacturers and their clients to maintain an awareness of this threat and to effectively manage the risks associated with their embracement of the next industrial revolution.

---

[7]www.hse.gov.uk/eci/cyber-security.htm

[8]https://securityboulevard.com/2020/09/surge-in-cyberattacks-puts-manufacturing-ot-systems-at-risk/

[9]www.scadafence.com/state-sponsored-hackers-target-big-pharmaceuticals/

[10]www.infosecurity-magazine.com/news/manufacturing-ransomware-payments/

The Industrial Revolution

The world of manufacturing has gone through three major industrial revolutions[11] with the first starting in the eighteenth century, and this industry is now entering its fourth revolution (aka Industry 4.0[12]):

- **First Industrial Revolution – 1765**

  Driven by the mass extraction of coal and mechanization, the industry began to replace agriculture as the backbone of the societal economy.

  - The invention of the steam engine led to the accelerated adoption of manufacturing operations.

  - The manufacturing of the railroads resulted in a considerable acceleration in the world economies.

- **Second Industrial Revolution – 1870**

  Once again, it was the discovery of a new energy source (electricity, gas, and oil) that drove the next wave of technological advancements. During this phase, we saw the invention of an array of technical advancements (e.g., internal combustion engines, automobiles, aircraft, etc.).

  - To date, this is considered to have been the most important period in this industry.

- **Third Industrial Revolution – 1969**

  Can you guess what has been the driver for this revolution? Yes, you've guessed it – the creation of another energy source: nuclear energy! During this period, we saw the rise of electronics, telecommunications, and IT systems, which opened the doors to such things as space expeditions, research, and biotechnology.

---

[11]www.historic-uk.com/HistoryUK/HistoryofBritain/Timeline-Industrial-Revolution/

[12]www.intechopen.com/books/industry-4-0-current-status-and-future-trends/
industry-4-0-what-is-it-

- **Fourth Industrial Revolution – Present day**

  Now, driven by the exponential growth of technology (as depicted in Figure 10-3[13]), in accordance with Moore's Law,[14] manufacturing companies are seeking to revolutionize the operations. By taking advantage of intelligence, virtualization, and digital performance capabilities, they can improve operational efficiency and integrate factory-wide systems.

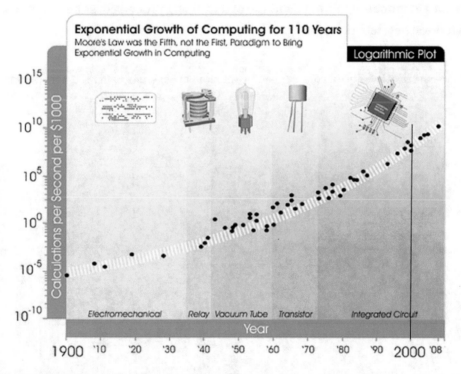

Figure 10-3. *Estimated technology growth*

---

[13]www.diamandis.com/blog/why-tech-is-accelerating

[14]www.technologyreview.com/2020/02/24/905789/were-not-prepared-for-the-end-of-moores-law/

Moore's Law[15]

This was a prediction made by American engineer Gordon Moore in **1965** that the number of transistors per silicon chip doubles every year.

With this exponential growth in the businesses and consumers embracing new technologies, we are seeing an equally increasingly rapid growth in the rates of cybercrime[16] (as depicted in Figure 10-4[17]).

As technology increased the data processing capabilities, the criminals adjusted their tactics to monetize this high volume of data being processed, stored, or transmitted through these new technologies.

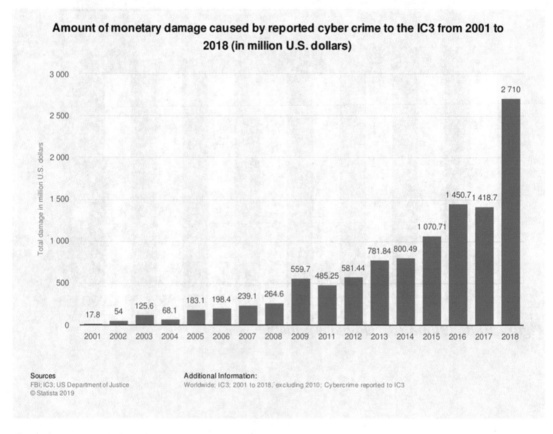

Figure 10-4. *Cybercrime monetary damage trends*

---

[15]www.britannica.com/technology/Moores-law

[16]www.webroot.com/blog/2019/04/23/the-evolution-of-cybercrime/

[17]www.weforum.org/agenda/2019/10/cyber-crime-and-security-business/

Consequently, considering the potential damage that can be caused by a compromised Industry 4.0 critical IT system, it becomes increasingly more important to ensure that these new technologies are proportionately protected.

Military Comparison

Although not a manufacturing business, military satellite operations rely on continuous or batched processing operations to keep their satellites functioning properly. This was evident during my time at RAF Oakhanger[18] (as depicted in Figure 10-5[19]), where the supporting IT systems and networks needed to be carefully managed and maintained.

Figure 10-5. *RAF Oakhanger*

---

[18]www.flightglobal.com/secure-communications/18495.article
[19]https://latitude.to/satellite-map/gb/united-kingdom/86999/raf-oakhanger

With the IT systems that support the satellite operations being so important, maintaining their security, operability, and resilience was never ignored. Instead, these were subject to rigorous change management, risk assessment, and prioritized schedules.

It all started by ensuring that the estate was fully understood (e.g., all network connections, authorized hardware and software, approved functions/ports/protocols/services, data types, data/communication flows and third parties having been identified). For any assets/operations that were deemed to be critical, alternate, and redundant, supporting services were established, based upon the results of the formal capacity and contingency planning.

Following up on this, each system component was then categorized for their importance to the satellite operations, and specific roles and responsibilities were formally assigned to ensure that appropriate security safeguard was established, as part of an integrated defense-in-depth security strategy.

Within this comprehensive strategy was the inclusion of periodic risk assessments and reviews to ensure the timely identification of any additional resources needed to mitigate any identified risks. These risk management practices would also address the agreement of well-timed conduct performance/load testing and penetration testing to ensure minimal impact on the satellite operations.

Being a highly specialist operation, you may imagine that not everything could be carried out using the "in-house" engineering teams, and there was a considerable reliance on third-party suppliers. Consequently, these suppliers were subject to robust management practices, where strict contractual clauses, covering the need to maintain effective protective security practices, were mandated, along with comprehensive risk assessments to ensure that these organizations would not be introducing unsafe/insecure working practices into the environment.

My role was to ensure the physical security defense-in-depth measures (at this and the other satellite locations) remained effective and that the team remained well trained to respond to and deal with any security incidents that could impact the 24/7 operations. The physical security architectural design had similarities to that seen in the Purdue model:[20]

---

[20]www.checkpoint.com/downloads/products/cp-industrial-control-ics-security-blueprint.pdf

Main Zone

- Level 5: Enterprise network

  Technically not part of the Satellite Operations environment, the enterprise zone had connectivity to the Satellite Operations environment.

- Level 4: Business logistics systems

  Enterprise resource planning (ERP) systems managed the business-related activities of the Satellite Operations. It supported the administration operations required to keep the Satellite Operations functioning.

  - DMZ

    This was the interconnect zone between Satellite Operations and operational technology (OT) systems; this zone acted as the buffer zone between the environments.

Satellite Operations Zone

- Level 3: Satellite Operations systems

  The purpose of level 3 systems is to manage production workflows to produce the desired products.

- Level 2: Control systems

  Level 2 systems supervised, monitored, and controlled the physical processes.

- Level 1: Intelligent devices

  Level 1 systems sensed and manipulated the physical processes.

Level 0: Physical Process

Level 0 systems defined the actual physical processes.

In Figure 10-6, you can see the similarities between the intent of the Purdue model for secure architecture and the physical architecture design at one of RAF Oakhanger's auxiliary satellite locations.

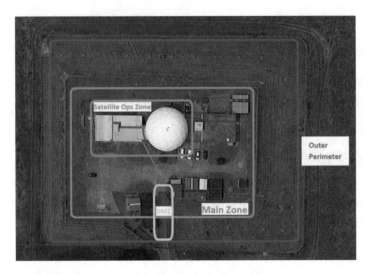

Figure 10-6. *Secure architecture at auxiliary site*

During this time, we carried out a full-blown practical exercise where the layered defenses helped us to effectively respond to a simulated terrorist attack. During the attack, improvised explosive devices (IEDs) had been detonated, and, while waiting for the arrival of the local emergency services (Police, Fire, and Ambulance), I was appointed into the role of "Silver Commander," responsible for supervising the immediate action drills to ensure the preservation of life and the containment of the scenes and the preservation of evidence while minimizing the impact on critical operations.

This exercise proved to be an extremely rewarding and helped to confirm the Joint Emergency Services team's ability to work together to ensure that the organization was suitably prepared, able to detect and analyze the situation and contain, eliminate, and quickly recover from the attack.

The exercise simulated an attacker who knew that the facility was a target of interest but was not privy to which parts of the facility were critical to the delivery of critical services.

Consequently, two large explosions were simulated in the buildings adjacent to the most critical areas of operations. This included the safe and secure use of pyrotechnics, smoke machines, and debris to provide a realistic "shock and awe" simulation (as depicted in Figure 10-7) for the teams to respond to.

Figure 10-7. *Explosion after effects*

The response teams needed to respond in such a manner that the situation could be contained, allowing minimal disruption and impact to the critical services, to help ensure that the delivery of the essential military satellite communications,[21] safely and effectively, could continue throughout this incident.

- **How varied are your security incidents?**

- **Have you considered a wide range of threats (both traditional and nontraditional)?**

- **Have you included the consideration for the impact of a terrorist attack scenario against your product development and production environments?**

Manufacturing Your Secure Environments

Much like the network and systems that supported the military satellite operations, there is a requirement for high availability, that is, these systems need to be permanently available (no matter what happens).

High availability relies on high-level redundancies and fault tolerances, and effective contingency planning/responses, to ensure that uptime is maintained.

---

[21]www.rafmuseum.org.uk/blog/the-original-skynet/

Within the manufacturing sector (as depicted in Figure 10-8[22]), there tend to be two types of industrial system control models:[23]

Figure 10-8. *Chemical processing plant*

- **Traditional**[24]

    A traditional model tends to be most prevalent in those conventional manufacturing businesses (as depicted in Figure 10-9[25]), such as those that have long-standing industrial plants (e.g., manufacture of specialty chemicals that are sold to various industries) and where the business executives only see the profits that these operational systems provide to the business.

---

[22]www.amarinth.com/specialist-industries/chemical/

[23]www.tradeandindustrydev.com/industry/manufacturing/traditional-industrial-vs-advanced-manufacturing-t-8304

[24]www.manufacturingglobal.com/technology/why-traditional-manufacturing-theories-dont-work

[25]www.shopfloor.org/2018/02/amgen-plans-build-new-300-million-biologics-manufacturing-plant-due-tax-reform/

Figure 10-9. *Traditional manufacturing plant*

In these types of operations, the supporting networks and architecture tend to be on stand-alone local area networks (LANs), without any external connections, and are only subject to the minimal upgrades and maintenance schedules. These environments tend to lean toward keeping the assets running with minimal investment and insignificant security measures implemented.

- In most cases, supporting IT Operations team have a confidence in delivering and supporting normal business systems but see industrial systems as a bit of an enigma. Consequently, because of their importance to the business, they adopt the bare minimum approach to ensure that the costs remain low and to ensure that they reduce the risks of their security program being the cause of an outage.

- In these types of models, the supporting systems tend to be completely isolated, with increasingly close to (or beyond) their end of life, with negligible failover measures and only a token gesture for risk and security management.

- Their mantra tends to be

If it isn't broken, then don't try and fix it!

- **Advanced**

    This is where the manufacturers have embraced the introduction of innovative technologies to help improve products or production processes.

    Many manufacturers may believe that they are embracing new technologies by moving their sales support systems to the cloud. However, their industrial systems continue to use the "safer" traditional model.

    The true advanced manufacturing models are those businesses that start to recognize the value of slowly replacing some of their traditional industrial systems with innovative technologies, to enhance their competitiveness and increase their value.

    Businesses that are considering, or implementing, advanced manufacturing plant equipment (as depicted in Figure 10-10[26]) are increasingly seeing the value of such things as[27]

- **Autonomous robots**

    A new generation of automation systems connects industrial robots with control systems through information technology. New robots and automation systems equipped with sensors and standardized interfaces have begun to supplement (and in some cases eliminate) labor in many processes. This allows manufacturers to cost-effectively produce smaller-scale products and improve their ability to improve quality.

- **Integrated Computational Materials Engineering (ICME)**

    By creating a computer model of a product and simulating its performance before the product is manufactured, instead of building and testing multiple physical prototypes, engineers and designers can develop products better, faster, and cheaper.

---

[26]www.novartis.com/stories/discovery/new-drug-manufacturing-tools-change-pharma-chemistry

[27]www.market-prospects.com/articles/what-is-advanced-manufacturing#:~:text=Advanced%20manufacturing%20is%20the%20use%20of%20innovative%20technologies%20and%20methods,and%20flexibility%20to%20the%20market

- **Digital manufacturing**

  Virtualization technology can be used to generate a complete digital factory that simulates the entire production process. Among other things, digital simulation can help engineers save time and money by optimizing factory layout, identifying and automatically correcting defects in each step of the production process, and modeling product quality and output. The entire assembly line can be copied to different locations at a relatively low cost.

- **Industrial Internet and flexible automation**

  Manufacturing hardware can be linked together so that machines can communicate with each other and automatically adjust production based on data generated by sensors. They can "see" the supply chain.

- **Additive manufacturing**

  The additive manufacturing process is commonly referred to as 3D printing, which creates three-dimensional objects based on digital models by continuously depositing thin layers of material. Such processes have already been used for prototyping in certain industries, including aerospace, automotive parts, and basic consumer products. In the future, it is expected that these processes will be used to manufacture small batches of a product made of solid material, such as hollow balls without seams.

Figure 10-10. *Advanced drug manufacturing plant*

Establishing the Baseline

Much the same as the methodology applied for effective Protective Security, you need to start by knowing the business context (e.g., How important is the continued production? Are there scheduled periods where acceptable reduced productivity or closedown operations are already in place? What are the future aspirations for the manufacturing side of the business?), understanding the perceived threats and initial risks (as depicted in Figure 10-11[28]), and identifying and categorizing the supporting assets based upon the importance of their role within the manufacturing operations.

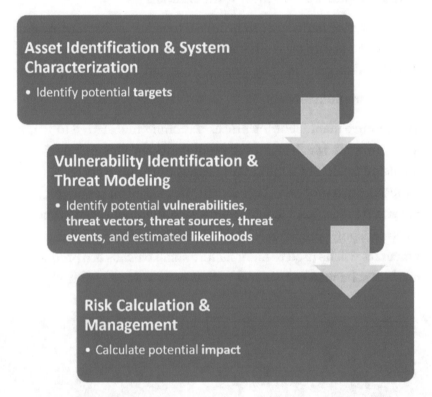

Figure 10-11. *ICS risk steps*

---

[28]Bodungen, C., Singer B, Scheeb, A., Wilhoit, K. and Scambray, J. (2017). Hacking Exposed Industrial Control Systems.

The Purdue reference model for ICS[29] describes the value of identifying all the major interdependencies and interworking between all major components in a major ICS environment. As shown in Figure 10-12,[30] these are categorized across zones and levels:

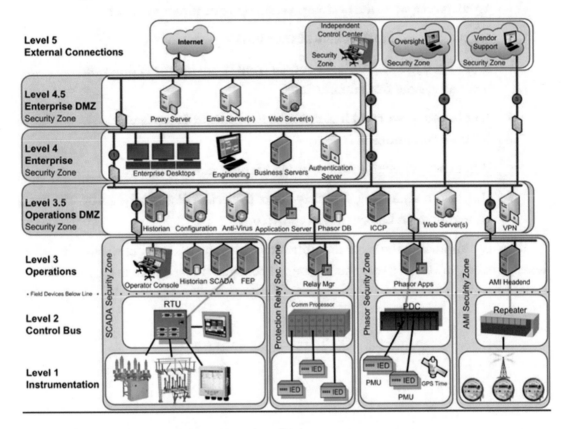

Figure 10-12. *Five-level ICS control architecture*

Whether the manufacturing element of your business is using the traditional or advanced models, or a hybrid of both, or you are deemed as being a critical national infrastructure operation[31] (or not), I think you will agree that this part of the organization is deemed to be a valuable part of the business.

---

[29]Johnson, Jay. (2017). Roadmap for Photovoltaic Cyber Security.

[30]www.pnnl.gov/main/publications/external/technical_reports/PNNL-20776.pdf

[31]www.cpni.gov.uk/critical-national-infrastructure-0

Consequently, if you agree that this is something that is critical for your business, wouldn't you want to ensure that it is well maintained and protected from harm? Think of it as being like the braking system on your car.

- **Would you ignore the braking system on your motor vehicle?**

- **Do you appreciate the value of your braking systems?**

- **Would you want to protect yourself from harm by protecting your braking system from tampering?**

- **Would you be worried if your brake fluid was to degrade or become contaminated?**

- **What about checking for corrosion of the brake lines?**

- **How about managing the lifecycles of the brake discs and pads by changing them before they are worn out?**

If you can appreciate the value for protecting your vehicle's braking systems (as depicted in Figure 10-13[32]), why should you not consider doing the same for your ICS environment?

---

[32]www.howacarworks.com/basics/how-the-braking-system-works#:~:text=A%20typical%20
dual%2Dcircuit%20braking,reservoir%20that%20keeps%20it%20full

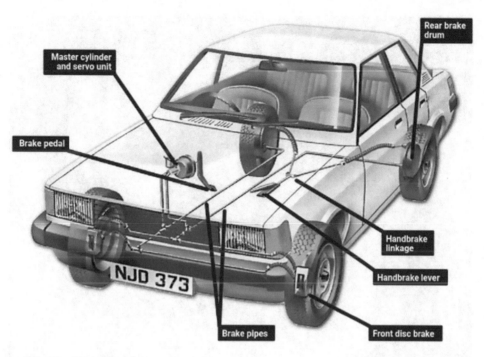

Figure 10-13. *Dual braking system*

Very much like the maintenance of a motor vehicle, you need to be periodically inspecting the systems for signs of tampering, wear and tear, and aging and to be monitoring their end of life.

Additionally, you should ensure that only approved personnel are allowed access to operate (or carry out maintenance on) the braking system.

Like owning a vehicle (as depicted in Figure 10-14), you should provide all personnel with a reference handbook and keep a record of the maintenance/change schedules.

Figure 10-14. *Vehicle owners' handbook and maintenance record*

This will help the individuals to understand and follow the rules and procedures associated with their role and be suitably trained to ensure that they are able to complete their tasks safely and securely.

Additionally, you should implement an appropriate Protective Security standard for your ICS operations. For example, you could choose to apply the countermeasures provided from the following industry controls standards[33]:

- **IEC 62443-4-2:2019**[34] – Security for industrial automation and control systems – Part 4-2: Technical security requirements for IACS components

- **NIST SP800-82**[35] – Guide to Industrial Control Systems (ICS) Security

---

[33]https://scadahacker.com/library/Documents/Standards/IEEE%20-%20Comparison%20of%20 SCADA%20Security%20Standards.pdf

[34]https://webstore.iec.ch/publication/34421#additionalinfo

[35]https://csrc.nist.gov/publications/detail/sp/800-82/rev-2/final

- **API Standard 1164**[36] – Pipeline SCADA Security, Second Edition

- **Australian Standard AS 7770**[37] – Rail Cyber Security

- **NISTIR 8183 Rev. 1**[38] – Cybersecurity Framework Version 1.1
  Manufacturing Profile

- **The Committee on National Security Systems Instruction (CNSSI),
  No. 1253, version 2**[39] – Security Categorization and Control Selection
  for National Security Systems

If you are a member of the board of directors, or other senior business decision-makers in a manufacturing type of business, or a client being provided manufactured products by such an organization, you should ensure that you have a clear understanding of the risks associated with the industrial control systems.

To effectively achieve this, you need to ensure that the following measures are in place (as depicted in Figure 10-15[40]):

- Assets have been identified and categorized, with connected systems being documented.

  - Asset inventory

  - Network diagrams

  - Communication flow diagrams

  - Data flow diagrams

- Threats have been identified and analyzed.

- Defined security objectives have been established and documented.

- Risks are analyzed and periodically reviewed/reassessed.

---

[36] https://scadahacker.com/library/Documents/Standards/API%20-%201164%20-%20
Pipeline%20SCADA%20Security%202nd%20ed.pdf

[37] https://scadahacker.com/library/Documents/Standards/Au-RISSB%20-%20AS-7770%20-%20
Rail%20Cyber%20Security%20v2.0.pdf

[38] https://csrc.nist.gov/publications/detail/nistir/8183/rev-1/final

[39] https://scadahacker.com/library/Documents/Standards/CNSS%20-%20Security%20
Categorization%20and%20Control%20Selection%20for%20National%20Security%20
Systems%20-%20CNSSI-1253R2.pdf

[40] https://serwiss.bib.hs-hannover.de/frontdoor/deliver/index/docId/1136/file/IT+Sec
urity+in+Production+Facilities_07-2017.pdf

- Individual countermeasures have been identified, and their effectiveness is being periodically assessed.

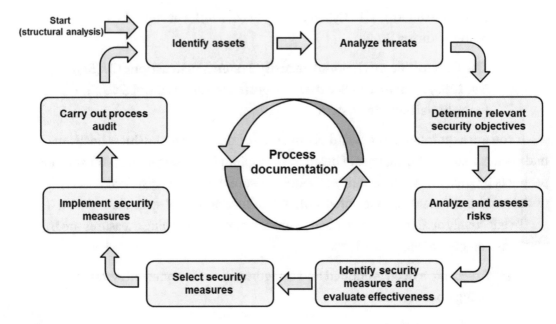

Figure 10-15. *ICS PDCA model*

Whether or not your ICS environment has a site-to-site or Internet connection, you need to ensure that the measures that are in place can provide a proportionate defense-in-depth protection from both the virtual and physical perspectives.

Without this, you will increase the risk of an opportunist attacker being able to exploit an unknown vulnerability, for example:

- If you invite specialist engineers in to carry out maintenance, have you closed their remote access?

- If the corporate IT teams carry out a remote task, have they terminated their connection between the ICS and the corporate environments (i.e., gone through the formal firewall change process before and afterward)?

- In a stand-alone LAN, there may be a greater confidence that the attack surfaces have been minimized. However, what if an organized or state-sponsored criminal group can infiltrate the physical environment?

- Criminals can gain unauthorized access (e.g., imitating a specialist engineer, cloning[41] a radio frequency identification (RFID) or near-field communication (NFC)[42] telemetry access card, etc. (as depicted in Figures 10-16[43] and 10-17[44])).

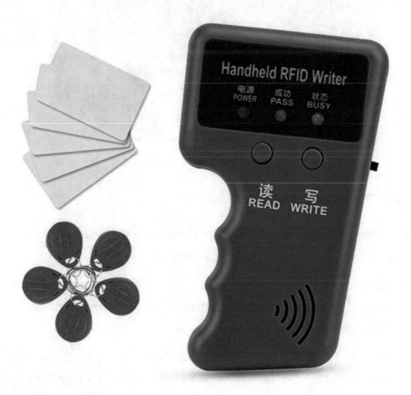

Figure 10-16. *Handheld RFID copier and writer*

---

[41]www.getkisi.com/blog/how-to-copy-access-cards-and-keyfobs
[42]www.getkisi.com/guides/rfid-access-control
[43]www.amazon.co.uk/dp/B07DQR7GW9/ref=cm_sw_em_r_mt_dp_wDCGFbC7E3GB8
[44]https://hackerwarehouse.com/product/proxmark3-kit/

Figure 10-17. *Proxmark3 kit*

- What about them just "tailgating" onto the authorized access credentials of an industrial site worker?

- How about a strategically placed rogue USB stick that could be picked up by an authorized industrial site worker and plugged into the stand-alone LAN?

- How about an industrial site worker being fed up not having the convenience of an Internet connection and so creating their own rogue access point (as depicted in Figure 10-18[45])?

---

[45]https://shop.hak5.org/

Figure 10-18. *Wi-Fi pineapple*

Remember that even in the military, there is never the thought that they are 100% secure. However, they understand that there is an ever-present threat and that they need to apply proportionate countermeasures to reduce the risks to within acceptable tolerances/appetites.

The same approach should be applied to any of your industrial environments, as these are most likely to be one of your valuable business assets and need to be proportionately protected from your opportunist attackers.

You only need to read the latest threat articles and reports (as depicted in Figure 10-19[46]) to get a better appreciation of just how prevalent the threat might be for your organization.

---

[46]https://ics-cert.kaspersky.com/reports/2020/09/15/the-state-of-industrial-cybersecurity-2020/

Industrial cybersecurity drivers in 2020

How the pandemic impacted businesses:

53%	24%	24%	23%
Increased levels of remote working	Reduced cybersecurity budgets	Developed cybersecurity plans for disasters	Experienced delays implementing cybersecurity measures

Tech trends forcing revised industrial cybersecurity practices:

55%	55%	36%	33%
Industrial IoT	Cloud and SaaS	Edge computing	5G

Ongoing digitalization

44% are working on cybersecurity initiatives for digital OT transformation

Prioritizing sustainable development

44% have or plan to introduce environment-related roles such as a Chief Sustainability Officer

98% believe that this role will elevate cybersecurity within their company

© 2020 AO Kaspersky Lab
Source: 'The State of Industrial Cybersecurity in the Era of Digitalization'. ARC Advisory Group and Kaspersky, 2020.

Figure 10-19. *The State of Industrial Cybersecurity 2020*

Building BRIDGES

Just like the importance a braking system plays into the ability for a motor vehicle to operate safely and ensure the protection of its occupants and other road users, the ICS environment can be just as important to its business and the organization's clients/partners.

Consequently, it is important to understand its importance and to ensure that this is appropriately managed. Once again, the BRIDGES acronym can be used to break down this part of the business.

Business Context

In the United Kingdom, chemical manufacturing is just one of the 13 critical national infrastructure types, which are required to meet a minimum level of regulatory expectations,[47] which help to clearly outline the business context for these types of organization:

- Chemicals
- Civil nuclear
- Communications
- Defense
- Emergency services
  - Police
  - Ambulance
  - Fire services
  - Coast Guard
- Energy
- Finance
- Food
- Government

---

[47]www.ncsc.gov.uk/section/private-sector-cni/cni

- Health

- Space

- Transport and water

The UK Government has defined critical national infrastructure organizations as being

Those critical elements of infrastructure (namely assets, facilities, systems, networks or processes and the essential workers that operate and facilitate them), the loss or compromise of which could result in:

a) *Major detrimental impact on the availability, integrity, or delivery of essential services – including those services whose integrity, if compromised, could result in significant loss of life or casualties – taking into account significant economic or social impacts; and/or*

b) *Significant impact on national security, national defense, or the functioning of the state.*

What if you are not one of these industry types or are not located in the United Kingdom?

Within the European Union, as from May 13, 2018, any critical national infrastructure entities, operating within the European Union, need to align with the network and information systems (NIS),[48] which has fines that are comparable to the General Data Protection Regulation (GDPR).[49]

A similar approach was taken by the United States when, on November 16, 2018, President Trump signed into law the Cybersecurity and Infrastructure Security Agency Act of 2018.[50] Additionally, there is InfraGard[51] which is a partnership between the Federal Bureau of Investigation (FBI) and members of the private sector designed to help with the protection of the US Critical Infrastructure.

However, if your business is not in a country that has regulatory requirements for critical national infrastructures or you're not one of these business types, it is still extremely likely that your key stakeholders will have an opinion on how important the manufacturing processing operations are to the business and its clients.

---

[48]https://ec.europa.eu/digital-single-market/en/network-and-information-security-nis-directive

[49]https://gdpr-info.eu/

[50]www.hsdl.org/?view&did=818949

[51]www.infragard.org/

Consequently, it is extremely important to reach out to these key stakeholders, so that you can ascertain an appreciation for their viewpoints. This will be particularly important to ensure that any strategy remains proportionate to the business perspectives.

Risk and Resilience

When evaluating the risk to your ICS environments, you need to consider the following subject areas:

- **Threat sources**

    This is the person or thing that initiates an event. Unlike a threat actor, this includes nonhuman-based events (i.e., natural disasters) and includes accidental actions, where no malicious intent was involved.

- **Targets**

    This is the person or asset that is affected by the threat source *(sometimes referred to as an asset)*.

- **Vulnerabilities**

    These are the conditions *(aka weakness)* which provide the opportunity for the threat source to affect the target.

- **Threat vectors**

    This is the path by which the threat source can access the vulnerabilities.

- **Threat events**

    This is when an event occurs that affects the target.

- **Probability**

    This is a forecast for the likelihood that a threat event will successfully affect the target.

The next two subject areas are often thought to be the same, but in an ICS environment, it is best to identify each of their specific distinguishing features.

- **Consequence**

  This is the direct result of a threat event, for example, the causal effect results in a system operating outside of its intended purpose (*disruption of services/operations, power outage, explosion, hazardous waste leakage, arbitrary code execution, etc.*).

- **Impact**

  This is the degree to which the consequence affects the business, third parties, operations, revenue, the environment, and so on.

During an ICS risk assessment, you should consider the stages depicted in Figure 10-20.

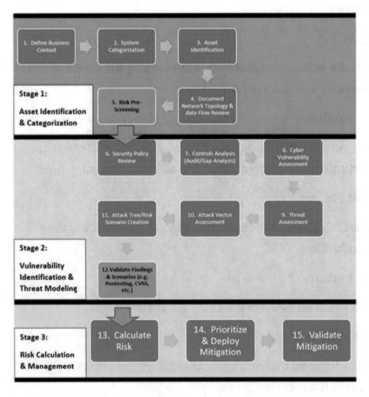

Figure 10-20. *ICS risk assessment steps*

Identify and Isolate

It is essential that all ICS assets are identified, categorized, and documented in asset inventories, network, and data flow diagrams to show the connections and clear delineation between isolated environments (as depicted in Figure 10-21[52]).

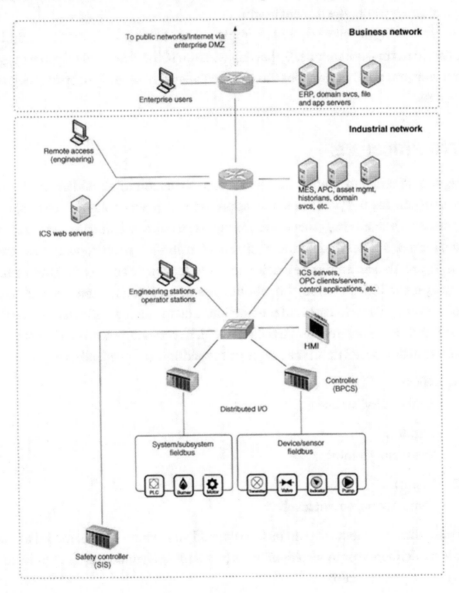

Figure 10-21. *High-level network diagram*

---

[52]Knapp, E., Langill, J. and Samani, R., 2015. Industrial Network Security. Amsterdam [etc.]: Elsevier/Syngress.

Detect Anomalies

Having an understanding of the business context and the assets that support the ICS environment(s), you are now able to feed this information into the monitoring processes, to ensure that your teams are able to quickly detect ABNORMAL activities or impactful events occurring within the ICS environment.

Any monitoring activities should be implemented in such a way that it minimizes the disruption to normal operations. By liaising with the ICS site managers, you can agree on a monitoring practice that provides the required degree of security oversight aligned to the business.

Govern Processes

Nothing should be left to chance, and, as a result, all personnel should be made aware of the rules (policies and processes) that apply to their specific roles and be subject to comprehensive onboarding procedures *(to include security familiarization/awareness training)* for new starters and periodic refresher/on-the-job security awareness training.

In the event that an employee carries out a nonmalicious activity that threatens the security of the ICS operation, they should be subject to further measures to remind them of the potential seriousness of their actions and to convey the message that this is something that the organization wants to avoid. In essence, you are seeking to apply levels of escalation based upon the severity or repetition of the mistakes made:

1. **Warn**
    Shift supervisor level

2. **Caution**
    Site manager level

3. **Report**
    Senior management level

All events and incidents should be investigated and, where it is deemed that the actions were deliberate or repeated offences (escalating beyond level 3), should be subject to disciplinary action.

Evaluate Security Controls

When evaluating the effectiveness of your security controls, you need to employ a combination of manual and automated approaches. The manual (audit) process should involve an agreed schedule to apply a combination of document reviews, process observations, and interviews to ascertain the effectiveness of the internal processes, which can be scored based on the perceived levels of maturity (as depicted in Figure 10-22[53]).

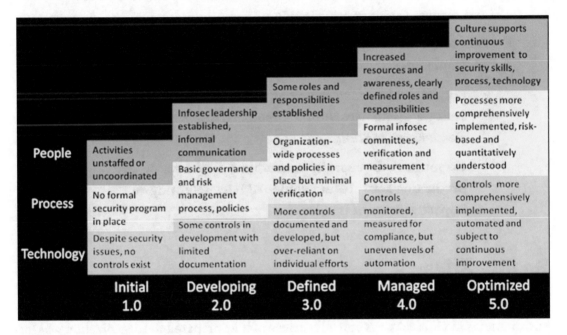

	Initial 1.0	Developing 2.0	Defined 3.0	Managed 4.0	Optimized 5.0
People	Activities unstaffed or uncoordinated	Infosec leadership established, informal communication	Some roles and responsibilities established	Increased resources and awareness, clearly defined roles and responsibilities	Culture supports continuous improvement to security skills, process, technology
Process	No formal security program in place	Basic governance and risk management process, policies	Organization-wide processes and policies in place but minimal verification	Formal infosec committees, verification and measurement processes	Processes more comprehensively implemented, risk-based and quantitatively understood
Technology	Despite security issues, no controls exist	Some controls in development with limited documentation	More controls documented and developed, but over-reliant on individual efforts	Controls monitored, measured for compliance, but uneven levels of automation	Controls more comprehensively implemented, automated and subject to continuous improvement

Figure 10-22. *Maturity levels*

There are several automated security tools available that can help you instantly gauge that the security controls[54] are effective. However, these should be treated as being complementary to the manual evaluations.

---

[53]https://security-architect.com/how-to-assess-security-maturity-and-roadmap-improvements/

[54]https://sectools.org/

Survive to Operate

Think that things will break or go wrong, so it is important to understand the impact of such events and to make plans that will reduce the effects of such an event. When deciding on what contingency measures are suitable, it is important to weigh this up against the potential cost of the occurrence of various scenarios.

- **How long will it take for your team to identify, respond to, contain, and recover from a specific incident?**

- **How long is an acceptable amount of time to have inoperable ICS environments?**

  - **Should you be considering redundancy, such as an Active Failover[55] (*aka Asynchronous Failover, Resilient Single, Active-Passive, or Hot Standby*)?**

  - **Do you have the capacity in another ICS to cover the lost production activities at another ICS site, following an impactful event or incident?**

Reality Bites

In the past few years, we have seen a rise in ransomware attacks that have impacted ICS environments in different ways and all because of how prepared the organization was for such an occurrence:

- **Honda[56]**

  In 2017, their ICS plant in Japan was forced to temporarily halt production after it suffered a cyber-attack from the same ransomware (WannaCry) that struck hundreds of thousands of computers worldwide last month.

---

[55]www.arangodb.com/docs/stable/architecture-deployment-modes-active-failover.html
[56]www.industryweek.com/technology-and-iiot/cybersecurity/article/22020489/
honda-halts-production-at-japan-plant-after-cyber-attacks

- Again, in 2020, Honda was impacted by another ransomware (snake) attack.[57]

- **Taiwan Semiconductor Manufacturing Company (TSMC)**[58]

  In 2018, almost 18 months after the MS17-10 security alert, this organization was crippled after an unpatched system (and connected to the ICS network) was infected by the WannaCry ransomware software.

  - The shutdown is believed to have cost the company roughly **$250 million** and will result in shipment delays.[59]

- **Norsk Hydro**[60]

  In 2019, the Norwegian aluminum giant Norsk Hydro was targeted by a ransomware (LockerGoga) attack, which forced the company to operate "using pen and paper," without the ability to rely on technology.

  - The attack cost Norsk Hydro up to **$75 million**.

- **Tesla**[61]

  In 2020, Tesla was the target of a ransomware attack. The criminals' plan was to use a Russian Tesla employee to target the electric car company's 1.9 million square meter factory in Sparks, Nevada (as depicted in Figure 10-23), which produces batteries for vehicles and energy storage units.

---

[57]www.bbc.co.uk/news/technology-52982427

[58]www.skyboxsecurity.com/blog/tsmc-wannacry/

[59]www.binarydefense.com/threat_watch/tsmc-hit-by-ransomware-attack/#:~:text=TSMC%20
said%20that%20a%20number,will%20result%20in%20shipment%20delays

[60]https://rusi.org/sites/default/files/20200928_braw_greyzone_exercises_web.pdf

[61]www.keepnetlabs.com/how-did-tesla-ransomware-attack-happen/

Figure 10-23. *Tesla Gigafactory*

However, owing to their effective security program, having an effective Protective Security program allowed this insider the opportunity to report this event back to the business, enabling the organization to avert this targeted attack.

- This clearly shows the value of embracing your "human communications network" to alert the business of any potentially harmful developments.

Key Takeaways

- There are three distinct rules that should define your ICS Protective Security strategy:

  - The belief that nothing is ever fully secure.

  - All software can be hacked.

  - The attackers will seek any opportunity to attack.

- As depicted in Figure 10-24,[62] an effective ICS security program must not be confined to being purely an IT-centric approach.

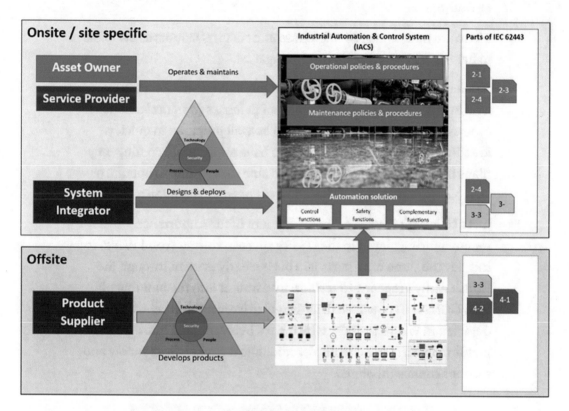

Figure 10-24. *IEC 62443 holistic Protective Security concept*

- The preventative/protective countermeasures need to be proportionate to the identified risks.

- It is extremely important to understand the potential attack paths and consequences against a variety of consequences.

- The ICS environment should be constructed using defined zones and levels, with access and changes being strictly controlled and subjected to risk assessments.

---

[62]Kobes, P. (2017). Guideline Industrial Security.

- The threats to the ICS operations are real, and the Protective Security bar needs to be set higher than for most corporate business environments.

- There are numerous ICS references and security standards available to help an ICS baseline themselves against.

- A determined, state-sponsored, or highly skilled attacker may be able to breach even the most robust of defenses *(and accidents will happen)*. Consequently, you need to be well prepared to quickly identify an impactful incident and to have appropriate contingency plans in place, to ensure that you are able to continue to operate or are able to quickly bounce back to near normal operations.

- Just like Joseph Stalin's acknowledgment of the importance manufacturing played in the USSR's success, during World War 2, to this day the same remains true. This is clearly evident through the British Army's recent **£16 million** investment into the building of the FUCHS are six-wheeled, all-wheel drive, armored vehicles (as depicted in Figure 10-25[63]), which have been adapted into a protected platform to carry out chemical, radiological, and nuclear survey and reconnaissance missions.

Figure 10-25. *Vehicle upgrade*

---

[63]https://des.mod.uk/fuchs-cbrn-vehicles-army-enhanced/?portfolioCats=69%2C735%2C29
0%2C734%2C726

CHAPTER 11

Securing Your Supply Chain

The line of supply may be said to be as vital to the existence of an army as the heart to the life of a human being.

Just as the duelist who finds his adversary's point menacing him with certain death, and his own guard astray, is compelled to conform to his adversary's movements, and to content himself with warding off his thrusts, so the commander whose communications are suddenly threatened finds himself in a false position, and he will be fortunate if he has not to change all his plans, to split up his force into more or less isolated detachments, and to fight with inferior numbers on ground which he has not had time to prepare, and where defeat will not be an ordinary failure, but will entail the ruin or surrender of his whole army.[1]

Colonel G.F.R Henderson (Figure 11-1[2])

---

[1]Henderson, G., Malcolm, N. and Roberts, F., 1933. The Science Of War. London: Longmans, Green.

[2]www.librarything.com/author/hendersongfr

© Jim Seaman 2021
J. Seaman, *Protective Security*, https://doi.org/10.1007/978-1-4842-6908-4_11

Figure 11-1. *Col. Henderson*

Introduction

The Defence Manual of Security (Joint Services Publication 440 (JSP 440))[3] defined an asset as being

> *Anything of value, either tangible or intangible that is owned or used by an organization or business.*
>
> *They can be documents and information; material such as buildings, equipment, valuables or cash; operating systems or personnel.*

Although these assets may not be owned by you, your third-party suppliers may be providing varying degrees of value to your business, and, thus, they need to be identified, categorized, and managed to ensure that these services are being proportionately protected in accordance with your risk tolerances.

There are more and more reports[4] showing an increase threat to your supply chain; it has never been more important to ensure that the third parties that you rely on do not become the "weakest link in your chain."

Imagine if your business has implemented and developed a robust Protective Security for all your in-house systems and processes, only to be undone by the failings of one of your suppliers.

---

[3]http://wla.1-s.es/uk-mod-jsp-440-2001.pdf

[4]www.checkpoint.com/downloads/resources/cyber-attack-trends-mid-year-report-2019.pdf

As an organization that is embracing the technology revolution, you may need to use a third party to support a specialist business operation or may see the use of a suitable third party as a means of reducing the resource burden and costs.

However, outsourcing the responsibility for the provision of services or operations to a third party does not negate that you remain accountable for ensuring that the services and operations that your business is paying for remain effective and secure.

- **Outsourcing is merely the transference of these services or operations, as a means of helping treat risk or meeting a business need.**

  Consequently, the decision to outsource services or operations should be carefully managed and needs to be treated as an extension to your in-house services or operations.

- **Why should you pay for a third-party delivering services or operations that may increase your risks or diminish your business efficiency?**

  TechTarget defines supply chain risk management (SCRM)[5] as being

  The coordinated efforts of an organization to help identify, monitor, detect and mitigate threats to supply chain continuity and profitability.

  Additionally, they go on to recommend the following key best practices:

1. Automate processes involved in supplier risk management (SRM) to collect, analyze, and manage supplier information.

2. Include supplier performance information in your analysis for insight into potential financial issues.

3. Identify red flags that may indicate problems and use technology to automate their early detection.

4. Integrate SCRM platforms with procurement and supply chain management (SCM) software systems including software for spend visibility, eSourcing, purchase-to-pay, contract management, and compliance.

---

[5]https://whatis.techtarget.com/definition/supply-chain-risk-management-SCRM

5. Provide dashboards that track and report on supply risk metrics to give the executive team access to real-time observations into risk factors.

Impact

Much like you would apply the ten Principles of Protective Security to help safeguard your in-house services and operations, the same ten principles should be extended to help risk manage your third parties:

---

1. Business alignment

Security is a business enabler. It supports the efficient and effective delivery of services.

- **Are third-party suppliers that are deemed to be business enablers known and understood?**

2. Board-driven risk

Risk management is key and should be driven from the board level. Assessments will identify potential threats, vulnerabilities, and appropriate controls to reduce the risks to people, information, and infrastructure to an acceptable level. This process will take full account of relevant statutory obligations and protections.

- **Do you periodically risk assess your outsourced services and operations?**

- **Are your third-party supplier risks documented and periodically reviewed?**

3. Risk ownership

Accountable authorities own the security risks of their entity and the entity's impact on shared risks.

- **Has someone within the business been assigned the role and responsibility for owning third-party supplier risks and escalating risks, when needed?**

442

4. Proportionality

Security measures applied proportionately protect entities' people, information, and assets in line with their assessed risks.

- **Are the suppliers categorized based upon the business importance of the services and operations that they provide?**
- **Are security measures applied based upon the supplier's criticality to your business?**

5. Security culture

Attitudes and behaviors are fundamental to good security. The right security culture, proper expectations, and effective training are essential.

- **Do the suppliers match, or exceed, your security expectations?**

6. Team effort

Security is everyone's responsibility. Developing and fostering a positive security culture is critical to security outcomes.

- **Do you have assigned supplier relationship managers to enable a collaborative approach?**

7. Cycles of action

Cycles of action, evaluation, and learning are evident in response to security incidents.

- **Do you and your suppliers share lessons learned from events/ incidents that may have occurred or from security incident scenario training?**

8. Robust protection

Protective security should reflect the widest security objectives of the business and ensure that the organization's most sensitive assets are robustly protected.

- **Do you have a reasonable level of assurance that the security measures applied are within your expectations?**

9. Transparency

Security must be a business enabler and should be framed to support the company's objectives to work transparently and openly and to deliver services efficiently and effectively, via digital services wherever appropriate.

- **Do your suppliers freely share regular key performance indicators (KPIs) and key risk indicators (KRIs) with you?**

10. Policies and procedures

Policies and processes will be in place for reporting, managing, and resolving any security incidents. Where systems have broken down or individuals have acted improperly, the appropriate action will be taken.

- **Do your suppliers have comprehensive document sets?**

The utilization of third-party services, development, production, and even asset management have become normal and routine operational elements for many businesses.

Often, the reason is that they can provide the ability to embrace specialist skills and equipment, with a cost savings over their internal equivalents.

Through the growth in the use of outsourced services and operations, businesses are increasingly exposing technology systems, information, and other high-value assets to enable the seamless and efficient flow of business processes.

The objective of an effective SCRM program is intended to help identify any risks associated with the actions of your third-party suppliers, the formalization of the third-party supplier relationships, and the ongoing management of those interdependencies and relationships.

All this should be suitably managed to ensure that appropriate Protective Security measures are being applied to sustain your outsourced services and assets, which are managed and delivered by external entities.

In essence, there are four main goals of an effective SCRM:

1. To identify and prioritize third-party supplier dependencies

2. To manage risks associated with your third-party suppliers

3. To formalize binding relationships with your outsourced services and operations

4. To monitor and manage third-party supplier performance against all contractual specifications, including those for Protective Security

Strengthening Your Supply Chain Links

Supply Chain Management (as depicted in Figure 11-2) starts with identifying and managing the risks.

Figure 11-2. *Components of Supply Chain Management*

Before doing anything else, you need to gain a clear understanding of what services you have transferred the responsibilities to third-party organizations. Without this, you will find it extremely difficult to ensure proportionate levels of Protective Security measures are being applied and that the appropriate amount of effort and resources are invested to achieve your goals.

Ask yourself:

- **Do you understand the sensitivity of the contracted services and operations for each of your third parties?**

- **Do you know the value of your information or assets that are managed by third parties (or to which they have access) as part of the contracted services and operations?**

- **Do you understand their potential impact on your business should they become compromised?**

  - *Confidentiality*

  - *Integrity*

  - *Availability*

  - *Authentication*

  - *Nonrepudiation*[6]

- **Have you created a prioritized list of your third-party suppliers based upon the importance of the contracted services and operations they provide to you?**

- **Have you identified the specific risks that pertain to each of your third-party suppliers?**

- **What Protective Security requirements have you included in the contracts (primary and subcontractors)?**

You should consider the benefits of formalizing, documenting, and getting agreement for an SCRM action plan. Through grouping and profiling your third-party suppliers (based upon their perceived risks to your business), you will be better placed to tailor your SCRM program to ensure that the measures reflect your business' view of the associated risks.

---

[6]Assurance that the sender of information is provided with proof of delivery and the recipient is provided with proof of the sender's identity, so neither can later deny having processed the information (NIST Glossary).

Having established your third-party "risk scales," you can then start to engage with each of your links in your Supply Chain and start to take control of the weaker links (as depicted in Figure 11-3).

Figure 11-3. *Taking control of supplier relationships*

Ask yourself:

- **Are you able to easily identify those suppliers who are continually failing to meet your Protective Security expectations?**

- **Do you have any high-risk single points of failure?**

  - *Single/specialist third parties*

  - *Suppliers that support business-critical assets*

- **Do your suppliers understand their Protective Security responsibilities for the services and operations that they are providing?**

- **Have you provided your suppliers with clear guidance on what is expected from them (and any subcontractors)?**

  - *Provide each supplier with details of the minimum Protective Security requirements, which are*

    - *Justified*

    - *Proportionate*

    - *Achievable*

- *These need to be comparable with the results of the supplier risk assessments.*

- **Are the minimum Protective Security requirements embedded into the procurement process?**

  - *Ensuring that all contractual agreements include the Protective Security (where needed) and that the prospective suppliers can provide evidence of their ability to meet your expected standards*

- **Have you established a constructive working relationship between your organization and your suppliers to ensure that you are working as a harmonious partnership?**

  - *Security risks are clearly explained to your third parties.*

  - *Protective Security information is shared across your supply chain to enable better understanding and anticipation of emerging security attacks.*

  - *In the event of a security incident, both entities will work in collaboration (if required) to help minimize the potential impact across your business or the wider supply chain.*

Building upon the taking control of your third-party suppliers, it is essential that you integrate appropriate assurance activities into your SCRM operations.

Ask yourself:

- Do your contracts include protective security clauses?

  - *Upward reporting of security performance and adherence to risk management policies and processes*

  - *Right to audit*

  - *When required, justified assurance requirements:*

    - Formal security certifications (e.g., SOC2, ISO 27001, PCI DSS, etc.)

    - External audits

    - Schedule of penetration testing

- Are you using KPIs and KRIs to monitor your supply chains?

- Do you follow up on any findings or lessons learned?

- Do you encourage good security behaviors in your supply chain?

Much like the IT environment, your supply chain will prove to be extremely dynamic and will evolve and change throughout your time with them. Consequently, you should ensure that your SCRM program encourages and supports continual improvement and maintenance of Protective Security.

Ask yourself:

- Are you actively encouraging and working with your third-party suppliers to continually improve their security postures?

  - *Consider the benefits of sharing the findings of external reconnaissance of their digital footprint (as depicted in Figure 11-4).*

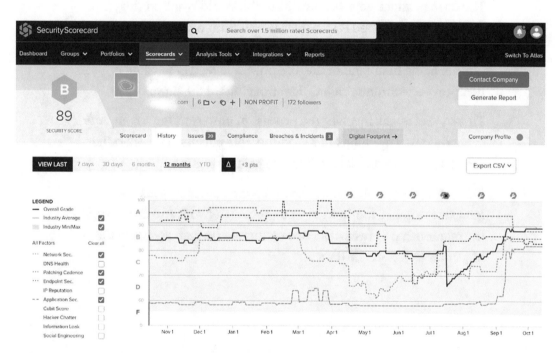

Figure 11-4. *Third-party 12-month historic risk profile*

- Do you actively work with your third parties to ensure that they appreciate and understand your minimum security expectations?

- Do you agree on remediation activities that include SMART (Specific, Measurable, Achievable, Realistic, and Time-bound) objectives?

- Are your supplier management activities embedded into your risk management practices to ensure that any performance issues, incidents, or reporting failures are escalated for risk assessment?

Supply Chain Attack Vectors

Attacks against the Supply Chain are constantly evolving, so it is important that you keep abreast of the latest attack methods that could be used against the links in your supply chain. Here is a short list of some of the supply chain attack types, but you should also consider other threats such as fraud, theft, and insiders:

- **Island hopping (as depicted in Figure 11-5[7])**

  The form of attack gets its name from the World War 2 strategy adopted by the United States in its island campaign against Japan. Forces gradually and strategically seized control of smaller islands outside of the mainland of the axis power instead of tackling it head-on – a technique called "leapfrogging" at the time.

  This style of attack involves the process of undermining a company's cyber defenses by going after its vulnerable partner network rather than launching a direct attack on the primary entity.

  Infiltrating the smaller and often less secure partner firms allows attackers to gain a foothold in a connected network and then exploit the relationship between the two companies to gain access to the bigger target's valuable data.

---

[7]www.researchgate.net/figure/An-instance-of-Island-hopping-attack_fig4_256840855

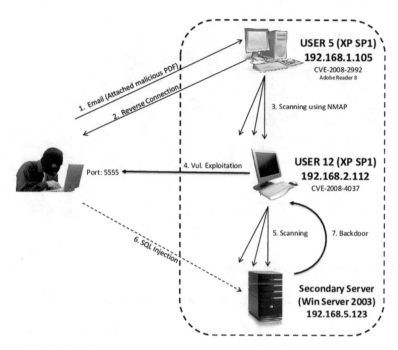

Figure 11-5. *Island hopping attacks*

- **Lateral movement (as depicted in Figure 11-6[8])**

    This is where a cyber-attacker, after gaining initial access, attempts to move deeper into a network in search of sensitive data and other high-value assets. After entering the network, the attacker maintains a clandestine and persistent presence and obtains increased privileges using various tools.

    Lateral movement has become a key tactic that distinguishes today's advanced persistent threats (APTs) from simplistic cyber-attacks of the past.

    Once the attacker has gained initial access to an endpoint (such as through a phishing attack or malware infection), the attacker impersonates a legitimate user and moves through multiple systems in the network until their objectives have been met. Attaining that objective involves gathering information about multiple systems and accounts, obtaining credentials, escalating privileges, and ultimately gaining access to the identified payload.

---

[8]www.beyondtrust.com/blog/entry/cybersecurity-strategies-to-stop-lateral-movement-attacks-leave-your-adversaries-marooned

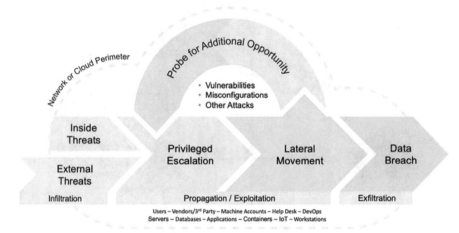

Figure 11-6. *Lateral movement attacks*

- **Software Supply Chain attack (as depicted in Figure 11-7[9])**

  In this form of attack, the attackers circumvent traditional cyber defenses to compromise software and delivery processes. The end goal is to enable successful, rewarding, and stealthy methods to subvert large numbers of computers through a single attack.

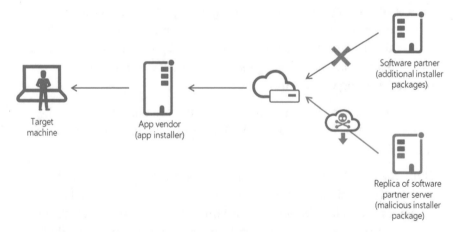

Figure 11-7. *Software Supply Chain attacks*

- **Watering holes (as depicted in Figure 11-8[10])**

---

[9]https://redpiranha.net/news/software-supply-chain-emerging-attack-vector
[10]https://cybersecurityglossary.com/watering-hole-attack/

In this style of cyber-attack, legitimate or popular websites of high-profile companies become the focus of watering hole attacks. An opportunist attacker lurks on legitimate websites, which are frequently visited by their targeted prey, before infecting these websites with malware and making their targets more vulnerable.

The attacker investigates the vulnerabilities associated with the websites and injects malicious programming code, often in JavaScript or HTML. The code then redirects the targeted groups to a different site where the malware or malvertisements are present. The malware is then ready to infect machines upon their access of the compromised website.

Most users unknowingly provide the tracking information while browsing. The tracking information gives the behavioral web patterns of the targeted victim groups. It also indirectly provides the attackers with information about browsing, cloud services access, and security policies of the organizations.

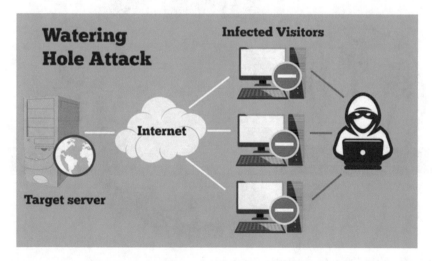

Figure 11-8. *Watering hole attacks*

- **Third-party data stores (as depicted in Figure 11-9[11])**

---

[11]www.ncsc.gov.uk/collection/supply-chain-security/third-party-data-stores

This is where a business has outsourced their aggregated data storage, processing, and brokering of information to a third-party organization.

The attackers then target vulnerabilities in the third-party data store to exfiltrate the sensitive data contained within. Such data is not limited to personal data but may also include

- Business structure

- Financial health

- Strategy

- Exposure to risk

- High-profile mergers and acquisitions

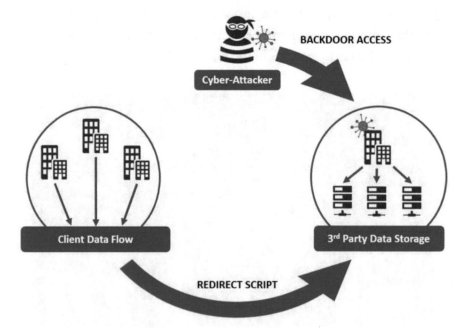

Figure 11-9. *Third-party data stores attack*

Assessing Your Supply Chain Security Links

The UK National Cyber Security Centre provides some very helpful good/bad examples (as shown in Table 11-1) which will assist you to compare yourselves against.

Table 11-1. *NCSC Table of Good/Bad Practices*

Good	Bad
You **understand the risks** suppliers may pose to you, your wider supply chain, and the products and services it offers. You know the sensitivity of information your suppliers hold and value of projects they are supporting.	You have a **poor understanding of the risks** that suppliers may pose to you, your wider supply chain, and the products and services it offers. You do not know what data they hold nor the value of projects they are supporting.
Know the full extent of your supply chain, including subcontractors.	**Only know your immediate suppliers**, but have limited/no knowledge of any subcontractors.
Know the security arrangements of your suppliers and routinely engage with them to confirm they are continuing to manage risks to your contract effectively.	Have no real idea about the security status of your supply chain, but **think they might be okay**. Fail to review this status.
Exercise control over your supply chain; exercise your right to audit and/or require upward reporting by your suppliers to provide security assurance that all is working well. An audit request would not be your first interaction with the supplier.	Exercise **weak control over your supply chain**, lose sight of subcontracting, fail to exercise audit rights, and do not seek upward reporting. Often, the first engagement of your security team with the supplier will be for an audit following an incident.
Based on your assessment of risks and the protections you deem are necessary, **set minimum security requirements for suppliers**, telling them what is expected in contracts.	**Fail to set minimum security requirements**, leaving it up to suppliers to do their own thing, even though they might not have the security awareness to understand what is needed or know how to do this effectively. Or set minimum security requirements, but fail to match these to your assessment of the risk – potentially making security unachievable for many of your suppliers.

(continued)

Table 11-1. (*continued*)

Good	Bad
Differentiate the levels of protection required to match the assessed risks to the specific contract. Ensure these protections are justified, proportionate, and achievable.	**Set a disproportionate "one size fits all" approach** for all suppliers, regardless of the contract and assessed risks. Fail to ensure these controls are justified and achievable – potentially causing suppliers not to compete for contracts with you.
Require that the **protections** you have deemed necessary in each case **are passed down throughout your supply chain**. Check to ensure it is happening.	Leave security to immediate suppliers to manage, but fail to mandate and/or check it is happening.
Meet your own responsibilities as a supplier (and challenge your customers for guidance where it is lacking). Pass your customer's requirements down and provide upward reporting.	**Neglect your responsibilities as a supplier**, or ignore any absence of customer guidance. Fail to pass requirements down and/or fail to provide upward reporting.
Provide some guidance and support to suppliers responding to incidents. Communicate lessons learned so others in your supply chain avoid "known problems."	**Offer no incident support to your suppliers.** Fail to act or spot where "known issues" might impact others in your supply chain nor to warn others about these issues – potentially leading to greater disruption, with known issues hitting many suppliers.
Promote improvements to the cyber awareness of your suppliers. Actively share best practice to raise standards. Encourage suppliers to subscribe to the free CISP threat intelligence service so they can better understand potential threats.	**Expect suppliers to anticipate developing cyber-attacks**, offering little or no support or advice, regardless of their security awareness and capabilities.

(*continued*)

Table 11-1. (*continued*)

Good	Bad
Build assurance measures into your minimum security requirements (such as Cyber Essentials Plus, audits, and penetration tests). These provide an independent view of the effectiveness of your suppliers' security.	**Fail to include assurance measures into your security requirements**, trusting that your suppliers will do the right thing – regardless of whether they have enough knowledge or experience to know what is expected of them.
Monitor the effectiveness of the security measures that are in place. Based on lessons learned from incidents, feedback from assurance activities, or from suppliers about issues, be prepared to revise or remove controls that are proving ineffective.	**Fail to monitor the effectiveness of security measures**. Fail to listen to feedback. Be unwilling to make changes, even when the evidence in favor of doing so is overwhelming.
Develop partnerships with your suppliers. If your suppliers adopt your approach to supply chain security as their own, there's much greater potential for success than if you simply mandate compliance.	**Dictate** requirements without consultation.
Get suppliers thinking about security from the outset by starting the discussion about security earlier than you would during traditional product assurance engagements.	Just **consider security to be a product assurance issue**.
Explain benefits of achieving the required security improvements to suppliers: i.e., that these will meet compliance requirements or offer the potential for the supplier to win other contracts.	Just **tell your suppliers what to do, but offer no explanation of benefits**: some suppliers may consequently be reluctant to bid for contracts.

(*continued*)

Table 11-1. (*continued*)

Good	Bad
Consider how you will enable suppliers who may require legitimate but ad hoc/occasional and/or limited **access to your business to do so without having to comply with your minimum security requirements for suppliers**. Document the procedures for these engagements and train all parties on their use.	**Make no provisions for such circumstances**, and either require them to meet your security requirements (even though there is little justification for this) or ignore it and let people make their own arrangements (hoping it will be okay).
Where required, **develop common contract artifacts** (i.e., risk assessment and self-assessment security questionnaire) to support the contracting process and to enable your suppliers to pass these down to subcontractors. Share these with your suppliers and train all staff on their use.	**Offer little/no advice on the contracting process**, allowing suppliers to do their own thing – and fail to understand the implications of this in terms of assurances about overall supply chain security.
Require these artifacts to be reviewed at appropriate intervals, such as at contract renewal, when there are significant changes, or in response to major incidents.	**Worry about the initial contract, but take little/no interest in subsequent contract renewals**: fail to spot changes/problems that may have arisen.

(*continued*)

Table 11-1. (*continued*)

Good	Bad
Ensure that security considerations are an integral part of the contract competition process and that they influence the choice of supplier. Require suppliers to provide appropriate evidence of their security status and ability to meet your minimum security requirements throughout the various stages of the contract competition: perhaps seeking basic assurances of your supplier's ability to meet legal and regulatory requirements, as a first gate, at initial contract advertisement, but requiring greater detail as the competition narrows to a choice of a few preferred bidders. Ensure these do not impose unnecessary workloads on prospective suppliers – particularly in the early stages of contracting when there are many applicants for the contract.	**Only worry about security at the end of the contracting process** – these considerations have little influence on your choice of supplier. Ask for more information than you need, can handle, or will use: potentially creating unnecessary workloads on potential suppliers when they have little chance of winning the contract. Be surprised when suppliers do not compete for contracts on these grounds.
When using a self-assessment security questionnaire to aid the contracting process, ensure this matches the minimum security requirements you have set – and reduces workloads on suppliers to a necessary minimum. Only require more detailed information when the supplier has progressed to the later contracting stages and is one of a very small number being considered for the contract.	**Just dust off an existing ISO 27001–based questionnaire** that you think might do and get suppliers to complete that: even if this has no resemblance to the minimum security controls you have used (i.e., Cyber Essentials or 10 Steps to Cyber Security). Fail to take account of the workloads this will create for suppliers, nor seek to match your requirements to the stage of the contract competition.

(continued)

Table 11-1. (*continued*)

Good	Bad
Allow suppliers time to achieve desired security improvements: develop risk criteria to manage this transition (i.e., require suppliers to provide a security improvement plan setting out how progress will be made) and stipulate when checks against progress have been made and should be performed.	**Set unrealistic deadlines** or have no clear or consistent risk criteria to inform decisions about suppliers who are unable to make these improvements within agreed timeframes. This may mean you are unable to work with such suppliers – potentially leading to a damaging fall in capability and reduced choice of suppliers.
Acknowledge any existing security certifications or prior/existing contract approvals that suppliers may have, and allow them to reuse such evidence to demonstrate how this might meet some of your minimum security requirements. But probe appropriately to confirm this is the case.	**Ignore any existing security certifications**, or contract approvals, requiring suppliers to achieve compliance with your minimum security requirements regardless. This could create unnecessary work and cost for suppliers, harming these relationships.
Expect all suppliers to achieve Cyber Essentials. But understand that some suppliers – even those who have existing security certifications like ISO 27001 – may find it difficult to meet the letter of the scheme. However, where the letter of the scheme cannot be met for whatever reason, you should seek to understand what steps the supplier is taking to manage these risks through, for example, alternative business processes or compensating security controls. You should check to confirm these are suitable.	Expect all suppliers to achieve Cyber Essentials, but **adopt a black-and-white approach, taking no account of special circumstances**. Do not acknowledge any difficulties and refuse to award contracts to suppliers who find Cyber Essentials certification difficult to achieve, further undermining your own capability and choice of suppliers.

(*continued*)

Table 11-1. (*continued*)

Good	Bad
Provide some mapping of the minimum security requirements you have chosen to common commercial security schemes to help suppliers reuse evidence and other customers to assess equivalences. This will also help suppliers demonstrate how they align with international schemes.	Provide no support and **expect suppliers to do this mapping themselves**: potentially increasing workloads and leading to inconsistencies – potentially undermining customers' trust in the evidence they provide.
Monitor and continually improve the process, discontinuing or refining processes that are disproportionate, ineffective, or unjustified.	Allow disproportionate, ineffective, or unjustified processes to remain unchanged. Fail to listen to consistent, justified calls for refinement.

Monitoring your supply chain ensures that any changes that could directly impact your organization are identified and tracked through the routine evaluations and monitoring. This will ensure they can be subject to timely risk assessments, so that the impact to your business is minimized.

Escalation for risk assessments can be the result of KPIs/KRIs, events, incidents, or a finding from an audit.

The NIST SP800-161: Supply Chain Risk Management Practices for Federal Information Systems and Organizations[12] provides a comprehensive overview of their recommendations for supply chain monitoring (as depicted in Figure 11-10).

---

[12]https://nvlpubs.nist.gov/nistpubs/SpecialPublications/NIST.SP.800-161.pdf

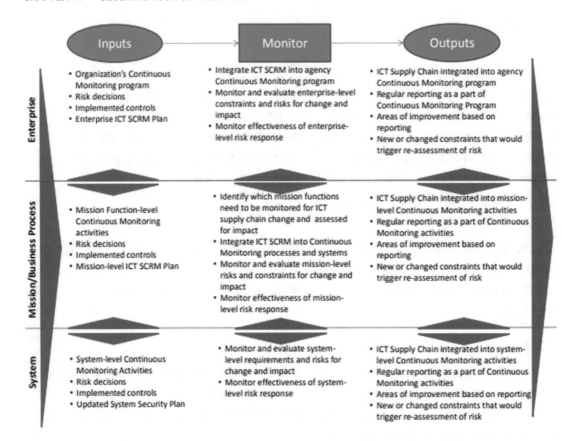

Figure 11-10. *Supply Chain monitoring*

An effective supply chain management program should look to limit the supply chain risk pertaining to the four aspects depicted in Figure 11-11.

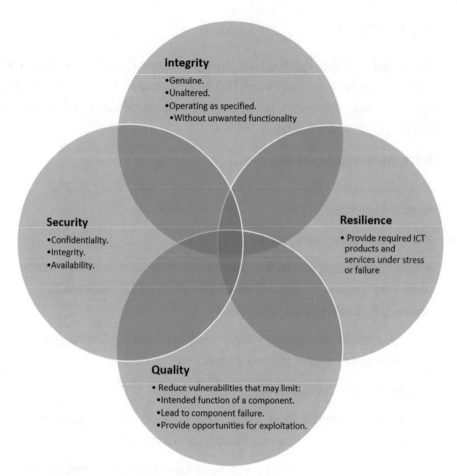

Integrity
- Genuine.
- Unaltered.
- Operating as specified.
  - Without unwanted functionality

Security
- Confidentiality.
- Integrity.
- Availability.

Resilience
- Provide required ICT products and services under stress or failure

Quality
- Reduce vulnerabilities that may limit:
- Intended function of a component.
- Lead to component failure.
- Provide opportunities for exploitation.

Figure 11-11. Focus areas of SCRM

Building BRIDGES

Once again, I will use the **BRIDGES** acronym to do a deep dive into a specific supply chain scenario.

Business Context

As part of the adoption of the digital model, an organization decides to investigate the opportunity of enhancing their supporting IT infrastructure architecture with a move to the cloud. However, in doing so, it is important that they understand the differences between the differing cloud models:

- **Infrastructure as a service (IaaS)**

  A cloud computing system, which delivers virtualized computing resources over the Internet

- **Platform as a service (PaaS)**

  A cloud computing model that provides customers with a complete platform *(hardware, software, and infrastructure)* for developing, running, and managing applications

  - *This reduces the cost, complexity, and inflexibility of building and maintaining that platform on-premises.*

- **Software as a service (SaaS)**

  A software delivery method, which allows data to be accessed from any device with an Internet connection and a web browser

  - *In this web-based model, software vendors host and maintain the servers, databases, and the code that is used for applications.*

Risk and Resilience

Dependent on which cloud model option is chosen, this can reduce the visibility *(aka Abstraction)* into the people, processes, and technologies supporting these digital assets.

A reduced level of visibility from the cloud service provider (CSP) makes risk assessment increasingly difficult, with each cloud model having its own cumulative levels of risk (as depicted in Figure 11-12[13]).

---

[13]ISACA, 2014. Vendor Management Using COBIT 5. ISACA.

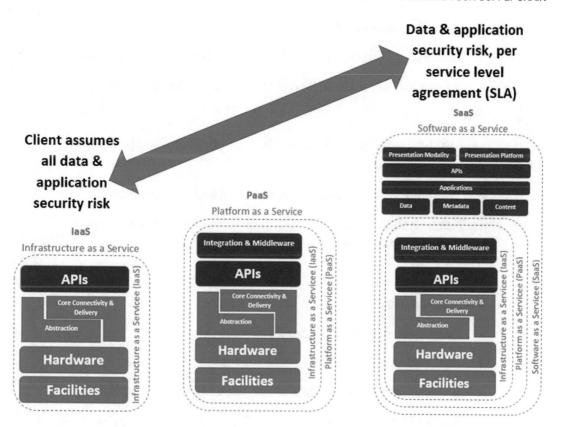

Figure 11-12. *Cloud models*

For each model, there are several factors that may increase your risks, such as

- **IaaS**

  - Transborder legal requirements

  - Multitenancy[14] +/or isolation failure

  - A lack of transparency for in-place technical security measures

  - A lack of disaster recovery or backup planning

  - The effectiveness of Physical Security measures

  - A lack of secure disposal practices

---

[14]https://whatis.techtarget.com/definition/multi-tenancy

- Volume of "offshored"[15] infrastructure

- Proficiency of the security maintenance of any virtual machines

- Robustness of the cloud provider's authentication measures

- **PaaS**

  - Misalignment between the applications and the cloud provider's capabilities

  - The compromise of the service-oriented architecture[16] library

  - Unavailability of applications (originals and backups) developed within the PaaS environments

- **SaaS**

  - Ineffective data ownership

  - Insecure data erasure/disposal procedures

  - Poor visibility of software systems development lifecycles (SDLC)

  - Insecure identity and access management (IAM) practices

  - A lack of an exit strategy

  - A broad exposure of applications

  - Poor release management practices

  - Insecure browsers

When looking to identify the risks to your Supply Chain links, it is important to be able to gain an understanding of their security culture and process maturities. Consequently, by carrying out some reconnaissance of their public-facing digital footprint, you will be able to gauge how well they manage their own assets to provide you with a starting baseline, for example, Supply Chain Security Scorecard (as depicted in Figure 11-13[17]).

---

[15]https://searchcio.techtarget.com/definition/offshore-outsourcing?_ga=2.127542600. 494336964.1602952807-1213537619.1588923015

[16]https://searchapparchitecture.techtarget.com/definition/service-oriented-architecture-SOA?_ga=2.47825634.494336964.1602952807-1213537619.1588923015

[17]assistance@cyberrescue.co.uk

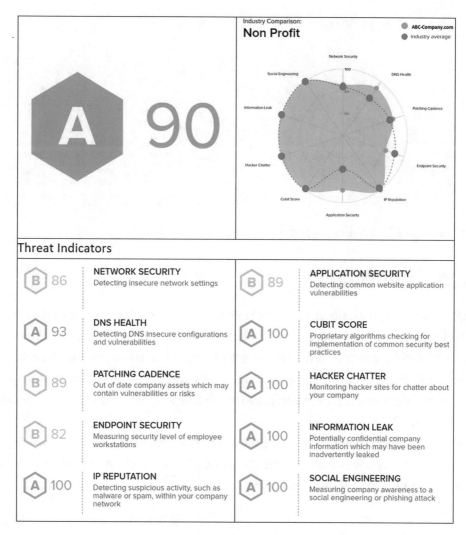

Figure 11-13. *Supply Chain Security Scorecard*

Detect Anomalies

Having established your baseline levels of risk, it is important to continue to proportionately monitor your suppliers through periodic security audits and security metrics reviews. For example, significant changes or omissions to the monthly security metrics reports could be an indicator of a change to internal processes, which could increase the risks to your organization (as depicted in Figure 11-14[18]).

---

[18]assistance@cyberrescue.co.uk

Security rating changes over a 12 month period

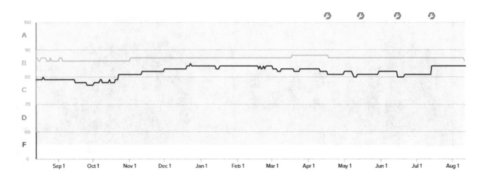

Figure 11-14. *12-month risk profile*

Govern Processes

Managing your supply chain links needs to be appropriate to the risks, and the greater the links in the chain, the more important it is to consider the potential benefits of a centralized SCRM platform – although for smaller supply chains, you may be able to manage this through an array of spreadsheets. However, when considering this option, it is important to consider the time and resource costs associated with the manual creation of summary dashboards.

Communication is essential to the effective management of your supply chain, ensuring that the suppliers embrace the ten principles of Protective Security, especially business alignment, team effort, and transparency.

Evaluate Security Controls

Based upon the criticality of the supply chain link, you should periodically reach out to them and request that they complete a security baseline questionnaire (as depicted in Figures 11-15,[19] 11-16 and 11-17,[20] 11-18,[21] and 11-19[22]).

---

[19]https://ihsmarkit.com/products/vendors-third-parties.html

[20]https://cset.inl.gov/SitePages/Home.aspx

[21]https://securityscorecard.com/resources/atlas-overview

[22]https://csrc.nist.gov/Projects/cyber-supply-chain-risk-management/
  interdependency_tool

ID	Control Objective	Control Area	Assessment Observations	Conclusion
35	Subcontractors hosting, storing, or processing clients' data as part of cloud deployment services are managed and the subcontractors' location(s) is specified	Info Sys & Security	**Observation**: The assessor could not validate the following due to lack of evidence or documentation based on publicly available information: - Whether or not Sample Cloud Vendor has established formalized procedures to manage subcontractors hosting, storing, and processing clients' data as part of cloud deployment services. - Whether or not Sample Cloud Vendor maintains a formal inventory of subcontractors supporting cloud deployment services and has identified and specified the subcontractors' location to ensure compliance with legal and regulatory requirements. Note: As part of the assessment procedures, the assessor noted the ISO 27001, PCI DSS, FEDRAMP and SOC 2 Type 2, certifications were not made available publicly for the assessor to observe, however Sample Cloud Vendor has published on their website that they have achieved certifications for the various standards and frameworks above.	Undetermined
40	Incident alert thresholds are established	Info Sys & Security	**Observation:** The assessor could not validate the following due to lack of evidence or documentation based on publicly available information: - Sample Cloud Vendor has established pre-defined thresholds configured on systems and tools used to generate alerts and notifications based on detected events. Note: As part of the assessment procedures, the assessor noted the ISO 27001, PCI DSS, FEDRAMP and SOC 2 Type 2, certifications were not made available publicly for the assessor to observe, however Sample Cloud Vendor has published on their website that they have achieved certifications for the various standards and frameworks above.	Undetermined
66	Organizational risk tolerance is determined and clearly expressed	Info Sys & Security	**Observation**: The assessor could not validate the following due to lack of evidence or documentation based on publicly available information: - Sample Cloud Vendor's enterprise-wide Risk Management Strategy includes a defined risk appetite. Note: As part of the assessment procedures, the assessor noted the ISO 27001, PCI DSS, FEDRAMP and SOC 2 Type 2, certifications were not made available publicly for the assessor to observe, however Sample Cloud Vendor has published on their website that they have achieved certifications for the various standards and frameworks above.	Undetermined

Figure 11-15. *Supply Chain security questionnaire*

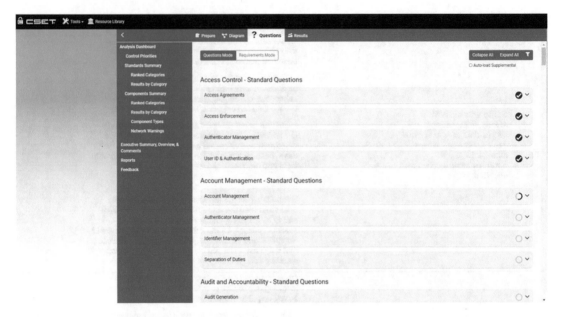

Figure 11-16. *CSET NIST SP800-161 questionnaire*

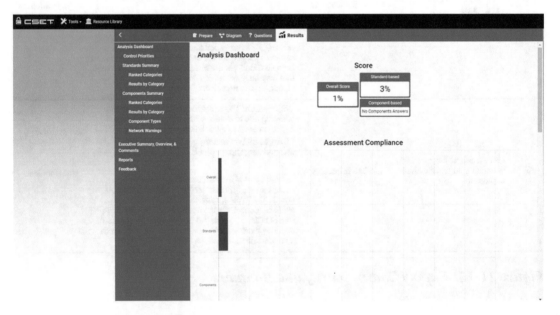

Figure 11-17. *CSET NIST SP800-161 results*

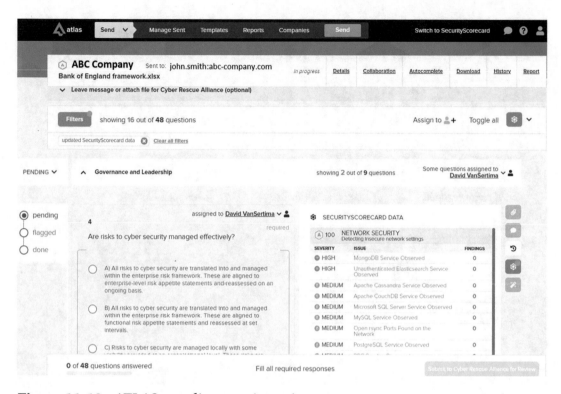

Figure 11-18. *ATLAS supplier questionnaire*

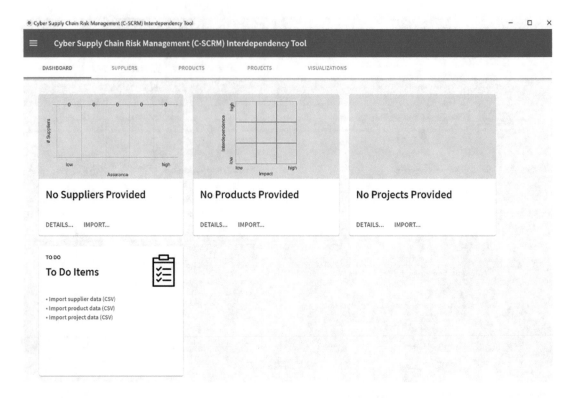

Figure 11-19. *NIST C-SCRM*

The results of the questionnaires should be reviewed and analyzed, with follow-up questions or onsite audits being implemented (where deemed appropriate) and the results being used to contribute to the corporate risk register[23] and risk management practices.

Survive to Operate

When outsourcing services or operations, it is essential that you do not forget the supply chain's contribution to your capability to continue operations, should something happen to disrupt these outsourced elements.

---

[23]https://acuitys3.s3.eu-west-2.amazonaws.com/s3fs-public/stream_for_supply_chain_risk_management_2017.pdf

Do you understand how mature their security incident practices (as depicted in Figure 11-20[24]) are or what contingency plans they have in place and how often they test their capabilities for ensuring they can "Survive to Operate"?

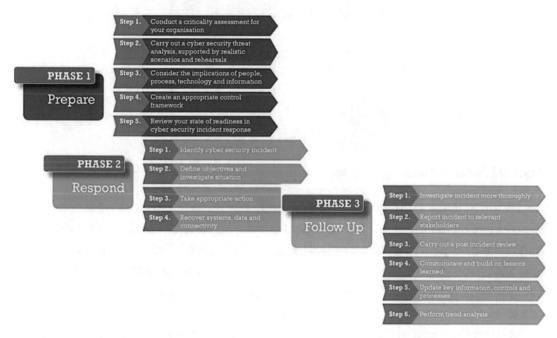

Figure 11-20. *CREST Cyber Security incident maturity assessment*

The importance of the supply chain's ability to "Survive to Operate" has never been so relevant than when seeing the impact that a global pandemic had on businesses, as the supply chain needed to move from efficiency to a more resilient approach.[25]

Military Comparison

During my counter intelligence field team (CIFT) tours of Afghanistan (Kandahar and Camp Bastion), a significant component involved the supply chain (as depicted in Figure 11-21).

---

[24]www.crest-approved.org/cyber-security-incident-response-maturity-assessment/index.html

[25]https://media.bitpipe.com/io_14x/io_148038/item_1970834/Supply_chain_management_balance_shifts_under_Covid.pdf

Figure 11-21. *Protecting the Supply Chain*

Within a "landlocked" country, such as Afghanistan, the supply chain becomes increasingly more important. The insurgents were well versed in the knowledge that if they could disrupt or stop the air or land supplies, they could seriously impact military operations. Additionally, they saw the supplies as a potential opportunity to use them as a "mule" to deliver malicious payloads or to gain unauthorized access to the military bases.

My final CIFT tour was as part of the Force Protection Wing at Camp Bastion. The military leaders had learned from previous mistakes and had tactically located this operating base in an isolated, flat terrain area, which provides a maximum defensive profile. As a result, the footprint area of the establishment had quadrupled in size, in as many years.

During my time there, the base was equivalent in size to the UK City of Reading, with around 30,000 personnel,[26] plus extensive mission-critical equipment, providing essential support to the other deployed operations. It even became the focus of many a television documentary, including a visit from one of TV's biggest "Petrol Heads" – Discovery's Mike Brewer.[27]

Well, as you may imagine, having to provide the logistics to support around 30,000 personnel and their equipment proved to be a mammoth task and could not be achieved with only the use of air supply chains.

---

[26]www.theguardian.com/uk/2011/aug/15/inside-camp-bastion

[27]www.discoveryuk.com/series/frontline-battle-machines-with-mike-brewer/

Consequently, a great deal of the supplies would come in across the land routes. However, with only two main routes in and out from the major sea ports, these supply convoys became easy targets to opportunistic criminals and insurgents.

Frequently, although provided limited private armed escorts, the local national haulage convoy drivers would often be targeted with small arms fire (rocket-propelled grenades (RPGs[28]), AK47s,[29] RPKs,[30] etc.) attacks (as depicted in Figure 11-22).

Often, the supplies deemed to be of increased importance[31] would be subject to enhanced protective security measures (as depicted in Figure 11-23[32]).

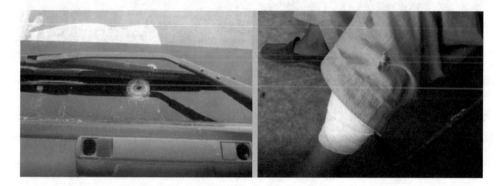

Figure 11-22. *Convoy driver casualty*

---

[28]https://williamamos.wordpress.com/2008/08/19/army-discovered-advanced-rpgs-in-afghanistan/

[29]www.reddit.com/r/GunPorn/comments/19r71w/confiscated_ak47s_in_afghanistan_1024x768/

[30]www.militaryimages.net/threads/rpk-rpk-74-and-its-derivatives-in-action.9105/

[31]www.oxfordmail.co.uk/news/10577570.afghanistan-conflict-troops-risking-lives-chance-normality/

[32]www.flickriver.com/photos/defenceimages/6940697111/

Figure 11-23. *Supply Chain convoy*

Part of the CIFT role[33] was to create an intelligence network, analyze intelligence feeds, and respond to and interview/investigate (as depicted in Figure 11-24) any events or incidents relating to the supply chain.

Figure 11-24. *CIFT interview*

---

[33]Para 231. https://assets.publishing.service.gov.uk/government/uploads/system/uploads/attachment_data/file/311572/20110830_jdp2_00_ed3_with_change1.pdf

By the end of a 6-month tour, we had delivered over 600 intelligence reports, with most of them being related to supply chain events/incidents and which ranged from deliberate actions to accidental or careless activities (as depicted in Figure 11-25) which increased the risk to the assets within the base.

Figure 11-25. *Dangerous loads*

Just my experiences in the CIFT role, at Camp Bastion, I could write another book. No incident was the same, and the complete myriad of threat types (as described in the Chapter 2) was experienced against the supply chain.

Ranging from insurgents planting improvised explosive devices (IEDs), on non-potable water tankers, to the delivery drivers trying to smuggle in prohibited items, or to the innocent actions of the innovative delivery drivers appearing to be suspicious and causing alarm.

I can recall a couple of the more intriguing incidents. The first is the discovery of empty ammunition cases and a charred wooden block (as depicted in Figure 11-26) in a delivery driver's vehicle cab.

Figure 11-26. *Charred wooden block*

When investigating this event, we soon learned that the explanation for having these items was completely innocent and demonstrated the practical and problem-solving thought processes of the Afghanistan heavy goods vehicle (HGV) drivers. The discarded empty ammunition cases just happened to be the correct diameter to punch holes in pieces of cardboard, which they could use as temporary gaskets, and the wooden block had a dual role – the punch block and the base for his portable stove, as he would often spend 2–3 months on the road and would often sleep under his trailer.

The second is related to an external patrol to liaise with the drivers waiting in the temporary village that had been established approximately 2 kilometers away from the main entrance *(adjacent to the main entry/egress road)*.

This had been a joint intelligence patrol (US Marines and the RAF Police) to investigate reports of building tensions and anger within the area. On arrival at the location, it was decided that the US Marines would go their way and that the RAF Police would be left to engage the locals in the manner that they preferred.

This approach yielded two polar opposite results:

1. The US Marines reported back that there was nothing to report and that all was peaceful.

2. However, through the CIFT's proactive engagement with the local nationals (as depicted in Figure 11-27), we had forged strong trust relationships and, as a result, had received the intelligence that people were planning a protest (as depicted in Figure 11-28).

    Rumors were being spread of the coalition forces going to the "burn pit" to destroy copies of the Quran, which had angered the locals.

Figure 11-27. *CIFT routine visits*

As you can imagine, the resulting intelligence reports had completely opposite implications. However, as a result of the CIFT's input, the base was able to arrange for further "hearts and minds" interventions (as depicted in Figure 11-29) to help avert such actions from happening.

Figure 11-28. *Protest planning*

Figure 11-29. *Hearts and minds engagements*

By the end of the 6-month tour, I had gained a comprehensive understanding and appreciation of the value of a proactive approach to Protective Security.

Reality Bites

In Sonatype's 2020 State of the Software Supply Chain report (as depicted in Figure 11-30[34]), they have seen a **430%** surge in the "next-generation" supply chain attacks.

---

[34]www.sonatype.com/hubfs/Corporate/Software%20Supply%20Chain/2020/SON_SSSC-Report-2020_final_aug11.pdf

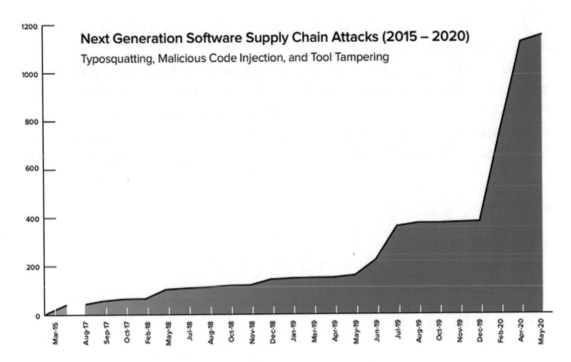

Figure 11-30. *Next-gen Supply Chain attacks*

Already in 2020, there have been many notable cyber-attacks that have been reported in the press. One of the most significant is the ransomware attack on Blackbaud,[35] which impacted hundreds of organizations.

The initial press release,[36] made by Blackbaud, made it sound as though they had averted the cyber-attack and that none of their customers' sensitive data had been compromised. However, it was later reported[37] that this was far from being the events that had occurred, with the supplier paying the ransom to the criminals to get their data back. This almost followed the same approach taken by Uber's chief information security officer (CISO)[38] in their ransomware attack, which led to his arrest.

---

[35]https://topclassactions.com/lawsuit-settlements/privacy/ransomware/blackbaud-ransomware-attack

[36]www.blackbaud.com/newsroom/article/2020/07/16/learn-more-about-the-ransomware-attack-we-recently-stopped

[37]www.bleepingcomputer.com/news/security/blackbaud-ransomware-gang-had-access-to-banking-info-and-passwords/

[38]www.csoonline.com/article/3584071/uber-breach-case-a-watershed-moment-for-cisos-liability-risk.html

Now, we are seeing several class action lawsuits being raised against Blackbaud for allowing the ransomware attack to happen.

Despite Tyler Technologies[39] providing ransomware protection advice (as depicted in Figure 11-31[40]), they were to suffer a ransomware attack. Days after the attack, some of their customers started noticing suspicious logins and the presence of malicious remote access Trojans on their networks and servers.[41] However, once again, the initial notice (as depicted in Figure 11-32[42]) failed to indicate as to the true gravity of this cyber-attack.

---

[39]www.tylertech.com/

[40]www.tylertech.com/resources/resource-downloads/ransomware-survival-guide

[41]www.zdnet.com/article/suspicious-logins-rats-reported-after-ransomware-attack-on-us-govt-contractor/

[42]https://web.archive.org/web/20200925001207/https://tylertech.com/

Ransomware Survival Guide

We've all seen the headlines. Ransomware attacks are escalating. It's essential that your organization has the proper controls in place to defend your organization against an attack.

But, defense strategies are not enough. It is important that your organization is prepared to confidently respond to, and survive, a ransomware attack. This survival guide will arm you with the knowledge you need to defend against and prepare for an attack.

In this survival guide you'll learn:

- The anatomy of a ransomware attack and typical delivery channels
- How to defend your organization against a ransomware attack
- Ransomware incident response preparation tips

Figure 11-31. *Tyler Technologies ransomware guide*

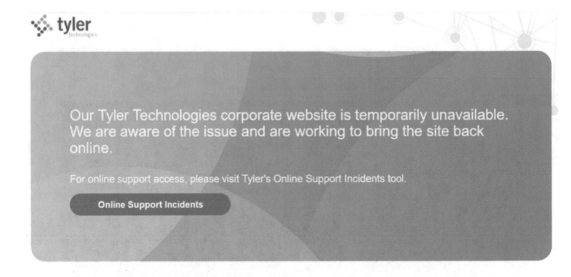

Information on Tyler's Security Incident Response

Figure 11-32. *Tyler Technologies security incident notice*

Other examples include

- Another incident involved multiple Zen customers being affected by an outage[43] caused by routing and core network problems.

- The Maharashtra Energy company suffered a power outage, where they stated that foul play or sabotage by external parties could not be ruled out.[44]

Key Takeaways

- It is important to acknowledge the importance risk management plays within effective supply chain management.

- The consequences of supply chain security incidents should be included into your organization's risk strategy.

---

[43]https://servicealerts.zen.co.uk/active/1/5589

[44]https://energy.economictimes.indiatimes.com/news/power/cant-rule-out-foul-play-sabotage-in-mumbai-power-outage-incident-maharashtra-energy-minister/78655039

- The supply chain risk strategy should define decisions, risk appetites, aims, methods, and procedures.

- Each link within the supply chain needs to be understood and their criticality ranked, with appropriate ongoing auditing programs implemented.

- Risks to the supply chain (both actual and potential) need to be identified.

- The probability of these risks occurring should be forecasted.

- The consequences of such an incident happening should be analyzed (e.g., expected values, risk relationships, events, responses, consequences, etc.).

- The results of the consequence analysis should be used to prioritize the identified risks.

- Proportionate responses should be designed, listing possible alternatives and identification of the best options.

- Any remediation plan should include the communication of any audit findings, assignment of responsibilities, staff training, defined procedures, and so on.

- Suppliers should be monitored and periodic KPIs/KRIs received and reviewed.

- As and when required, appropriate response plans should be actioned to help manage the risks.

- Control responses should be reflected in the updates to the risk register.

CHAPTER 12

Developing Your Human Firewall

Cheshire's informality suited men and women whose shared experience had begun to dissolve many of the class barriers which had divided pre-war Air Force.

For example:

A young wireless operator, who had arrived at Linton the previous day, was climbing into the truck for dispersals when he felt Cheshire's arm round his shoulder. "Good luck, Wilson." All the way to the aircraft, the wireless operator pondered… "How the hell did the Commanding Officer know my name?"

Or:

"Hello Read." I did not know he knew my name. "Hear you had a few problems tonight… Would you like to come and have a chat about it?" My first meeting with the nicest and most considerate squadron commander I ever met. "I needed help and advice and he was ready to give it."

His rapport with ground crews became legendary. "He could get men to do anything. If he went into a billet on a Saturday morning, with airmen getting ready to go into York, and ask for eight volunteers, he'd get the lot." He always believed he could learn more about the planes by talking to the ground staff than form 'other personnel'. Mechanics on engine stands grew accustomed to Cheshire climbing up beside them to discuss what they were doing and why. On Christmas Day two radar mechanics were inspecting a remote dispersal:

…it seemed a good idea to get some fresh air after a few drinks on Christmas Eve.

© Jim Seaman 2021
J. Seaman, *Protective Security*, https://doi.org/10.1007/978-1-4842-6908-4_12

We heard someone going through the plane but took no notice as we assumed it was another mechanic. It was in fact Wg Cdr Cheshire (as depicted in

Figure 12-1[1]) who wished us "a very merry Christmas," had a few words with us and suggested we "jack it in for the day and get back for Christmas dinner." He did, in fact, go around various dispersals on that Christmas morning and had a few words with everyone.

Figure 12-1. *World War 2 legend Leonard Cheshire, right, and his equally famous wife, Hollywood star Constance Binney*

Introduction

Increasingly, we see the insider threat as being the greatest cause of security incidents and data loss. From a benchmarked sample, across 13 industries (as depicted in Figure 12-2[2]), the average cost of the insider threat was identified at **$11.45 million** *(astonishingly, this equates to a **47% increase** in the last 2 years).*

---

[1]www.yorkpress.co.uk/news/14302088.in-search-of-terence-rattigan-and-leonard-cheshire/

[2]www.observeit.com/wp-content/uploads/2020/04/2020-Global-Cost-of-Insider-Threats-Ponemon-Report_UTD.pdf

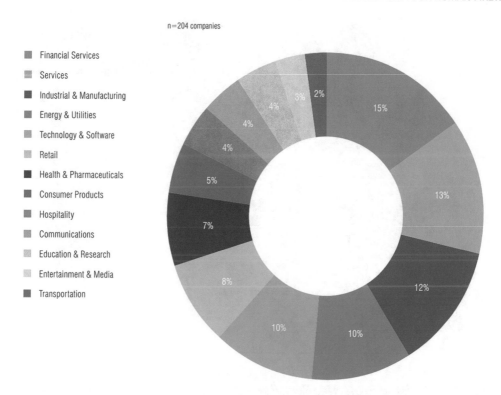

n=204 companies

- Financial Services
- Services
- Industrial & Manufacturing
- Energy & Utilities
- Technology & Software
- Retail
- Health & Pharmaceuticals
- Consumer Products
- Hospitality
- Communications
- Education & Research
- Entertainment & Media
- Transportation

Figure 12-2. *Industry sectors of participating organizations*

If your business is looking to embrace new digital technologies, it is important that you risk assess the potential impact on your users of these new technologies. Dependent on the demographics and capabilities of your personnel, the safe and secure use of these technologies can widely vary.

It is this variance in people's capabilities that provides the opportunities for the criminals. Remember that, although you will have a threat for the malicious insider, not all your personnel are hell-bent on carrying out actions that will lead to a compromise of these digital systems or the sensitive data being processed by them.

- **95%** of security breaches are caused by human error.[3]

Consequently, you should consider the complexities of your "Human Firewall"[4] and how you can best securely configure them to ensure that they remain as effective as the other components of your Protective Security program (as depicted in Figure 12-3).

---

[3]www.e-zu.co.uk/2020/06/16/95-of-cyber-security-breaches-are-due-to-human-error/
[4]www.reddit.com/r/Humanfirewall/comments/fax9rk/human_firewall_laymans_definition/

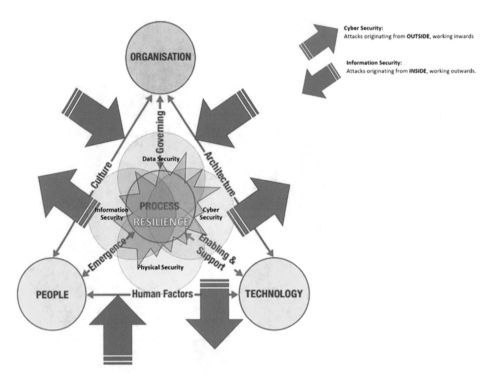

Figure 12-3. *Holistic Protective Security*

With the insider threat representing such a significant cost and impact to an organization, why does it still appear that there continues to be such a sizeable difference between what businesses are doing and what is needed to reduce this risk to within acceptable parameters?

Human Firewall

Developing an effective "Human Firewall" involves far more than just creating a documentation suite of policies and procedures and expecting everyone to understand and abide to these rulesets.

The Infosec Institute defines a Human Firewall (as depicted in Figure 12-4) as being[5]

---

[5]https://resources.infosecinstitute.com/how-to-create-a-human-firewall-top-7-elements-required-for-success-in-2018/

A commitment of a group of employees to follow best practices to prevent as well as report any data breaches or suspicious activity.

The more employees you have committed to being a part of the firewall, the stronger it gets.

Remember that a human firewall is different from a Security Champion[6] in that Security Champions are more about education and awareness. However, a human firewall can include Security Champions.

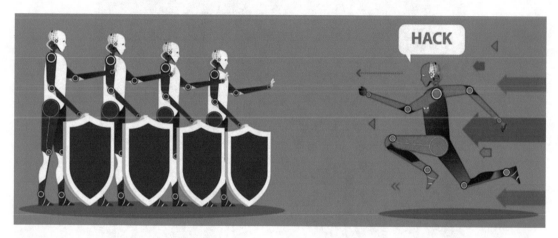

Figure 12-4. *Human Firewall*

A major part of this objective is understanding your employee demographics, the role that they do within the business, and the IT software and hardware assets that they use.

In essence, your "Human Firewall" could be regarded as adding extra layers to the open system interconnection (OSI) (as depicted in Figure 12-5[7]) and your defense-in-depth (as depicted in Figure 12-6[8]) models.

---

[6]https://resources.infosecinstitute.com/what-is-a-security-champion-definition-necessity-and-employee-empowerment/

[7]https://regmedia.co.uk/2013/06/04/10_layers_of_7_layer_osi_model.png

[8]www.malwarefox.com/wp-content/uploads/2017/02/Layered-Security.jpg

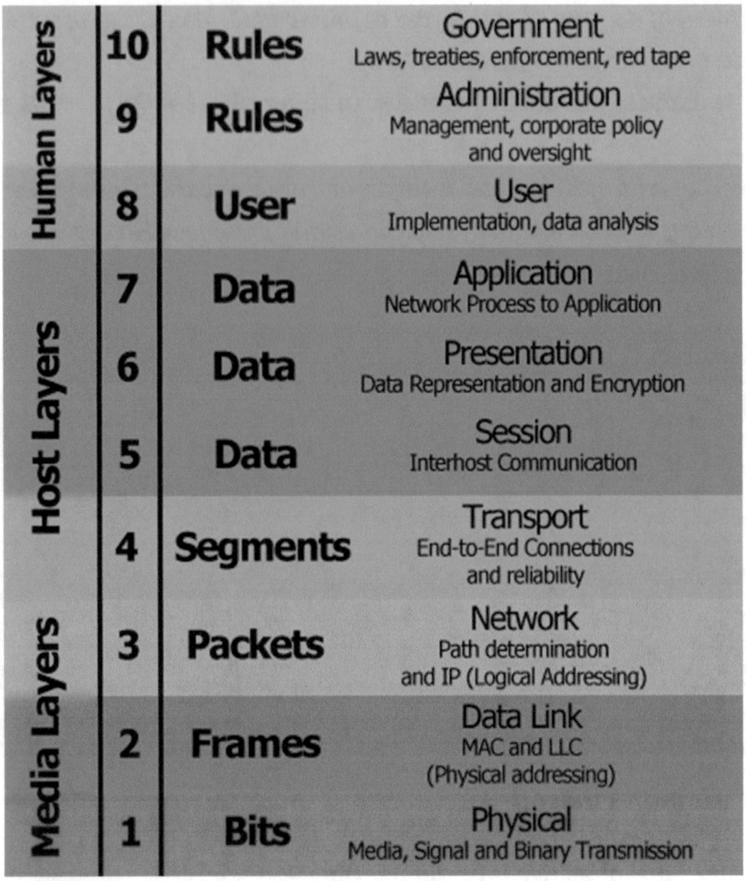

Human Layers	**10**	**Rules**	**Government** Laws, treaties, enforcement, red tape
	9	**Rules**	**Administration** Management, corporate policy and oversight
	8	**User**	**User** Implementation, data analysis
Host Layers	**7**	**Data**	**Application** Network Process to Application
	6	**Data**	**Presentation** Data Representation and Encryption
	5	**Data**	**Session** Interhost Communication
	4	**Segments**	**Transport** End-to-End Connections and reliability
Media Layers	**3**	**Packets**	**Network** Path determination and IP (Logical Addressing)
	2	**Frames**	**Data Link** MAC and LLC (Physical addressing)
	1	**Bits**	**Physical** Media, Signal and Binary Transmission

Figure 12-5. Ten-layer OSI model

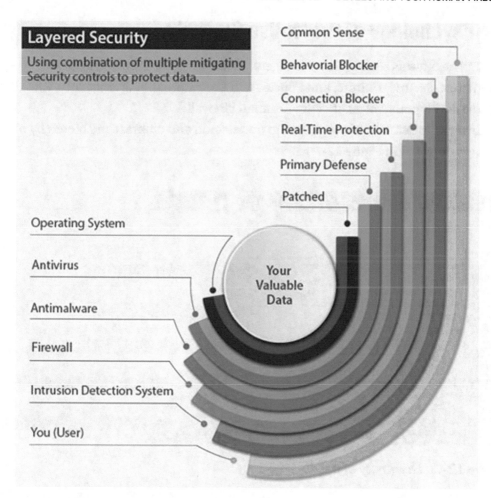

Figure 12-6. *Defense-in-depth model*

At the heart of the development of these additional layers is the engagement and two-way communication with the employees. Often, this is more aligned with psychology (rather than security) as one willing volunteer is far more effective than ten pressed *(compliant)* people.

- An effective "Protective Security" program requires the development of a network of "securely configured" human components.

- These become your extended network of "eyes and ears," helping detect and notify you of suspicious activities while helping to police your business operations.

The Psychology of Protective Security

We often hear terms such as Risk Management, Stakeholder Communications, Governance, Security Culture, and Policies and Procedures being associated with the effective development of an effective "Human Firewall."

However, to achieve this, you need to understand and embrace the hierarchy of needs (as depicted in Figure 12-7[9]).

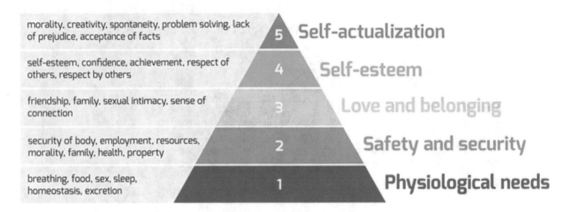

Figure 12-7. *Hierarchy of needs*

Through the documented policies and procedures and annual security awareness training, you will only enter the business and employees' hierarchy of needs at the fundamental levels (levels 1 and 2 (basic needs)).

To really engage with the "Human Factor," you should be looking to connect with your employees and make "Protective Security" a more personalized approach. Start to engage with the various business departments and their personnel to begin two-way communication channels.

This involves engaging at the high levels of the Maslow Pyramid (as depicted in Figure 12-8[10]).

---

[9]www.simplypsychology.org/maslow.html
[10]www.simplypsychology.org/maslow.html#needs7

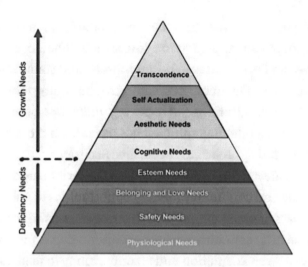

Figure 12-8. Maslow's motivation model

1. **Biological and physiological needs** - air, food, drink, shelter, warmth, sex, sleep, etc.

2. **Safety needs** - protection from elements, security, order, law, stability, freedom from fear.

3. **Love and belongingness needs** - friendship, intimacy, trust, and acceptance, receiving and giving affection and love. Affiliating, being part of a group (family, friends, work).

4. **Esteem needs** - which Maslow classified into two categories:

   (i) esteem for oneself (dignity, achievement, mastery, independence) and

   (ii) the desire for reputation or respect from others (e.g., status, prestige).

5. **Cognitive needs** - knowledge and understanding, curiosity, exploration, need for meaning and predictability.

6. **Aesthetic needs** - appreciation and search for beauty, balance, form, etc.

7. **Self-actualization needs** - realizing personal potential, self-fulfilment, seeking personal growth and peak experiences. A desire "to become everything one is capable of becoming".

We are increasingly seeing the effects that new technologies are having on people, so it is beneficial to adapt your approach to address their difficulties, rather than just expecting the policies and procedures to be appropriate and suitable for all.

With the increased use of technologies leading to shortening attention spans[11] and the embracement of new applications *(all requiring individual logins and passwords)* and a wide range of end user demographics, it has never been more important to develop a human-centered approach to "Protective Security."

This can only be achieved through an adaptive and flexible model, where you can engage with the people and continually identify opportunities to enhance this model.

One of the best ways of doing this is through engagement and the establishment of an enterprise-wide security committee, where representation from across various areas of the business are given representation and an opportunity to feedback any issues which their departments might be facing.

The purpose of developing your "Human Firewall" is to help minimize or reduce the risks to your business, so it is essential to ensure that these firewalls are securely configured.

Configuring Your "Human Firewalls"

Much the same as you should establish the appropriate policies and rulesets for your "Technology Firewalls," the same principles need to be applied to the human version.

A single configuration standard may not be suitable for application across all your people assets. Consequently, the configuration needs to be flexible and adapted to suit the make (roles), model (responsibilities), version no. (age), and so on.

There are a great deal of similarities that can be seen between the driver safety and business "Protective Security," with the younger generation being perceived as being more reckless and being the risk takers, whereas the elderly struggle to adapt to the technological advancements (as depicted in Figure 12-9[12]).

---

[11]`www.webwisewording.com/shorter-attention-span-technology/`
[12]Seaman, J. (2020). Apress. New York City. PCI DSS : An Integrated Data Security Standard Guide.

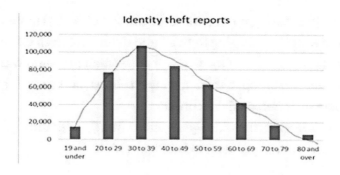

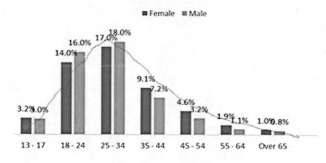

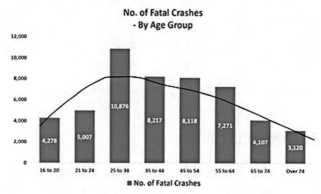

Figure 12-9. *Risk demographics*

Consequently, to ensure suitable secure configuration states, the approach needs to be tailored and adapted for the wide-ranging demographics. Additionally, it is important to engage with the wide-ranging demographic group to understand whether the configuration practices remain effective for most of the demographic groups.

Your approach to ensuring the secure configuration of your "Human Firewalls" needs to be able to adapt to changing trends[13] and influences from external influences.[14]

Increasingly, it is reported that the younger generation have embraced the technology revolution, resulting in them having an almost laissez-faire approach to their willingness to share their personal data online.

On the contrary, much of the older generation struggle with the rapid rate of technological advancements (as depicted in Figure 12-10[15]).

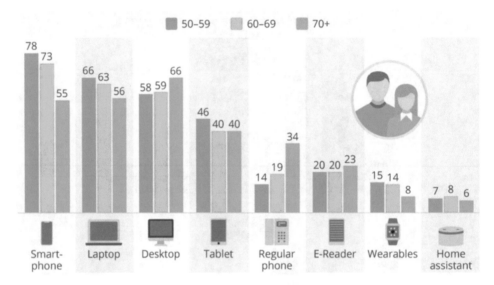

Figure 12-10. *Device ownership (2017), by age group, in %*

Selling Protective Security

Building an effective "Human Firewall" is very much like trying to sell something to someone; they need to have an appreciation for buying into the concept and to understand what the benefits are to them and the organization.

The "sales pitch" needs to be tailored to the audience, and the traditional way of developing and delivering is no longer an effective way of doing this.

---

[13]www.similarweb.com/corp/reports/2020-digital-trends-report/

[14]www.bloomberg.com/news/articles/2020-06-13/businesses-transformed-by-covid-19-plan-to-keep-the-changes

[15]www.statista.com/chart/13206/device-ownership-among-baby-boomers/

While there is little doubt that as a security professional you will have the knowledge to develop a security awareness presentation, do you have the time available and the development skills and software needed to create current, thought-provoking, and professional-looking material that can be delivered to your wide audience demographics?

I'm not saying that the traditional approach should be completely disregarded, but as an inefficient model, it should be limited to your key stakeholders or persons who hold more critical roles and responsibilities, where the traditional presentations can be made relevant to their roles.

Remember that "Protective Security" is everyone's responsibility, so to make your life easier and help you to gain access to instantly available professional material, consider investing in an outsourced security awareness solution.

By investing in such a solution, you benefit from "mass-produced" security awareness libraries[16] which you can choose from and implement to meet your needs. For example, if you are worried about mobile device security, data privacy, or phishing attacks, these library resources are readily available to you in a variety of formats:

- **Interactive training modules** (as depicted in Figure 12-11)

Figure 12-11. KnowBe4 training modules

[16]`www.knowbe4.com/training-preview`

- **Games** (as depicted in Figure 12-12)

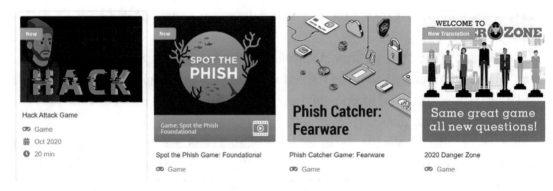

Figure 12-12. *KnowBe4 games*

- **Videos** (as depicted in Figure 12-13)

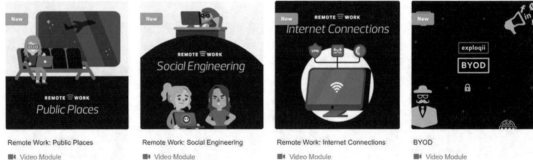

Figure 12-13. *KnowBe4 videos*

- **Posters and artwork** (as depicted in Figure 12-14)

224 Results

Security Awareness Is A Journey

  Posters & Artwork

Poster: Standups 4 Security Series

  Posters & Artwork

Poster: Cyber Essentials Series

  Posters & Artwork

Poster: Privacy Series

  Posters & Artwork

Figure 12-14. *KnowBe4 artwork and posters*

- **Newsletters** (as depicted in Figure 12-15)

236 Results

November 2020 Security Awareness Newsletter: Scavenger Hunt

November 2020 Security Awareness Newsletter: Email Security

Physical Security Crossword

  Newsletter & Security Docs

Where's the Security Desk

  Newsletter & Security Docs

Figure 12-15. *KnowBe4 newsletter*

- **Assessments** (as depicted in Figure 12-16)

2020 Security Culture Survey

▤ Assessment

Security Awareness Proficiency
Assessment

▤ Assessment

Figure 12-16. *KnowBe4 assessment*

The greater the number of "security savvy" end users that you have, the harder it becomes for the opportunist attackers.

- Secure Backend Operations

- Secure Frontend Operations

The primary objective for developing an effective "Human Firewall" is to create the feeling, among the end users, that they are making a positive contribution to the defense of the valuable business assets.

Much the same as health and safety initiatives, to help make this relevant to the end user, it requires a team effort, where Security Champions are encouraged and supported by senior management and department managers to promote interdepartmental security cultures.

End users are inspired to be the "eyes and ears" of an organization to support good practices within their teams and to report any harmful or malicious activities.

Military Comparison

A significant part of the Counter Intelligence role involved helping people to feel that they were making a positive contribution to the defense of mission-critical assets and operations.

Consequently, the "hearts and minds" element was a key factor in the effectiveness of the Counter Intelligence operations, and the gathering of information from service personnel (for analysis into actionable intelligence) was deemed to be crucial to effective "Protective Security."

During the homeland role, we assumed a role that was more akin to that carried out by the Home Office Special Branch and Intelligence Units,[17] and, as a result, the Regional Units were also known as the RAF Police Special Branch.

During overseas operations, this was a given. However, this was also the case for the homeland Counter Intelligence role. Consequently, for the role on Counter Intelligence Regional Operations, to help enhance our capabilities, we would receive additional training that would prove to be invaluable for both homeland and overseas Counter Intelligence operations.

For example:

- Attending a Home Office Level 2 Source Handlers course (Kent Constabulary) to ensure that we could gather Human Intelligence in a safe, secure, and legal manner[18] (certificate depicted in Figure 12-17)

---

[17]Staniforth, A., Ratcliffe, M., Rabenstein, C., Walker, C., Osborne, S. and Police National Legal Database (England (2013). Blackstone's counter-terrorism handbook. Oxford: Oxford University Press, Cop.

[18]https://assets.publishing.service.gov.uk/government/uploads/system/uploads/attachment_data/file/920537/CHIS_Code_-_Bill_amendments.pdf

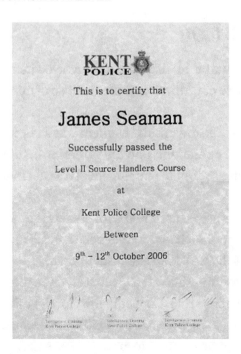

Figure 12-17. *Kent College training*

- Being provided with Home Office–approved Counter Terrorism (Special Branch) training, with the South West Regional Intelligence Cell (RIC) (certificate depicted in Figure 12-18)

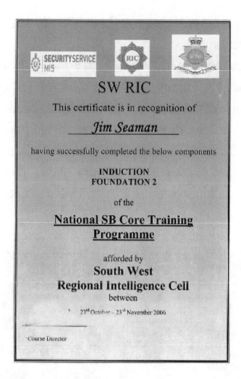

Figure 12-18. South West RIC training

Up until this point, the Source Handling course was the most enjoyable and informative training course that I had ever attended. The course consisted of some frontend theory training before the practical phase where the course was divided into teams of two, and we were given several practical scenarios to test our understanding and application of the principles.

Well, I was teamed up with a member of the British Transport Police, and our first scenario was the initial engagement with a potential intelligence "source." Talk about being completely out of our comfort zone.

The initial engagement was met with a hostile response, with the potential source taking an instant disliking to my team colleague. However, eventually, we managed to win them around and start to make the atmosphere a little friendlier.

The next day, we were to plan for a safe follow-up engagement with this potential source. However, the course instructors had informed us that they would be deploying undercover police units in the region to act as criminals looking to compromise our interventions.

With this in mind, that evening we decided to carry out reconnaissance and planning for the next morning's meeting. We had been allocated the North Eastern region of

Maidstone, Kent, and so that evening we sought to identify some suitable meeting places for the follow-up intervention.

During our reconnaissance, we identified what we thought was a suitable venue. We came up with the idea of arranging to meet in the Coffee Shop of a Garden Center, where (to break down some of the barriers) my colleague would approach the "source" carrying a tourist flyer and ask for directions. During this engagement, he would open the tourist flyer to reveal a note, instructing the "source" to meet us in the car park of the crematorium, across the road (as depicted in Figure 12-19). The purpose being that we could get ourselves into a suitable position to identify if the 'source' was being followed by the undercover police units.

Figure 12-19. *Maidstone*

Well, although we thought we had come up with a fairly good strategy, things did not go quite as planned. That morning, after making the telephone call to confirm the arrangements, I dropped my colleague at the front of the Garden Center and waited at the back of the Garden Center.

Ten or so minutes, an incredibly angry and infuriated team colleague returned to the vehicle. When I asked what had happened, he stated that the "source" had been deliberately obstructive, having sat at a table furthest away from the Coffee

Shop's entrance. The Coffee Shop had been full, meaning that to carry out the planned interaction, he would have had to walk past and ignore everyone else to very suspiciously choose the "source" to ask for tourist information.

Consequently, on seeing this (as he entered the Coffee Shop), he had angrily walked through the Coffee Shop and forcefully threw the tourism flyer onto the "source's" table, angrily shouting

Here!

Of course, the "source" was completely unaware that there was a note inside the tourism flyer, and so it was only a few minutes later when I received a telephone call from an irate "source," who was far from pleased at being messed around.

Next thing, we were doing a drive-by collection of the "source," and after bundling them into our vehicle, we made a quick exit toward the crematorium.

It didn't get any easier from here on either. I turned left out of the Garden Center, down to the roundabout and back up to the crematorium, opposite. On arrival, I was greeted by a queue of vehicles entering the crematorium *(there only happened to be a service going on)*.

A swift change of plan, I carried on up the road, all the way back round the next roundabout and back to the Garden Center. Here, we decided to carry out the interview in a quiet corner of the car park. Now, it is important to remember that our senses were heightened, as we believed that there were undercover police units looking to compromise our "source."

Well, as we approached the far end of the car park, there was an adjacent hand car wash facility. Wouldn't you know it, as we were looking for somewhere to park, a worker from this facility drove straight out in front of us, without looking, causing me to brake sharply.

Boom! That was it; the heart started racing.

- *Was that the undercover police units?*

- *Had our cover been blown?*

- *Was our "source" safe?*

With the nerves racing and elevated breathing, I quickly parked up, and we waited for what we thought was going to be the inevitable escalation, which was bound to come next.

A couple of minutes went by and nothing *(false alarm)*, so we started to calm down and decided it was safe to continue to have the chat with the "source."

Well, that set the benchmark for the next planned intervention for the next day, which, once again, did not go to plan!

However, the lessons learned from this course proved invaluable for me, during other Counter Intelligence operations, to help me develop my "people skills" later along in my RAF Police career (both in the overseas and homeland roles).

There are three notable examples that spring to mind:

1. Being tasked to investigate an incident that occurred during a reoccurring NATO exercise, being held in Belgium, Europe
    During their "downtime," a junior member of the RAF had been socializing in the local town and, at the end of the night, leaving on their own, had decided to take a "taxi" back to his accommodation. However, soon after the journey had begun, the "taxi" had turned off the main street into a side street. Here, there were four unknown males waiting for the "taxi."

    As the taxi came to a stop, all four males worked in harmony to rob the junior member of the RAF, at knifepoint.

    Coincidentally, during the previous exercise, the very same thing had occurred to another member of the RAF. I was tasked to carry out a fact-finding interview to ascertain whether this had been an orchestrated attack against this NATO exercise and its personnel.

    During the interview, the junior member of the RAF had provided a comprehensive overview of the events leading up to, and during, this incident. It turns out that the individual had gotten into a vehicle that he had believed (but could not confirm) was a genuine taxi, which had parked outside the wine bar that they had been frequenting. However, when going into the finer detail, they suddenly came to realize that he may have gotten into a bogus "taxi."

    Consequently, this task proved to be invaluable in ascertaining that this was increasingly likely to be organized crime, as opposed to being something that was specific to these NATO exercises. A mitigation measure that was implemented, as a result of this engagement, was the requirement for all deployed personnel to receive travel security briefings and be reminded of the importance of familiarizing themselves with the travel advice made available to them by the Foreign and Commonwealth Office (FCO):[19]

"If you travel by taxi, use official, licensed taxis or a pre-booked minicab. We recommend that you avoid hailing taxis on the street, and do not use taxis that stop but were not specifically hailed."

2. Being part of the security debriefing team, tasked to carry out fact-finding interviews with the 15 Royal Navy and Royal Marines service personnel, held by the Iranian authorities for a period of 15 days (as depicted in Figure 12-20[20])

Figure 12-20. *2007 Iranian security incident*

The objective of this assignment was to produce a comprehensive security report, which would detail any potential events that could have compromised either the military service operations or the individuals or their families.

---

[19]www.gov.uk/foreign-travel-advice/belgium/safety-and-security
[20]www.dailymail.co.uk/news/article-444202/Fifteen-Royal-Marines-sailors-taken-hostage-Iran.html

3. Receiving vital intelligence about illegal cigarette smuggling
    activities

    Having completed an assignment on the Central Region, Counter
    Intelligence operations, I had returned to the Counter Intelligence
    operations for an RAF establishment in North Yorkshire.

    One afternoon, while carrying out the routine daily Counter
    Intelligence operations, I received a telephone call from the Guard
    Commander at the main entry gate. I was informed that there
    was a member of the public there, who was wanting to speak to a
    member of the RAF Police. I promptly went down to meet with the
    individual, and from the initial discussions, I decided that it would
    be best if I took them back to the RAF Police Flight for a further
    interview.

    It turns out that my experiences on the Central Region would once
    again prove to be valuable. This individual provided me with some
    vital intelligence, from a conversation that they had overheard,
    involving three RAF service personnel illegally smuggling cigarettes
    into the United Kingdom[21] (as depicted in Figure 12-21[22]).

---

[21]www.bbc.co.uk/news/uk-england-12369894

[22]www.theguardian.com/uk/2010/dec/08/raf-servicemen-admit-smuggling-cigarettes

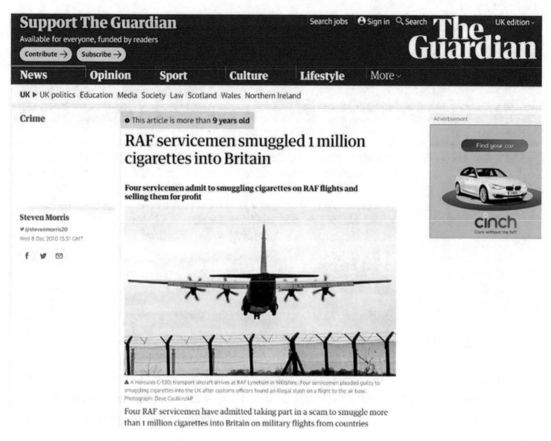

Figure 12-21. *RAF illegal cigarette smuggling*

However, when looking to develop an effective "Human Firewall," it is important to remember that it is a two-way process, and it is essential that the application is proportionate to the local situation.

I recall an occasion when I felt it necessary to apply additional measures to those that had been expected from, by the overseeing RAF Police Squadron *(not privy to the local situation)*. The RAF establishment had been planning for a public military event (PME), involving the funeral (as depicted in Figure 12-22[23]), at a local Cathedral, for an RAF Officer and a close friend of the Station Commander.

---

[23]www.pprune.org/military-aviation/366407-sqn-ldr-pete-mcnamara.html

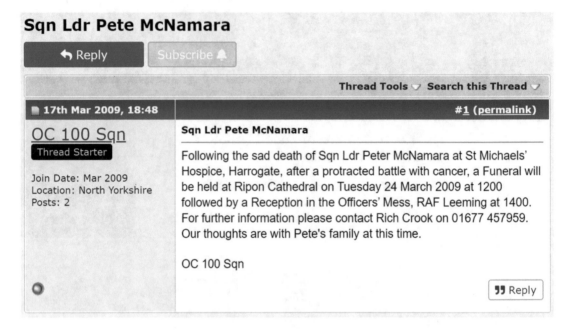

Sqn Ldr Pete McNamara

↩ Reply   Subscribe 🔔

Thread Tools ▽   Search this Thread ▽

🔲 17th Mar 2009, 18:48   #1 (permalink)

OC 100 Sqn
[Thread Starter]

Join Date: Mar 2009
Location: North Yorkshire
Posts: 2

Sqn Ldr Pete McNamara

Following the sad death of Sqn Ldr Peter McNamara at St Michaels' Hospice, Harrogate, after a protracted battle with cancer, a Funeral will be held at Ripon Cathedral on Tuesday 24 March 2009 at 1200 followed by a Reception in the Officers' Mess, RAF Leeming at 1400. For further information please contact Rich Crook on 01677 457959. Our thoughts are with Pete's family at this time.

OC 100 Sqn

❝ Reply

Figure 12-22. *Funeral notification*

Based on the local factors *(and being something that was close to my heart)*, against the instructions of the Squadron Warrant Officer, I had sought approval from my boss (Officer Commanding RAF Police Flight) to provide additional security measures for this event.

The funeral proceeded very well, but, as you might well imagine, the Squadron Warrant Officer had not been pleased to hear that I had gone against their instructions not to provide any additional security measures.

However, as it turns out, these actions proved to be the correct decisions, as on the following morning, the Officer Commanding Admin Wing had sought to reprimand my boss for not having provided additional support for this sensitive PME.

Fortunately, my boss had been in the fortunate position of being able to defend themselves against this reprimand, with the reference to the letter of thanks that the Station Commander had sent to me, that very same morning (as depicted in Figure 12-23).

From: Group Captain ▮▮▮▮▮▮▮▮▮▮▮▮▮▮▮

Station Commander, Royal Air Force Leeming,
NORTHALLERTON, North Yorkshire, DL7 9NJ

Tel: ▮▮▮▮▮▮ Fax: ▮▮▮▮▮▮
E-mail: ▮▮▮▮▮▮▮▮▮▮r@leeming.raf.mod.uk

Sergeant J Seaman
RAF Police Section
Royal Air Force
Leeming
NORTHALLERTON
North Yorkshire
DL7 9NJ

25 March 2009

Dear Sergeant Seaman,

I write to convey my thanks for making the security arrangements for the Funeral of Sqn Ldr McNamara that took place in Ripon Cathedral yesterday. I am well aware of the short notice that you were given and the amount of work that you put in behind the scenes to make the day run so smoothly.

It was no mean feat easing the access of over 200 people on to the Station and ensuring that they were able to park with minimal fuss. It was also comforting to know that you were providing a security presence at the Cathedral. Additionally, your staff were impeccable in appearance and attitude, which reflected very well on the high standards that you demand.

The fact that the arrangements met the expectations of the family was due in no small measure to the efforts of you and your staff. I would be grateful if you would pass on my thanks to all involved.

Yours sincerely

Figure 12-23. *Letter of appreciation*

From my personal experiences, within the Royal Air Force, I have experienced the extensive returns and benefits that can be gained through an appropriate investment in developing your "Human Firewall."

However, it is important that this involves much more than just having a set of documented policies and procedures, and it requires a "Top-Down" and "Bottom-Up" approach, where the end users are suitably engaged and feel that they can actively contribute to the defense of the organization, they understand the intent and reason for any rules, and are periodically reminded about these rules and procedures *(continuing engagement, communication, and security awareness training)*.

The "insider threat" remains an ever-present risk for the military, and, consequently, they continue to carry out research[24] into this very same subject and continue to report on this subject costing the UK military £60 million per year (as depicted in Figure 12-24[25]).

Figure 12-24. *Extract from Soldier Magazine*

Building BRIDGES

When looking at developing your "Human Firewall," there are numerous departments that can make a positive contribution to your organization's defensive efforts. In this section, we will use the **BRIDGES** acronym to highlight one higher-risk business department.

---

[24]https://dsb.cto.mil/reports/2020s/CI_ExecutiveSummary.pdf

[25]https://edition.pagesuite-professional.co.uk/html5/reader/production/default.aspx?pubname=&edid=f8a8c4f3-ea6a-4e2e-b592-39de6e001776&pnum=24

An organization has identified that their in-house software development team needs to be assessed to ensure that it is being afforded appropriate levels of protection and to safeguard that the developed software is not vulnerable.

Business Context

As an organization that has an in-house software development team, it is extremely important to ensure that any in-house developed software/applications have security requirements incorporated into them.

Risk and Resilience

No new software/applications should be introduced into the live environments, which contain any vulnerabilities which could increase the risk to the organization.

Where these vulnerabilities are unable to be remediated, based upon the business needs, the senior management should be involved in the risk assessment process to ensure that the business is able to make an informed decision regarding any inherited risks.

If the business requires the introduction of vulnerable software/applications, mitigation courses of action should be presented to the business and the most suitable options implemented to reduce the risks to within the organization's risk appetite levels.

Identify and Isolate

When looking to introduce secure development practices, it is essential that you identify the various software development responsibilities and ensure that there is an established separation of environments and duties, across the development, testing and production environments.

Additionally, formal software development standards should be developed, and all software development personnel should be included in the creation of a suitable standard to ensure that they feel that they have contributed, with the opportunity to make recommendations and to provide feedback.

The secure software development standard should provide clear detail on what steps must be followed during their software development roles, for example:

- Coding practices

- Input validation

- Output encoding

- Authentication and password management

- Session management

- Access control

- Cryptographic practices

- Error handling and logging

- Data protection

- Communications security

- Systems configuration

- Database security

- File management

- Memory management

- Development lifecycle

- Code quality

- Open source

Detect Anomalies

You should look to ensure that there is an established process to ensure that security considerations are addressed throughout the development lifecycle. This should enforce independent oversight to ensure that the possibility of someone "marking their own homework" is eliminated or reduced to within acceptable levels.

Security stories and relevant acceptance criteria should be added to development teams' backlogs upon project initiation.

These may be identified at various checkpoints during the development and test stages of the lifecycle, but all must be implemented (or risk assessed and accepted) by the time the development moves into production.

Consider the benefits of using automated code analysis and vulnerability scanning tools.

Static Code Analysis Tools

- Raxis[26]

- RIPS Technologies[27]

- PVS-Studio[28]

- Kiuwan[29]

- Embold[30]

Vulnerability Scanners

- Burp Suite[31]

- OWASP Zed Attack Proxy (ZAP)[32]

- WhiteHat Security[33]

- Veracode[34]

- Checkmarx[35]

Govern Processes

It is important that a program is established to ensure that the software developers are periodically reminded of what secure development operations should be and to encourage their participation in secure software development education events, for example:

---

[26]https://raxis.com/code-review

[27]www.ripstech.com/product/

[28]www.viva64.com/en/pvs-studio-download/?promo=top40

[29]www.softwaretestinghelp.com/Kiuwan-static-code-analysis

[30]https://embold.io/

[31]https://portswigger.net/burp

[32]www.zaproxy.org/

[33]www.whitehatsec.com/

[34]www.veracode.com/

[35]www.checkmarx.com/

- OWASP[36]

    - SecureFlag Open Platform[37]

The team should have an established hierarchy, where all the software developers understand the responsibilities of their roles and there are identifiable management roles that are deemed accountable for ensuring secure development practices are being followed and escalating issues for risk assessment (when required).

Evaluate Security Controls

Having established the "SecDevOps Standard," it is important to ensure that the embedded controls are independently assessed to ensure continued adherence, and any "in production" software/applications should be subject to periodic testing by an independent software/application tester.

- Synopsys[38]

- Checkmarx

- Micro Focus[39]

- Veracode

- WhiteHat Security

Survive to Operate

It is important that you remain alert to the possibility that things may go wrong and that you need to be prepared for such events. Being able to identify, quickly respond to, and contain activities or incidents that could prove to be of high risk, or provide an opportunity to your attackers, is essential for keeping business operations safe.

Developing your "Human Firewall" is a key part of being able to Survive to Operate, having a set of "eyes and ears" to help you monitor the internal processes, which could prove to be detrimental to your organization.

---

[36]https://owasp.org/

[37]https://owasp.org/www-project-secureflag-open-platform/

[38]www.synopsys.com/

[39]www.microfocus.com/en-us/home

Your "Human Firewall" should be encouraged to monitor their internal processes and to report any serious or deliberate dangerous practices. Additionally, your "Human Firewall" can provide valuable inputs into possible contingency plans, which are appropriate to their department, roles, and responsibilities.

Reality Bites

In the Ponemon Institute's 2020 research into the Costs of Insider Threats: Global Report,[40] they identified that the cost of the insider threat was significantly different based upon the type of incident.

The estimated costs had a range from

- **$307,111 to $871,686 per incident**

Despite this and although **97%** of IT leaders are reported to be worried about the "insider threat"[41] and this being purported to be the "Biggest Cyber Risk You Can't Ignore"[42] and the percentage rates of insider-related incidents (as depicted in Figure 12-25[43]), there appears to be a disparity between the business and industry concerns and the investment being made to mitigate this threat.

---

[40]https://securityintelligence.com/posts/gaining-insight-into-the-ponemon-institutes-2020-cost-of-insider-threats-report/

[41]www.helpnetsecurity.com/2020/02/24/insider-data-breaches/

[42]www.bloomberg.com/press-releases/2020-09-29/inside-jobs-why-insider-risk-is-the-biggest-cyber-threat-you-can-t-ignore

[43]https://securityintelligence.com/posts/gaining-insight-into-the-ponemon-institutes-2020-cost-of-insider-threats-report/

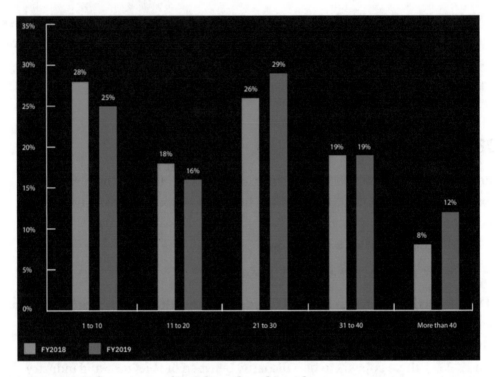

Figure 12-25. *% frequency of insider-related incidents per company*

All too often, it is after the "insider threat" becomes a reality to an organization that they start to consider making improvements to the development of their "Human Firewall."

There's an apt quote from Sir Richard Branson[44] that is truly relevant to the development of an effective "Human Firewall":

Train people well enough so they can leave.

Treat them well enough so they don't want to.

In a recent article by Thrive Global,[45] they open with this very same quote and go on to explain that your employees are your greatest asset and that the greatest investment you can make is in your people.

---

[44]www.virgin.com/branson-family/richard-branson-blog

[45]https://thriveglobal.com/stories/train-people-well-enough-so-they-can-leave-treat-them-well-enough-so-they-dont-want-to-richard-branson/

Other than accidental or negligent acts, which can cause damage to your organization, there are many things that can happen in an employee's life, which might influence them to carry out deliberate and malicious actions, for example:

- Debt

- Greed

- Disaffection

- Blackmail

- Gambling

- Bribes

Consequently, with such an array of external factors that could influence an (perhaps once loyal and trusted) employee to carry out a willful act, the importance of an effective "Human Firewall" becomes ever more relevant.

For instance, if you look at the details behind the UK Morrisons Supermarket data breach,[46] a disgruntled senior internal auditor abused their role to compromise the details of almost 100,000 supermarket staff.

In fact, this is not an isolated example, and I'm sure it is possible to author an entire book on the "insider risks/threats," containing extensive examples.

However, I would like to provide a real-life example of when the "Human Firewall" had proved to be effective in preventing a considerable data breach of a very successful US-based technology company.

A Russian criminal had plotted to use an employee from the Tesla Gigafactory to allow them to deliver ransomware to compromise the supporting IT infrastructure (as depicted in Figure 12-26[47]).

---

[46]www.bbc.co.uk/news/uk-england-leeds-33566633

[47]www.teslarati.com/tesla-employee-fbi-thwarts-russian-cybersecurity-attack/

Figure 12-26. *Tesla Gigafactory*

For the employee's participation in this attack, they would receive $1 million (raised from the initial offer of $500,000). It turns out that despite this lucrative offer, after refusing the offer, it was the employee who reported this to the Tesla authorities.

An amazing story and one that had all the excitement and nail-biting elements you would find in a modern spy/crime fiction movie.

Key Takeaways

- The development of an effective "Human Firewall" is just as (if not more) important as the technology-based Protective Security measures.

- An effective "Human Firewall" requires a Top-Down, Bottom-Up approach, where all employees are encouraged to contribute.

- The "Human Firewall" strategy should embrace the employees' sense of self-actualization.

- The strategy should involve a widespread representation from the business and should not be restricted to only representatives from IT.

- An effective "Human Firewall" requires a team effort, with everyone coming together to encourage a good security culture across the organization.

- The strategy should support the continual investment in formal training and awareness to ensure that everyone knows the rules and procedures.

- An effective "Human Firewall" strategy requires a far more proactive approach than just the creation and publication of policies and procedures.

- Personnel should be encouraged to be engaged in the protection of the business assets and to provide feedback, where the rules and procedures could be improved.

- Two-way communication is an essential element of a successful strategy, ensuring personnel are engaged across cross-disciplines.

- Senior management need to be supportive of the program to ensure that appropriate resources are made available to ensure that everyone has a baseline understanding.

CHAPTER 13

Strict Access Restrictions

Today, therefore, a commander must ensure that his troops always know what they are being asked to do, and how that fits into the larger plan. I have always insisted that before a battle the essentials of the plan are known right through the chain of command, and finally down to the rank and file. The troops must know how a commander is going to fight the battle and what they are to play in it; this must be explained to them by word of mouth, for that counts far more than the written word.

And then when the battle has been won, and the troops see that the battle has gone as the commander said it would be, their confidence in the high command will be very great.

This confidence is beyond price.

Military commentator and correspondent from Thoughts on War, 1944[1]

---

[1]Henry, B. (1999). Thoughts on war. Staplehurst: Spellmount.

J. Seaman, *Protective Security*, https://doi.org/10.1007/978-1-4842-6908-4_13

Figure 13-1. *Captain Liddell Hart*

Introduction

Captain Liddell Hart's words have never been truer than when looking to create strict access restrictions for a business' digital solutions. Every time a login screen is made available to the wider audience, it is like sending troops into war, with the Internet representing the battle fields.

Consequently, it is essential that everyone knows the importance of strict access control and how secure access credential management practices assist a digital business to fight their battles.

As mentioned by Hart, this cannot be achieved by written word alone (policies), and this needs to be effectively communicated to all those who are granted access, those who authorize the access, or those personnel who are responsible for the secure management of the access system.

- Secure access management is a team effort.

Background

The NIST[2] provides several definitions for access control; here is just a small selection of them:

The process of granting or denying specific requests to:

1) *obtain and use information and related information processing services; and*

2) *enter specific physical facilities (e.g., federal buildings, military establishments, border crossing entrances).*

NIST SP800-12 Rev. 1 (An Introduction to Information Security)[3]

The process of permitting or restricting access to applications at a granular level, such as per-user, per-group, and per-resources.

NIST SP800-113 (Guide to SSL VPNs)[4]

The process of granting access to information technology (IT) system resources only to authorized users, programs, processes, or other systems.

NIST SP800-47 (Security Guide for Interconnecting Information Technology Systems)[5]

How access to the cryptographic devices or applications are to be authorized, controlled, and validated to request, generate, handle, distribute, store, use and/or destroy keying material. Any use of authenticators, such as passwords, personal identification numbers (PINs) and hardware tokens, should be included. For example, in PKI cryptographic applications, role and identity-based authentication and authorization, and the use of any tokens should be described.

NIST SP 800-57, Part 2 (Recommendation for Key Management)[6]

---

[2]https://csrc.nist.gov/glossary/term/access_control
[3]https://doi.org/10.6028/NIST.SP.800-12r1
[4]https://doi.org/10.6028/NIST.SP.800-113
[5]https://nvlpubs.nist.gov/nistpubs/Legacy/SP/nistspecialpublication800-47.pdf
[6]https://nvlpubs.nist.gov/nistpubs/SpecialPublications/NIST.SP.800-57pt2r1.pdf

Alternatively, Techopedia[7] defines access control as being

A way of limiting access to a system or to physical or virtual resources. In computing, access control is a process by which users are granted access and certain privileges to systems, resources, or information.

In access control systems, users must present credentials before they can be granted access. In physical systems, these credentials may come in many forms, but credentials that can't be transferred provide the most security.

All these definitions state the requirement for limiting and managing access to systems, applications, buildings, rooms, and so on to only authorized personnel.

However, as simplistic as this may appear, secure access management continues to be highly problematic for today's digital business and, as a result, is increasingly being leveraged by criminals as a successful attack vector.

Why is this? Simply put, it is because it relies on a securely configured and managed backend operation (e.g., Active Directory and User Access Management) and consumer/user secure password management.

Let's face it; secure access management can prove exceedingly difficult to manage and may become an inconvenience for the consumer/user. This then impacts their experience, which can then affect the convenience and usability of the digital interfaces – which, by addressing this often, makes them increasingly vulnerable and favored as a potential attack vector.

The greater the number of digital applications that rely on sensitive information, the greater the appeal for today's criminals. Additionally, the greater the number of digital interfaces and web/cloud-based applications, the increasingly difficult it is for the consumer/user to commit the access credentials to memory.

It has become increasingly difficult for consumers and end users to commit their strong access credentials to memory (e.g., passwords, PINs, answers to security questions, etc.), and, as a result, they are either reusing the same "strong password" across multiple logins, are creating sequential passwords (e.g., P@ssword1, P@ssword2, Password3, etc.), or are using easy-to-remember passwords.

---

[7]www.techopedia.com/definition/5831/access-control

NIST's SP800-63B (Digital Identity Guidelines: Authentication and Lifecycle Management)[8] provides the following guidance regarding passwords:

- **Length**

  The minimum password length that should be required depends to a large extent on the threat model being addressed. Online attacks where the attacker attempts to log in by guessing the password can be mitigated by limiting the rate of login attempts permitted.

  For example:

  Payment Card Industry Data Security Standards (PCI DSS)

  - Minimum of seven characters

- **Complexity**

  Composition rules are commonly used to increase the difficulty of guessing user-chosen passwords. Research has shown, however, that users respond in very predictable ways to the requirements imposed by composition rules.

  Consequently, the difficulties faced by the consumers/end users in maintaining secure password management make these an extremely rewarding attack vector for today's criminals.

  A mix of characters:

  1. Lowercase

  2. Uppercase

  3. Numbers

  4. Symbols (special characters)

Table 13-1 demonstrates the differences between chosen passwords.

---

[8]https://nvlpubs.nist.gov/nistpubs/SpecialPublications/NIST.SP.800-63b.pdf

Table 13-1. *Password Comparisons*

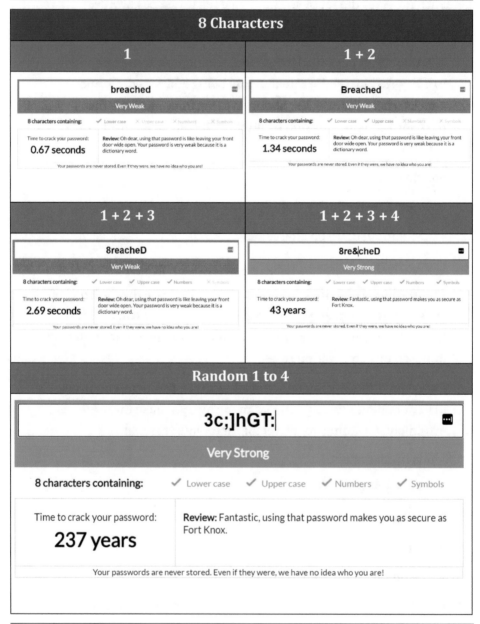

(continued)

Table 13-1. (*continued*)

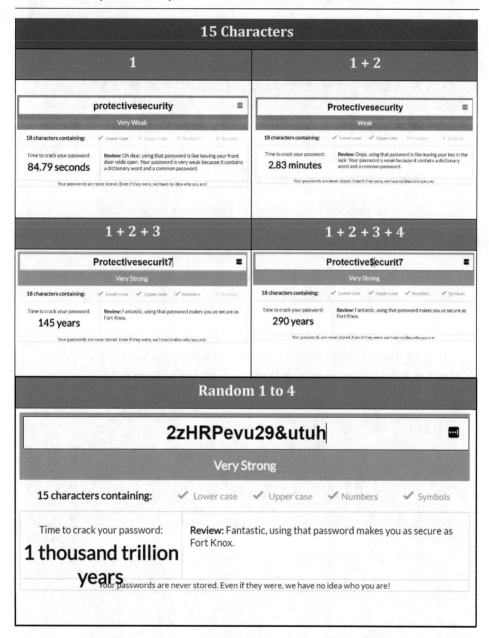

Easy passwords are easily cracked (as depicted in Figure 13-2[9]).

---

[9]www.my1login.com/resources/password-strength-test/

How secure is your password?

Tip: Try to make your passwords at least 15 characters long   Show password: ☑

Password1	⬛
Very Weak	

9 characters containing: ✓ Lower case   ✓ Upper case   ✓ Numbers   ✗ Symbols

Time to crack your password: **0 seconds**	**Review:** Oh dear, using that password is like leaving your front door wide open. Your password is very weak because it contains a common password and a dictionary word.

Your passwords are never stored. Even if they were, we have no idea who you are!

Figure 13-2. *My1Login password strength test*

- With reused strong passwords, once one password is compromised, all other applications using the same password are compromised.

Note.

By using haveibeenpwned, you can check if one of your online accounts has been compromised (as depicted in Figure 13-3[10]).

Figure 13-3. *Have I Been Pwned website*

---

[10]https://haveibeenpwned.com/

532

Defending from the Enemy at Your Gates

Imagine that your corporate environment as being like a deployed operating base (much like Camp Bastion, as depicted in Figure 13-4[11]).

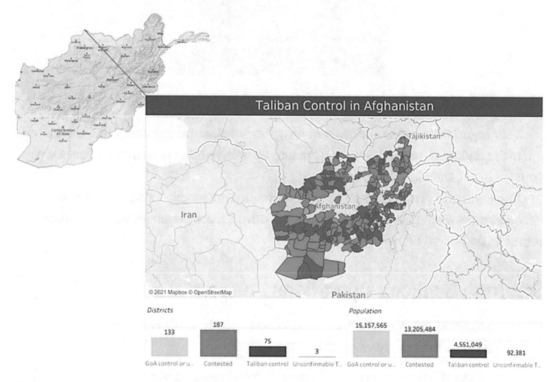

Figure 13-4. *Camp Bastion location*

Your business is sited within a hostile environment, with the enemy encamped within the boundaries of your business and indistinguishable from the friendlies (as depicted in Figure 13-5).

---

[11]www.longwarjournal.org/mapping-taliban-control-in-afghanistan

Figure 13-5. *Enemy at the gates?*

Your organization still needs to remain operational, requiring assets to move in and out of the badlands, while preventing the enemy from gaining unauthorized access to your environment and valuable assets.

Consequently, ensuring strict access restrictions are enabled and maintained becomes an essential part of an effective Protective Security strategy, which requires robust Backend and Frontend Operations.

Securing Backend Operations

I'm going to avoid differentiating between logical and physical access control management, as the principles are the same:

- **The effective utilization of access control systems to prevent unauthorized access to business assets while allowing the managed access of approved individuals, who have a legitimate business need to access these business assets**

This requires an effective "gate keeper" process (Backend Operations) to manage and monitor the access control system while ensuring that the "keys" (passwords, proximity cards, etc.) and additional authentication requirements (e.g., multifactor authentication (MFA)) are only established for authorized individuals (Frontend Operations).

Effective Backend Operations need to be formalized through documented policies and procedures, with all responsible personnel knowing how these policies apply to their role, in support of these Backend Operations.

The objective of the Backend Operations is to strictly restrict access to sensitive business assets, to monitor its effectiveness, and to respond to any **ABNORMAL** activities.

Account Management

Account types are identified and selected based upon legitimate support of business missions/functions, and account managers are assigned to ensure conditions for group and role membership are established, including specifics for authorized users, and ensure all access requires formal approval.

The account managers are responsible for the creation, enablement, modification, disablement, and removal of the live accounts and for actively monitoring the use of the accounts (being proactive rather than reactive).

Department managers will work with the account managers to ensure that accounts are disabled when no longer needed (e.g., termination/transfer), and access is granted based on strict need to know/access criteria.

Only access to these assets will be enabled using a valid authorization (e.g., unique ID, assigned password/PIN/biometrics, proximity access card, etc.) and for the intended use, based upon defined business missions/functions.

An audit trail should be established that ensures that access can be assigned to an individual, and the use of privileged user accounts should be strictly limited to specific business missions/functions.

- **Avoid the unnecessary use of privileged accounts for duties that can be achieved through standard access. Access should be based upon the principle of "least privilege."[12]**

    - *If it is convenient for the employer, it can prove convenient to the opportunist attacker.*

Logical and physical access should strictly enforce access restrictions based upon approved authorizations.

---

[12]https://csrc.nist.gov/glossary/term/Principle_of_Least_Privilege

All access for employees, customers, suppliers, and so on should be robustly monitored to quickly identify potential malicious activities, for example:

- Unsuccessful access attempts/logins

    - End user difficulties or something more sinister, for example:

        - An attempted brute-force[13] attack

- System use/misuse

    - Using a fire extinguisher to prop open a physical access control barrier

    - Logins outside a user's normal times or from an unexpected location.

        - Are the actions deemed acceptable or expected?

        - Are the actions unusual for that end user's role?

- Remote access

    - Is this usual for this end user?

        - Location

        - Time

        - Duration

- Wireless access

    - Is this an authorized device accessing via wireless?

- Mobile devices

    - Is this an authorized mobile device?

- Use of external information systems

    - Are the activities what you would expect of this end user?

---

[13]https://attack.mitre.org/techniques/T1110/

All end users should receive an appropriate level of training (appropriate to their roles) to ensure that they understand the importance they play (as key custodians) in safeguarding their access, what is expected of them, and how they should report any suspicious activities or potential loss/compromise of their access credentials (keys).

Whether this is an automated logical access control system (e.g., Active Directory) or physical electronic automated access control system (EAACS), it is essential that the logs are subjected to periodic sampling reviews to help in the proactive identification of potential **ABNORMAL** activities, compromised access credentials, or misuse of end user privileges.

The logs should clearly identify individual access attempts, so that in the event of a compromise or breach, the root cause or culprit can be easily identified. Consequently, your access control (physical and logical) system logs should work in harmony with any closed-circuit television (CCTV) monitoring and time synchronization technologies (e.g., times for the physical access, logical access, and CTTV are consistent across all monitoring systems).

- How easily and quickly could you identify unusual physical access activity or malicious attempts to circumvent the physical access controls?

- Do you proactively monitor the access logs for both your physical and logical access control systems?

- Are you solely reliant on the logical and access control systems to enforce access restrictions?

- Do you appreciate the value that the access control (physical and logical) system logs provide to your organization in helping to identify the **ABNORMAL**?

- How frequently do you carry out audits of your access control (physical and logical) system logs?

    - Periodic sampling?

    - After the event/incident audit trails?

        - Who might have done what and when?

Frontend Operations

Working in harmony with the Backend Operations, any individual who is deemed to be approved for authorized access owns a shared responsibility to ensure that the "keys to the gate" remain protected and that they respect the fact that they are a target for criminals.

Consequently, it is essential that secure keys (authentication protocols) are generated and used as per the organization's access control policies and procedures. This is what I call "Frontend Operations" (as depicted in Figure 13-6), for example:

- Access credential management

- End user account management

- End user device management

- End user acceptable use

- Eavesdropping management

Figure 13-6. *Frontend Operations*

Today's criminals have recognized that most organizations have trust in their employees and as a result may pay less attention to monitoring their "trusted assets." Consequently, these "trusted assets" are regarded as opportunist attack vectors that the criminals can use to evade or undermine a business' defensive efforts.

The criminals have identified that human behavior provides them a unique opportunity to exploit poor habits, for example:

- Enticing an employee to click a malicious link or download some harmful software

- Providing unauthorized access to sensitive data through careless habits, for example:

  - Having a sensitive conversation in a public place

    - Overhearing

  - Accessing sensitive data on a mobile device in a public place

    - Overseeing

- Being careless with or struggling to maintain their secure and robust keys, which allow them authorized access to the valued business assets

- Accessing sensitive areas via insecure network environments

- Being unaware of the dangers of publishing far too much personal or sensitive data on social media websites, which (much like pieces of a jigsaw puzzle) are collected up and pieced together by the criminals

- Being overtrusting and helpful of people, resulting in them bypassing the access control measures to allow unauthorized access

  - Let's face it; it is not in most people's nature to challenge others or to be untrusting of others.

    - This is exactly why criminals' use of social engineering has proven so successful for them and is regarded as the weak link in the business security chain (Chapter 2: Social Engineering Penetration Testing[14]).

---

[14]Watson, G., Ackroyd, R., Mason, A. and Seaman, J. (2014). Social Engineering Penetration Testing. Syngress.

Indeed, having robust and strong Frontend Operations in ensuring strict access restrictions has become as equally important as having the effective Backend Operations and clearly requires the three-pillar approach (as depicted in Figure 13-7[15]) to be applied across the Backend and Frontend perspectives.

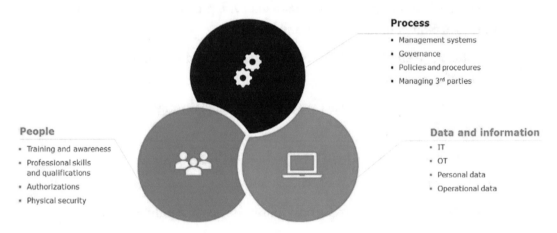

Figure 13-7. DNV-GL 3 pillars

It is no longer appropriate just to expect the Frontend Operations to run efficiently and effectively without some investment of time and resources to identify the specific risks to the Frontend and to provide proportionate mitigation controls to reduce these risks to within acceptable tolerances and to act as a complement to the Backend Operations.

As an example, if you were to engage with your sales team or senior management, you may discover that they have a business requirement to carry out work while traveling on public transport and, as a result, have an increased risk of being overlooked. However, for a relatively small investment, this risk could be reduced through some security awareness training and the procurement of privacy screen filters (as depicted in Figure 13-8[16]) that can be used with their mobile devices.

---

[15]www.dnvgl.com/article/the-three-pillar-approach-to-cyber-security-data-and-information-protection-165683

[16]www.3m.com/3M/en_US/privacy-screen-protectors-us/comply/

Figure 13-8. *Privacy protection screens*

Additionally, another area of difficulty for the Frontend Operations is the management of their access credentials, and this is often not helped by some organizations' insistence on enforcing rigorous access credential management requirements, for example:

- Password must meet strong criteria:

  - Lengthy string

    - **15 characters or more**

  - Must include a combination of

    - **Uppercase characters**

    - **Lowercase characters**

    - **Numbers**

    - **Symbols (special characters)**

  - Must be changed frequently:

    - **Every 30 calendar days (20 working days)**

- Must not be a previously used password.

  - **Not the same as the one used in the past four passwords.**

- Passwords must not be written down.

- Passwords must not be commonly cracked passwords (as depicted in Figure 13-9[17]).

Position	Password	Number of users	Time to crack it	Times exposed
1. ↑ (2)	123456	2,543,285	Less than a second	23,597,311
2. ↑ (3)	123456789	961,435	Less than a second	7,870,694
3. (new)	picture1	371,612	3 Hours	11,190
4. ↑ (5)	password	360,467	Less than a second	3,759,315
5. ↑ (6)	12345678	322,187	Less than a second	2,944,615
6. ↑ (17)	111111	230,507	Less than a second	3,124,368
7. ↑ (18)	123123	189,327	Less than a second	2,238,694
8. ↓ (1)	12345	188,268	Less than a second	2,389,787
9. ↑ (11)	1234567890	171,724	Less than a second	2,264,884
10. (new)	senha	167,728	10 Seconds	8,213

Figure 13-9. *Commonly cracked passwords*

Consequently, while the end user is struggling to remember and manage this and all the other access credentials *(typically more than **40**)*, they end up doing the following: Establishing password chains:

- Creating memorable corresponding strings

- Reusing the same "strong" passwords across multiple logins

- Creating convenient passwords that are easy to compromise

As a business, you need to allow the Frontend Operations to interact with the "badlands," providing the opportunity to use these interfaces as a "mule" to help deliver malicious payloads or to act as a conduit to gain unauthorized access to the inner sanctums.

---

[17]https://nordpass.com/most-common-passwords-list/

Why wouldn't you consider the benefits of reducing these risks through such things as

- Adjusting the access credential requirements (as per the NIST guidance[18]) or providing the Frontend Operations with supporting technical solutions (e.g., password managers[19])

- Providing additional protective measures

- Providing suitable levels of training to help them to be a more effective contribution to Frontend Operations

Two/Multifactor/Strong Customer Authentication

Another enhancement to Frontend Operations is the use of an additional layer of access protection, where the user is required to use an additional method to authenticate themselves:

1. Something you know (e.g., password, PIN, etc.)

2. Something you have (e.g., token, smart card, etc.)

3. Something you are (e.g., fingerprint, retinal scan, etc.)

By employing two or more of these requirements to meet the two-factor authentication (2FA),[20] multifactor authentication (MFA),[21] or strong customer authentication (SCA),[22] you are providing an additional barrier to the opportunist criminals. Rather than just needing to compromise the passwords, they need to compromise the other authentication elements.

A compromised username and password, via a phishing email, will not allow unauthorized access to the accounts.

---

[18]www.isaca.org/-/media/files/isacadp/project/isaca/articles/journal/2019/volume-1/nists-new-password-rule-book_joa_eng_0119.pdf

[19]https://digital.com/password-managers/

[20]www.liquidweb.com/blog/what-is-two-factor-authentication/

[21]www.centristic.com/2020/07/06/mfa-is-quite-simple/

[22]www.signifyd.com/psd2-strong-customer-authentication/

Note.

Despite several social media accounts offering (not by default) this enhanced authentication model (as depicted in Figure 13-10[23]), many users/consumers regard the additional hassle, for using further authentication requirements, as an inconvenience and do not take up this option.

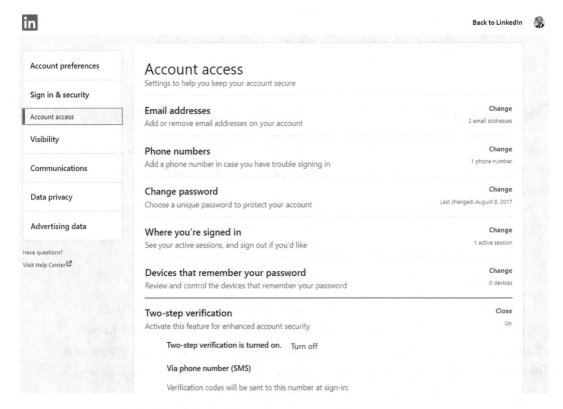

Figure 13-10. *LinkedIn two-step verification setting*

However, it is important to remember that this is a case of balancing this inconvenience with the risks/threats. If you value the data that resides within, you should promote the value and benefits multilayered access controls bring.

- **If it is easy and convenient for the user, it is likely to be easy and convenient for the opportunist attacker.**

---

[23]www.linkedin.com/help/linkedin/answer/544/turning-two-step-verification-on-and-off?lang=en

Military Comparison

Having served 22 years in military service, in the RAF Police, I have been directly involved in, or the supervision of, enforcing strict access restrictions and especially (prior to the UK Government's Options for Change[24]) regarding the control of access to several RAF establishments:

- RAF Brize Norton

- RAF Marham

- RAF Leeming

- RAF Oakhanger

- RAF Aldergrove, Northern Ireland

- RAF Linton On Ouse

- RAFO Thumrait, Oman

Whether this was controlling the access at the main gate of the establishment or an internal access gate or an aircraft apron,[25] the principles were the same. Ensure that the individual could be identified (RAF Form 1250/MOD 90 identity card) and was authorized to access the environment (e.g., access control list, "PIT" tag exchange, etc.).

If I had a pound (£) for every time I had used the phrase:

Sir, please do not confuse your rank, with my authority!

I would have been an extraordinarily rich man.

Consequently, I have endless tales providing the value of effective access restrictions, ranging from some of the incidents that occurred in Camp Bastion (potential suicide bomber, local national caught in the perimeter fence line, etc.), as mentioned in my book about Payment Card Security (*PCI DSS: An Integrated Data Security Standard Guide*[26]).

However, rather than focus on retelling the same accounts, I will focus on my first role as a Counter Intelligence operative, where I not only had oversight responsibilities for the main access/egress but also had responsibility for maintaining the internal strict access restrictions.

---

[24]www.rafpa.com/history.htm

[25]www.forces.net/military-life/fun/guide-understanding-raf-slang-and-terminology

[26]Seaman, J. (2020). PCI DSS : an integrated data security standard guide. S.L.: Apress.

This was enabled using various security graded buildings, rooms, and containers. Where there was a need to retain hardcopy media, containing sensitive data assets, these needed to be retained securely but made accessible to those who had a legitimate need to access the data.

To enable this, I had the responsibility for managing and maintaining a large estate of mark 4 manifoil combination locks (MCL; as depicted in Figures 13-11[27] and 13-12[28]) and their containers.

Figure 13-11. *Mark 4 MCL*

Figure 13-12. *MCL use*

---

[27]http://safe-opening.co.uk/manifoil_mk4.htm

[28]www.youtube.com/watch?v=vjtiy2r6wDE

As the custodian for this estate of MCL, I had the responsibility for carrying out servicing and maintenance of the locks and ensuring that the combinations were periodically changed and an effective recovery process (in case of authorized users forgetting the combination) was established.

Now, much like some of your growing number of applications and systems, to which you need to commit to memory a unique access code or password, some of these containers may only have needed to have been accessed on exceedingly rare occasions.

To access the contents of these secure cabinets, authorized users needed to enter a unique combination (## – ## – ## and opening digits ##, e.g., 21 – 32 – 43 – 75). However, you didn't want to make these combinations too easy to guess, but they needed to be committed to memory.

Consequently, based around the Battle Code concept (aka BATCO, as depicted in Figure 13-13[29]), I would place a grid (as depicted in Figure 13-14) on the wall adjacent to the locks, which they could use as a prompt to help them remember the combination code.

EDITION NO. 819   PAGE NO. 21   COPY NO. 001
PERIOD OF USE: FROM   TO

	2	3	4	5	6	7	0	0	1	2	3	4	5	6	7	8	9	CH	.
O	F	T	R	H	X		VU	PS	OZ	BX	IQ	ME	KG	DF	YH	RA	JL	WN	TC
X	O	X	J	D	T		CF	VG	SK	YL	IA	RJ	EB	ZP	WU	NH	QD	DT	XM
I	P	H	C	V	A		NT	RZ	OC	FK	PQ	NH	YS	LX	GE	VJ	MU	IW	DB
Y	V	F	L	N	H		YA	KM	BN	EX	ZO	RS	DW	HU	QC	JT	PV	LI	GF
D	Z	Z	Y	G	W		XV	EN	SF	AT	BG	MZ	QO	PY	HW	UI	JD	LR	KC
H	W	J	B	I	K		HY	AF	ZP	MT	XI	JG	DN	QB	LR	OE	KU	CW	SV
U	E	W	T	J	I		VX	GF	LS	OT	MW	CP	DE	QR	KA	YN	UZ	BH	IJ
J	I	C	N	C	S		CJ	TM	DZ	QY	BK	WO	UG	SR	EH	IX	LP	AN	FV
K	G	N	U	P	G		PW	KN	HF	EY	ZU	TR	OC	BA	SG	XL	ID	JQ	VM
N	X	O	K	L	L		DY	TH	WR	XU	SF	BL	OM	PQ	CZ	GJ	KE	AN	VI
S	S	V	W	K	R		QZ	XN	LK	HR	JP	CY	AE	IS	OW	UT	FV	DM	BG
M	R	Q	Z	B	D		JF	EH	NT	DS	MR	AC	WY	UG	VX	OQ	LI	PB	ZK
T	A	M	H	R	Q		LE	QI	BK	TY	WA	NC	MU	JG	XR	DZ	HP	VT	SO
L	B	K	S	T	P		NQ	GC	FI	YZ	BJ	RM	WP	TL	DX	VH	ES	UO	AK
R	Y	D	Q	E	B		OM	ED	GX	IF	RW	YT	QN	UA	JL	BH	KS	PV	ZC
C	D	P	G	O	Y		LS	JN	OG	IE	BX	WD	CH	ZY	UP	FN	QA	RT	VK
A	C	G	D	S	J		JZ	GV	LW	YF	EN	MD	PX	TC	BQ	UH	IK	RO	SA
E	N	E	O	M	Z		UM	ZR	BO	EW	SH	IT	AD	YX	PN	QJ	VK	LF	CG
G	L	R	P	Y	M		UY	QF	XO	TE	LJ	MV	WP	NK	IG	SD	RC	ZB	HA
P	K	Y	A	U	C		AC	UW	FD	VS	KZ	PY	QB	GI	LT	RO	HE	NX	MJ
B	H	I	M	Z	N		JN	VH	KA	UI	ZW	EO	SP	BQ	XM	RF	LD	TY	GC
Q	M	U	I	X	E		RX	CJ	BI	UM	WA	OQ	YT	DS	GP	VN	FH	IZ	EK
F	Q	B	X	Q	F		DA	ZS	HF	QX	TN	WG	VY	IE	UP	BO	CR	LM	KJ
V	U	S	V	F	U		QX	OC	MU	DS	NF	EA	IT	YV	ZL	JP	BH	WR	KG
W	J	A	E	A	V		CE	MD	AU	QS	VX	JO	PY	RK	FN	IG	HW	TB	ZL
X	T	L	F	W	O		TN	DZ	FV	EC	JM	HB	GR	AS	WX	PL	KU	OQ	IY

	8	9	3	5	1	6		0	1	2	3	4	5	6	7	8	9
2	E	G	M	V	L	P	4	73	31	21	14	43	81	01	90	42	89
4	O		W	A	H		1	40	36	64	32	63	15	98	74	44	47
9	S	F	C		B	J	5	37	70	57	48	07	62	02	99	39	76
3	T	R	N	Q	K	D	2	30	34	03	75	52	51	60	92	49	58
7		X	U	Z	Y	I	9	50	13	35	17	04	23	69	78	72	24

H	I	X	V	A	L	U	D	C	F	R	N	S	Q	Y	O	T	B	J	W	K	P	M	E	G
2	3	4	3	4	3	4	3	3	3	4	2	2	2	3	3	4	4	2	3	4	4	2	3	4

Figure 13-13. BATCO grid

---

[29]https://military.wikia.org/wiki/BATCO

	A	B	C	D	E	F	G	H	I	J	K	L	M
N	0	9	5	2	4	1	7	8	3	6	5	3	8
O	8	1	2	7	5	6	9	0	3	4	2	8	7
P	1	6	2	8	7	5	3	9	0	4	5	6	9
Q	4	6	8	1	5	9	7	0	3	2	4	0	9
R	2	4	0	9	3	5	7	6	8	1	7	8	1
S	3	5	8	7	1	9	0	6	2	4	9	1	6
T	0	3	4	9	1	2	7	6	8	5	5	3	1
U	3	8	4	2	7	0	1	5	9	6	7	9	3
V	4	8	2	3	9	6	0	1	5	7	6	4	5
W	3	7	5	6	9	2	1	8	0	4	9	0	6
X	0	8	1	6	3	4	9	7	2	5	7	9	3
Y	9	5	6	3	7	2	1	4	8	0	3	0	9
Z	1	7	6	9	8	3	5	2	4	0	4	5	0

S	E	C	U	R	E
3	4	5	3	2	4

L	O	C	K	E	D
3	8	5	5	4	2

Figure 13-14. *MCL grid*

These security containers were only to be used for the storage of sensitive data, and it was prohibited for using the containers for another purpose (segregation of use), that is, secure storage of the Squadron Team Bar funds.

Access to these security containers was strictly restricted, based upon an access control list, provided by the unit security officer (USyO)/branch security officer (BSyO). Other than the scheduled combination changes, the combinations would also be immediately changed when someone had their access revoked (e.g., change of role, termination, etc.) or if compromise was suspected.

Using the same principle, you can make it easier to create and remember secure authentication data, without having to write the passwords down.

For example, by applying a memorable pattern or reference, you can easily create and remember secure passwords (as depicted in Figure 13-15).

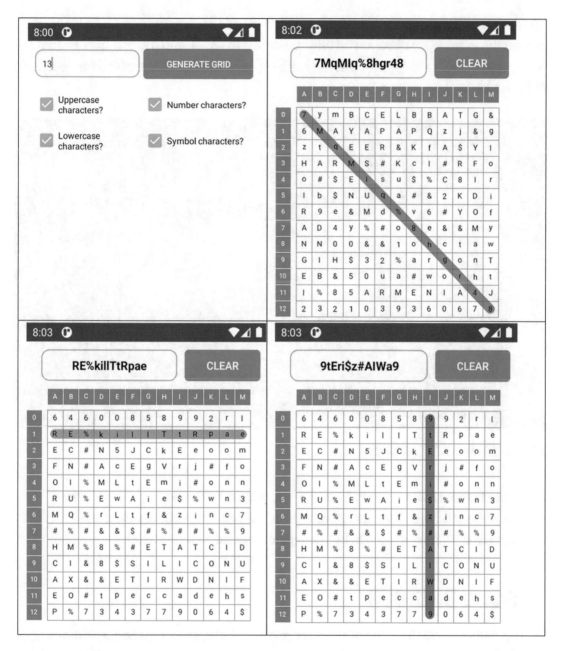

Figure 13-15. *Grid-lock application*

In preparation for these duties, we had this included within the 10-week residential Counter Intelligence training course, which also included the stripping down and reassembling of these complex locks. However, this was the phase of the training I had missed out on because of the sudden death of my father. Fortunately, the instructor gave up some of his time over the weekend to deliver one-to-one mentoring to enable me to answer the exam essay question on how to operate the MCL and the practical evaluation of being faced with a stripped-down lock, which needed to be reassembled (as depicted in Figure 13-16[30]).

Figure 13-16. *MCL maintenance*

I have learned many lessons from the management of the MCL property estate, which can be seen to be directly applicable for the enhancement of strict access restriction requirements, used to help safeguard valued business assets.

Building BRIDGES

To help demonstrate the value of strict access restrictions, I will now convey this using the **BRIDGES** acronym for a specific business area of operation.

---

[30]www.youtube.com/watch?v=UFFRUH_3fPO

Business Context

ABC Company has a sales team which is deemed an essential component of their profitability. A primary role of the sales team, as you can well imagine, involves the extensive interaction with customers and their personal details.

Consequently, the organization wants to ensure that the sales team remains safe, secure, and trustworthy, which requires the assurance that this part of the business has a reduced risk for the compromise of the customers' personal data.

Risk and Resilience

The sales team has proven particularly good at customer relations, but their security culture had not, previously, been regarded as a risk. However, following a review of the sales operations, there were several issues observed regarding their Frontend Operations. This, in turn, could significantly undermine the efforts of the Backend Operations.

For example, they were seen to have a very relaxed attitude to the access controls around their Frontend IT assets:

- For convenience, they would share access credentials into the network-connected business IT systems.

- Often, the business IT systems would be left "unlocked" while unsupervised but in the presence of a customer (stranger).

- They would frequently leave customers alone, for periods of time, with uncontrolled access to the payment card reader devices and business IT systems.

    - *Allowing an opportunist stranger to place a clandestine hardware keyloggers (as depicted in Figure 13-17[31]) between the keyboard and the business IT systems (capturing every keystroke) to allow the circumvention of any access restriction controls*

---

[31]www.keelog.com/airdrive-keylogger/

Figure 13-17. *Hardware keylogger*

Identify and Isolate

The business needs to ensure that all the sales teams receive security awareness training regarding the requirements for restricting access to the payment card devices and business IT systems and the risks that they are presenting by not strictly restricting the access to authorized personnel.

The payment card devices and business IT systems should be isolated and stored away, when not required. This can easily be achieved by relocating the business IT systems into an out-of-site location, for example, under the sales desk (as depicted in Figure 13-18[32]).

Figure 13-18. *Under-desk IT workstation rack*

---

[32]www.arengineering-onlineshop.co.uk/index.php?route=product/product&product_id=54

Detect Anomalies

Having established the strict access restriction controls, it would then be a requirement for the Backend Operations and the sales managers to carry out monitoring for any ABNORMAL activities or contraventions to these mitigation controls.

Govern Processes

Established roles and responsibilities should be developed, which include the strict access restriction requirements. These should be periodically communicated to the sales team members through security awareness training, policies, and procedures.

Where a member of the sales team fails to adhere to the corporate rules, this should be investigated and the offending individual's mens rea[33] or understanding of the rules investigated.

Where there was no evidence of malicious, deliberate, or criminal intent, the individual should receive refresher training. However, disciplinary action should always be a consideration where evidence is discovered.

Evaluate Security Controls

Independent periodic reviews should be established to ensure that all these mitigation access restriction controls remain effective, ensuring that the perceived risks to the sales team operations remain within the business' risk appetite levels.

Survive to Operate

Many successful business leaders appreciate the value of accepting when times are good but preparing for when bad things happen, and business may be impacted (e.g., COVID-19 pandemic).

---

[33]"A fundamental principle of Criminal Law is that a crime consists of both a mental and a physical element. Mens rea, a person's awareness of the fact that his or her conduct is criminal, is the mental element, and actus reus, the act itself, is the physical element."
Source: https://legal-dictionary.thefreedictionary.com/mens+rea

Forward-thinking leaders will accept this and will embrace the need to plan contingencies for when such events occur. This is no different with the restriction of access; things will not always go smoothly with the Backend and Frontend Operations, and these gear cogs will get out of sync or become misaligned.

Being prepared for such events can be the game changer for minimizing the impact on the business. In the event of a compromise of an email or end user account, what damage could occur?

- Could unauthorized access lead to further account compromises?

- Could a compromised account allow an attacker to move laterally across the network?

- Could an attacker use a compromised account to provide them with further credibility to launch further attacks that cause greater damage?

- What contingency plans do you have in place to limit this damage?

- How quickly could you identify and respond to a compromised end user account or an unauthorized escalation of user privileges?

Reality Bites

There are many accounts spanning throughout historic events that have clearly demonstrated how poor access control practices have undermined the strongest of defenses.

Take, for instance, the fall of the city of Constantinople,[34] which had been described as an impenetrable fortress. Despite a formidable array of physical defensive layers, after many failed attempted sieges and hundreds of years, the city was eventually compromised, as the attackers exploited the weakest points – the access/egress gates!

---

[34]www.britannica.com/event/Fall-of-Constantinople-1453

One of the most recent and notable incidents, relating to a compromise of the Frontend Operations, can be seen in the cyber-attack on The North Face.[35] The organization's web-based operations[36] had been compromised after the attacker used compromised customer credentials from other data breaches against The North Face customer logins (aka credential stuffing[37]).

Where customers had reused the same access credentials (Frontend Operations) across multiple accounts, the attackers had been able to use these to compromise their North Face logins. Therefore, The North Face's Backend Operations had to instigate their "Survive to Operate" activities and reset all their customer logins.[38]

I have a personal account of an incident which could have been avoided, had the business have listened to my concerns. I had only recently started with an organization that had just moved to Microsoft's cloud-based Office 365.

I was surprised to discover that they were allowing end user access to their accounts from any device, anywhere in the world, with the only reliance being on the unique user ID (e.g., no conditional access, multifactor authentication (MFA), etc.). However, when I voiced my concerns to the IT Operations Director and the chief information officer, I was basically "shot down in flames," being informed in no uncertain terms that this was not regarded as a risk, that it was a matter of business convenience, and that the criminals would not be interested in attacking a business-to-business (B2B) organization like theirs.

Clearly, they had not considered the risks and the additional mitigation costs needed for a secure transition to the use of Office 365 and did not want to consider the embarrassment of having to go back to the board members to get approval for the additional costs to mitigate the extra risks that they had overlooked or omitted from their initial business case, for moving the business onto Office 365.

You can probably guess what happened next; this process became convenient for the opportunist criminals!

---

[35]https://oag.ca.gov/system/files/VF%20Outdoor%20-%20Sample%20Notice%20%28CA%29.pdf
[36]www.thenorthface.com
[37]https://owasp.org/www-community/attacks/Credential_stuffing
[38]www.forbes.com/sites/leemathews/2020/11/14/
the-north-face-resets-customer-passwords-after-hackers-attempt-to-break-in/

Seven months later, three employees received a malicious email from one of the B2B customers. The email was requesting the urgent review of an attached document, access via a link. Once the link was clicked, an Office 365 login page (as depicted in Figure 13-19[39]) was presented, and the end user would enter their Office 365 credentials.

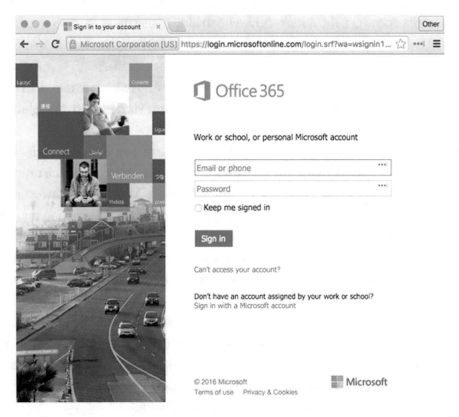

Figure 13-19. *Office 365 login web page*

The email had originated from a compromised email account from a business customer, and the link to the Office 365 login page was malicious. Of the three recipients, two ignored the email, while the third forwarded the malicious email to one of their junior assistance (who happened to have been one of the two who had originally ignored the email) and told them to

- "Deal with it, as I'm too busy!"

---

[39]www.bettercloud.com/monitor/the-academy/7-ways-identify-protect-phishing-emails/

Well, the junior assistant then clicked the link and entered their access credentials into the malicious Office 365 web page and clicked the sign-in button. However, they were then greeted with an error page and so just discounted it and carried on with their day.

Exactly 30 days later, less than 5 minutes after logging out of their Office 365 account, an unknown and unauthorized individual logged in to the account *(IP address originating from Nigeria)* and, using the considerable information available in the business email account, spent around 1 hour sending out more malicious Office 365 emails.

After around 1 hour, they logged out and another logged in, this time with an IP address originating from London, United Kingdom. This activity went on for around 4 hours, that evening *(with the attackers even responding to any emails received within this time)*, until they had sent out over 500 malicious emails.

As soon as this incident had been discovered, the response was to immediately identify any of the business' employees who could have received this email and to lock their accounts, requiring password resets. However, the distribution list for these malicious emails had not been limited to just the business' employees, and so an email had to be sent out to all those external recipients to ensure that they were made aware of the issue.

With this incident being regarded as a "near miss" for the organization, the business decision was made to upgrade the end user accounts so that conditional access[40] could be enabled.

Consequently, all access was then limited to registered devices, preventing unauthorized access in the event that an end user has their access credentials compromised. Additionally, once implemented, the users would be presented with a company-branded login web page (as depicted in Figure 13-20).

---

[40]https://techcommunity.microsoft.com/t5/azure-active-directory-identity/
introducing-conditional-access-for-the-office-365-suite/ba-p/1131979

Figure 13-20. Bespoke Office 365 login web page

However, this did not turn out to be the end of this. It took a considerable length of time to upgrade all the accounts, and the Office 365 was set up to employ single sign-on between the different Microsoft business applications, and some of the board members found changing their account passwords, or not being able to reuse the same "secure password," a great inconvenience for them.

Approximately 1 week before the conditional access was ready to be implemented (several months later), a payment clerk received several communications, across a few different mediums, purporting to be from three of the board members.

These communications were stressing that there was an urgent invoice, for around $50,000, that needed to be paid immediately. However, in one of the communications, the unknown attackers had made the mistake of addressing the recipient by their surname, when they were on first-name terms. This had made the payment clerk suspicious, resulting in him making a telephone call to the alleged originator of the communication.

Of course, once again, this had been compromised accounts that were being used by the criminals to try and get a fraudulent payment. On discovery, the payment clerk contacted me immediately to raise the alarm.

Having responded and contained the incident, the ensuing investigation revealed that none of the board members could recall having received the initial email and having compromised their accounts, and the access logs did not go back far enough to identify when this compromise may have occurred.

However, it is probably safe to assume that these senior management exceptions to the access restriction rules had allowed them to gain a clandestine persistent presence of their accounts.

The attackers even identified that my role was a threat and even took the opportunity to create a rule in the senior management's email accounts, so that if they received any emails from me, they would be moved directly into the trash.

- **Another avoidable "near miss!"**

Key Takeaways

- Strict access control is an essential component of a defense-in-depth[41] model.

- An effective access control program should be regarded as an integration between Backend and Frontend Operations.

- Backend and Frontend Operations are complementary to each other and should work in harmony with each other.

- Restrictions of access should be based on strict role or business requirements.

- Access control should include a degree of inconvenience.

- Your access control program should implement the principle of least privilege.

- Privileged access should only be used for specific requirements.

  - Where job functions can be achieved through a standard level of access, these accounts should be used.

---

[41]www.techopedia.com/definition/16509/defense-in-depth

- Backend Operations should be able to proactively detect ABNORMAL activities.

- Frontend Operations are a highly effective additional layer of defense. However, they need to understand what is acceptable and how they should report any difficulties or signs of ABNORMAL activities on their account.

- End users should be educated on the risks and receive mentoring on ways to improve the management of their account access credentials.

- Any changes to the access control measures should be risk assessed.

- Business leaders should consider the benefits of implementing measures to assist with the secure management of the Frontend Operations.

CHAPTER 14

Building Resilience

During operations, the ship's company had answered the call to action for twenty-five days. Everyone had withstood horrendous hours on duty, the pressure of attack, endlessly malfunctioning equipment, and, during off-watch periods, uncertainty about what was happening.

They had responded to praise, cajoling, and, of course, during quiet periods, reassurance that everything was going to be all right – they depended on that. But during the attack's immediate aftermath, leadership methods had to be much more direct.

Evacuation and survival need a much firmer, and louder, leadership style. There is no single approach to command. Command must adapt to the situation.

The Human in Command (as depicted in Figure 14-1[1])

Commander R A Lane
Officer Commanding HMS Coventry
Falklands Conflict, 1982

---

[1]Mccann, C. and Pigeau, R. (2000). The human in command: exploring the modern military experience. New York: Kluwer Academic/Plenum Publishers.

J. Seaman, *Protective Security*, https://doi.org/10.1007/978-1-4842-6908-4_14

Figure 14-1. *The Human in Command*

Introduction

Commander Lane's description clearly shows the resilience needed, during the Falklands conflict. Resilience is incorporated into an effective Protective Security strategy, ensuring that where the business mission or objectives require a resilient capability, this is factored into the Protective Security strategy.

Now, many new regulations incorporate the need to ensure that business and data processing operations are resilient.

European Union General Data Protection Regulation (EU GDPR)

Article 32[2]

1. Taking into account the state of the art, the costs of implementation and the nature, scope, context and purposes of processing as well as the risk of varying likelihood and severity for the rights and freedoms of natural persons, the controller and the processor shall implement appropriate technical and organisational measures to ensure a level of security appropriate to the risk, including inter alia as appropriate:

---

[2]www.privacy-regulation.eu/en/article-32-security-of-processing-GDPR.htm

(a) the pseudonymisation and encryption of personal data;

*(b) the ability to ensure the ongoing confidentiality, integrity, availability and **resilience** of processing systems and services;*

(c) the ability to restore the availability and access to personal data in a timely manner in the event of a physical or technical incident;

(d) a process for regularly testing, assessing and evaluating the effectiveness of technical and organisational measures for ensuring the security of the processing.

UK Financial Conduct Authority (FCA)[3]

*The Bank of England (the Bank), Prudential Regulation Authority (PRA) and Financial Conduct Authority (FCA) have published a shared policy summary and co-ordinated consultation papers (CPs) on new requirements to strengthen **operational resilience** in the financial services sector.*

European Union Directive on Security of Network and Information Systems (EU NIS Directive)[4]

*(13) Operational risk is a crucial part of prudential regulation and supervision in the sectors of banking and financial market infrastructures. It covers all operations including the security, integrity and **resilience** of network and information systems.*

The requirements in respect of those systems, which often exceed the requirements provided for under this Directive, are set out in a number of Union legal acts, including:

- *rules on access to the activity of credit institutions and the prudential supervision of credit institutions and investment firms, and rules on prudential requirements for credit institutions and investment firms, which include requirements concerning operational risk;*

- *rules on markets in financial instruments, which include requirements concerning risk assessment for investment firms and for regulated markets;*

---

[3]www.fca.org.uk/publications/consultation-papers/cp-19-32-building-operational-resilience-impact-tolerances-important-business-services

[4]https://ec.europa.eu/digital-single-market/en/network-and-information-security-nis-directive

- *rules on OTC derivatives, central counterparties and trade repositories, which include requirements concerning operational risk for central counterparties and trade repositories;*

- *rules on improving securities settlement in the Union and on central securities depositories, which include requirements concerning operational risk.*

Furthermore, requirements for notification of incidents are part of normal supervisory practice in the financial sector and are often included in supervisory manuals. Member States should consider those rules and requirements in their application of lex specialis.

European Union Cybersecurity Act[5]
Article 4

3. ENISA shall support capacity-building and preparedness across the Union by assisting the Union institutions, bodies, offices and agencies, as well as Member States and public and private stakeholders, to increase the protection of their network and information systems, to develop and improve cyber __resilience__ and response capacities, and to develop skills and competencies in the field of cybersecurity.

United States Protective Security Advisor Program[6]

The PSA Program's primary mission is to proactively engage with federal, state, local, tribal, and territorial government mission partners and members of the private sector stakeholder community to protect critical infrastructure through five mission areas:

- *Planning, coordinating, and conducting security and **resilience** surveys and assessments of nationally significant critical infrastructure through Assist Visits, Infrastructure Survey Tool, Rapid Survey Tool, and the Regional **Resiliency** Assessment Program.*

---

[5]https://ec.europa.eu/digital-single-market/en/eu-cybersecurity-act
[6]www.cisa.gov/protective-security-advisors

- *Planning and conducting outreach activities and providing access to critical infrastructure security and **resilience** resources, training, and information for critical infrastructure owners and operators, community groups, and faith-based organizations.*

- *Supporting National Special Security Events (NSSEs) and Special Event Assessment Rating (SEAR) Level I and II events, such as Super Bowls, Presidential Inaugurations, and Democratic and Republican National Conventions.*

- *Serving as liaisons between federal and local government officials and private sector critical infrastructure owners and operators during and after an incident.*

- *Coordinating and supporting improvised explosive device awareness and risk mitigation training, as well as CISA's Cybersecurity Division assessments and resources.*

Australian Protective Security Policy Framework[7]

Information Security

Robust ICT Systems

Guidance

Secure ICT systems at all stages of their lifecycle

An ICT system is defined as the related set of hardware and software used to process, store or communicate information, and the governance framework in which it operates.

As mandated in the core requirement, entities must ensure the secure operation of each ICT system the entity operates or outsources, and manage the associated security risks during all stages of the lifecycle of the system.

*This approach will improve both the trustworthiness and **resilience** of ICT systems (and associated components) that government relies on to protect information from compromise and ensure the secure and continuous delivery of Australian Government operations.*

---

[7]www.protectivesecurity.gov.au/

New Zealand Protective Security[8] Requirements

Governance

Business Continuity Management

Review your business continuity management programme

Reviews help you to evaluate your policy, plans, and processes to ensure they remain appropriate and effective, and to identify areas for improvement. Types of review include:

- *audit*

- *self-assessment*

- *quality assurance activities*

- *supplier performance review*

- *management review*

- *appraisal of performance against business continuity roles and responsibilities.*

Your recommendations from the review process should focus on improving **resilience**.

Integrate your business continuity plans

Business continuity is not just about having a plan. It's a process with practical steps for becoming more **resilient**, and proactively minimizing the impact of any disruption, regardless of cause.

To be successful, business continuity management can't occur in isolation. You must integrate your program with the response processes of the other teams that protect your organization's operations — such as security, health and safety, emergency management, information management, and risk management. If you integrate these functions, you'll enhance your organization's **resilience**.

With an increasing number of laws and regulations, referencing or requiring resilience, it is important to understand and appreciate what resilience is and what is involved in building resilience.

---

[8]https://protectivesecurity.govt.nz/

What Is Resilience?

There are several definitions of the term "Resilience," and here is just a selection of them:

- **Cambridge Dictionary**[9]

  The quality of being able to return quickly to a previous good condition after problems.

- **Youmatter**[10]

  Business resilience is a business-wide term that comprises crisis management and business continuity and that represents the ability of organizations to rapidly adapt and respond to all types of risks – such as natural disasters, cyber-attacks, supply chain disruptions, among others.

- **NIST Operational Resilience**[11]

  The ability of systems to resist, absorb, and recover from or adapt to an adverse occurrence during operation that may cause harm, destruction, or loss of ability to perform mission-related functions.

- **NIST Cyber Resiliency**

  The ability to anticipate, withstand, recover from, and adapt to adverse conditions, stresses, attacks, or compromises on systems that use or are enabled by cyber resources.

- **NIST Network Resilience**[12]

  A computing infrastructure that provides continuous business operation (i.e., highly resistant to disruption and able to operate in a degraded mode if damaged), rapid recovery if failure does occur, and the ability to scale to meet rapid or unpredictable demands.

---

[9]https://dictionary.cambridge.org/dictionary/english/resilience
[10]https://youmatter.world/en/definition/definitions-resilience-definition-meaning-examples/
[11]https://csrc.nist.gov/glossary/term/operational_resilience
[12]https://csrc.nist.gov/glossary/term/network_resilience

Despite all these differing definitions, they all have commonalities:

Preparing and protecting your business valuable assets, to ensure the organization is capable to deliver continued business operations, in the event of adverse occurrences happening, and being able to quickly respond to and quickly bounce back from significant incidents.

What Is Involved in Building Resilience?

Many of the components of building resilience will be covered by your Information Security, Cyber Security, and Physical Security programs. However, the resilience element requires a far greater focus on the delivery of critical or business essential services/assets, where a breach of confidentiality, integrity, or availability of these services/assets would have a significant impact on your business and other third parties (e.g. customers, third-party clients, government, etc.).

By using CERT's resilience maturity model (CRMM) v1.2, they've helpfully compartmentalized resilience into its constituent parts (as depicted in Figure 14-2).

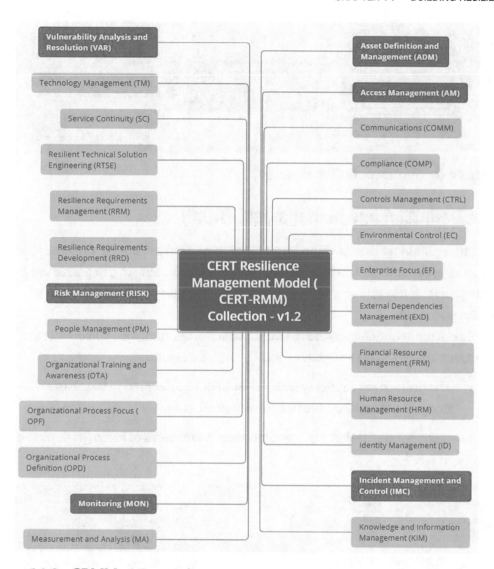

Figure 14-2. *CRMM v1.2 overview*

The Resilience Building Blocks

As you can see from Figure 14-2, there are lots of component parts to building an effective resilience program. Consequently, I have selected half a dozen of these (as depicted in Figure 14-3), which I would recommend as the areas to start your focus on:

- **The "building blocks" for an effective resilience program**

Figure 14-3. *Resilience building blocks*

Asset Definition and Management (ADM)

Your starting building block should be on identifying, understanding, documenting, and managing your organizational assets. The goal is to be able to categorize the assets, based upon their importance, or their potential impact, on your valuable/critical business operations.

Only once you understand the risks and what is important, can you enable the proportionate application protective security controls against.

- The protective security controls should not be deemed to be greater than the potential costs of a compromised asset.

Consequently, the **ADM** component has three main areas of focus (as depicted in Figure 14-4[13]).

Figure 14-4. *CRMM-ADM*

---

[13]http://resources.sei.cmu.edu/library/asset-view.cfm?assetid=514737

1. **ADM:SG1 Establish Organizational Assets**

   Organizational assets (people, information, technology, and facilities) are identified, and the authority and responsibility for these assets are established.

   - **ADM:SG1.SP1 Inventory Assets**

     Organizational assets are identified and inventoried.

   - **ADM:SG1.SP2 Establish a Common Understanding**

     A common and consistent definition of assets is established and communicated.

   - **ADM:SG1.SP3 Establish Ownership and Custodianship**

     Authority and responsibility for assets are established.

2. **ADM:SG2 Establish the Relationship Between Assets and Services**

   The relationship between assets and the services they support is established and examined.

   - **ADM:SG2.SP1 Associate Assets with Services**

     Assets are associated with the service or services they support.

   - **ADM:SG2.SP2 Analyze Asset-Service Dependencies**

     Instances where assets support more than one service are identified and analyzed.

3. **ADM:SG3 Manage Assets**

   The lifecycle of assets is managed.

   - **ADM:SG3.SP1 Identify Change Criteria**

     The criteria that would indicate changes in an asset or its association with a service are established and maintained.

   - **ADM:SG3.SP2 Maintain Changes to Assets and Inventory**

     Changes to assets are managed as conditions dictate.

Risk Management (RISK)

Once you have completed the first step, to understand and appreciate the assets which need to respond to and bounce back from occurrences, you then need to identify, analyze, and respond to their risks, which could adversely affect the operations and delivery of services that they support. The **RISK** segment consists of six key areas (as depicted in Figure 14-5[14]).

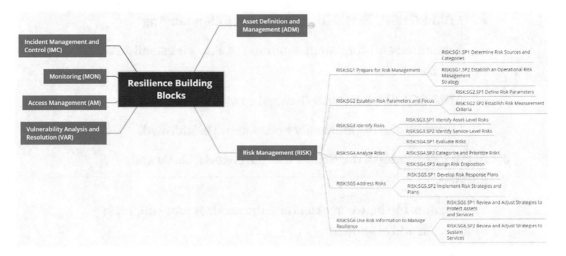

Figure 14-5. *CRMM-RISK*

1. **RISK:SG1 Prepare for Risk Management**

    Your organization develops and maintains a strategy for identifying, analyzing, and responding to operational risks.

    - **RISK:SG1.SP1 Determine Risk Sources and Categories**

    The sources of risk to assets and services are identified, and the categories of risk that are relevant to the organization are determined.

- **RISK:SG1.SP2 Establish an Operational Risk Management Strategy**

  A strategy for managing operational risk relative to strategic objectives is established and maintained.

2. **RISK:SG2 Establish Risk Parameters and Focus**

   The organization's risk appetite and tolerance levels are identified and documented, and the focus of risk management activities is established.

   - **RISK:SG2.SP1 Define Risk Parameters**

     The organization's risk parameters are defined.

   - **RISK:SG2.SP2 Establish Risk Measurement Criteria**

     Criteria for measuring the organizational impact of realized risk are established.

3. **RISK:SG3 Identify Risks**

   An organization's operational risks are identified.

   - **RISK:SG3.SP1 Identify Asset-Level Risks**

     Operational risks that affect assets that support services are identified.

   - **RISK:SG3.SP2 Identify Service-Level Risks**

     Operational risks that potentially affect services are identified.

4. **RISK:SG4 Analyze Risks**

   The business analyzes any risks to determine priority and importance.

   - **RISK:SG4.SP1 Evaluate Risks**

     Risks are evaluated against risk tolerances and criteria, and the potential impact of risk is characterized.

   - **RISK:SG4.SP2 Categorize and Prioritize Risks**

     Risks are categorized and prioritized relative to risk parameters.

- **RISK:SG4.SP3 Develop Risk Disposition Strategy**

  The strategy for disposition of each identified risk is established and maintained.

  - Possible risk dispositions include

    - **Avoid**

    - **Accept**

    - **Monitor**

    - **Research/defer**

    - **Transfer**

    - **Mitigate**

5. **RISK:SG5 Address Risks**

   The company addresses any risks to the identified assets and services to prevent disruption.

   - **RISK:SG5.SP1 Develop Risk Response Plans**

     Risk response plans are developed.

   - **RISK:SG5.SP2 Implement Risk Strategies and Plans**

     Risk strategies and response plans are implemented and monitored.

6. **RISK:SG6 Use Risk Information to Manage Resilience**

   The organization uses the information gathered and realized from the risk processes to improve the operational resilience management system.

   - **RISK:SG6.SP1 Review and Adjust Strategies to Protect Assets and Services**

     Protection strategies implemented to protect assets and services from risk are evaluated and updated as required based on risk information.

- **RISK:SG6.SP2 Review and Adjust Strategies to Sustain Services**

  Sustainment strategies are developed to ensure services are sustained and plans are evaluated and updated as required based on risk information.

RISK is a continual process and should be periodically reviewed and updated because of occurrences of findings, such as new vulnerabilities being discovered during the vulnerability analysis and resolution (VAR).

Any **RISK** activities should track the risk ratings before the risk disposition controls have been applied (Inherent) and the changes in the risk ratings after the chosen risk dispositions have been applied (Residual).

Vulnerability Analysis and Resolution (VAR)

By its very nature, operational resilience is extremely dynamic, and to ensure that the supporting assets can continue to operate without disruption, it is essential that proactive **VAR** is carried out.

The objective of the **VAR** process is to identify, analyze, and manage the business' operating environments to ensure that any vulnerabilities are remediated against in a timely manner, before they can impact operations.

VAR consists of four key areas (as depicted in Figure 14-6[15]).

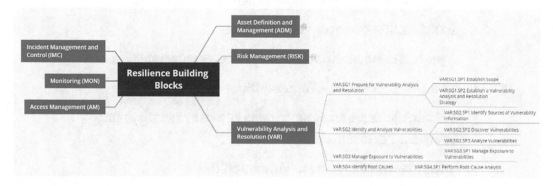

Figure 14-6. *CRMM-VAR*

---

[15]https://resources.sei.cmu.edu/asset_files/BookChapter/2016_009_001_514965.pdf

1. **VAR:SG1 Prepare for Vulnerability Analysis and Resolution**

   For **VAR** activities to be effective, it is important that the business makes adequate preparations to ensure that the strategy for identifying, analyzing, and appropriately remediating the vulnerabilities has been agreed and documented in a vulnerability management plan.

   - **VAR:SG1.SP1 Establish Scope**

     The assets and operational environments that must be examined for vulnerabilities are identified.

   - **VAR:SG1.SP2 Establish a Vulnerability Analysis and Resolution Strategy**

     An operational vulnerability analysis and resolution strategy is established and maintained.

2. **VAR:SG2 Identify and Analyze Vulnerabilities**

   The organization establishes and maintains a process for identifying and analyzing vulnerabilities.

   - **VAR:SG2.SP1 Identify Sources of Vulnerability Information**

     The sources of vulnerability information are identified.

   - **VAR:SG2.SP2 Discover Vulnerabilities**

     A process is established to actively discover vulnerabilities.

   - **VAR:SG2.SP3 Analyze Vulnerabilities**

     Vulnerabilities are analyzed to determine whether they must be reduced or eliminated.

3. **VAR:SG3 Manage Exposure to Vulnerabilities**

   The company develops a strategy for the effective management of the potential exposure limitations for identified vulnerabilities.

4. **VAR:SG4 Identify Root Causes**

    The business examines the root causes of any identified
    vulnerabilities to help improve the **VAR** process and to reduce the
    organizational exposure.

    - **VAR:SG4.SP1 Perform Root-Cause Analysis**

        A review of identified vulnerabilities is performed to
        determine and address underlying causes.

All too often, I have seen organizations where their **VAR** process is regularly scanning
the entire enterprise; however, there is little or no analysis of the findings.

Consequently, the businesses are unable to see "the wood for the trees," and all they
know is that there are several thousand/hundred critical/high category vulnerabilities
that have been identified.

Unfortunately, without any context regarding the assets that are associated with the
identified vulnerabilities, there is no way to understand the implications so that they can
prioritize their efforts. As a result, this merely becomes a number game.

- This can then become very demoralizing, as month on month they
    appear to be making little difference to their vulnerabilities profile.

Access Management (AM)

Having identified and categorized your assets, while effectively managing the risks and
vulnerabilities associated with these assets, it is essential that access to these assets is
strictly limited to those with a legitimate business need for access.

The greater the number of personnel and third parties granted access, the greater the
opportunity that a vulnerability, in one of these accounts, may be used to compromise
the assets.

Consequently, it is essential that **AM** is effective for controlling this access.

The **AM** module incorporates one key domain, consisting of four subdomains (as
depicted in Figure 14-7[16]).

---

[16]https://resources.sei.cmu.edu/asset_files/BookChapter/2016_009_001_514743.pdf

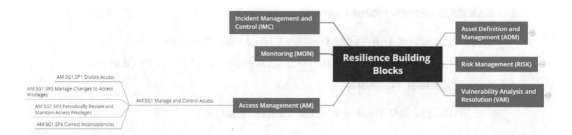

Figure 14-7. CRMM-AM

1. **AM:SG1 Manage and Control Access**

   Access to the identified assets are strictly managed and controlled to ensure that access privileges are commensurate to the individual's job responsibilities and the business and resilience requirements of the asset.

   • **AM:SG1.SP1 Enable Access**

     Appropriate access to organizational assets is established based on resilience requirements and appropriate approvals.

   • **AM:SG1.SP2 Manage Changes to Access Privileges**

     Changes to access privileges are managed as assets, roles, and resilience requirements change.

   • **AM:SG1.SP3 Periodically Review and Maintain Access Privileges**

     Periodic review is performed to identify excessive or inappropriate levels of access privileges.

   • **AM:SG1.SP4 Correct Inconsistencies**

     Excessive or inappropriate levels of access privileges are corrected.

The **AM** domain requires secure management for the granting and timely removal of excessive access privileges. Attackers will seek to exploit poorly managed access accounts and often look for opportunities to use privileged user accounts or to escalate privileges to enable them "power user" capabilities.

Consequently, it is essential that the authorized accounts are strictly controlled so that unusual or malicious account activities are easier for the **Monitoring (MON)** team to detect.

Monitoring (MON)

Having established and matured these earlier domains, proactive **MON** will help to ensure that NORMAL and **ABNORMAL** activities are collected, recorded, and distributed/reported on, in a timely manner.

During the **MON** domain, we are looking to be able to quickly and efficiently identify suspicious, unusual, or malicious activities, occurring within the organization, and to ensure that such events/incidents are immediately investigated to ensure that minimal disruption can occur to impact the operational resilience management system.

The **MON** domain consists of two overarching components (as depicted in Figure 14-8[17]).

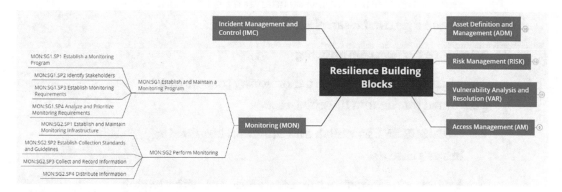

Figure 14-8. *CRMM-MON*

1. **MON:SG1 Establish and Maintain a Monitoring Program**

   Your business will establish and maintain a program for identifying, recording, collecting, and reporting important resilience information.

[17]https://resources.sei.cmu.edu/asset_files/BookChapter/2016_009_001_514852.pdf

- **MON:SG1.SP1 Establish a Monitoring Program**

  A program for identifying, collecting, and distributing monitoring information is established and maintained.

- **MON:SG1.SP2 Identify Stakeholders**

  The organizational and external entities that rely upon information collected from the monitoring process are identified.

- **MON:SG1.SP3 Establish Monitoring Requirements**

  The requirements for monitoring operational resilience management processes are established.

- **MON:SG1.SP4 Analyze and Prioritize Monitoring Requirements**

  Monitoring requirements are analyzed and prioritized to ensure they can be satisfied.

2. **MON:SG2 Perform Monitoring**

  The organization establishes a monitoring process that is performed throughout the enterprise.

- **MON:SG2.SP1 Establish and Maintain Monitoring Infrastructure**

  A monitoring infrastructure commensurate with meeting monitoring requirements is established and maintained.

- **MON:SG2.SP2 Establish Collection Standards and Guidelines**

  The standards and parameters for collecting information and managing data are established.

- **MON:SG2.SP3 Collect and Record Information**

  Information relevant to the operational resilience management system is collected and recorded.

- **MON:SG2.SP4 Distribute Information**

  Collected and recorded information is distributed to
  appropriate stakeholders.

Think of the **MON** process as being like a security observation tower (as depicted in
Figures 14-9 to 14-11[18]), where you are seeking to be able to have a high-level overview of
the estate, so that you can efficiently identify activities that could potentially impact your
ability to remain operational.

Figure 14-9. *Digital representation of RAF Bruggen*

---

[18]www.fsdeveloper.com/forum/threads/raf-br%C3%BCggen-redu_x.438261/page-3

Figure 14-10. *RAF Bruggen observation tower*

Figure 14-11. *Monitoring ingress and egress routes*

As you can see from the digital images of the observation tower, monitoring RAF Bruggen's quick reaction aircraft (QRA) secure site, the high-level observation tower provides a 360° view of the QRA location as well as extensive views of the wider infrastructures.

Consequently, they can monitor farther out to detect suspicious or malicious activities occurring outside the confines of the QRA location. This enables them to notify the resident quick reaction force (QRF), to investigate and intercept any such activities, and to contain these before they can impact the operations.

Incident Management and Control (IMC)

The output from the previous domains, along with proportionate and appropriately placed detective security controls, provides the essential elements required to support your QRF (incident response).

This will help ensure that your business can establish effective processes to quickly identify and analyze events, detect incidents, and determine the most appropriate organizational responses, so as to minimize the potential impact/damage to the business' operations.

The **IMC** consists of five overarching domains (as depicted in Figure 14-12[19]).

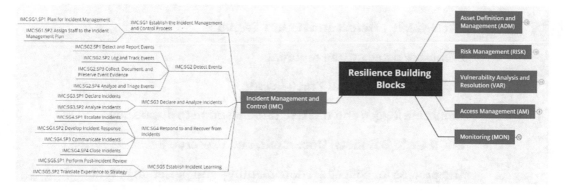

Figure 14-12. *CRMM-IMC*

1. **IMC:SG1 Establish the Incident Management and Control Process**

   Having an effective and established QRF process is integral to an effective **RISK** function to ensure that the identification, analysis, response to, and learning from **IMC** operations help to minimize the potential impact/damage that can be caused by an event/incident.

---

[19]https://resources.sei.cmu.edu/asset_files/BookChapter/2016_009_001_514842.pdf

- **IMC:SG1.SP1 Plan for Incident Management**

  Planning is performed for developing and implementing the organization's incident management and control process.

- **IMC:SG1.SP2 Assign Staff to the Incident Management Plan**

  Staff are identified and assigned to the incident management plan.

2. **IMC:SG2 Detect Events**

An event is the starting point for something that could initially be something small but can soon aggregate into something more sizeable in nature.

Consequently, it is essential that the organization establishes and maintains a capability for detecting, reporting, and analyzing events.

- **IMC:SG2.SP1 Detect and Report Events**

  Events are detected and reported.

- **IMC:SG2.SP2 Log and Track Events**

  Events are logged and tracked from inception to disposition.

- **IMC:SG2.SP3 Collect, Document, and Preserve Event Evidence**

  The process for collecting, documenting, and preserving event evidence is established and managed.

- **IMC:SG2.SP4 Analyze and Triage Events**

  Events are analyzed and triaged to support event resolution and incident declaration.

3. **IMC:SG3 Declare and Analyze Incidents**

Even a seemingly insubstantial event needs to be investigated to ensure that it is a benign event or something that needs to be declared as an incident to ensure that it can be appropriately handled and responded to.

- **IMC:SG3.SP1 Declare Incidents**

  Incidents are declared based on criteria that are established and maintained.

- **IMC:SG3.SP2 Analyze Incidents**

  Incidents are analyzed to support the development of an appropriate incident response.

4. **IMC:SG4 Respond to and Recover from Incidents**

   Your business should have an effective process in place to ensure that there are suitable capabilities for responding to and recovering from incidents:

   - To immediately limit and contain the incident

   - The development and implementation of appropriate responses to minimize the prolonging of the incident

     - Reducing the potential impact and damage caused by the incident

   - **IMC:SG4.SP1 Escalate Incidents**

     Incidents are escalated to the appropriate stakeholders for input and resolution.

   - **IMC:SG4.SP2 Develop Incident Response**

     A response to a declared incident is developed and implemented to prevent or limit organizational impact.

   - **IMC:SG4.SP3 Communicate Incidents**

     A plan for the communication of incidents to relevant stakeholders and a process for managing ongoing incident communications are established.

   - **IMC:SG4.SP4 Close Incidents**

     Incidents are closed after relevant actions have been taken by the organization.

5. **IMC:SG5 Establish Incident Learning**

   Just because you have managed to get the organization back up and running, this does not mean that this is the "job done." It is essential that the incident is reflected upon and areas for improvement are identified, so that the incident response plan can be enhanced and refined.

   This will translate into actions that can be implemented to improve your strategies for protecting and sustaining your valuable business assets and operations.

   - **IMC:SG5.SP1 Perform Post-Incident Review**

     Post-incident review is performed to determine underlying causes.

   - **IMC:SG5.SP2 Translate Experience to Strategy**

     The lessons learned from incident management are analyzed and translated into improvements.

You may wish to evaluate the maturity of your incident response process, through response testing integration with your penetration testing strategies (Blue Team vs. Red Team testing[20]) and/or using the CREST penetration testing maturity assessment (PTMA) tool[21] (as depicted in Figure 14-13).

---

[20]www.domaintools.com/resources/blog/what-is-a-red-blue-purple-team
[21]www.crest-approved.org/2018/07/20/penetration-testing-maturity-assessment-tools/index.html

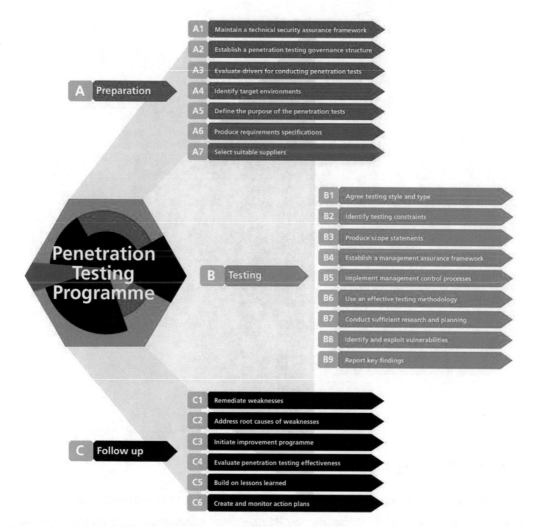

Figure 14-13. *CREST penetration testing program*

Very much like the nervous system of the human body (as depicted in Figure 14-14), resilience needs to be engrained throughout your organization so that your business' "vital organs" are adequately protected.

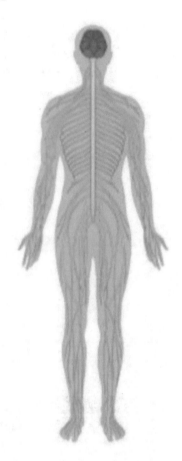

Figure 14-14. *Nervous system*

However, unlike the human body, in the business environment, resilience needs to be conditioned throughout the organization, so that it becomes a business-as-usual activity and not something that is treated as a compliance (tick box) endeavor.

In a growing number of digitalized businesses, it is no longer acceptable for these companies to not have the capability to "bounce back" from incidents. It is no longer acceptable to use such terms as

- "**it happens!"

- "It was unexpected!"

- "These things happen!"

- "It was a problem with our third-party supplier!"

    - **Note.** This is now a shared responsibility.

Military Comparison

While writing this book, and especially this chapter, I realized that throughout my military service, the training and unique experiences *(which can only be gained from military life)* had conditioned for me to have increased levels of resilience.

The demands of providing Protective Security services for more than 22 years have given me a greater appreciation for the term resilience.

The military is very good at learning the lessons from their past and developing suitable training to ensure that any personnel, likely to face such an activity, will know how to recognize this and be adequately prepared to respond to it.

All this extensive training, for numerous different types of events/incidents, ensures that the individual is better prepared and vigilant to other unexpected incidents.

Even the manner hours of continuation training (CT) and night training exercises, as a dog handler, were designed to make me a far more effective defensive solution, able to rapidly adapt to different situations and conditions.

At the age of 22 years, I was selected to represent the RAF Brize Norton Dog Section at the Provost Marshal's UK Dog Trials. Rather than being just a single day of evaluation (Annual Station Dog Efficiencies), this involved the top 22 RAF Police dog teams competing in a full week of daytime and nighttime evaluations, including

- Dog and equipment inspection
- Timed fitness test (dog and handler)
- Obedience and obstacles
- Two-criminal attack and arrest
- Wind scent
- Hangar (unlit) search
- Four-tonner test

Consequently, extensive preparatory training was provided to me by the seasoned senior noncommissioned officer (SNCO) and junior noncommissioned officers (JNCOs) to help Jake (my German Shepherd dog (GSD)) and I (as depicted in Figure 14-15) be as competitive as we could be.

Figure 14-15. *Jake and I*

Well, to say this was a nerve-racking experience was an understatement. Although the preparatory training was extremely helpful, it proved to provide limited benefits when it came to the nighttime four-tonner exercise.

We had trained for this test; however, the training did not quite cover the exact scenario that I was to face. Each competing dog team would be taken out to a deserted airfield, where they would sit and wait for their turn to participate in the test. However, as each team was called up, they would never return so you never knew how well each had done (not until you got back to the accommodation).

The objective of the exercise was to patrol an area of land and to protect three four-tonner military trucks, which would be parked up in a triangular formation, approximately 75–100 meters apart from each other (as depicted in Figure 14-16).

Figure 14-16. *Four-tonner test*

The exercise would not commence until the summer night had become sufficiently dark and would last for 20 minutes. In this time, each dog team had to try and prevent or detect the intruder.

The intruder's objective was to try and get in and out of the environment, plant an improvised explosive device (IED) on one of the vehicles, and to get out without being detected.

Let me tell you, this is the most physically and mentally demanding 20 minutes of my life. You've 20 minutes to continually risk assess the situation, while speed patrolling, using the wind, periodically dropping to the ground (to try and silhouette the intruder against what little light there was), applying irregular patrol patterns to try and ensure that all three vehicles were provided adequate protection.

- If you concentrated on a particular line between two of the military trucks, were you leaving the third truck vulnerable?

- If you went to check on the third military truck, would you be leaving the other two trucks vulnerable?

There were three realistic outcomes:

1. You discover the intruder.

2. You hear a single long blast on a whistle.

    - *The intruder managed to get in and out of the area undetected.*

3. You hear three blasts of the whistle.

    - *The time has ended, and you have managed to prevent the intruder from getting into the area.*

By the end of the exercise, you are exhausted, and if outcome one does not become your reality, although demoralizing, just hearing the long single blast of the whistle still comes as some relief – signaling the end of this torment.

For this year, of the 22 competing dog teams, only four teams managed to detect the intruder *(one tripping over the intruder as they made their way out of the area (after having planted the IED))*.

- All the other 18 competing dog teams (including me) were unfortunate enough to hear that daunting single long blast whistle sound.

However, despite this setback and disappointment, I still did enough to be placed in sixth place at the end of the week of evaluation. The final six would compete in front of the public on the final day of the trials.

By the end of my first year competing in the Provost Marshal's UK Dog Trials, I was to increase a place and would finish in fifth place.

Fortunately, the following year, Jake was good enough to be selected to compete in the next year's competition. This year, we were on fire and entered the final day of the competition placed in first place.

During the week, the four-tonner test had been perfect and even faced with an extremely tricky wind scent test; we had an exceptional week. For the wind scent test, each competitor had been faced with the task of clearing the disused airfield, at RAF Syerston, where an intruder had been hiding. The objective of the exercise was to use the dog's powerful scenting capabilities and the wind to detect and arrest the hiding intruder.

Well, prior to going into the test, there had been some horrendous tales of the experiences that had been had by the earlier participants, including where the dogs had lost the scent after being released and with one even running away in the opposite direction from where the intruder was hiding.

As you patrolled/cleared the field, at the point that the dog indicated that they had detected the scent of the intruder, you had to take a few steps into the scent cone,[22] stop, turn into the direction of the intruder, and to shout out the challenge, before releasing your dog to chase down the scent to flush out and attack the hiding intruder.

---

[22]https://scentsabilitiesnw.com/blog/what-is-a-scent-cone-really/

I started the exercise by testing the wind direction, using a DKP2 puffer bottle (as depicted in Figure 14-17) to use the fuller's earth to test and confirm the direction of the prevailing wind.

Figure 14-17. *DKP2 puffer bottle*

With the prevailing wind blowing into my right ear, I set off on patrol legs that parallelly traversed the grass field (as depicted in Figure 14-18). At the end of each leg, I would expect to turn up the field, walk 10 meters, and retest the wind direction, before commencing my next return leg (with the wind blowing into the left ear).

Figure 14-18. *Wind scent area*

This would be repeated until the intruder had been flushed out or detected or the field was deemed to be clear.

Okay, so I set off, and just halfway into my first leg of the wind scent (with Jacob at heel on my left-hand side), suddenly Jacob raised his nose and pulled right across the front of me, pulling to the full extent of the lead – a clear indication that he had detected something in the air. I took two or three more steps into the scent cone, before taking a firm grip of Jacob's leather collar and shouting the challenge:

Air Force, halt, hands up!

Halt hands up!

Halt, or I shall release my dog!

After waiting for a few seconds (allowing the intruder to show themselves and surrender), I released Jacob from the restraint of the dog lead. He set off at a blistering pace, for around 75 meters, before slowing to an almost stop. My heart started racing and I completely stopped breathing, as it appeared that Jacob had lost the intruder's scent (something that had never happened to me before!) – my heart sank!

- Had I misread his indication?

- Had I released him too early?

- To give Jacob a better chance, should I have continued to do another leg, so that we were deeper into the scent cone?

All these questions started rushing through my head, as I desperately started to scan the horizon to see if I might be able to see the location where the intruder was hiding – perhaps, in the vain hope that I might be able to subconsciously communicate this hiding place to Jacob.

Jacob had started to circle (completing a full 360°) in the middle of the airfield, with his nose extended and neck stretched to its full reach in the air, when suddenly he set off again at full sprint for another 100 meters or so, and I was relieved to see (out of the grass) the intruder sprang to his feet, just before Jacob (a 45 kg GSD), traveling at around 30mph, connected his 120 lbs per inch^2 bite to the intruder's right padded arm. I had never been more overjoyed and relieved.

Immediately after this test, the judges had gone out to the middle of the airfield and tested the wind direction. Here, they discovered that the scent cone was being disturbed into a swirling direction and that Jacob had clearly worked this out and had manage to follow the swirling scent back into the scent cone.

Also, during that same week, I was faced with the nighttime exercise to clear a completely unlit Type C Aircraft Hangar (as depicted in Figure 14-19[23]).

Figure 14-19. *Type C Aircraft Hangar*

It was after midnight, on a summer's night, when I would be waiting for my turn to try and locate the hidden intruder within the hangar. Outside the hangar was dimly lit by the ambient street lights. However, inside was a completely different matter with the changes in lighting between outside and inside, making the inside of the hangar appear as if you had entered a black hole.

Each competitor was given 40 minutes to carry out a free search of the hangar, in an attempt to locate and detain the intruder hiding within.

My time soon came, and when the judges signaled for me to start, Jacob and I approached the main entrance to the hangar and stepped into its depth of darkness. I firmly grasped hold of Jacob's leather collar, unclipped him from the lead, and gave out the first part of the challenge. Instantly, Jacob became excited and started barking

---

[23]www.challoner.com/aviation/hangars/type-c.html

and explosively lunging to try and break free of my hold. The sound of my shouting the first line of the challenge ("Air Force, come out with your hands up!) and Jacob's excited barking reverberated and echoed through the still air of the hangar.

I paused to allow the echoes to subside, before shouting out the next line of the challenge ("Come out with your hands up!"), and then another pause to once again allow the echoes and Jacob's barking to dissipate.

Finally came the third line of the challenge ("Come out with your hands up, or I shall release my dog!") and the 30-second wait *(allowing time for the hidden intruder to reveal themselves and surrender)*, before I could release Jacob into the darkness.

Now, Jacob had a distinct advantage over me as his exceptional hearing and sense of smell allowed him to sprint around the darkened bowels of the hangar, while I slowly stumbled around the hangar *(trying not to make too much noise or to bump into anything)*, trying to follow the sound of his scrambling paws and the eventual barking and the noise of him jumping up at the side of a hangar office *(as he tried to tell me that he had found something)*.

Out of the darkness, I made out the vague silhouette of Jacob, and as I reattached Jacob to the patrol lead/leash, I looked in the direction that Jacob was indicating, switched on my torch, and shouted out:

Come out with your hands up and show yourself!

At this point, my torch beam should have clearly illuminated the hidden intruder, but to my amazement at that point, I was unable to see anyone within my torch's light. Instantly, I started to fear that I had messed this exercise up, when seconds later, from the far side of the roof of the hangar office module up came a head and the reflection of the intruder's eyes into the path of my torch beam. I let out such a deep breath of relief, as I realized that Jacob had done me proud and had indicated on the intruder's scent, as it had traveled from the back of the office roof and down its leading edge to the front.

All the week's efforts had placed me in good standing for the final day of the week's competition, going into this day placed in first place to compete against the other top five placed competitors with an obedience and agility event (as depicted in Figure 14-20) and two-criminal attack workout as depicted in Figure 14-21) to finalize the places for this year.

Figure 14-20. Agility event

Figure 14-21. Two-criminal attack

Figure 14-22. UK Trials march-on

Well, part of being resilient is being able to react and respond to unexpected events, and this Saturday was certainly going to test our resilience. As the entire 22 dog teams marched out onto the arena (as depicted in Figure 14-22), it was clear that this was going to be a far more challenging day than I had experienced in the previous year.

That Saturday turned out to be a scorching, blazing hot summer's day, which is not the most suitable conditions for a thick-haired GSD, such as Jacob.

Well, they say you should never work with children or animals, and this was proven to me on this day. From the outset, Jacob was clearly struggling, and this was not helped by us having placed to compete in the height of this summer day.

We got through most of the obedience event okay, but as we got three quarters of the way through the agility round, we were faced with a combination of obstacle (tire jump and tunnel) to negotiate.

Now, the objective was to bring Jacob neatly to a sit in front of the tire obstacle. Here, I was to command him to jump through the tire, and I was to remain on here, while Jacob was to go through the second tunnel obstacle.

Okay, so I brought Jacob to a well-presented sit and gave him the command "up" (so that he knew to go through the tire). However, Jacob decided to duck under the tire jump and ran through the tunnel, and as I tried to recover the situation (by giving the command "sit"), he chose to walk off to the right, under the rope barrier of the arena, into the crowd (it's amazing how quickly a working RAF Police Dog can clear a path an audience!) and come smartly to a sit position, directly in front of an elder woman, who had been sat in a deck chair watching the competition while eating a very inviting ice cream!

Having composed myself and shrugged off the embarrassment, I rejoined Jacob in the crowd and continued to complete this part of the competition.

It would turn out not to be my day, and by the end of that day, I had dropped back down to retain a fifth-place finish, for a second year.

Additionally, during my two counter intelligence tours in Afghanistan, I experienced the changes made by the Ministry of Defense (MoD), in response to the insurgents' tactics, to ensure that off-base patrols could continue to be carried out, as safely as possible.

During my first deployment, attached to the resident Force Protection Wing, all off-base patrols would be carried out in soft-skinned Land Rovers (as depicted in Figure 14-23), Pinzgauer 6×6 (as depicted in Figure 14-24), and Land Rover Weapons Mounted Installation Kit (WMIK), Mark 1 (as depicted in Figure 14-25[24]).

---

[24]www.britmodeller.com/forums/index.php?/topic/234953882-wmik-comms-fit/

08/05/2007

Figure 14-23. *Agile Land Rover patrol vehicles*

Figure 14-24. *Pinzgauer 6×6*

Figure 14-25. *Land Rover WMIK*

Although these were extremely versatile, lightweight, agile, and capable patrol vehicles, which reduced the likelihood of a patrol being involved in an IED strike, this also increased the potential impact should such an incident occur (as depicted in Figure 14-26[25]).

---

[25]https://pakconnect.files.wordpress.com/2011/10/wimik-vehicle-destroyed-after-tripping-a-mine-central-helmand-province.jpg

WIMIK vehicle destroyed by bomb detonation- Nadi Ali

WIMIK vehicle destroyed after tripping a mine-Central Helmand province

Figure 14-26. *Post-IED destruction*

Consequently, the MoD revolutionized the patrol vehicles with the rapid development and introduction of the heavily armored "Mastiff" patrol vehicle (as depicted in Figure 14-27[26]).

Figure 14-27. *Mastiff patrol vehicle*

---

[26]www.dailymail.co.uk/news/article-2408715/Taliban-tunnelled-THREE-WEEKS-plant-huge-bomb-killed-British-soldiers-armoured-vehicle-thought-bomb-proof.html

However, although initially regarded as a "game changer" for the off-base patrols, it soon became apparent that the patrols would become overconfident in the capabilities of the vehicles, and rather than deploy from the safe confines of their vehicle to manually clear a choke point, for potential IEDs, they might prefer the option of using the vehicle to detect for any devices.

The outcome would be that although the occupants might survive, they could sustain some injuries from the force of the IED blast and that the vehicle would be made unavailable for a lengthy period, while it underwent repairs. In fact, at one point, the senior commanders had to issue orders to the troops reminding them that they were not to use the vehicles for clearing the choke points.

Add to this, the reality that the "Mastiff" patrol vehicles were less agile, meaning that the capability for taking more varied and different route options was limited, and that they carried more personnel, the insurgents would have greater success in their attacks by placing larger IEDs in locations where they knew a "Mastiff" had to pass over.

Consequently, the MoD responded to these changing threats to the patrol vehicles with the development and introduction of new agile patrol vehicles, such as

- The "Foxhound" (as depicted in Figure 14-28)

- The "Husky" (as depicted in Figure 14-29)

- The "Panther" (as depicted in Figure 14-30)

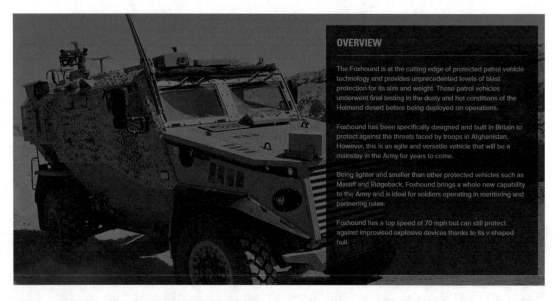

Figure 14-28. Foxhound patrol vehicle

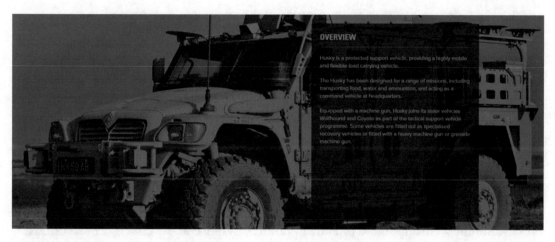

Figure 14-29. Husky patrol vehicle

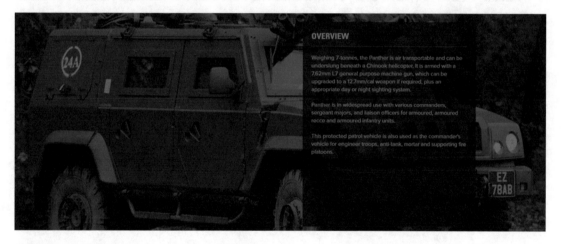

Figure 14-30. Panther patrol vehicle

This clearly demonstrated the military's capability and willingness to adapt to the changing threat landscape to ensure that they could continue to support the mission objectives and to continue to provide support to overseas operations.

Lessons Learned from World War 2

An excellent example of the importance of getting your asset management correct can be seen during the attempts to make the allied coalition aircraft more resilient to enemy fire.

In deciding where to add the additional armor to the aircraft, while ensuring that the aircraft remained effective and operational *(adding armor adds weight, and planes can only take off with a certain amount of weight that needs to be balanced between plane and crew, ammo, fuel, and armor. Add too much armor, and you have a super safe bomber that can't carry any bombs[27])*, it was essential to ensure that only the bare essential enhancements were applied to provide additional defense to the aircraft's most critical components.

Initially, the idea was to carry out the analysis based on the damage sustained by the returning aircraft (as depicted in Figure 14-31[28]).

---

[27]www.wearethemighty.com/mighty-history/abraham-wald-survivor-bias-ww2/

[28]https://medium.com/datashop/how-to-lie-with-big-data-7eff06bd349e

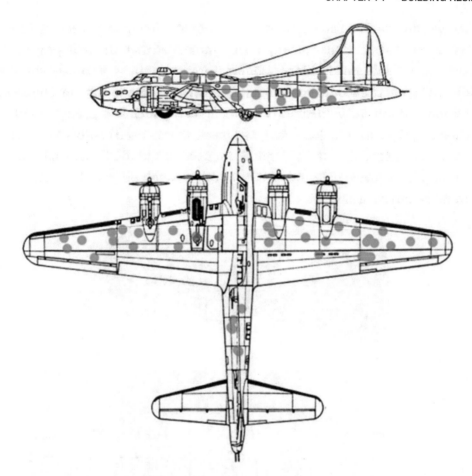

Figure 14-31. *Aircraft damage analysis*

However, it was the observations of the mathematician "Abraham Wald"[29] which proved to be a game changer in affording appropriate protection for the aircraft and their crew. He identified that analyzing the damage sustained by the returning aircraft was not the correct approach for ensuring that the additional armor was implemented to protect the most critical parts of the aircraft.

No, he surmised that the fact that these aircraft had continued to fly and land back safely meant that these areas of damage did not impact the resilience of these aircraft and that it is the damage sustained by the less fortunate aircraft that held the secrets as to where to add the additional armor.

---

[29]www.wearethemighty.com/mighty-history/abraham-wald-survivor-bias-ww2/

However, the problem was that most of the doomed aircraft would end up in enemy territory or be lost at sea. Consequently, he recommended that when carrying out the risk assessments for where to add the additional armor, the areas of damage sustained by the surviving aircraft should be eliminated and to focus on the areas that he defined to be the most critical and vulnerable components of the aircraft (e.g., engine and fuel systems, cockpit, aircraft flaps, etc.). As a result, the changed approach to the risk assessments meant that the places identified for needing the additional armor were more focused (as depicted in Figure 14-32[30]) and completely different from the damaged areas from the surviving aircraft.

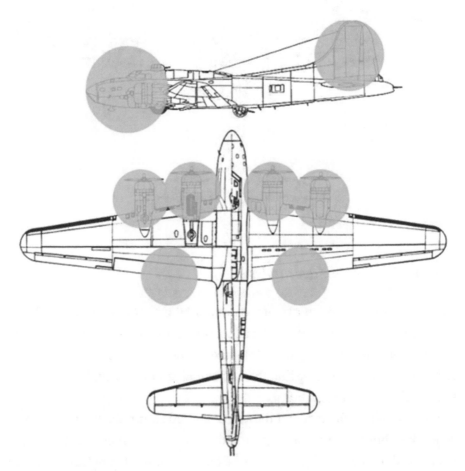

Figure 14-32. *WW2 aircraft analysis*

---

[30]https://medium.com/datashop/how-to-lie-with-big-data-7eff06bd349e

Consequently, through the adoption of Abraham's advice, the armor needed was reduced, and the number of surviving aircraft increased.

When you look at your digital business, are you focusing on the appropriate levels of protection for your business-critical assets or are you trying to apply armor to the whole of your business?

Building BRIDGES

The value of embedding resilience within an organization can be clearly demonstrated using the **BRIDGES** acronym, where I will apply it to a UK financial services business operation.

Business Context

As a financial services organization, located in the United Kingdom, it is a requirement to adhere to the Financial Conduct Authority's (FCA) requirements.

One of these requirements is to build operational resilience:[31]

> *Identify important business services that if disrupted could cause harm to consumers or market integrity, threaten the viability of firms or cause instability in the financial system.*

> *Set impact tolerances for each important business service, which would quantify the maximum tolerable level of disruption they would tolerate.*

> *Identify and document the people, processes, technology, facilities, and information that support their important business services.*

> *Take actions to be able to remain within their impact tolerances through a range of severe but plausible disruption scenarios.*

Consequently, for these types of businesses, building operation resilience may be regarded as being of considerable importance, as failure to do so could result in extensive financial and reputational costs.

---

[31]www.fca.org.uk/news/press-releases/building-operational-resilience-impact-tolerances-important-business-services

Risk and Resilience

Does your business understand the vulnerabilities, threats, and impacts to your organization and which parts of the company need the most resilience operations?

In the event of poor resilience preparations and practices happening, has your organization quantified the risks?

Identify and Isolate

Have you identified and categorized your assets based upon their resilience implications, and are there any associated or linked assets that could impact the effectiveness of your resilience building efforts?

Are these assets assessed for their associated threats, vulnerabilities, and potential impacts, and are you confident that this is with your organization's risk appetite and tolerance levels?

If the identified assets are associated with the services or products provided by a third party (another asset type), have you communicated to them the importance of maintaining the good levels of resilience, and is this covered in your contracts?

Detect Anomalies

Do your monitoring capabilities reflect the importance of effectively detecting **ABNORMAL** activities which could impact the resilience of these assets/processes?

Govern Processes

Do your policies and procedures include the importance of having resilient systems and operations, and which parts of the business need to have resilience embedded into BAU?

Evaluate Security Controls

Does your audit process include the evaluation of the business assets, systems, and operations that are deemed to be needing to be resilient?

Does your audit process convey the status of their security controls, within the context of their ability for being resilient?

Survive to Operate

If these "resilient" systems go wrong *(as no doubt they will)* what are your accepted recovery point objectives (RPO[32]) and recovery time objectives (RTO[33]), and are these acceptable to both the business and the regulators?

What contingency plans have you got to ensure that your identified assets are able to "bounce back" quickly and effectively, ensuring minimal impact?

Reality Bites

Despite the importance of some UK banking services, some banks continue to "scrimp and save" or poorly manage the supporting IT systems, with the organizations appearing to not understand the importance that these IT systems provide to their customers.

Consequently, there are an increasing number of reports where UK banks have suffered lengthy outages,[34] which have significantly impacted their customers' ability to use these services at the very time that they urgently need them.

Imagine a situation where several UK banks were to build their new digitalized bank services, so that they all are reliant on a central mainframe. Now, the procurement and maintenance of the mainframe is a considerable expense[35] for a single bank to absorb.

Consequently, they outsource this responsibility to a specialist third-party supplier. However, they have not stipulated that this mainframe can only be used to serve their services, and, as a result, the third-party supplier makes this expensive mainframe available to support other banks' services.

Before you know it, there are several banks that are reliant on this third party's mainframe for the delivery of their customers' digital services. The next thing you know, the third party carries out a planned update of the server but fails to reach out to their bank clients, so that they are able to carry out an assessment of the risk and potential contingency plans, should the system update adversely affect their digital services.

[32]www.techopedia.com/definition/1032/recovery-point-objective-rpo
[33]www.ibm.com/services/business-continuity/rto
[34]www.theguardian.com/business/2020/jan/01/lloyds-halifax-and-bank-of-scotland-online-banking-systems-crash
[35]https://gauravtiwari.org/mainframe/

The third party applies the update, and all the connected bank services stop working. Before the banks know it, they have thousands of irate customers who are unable to complete their online banking or pay for goods and services via these digitalized services.

How about the impact on the banks' customer digital services when several of them are reliant on the same third-party supplier? What would be the potential impact on these services, should this critical third-party supplier become the victim of a ransomware attack (such as the incident with Travelex[36])? How reassured are you in the capabilities of your critical third parties (as depicted in Figure 14-33[37])?

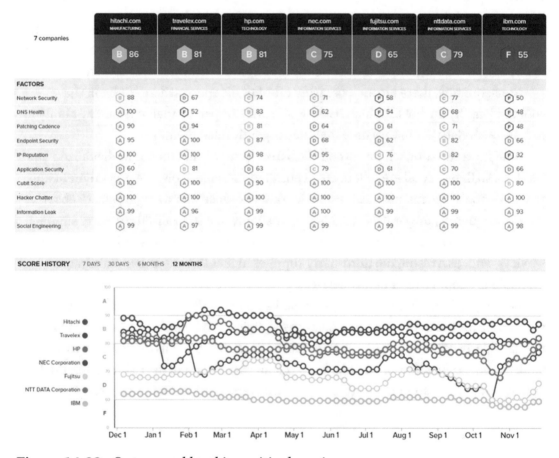

Figure 14-33. *Outsourced banking critical services*

---

[36]www.cnbc.com/2020/01/09/british-banks-hit-by-hacking-of-foreign-exchange-firm-travelex.html

[37]assistance@securityscorecard.co.uk

- Could your organization be subject to a similar type of event and, if so, how prepared are you for such an incident happening?

Key Takeaways

- Resilience is the capability for an organization's business operations to "bounce back" from disruptive events.

- The resilience capabilities need to be commensurate with the perceived value and impact of the assets.

- Much like the human anatomy's nervous system, resilience needs to be embedded into the business as a BAU activity.

- There are an increasing number of legal and regulatory frameworks which require resilient operations.

- Resilience incorporates many of the components of other industry terms:

  - **Cyber Security**

  - **Information Security**

  - **Physical Security**

  - **Network Security**

  - **Risk Management**

  - **Data Protection**

  - **Compliance**

- Resilience requires a team effort and effective leadership to ensure that the scope and expectations for resilience are supported and can be met and maintained.

- CERT has created a helpful resilience maturity model (CRMM), v1.2.

- From the CRMM, there are six key areas which have been identified as the building blocks for operational resilience:

    1. Asset definition and management **(ADM)**

    2. Risk management **(RISK)**

    3. Vulnerability analysis and resolution **(VAR)**

    4. Access management **(AM)**

    5. Monitoring **(MON)**

    6. Incident management and control **(IMC)**

CHAPTER 15

Demonstrating the Protective Security Return on Investment (ROI)

An equally important project was the establishment of a broadcasting station, specially for the Gulf Forces. Until we got one, the servicemen had nothing to listen to except American Forces programmes and the fearful harridan known as Baghdad Betty, who, between pop music records, broadcast doses of crude propaganda from the Iraqi capital and from an unidentified building in Kuwait.

It was clear to me from the start that we needed a station of our own, so that we could keep our forces properly informed about what was happening and so that I myself could talk to them from time to time. To me, a radio was essential – but to persuade London of the necessity was another matter.

Because the station would have to be mobile, we were going to need new equipment, which would cost between half and three-quarters of a million pounds. With Paddy Hine[1]'s help, I put together a case for the radio and submitted it to the Ministry of Defence (MoD).

Tom King (Secretary of State for Defence)[2] quickly appreciated the need and backed my request, but Whitehall failed to understand the importance of the radio station in such a wide-spread command.

---

[1] https://military.wikia.org/wiki/Patrick_Hine

[2] https://en.wikipedia.org/wiki/Tom_King,_Baron_King_of_Bridgwater

© Jim Seaman 2021

J. Seaman, *Protective Security*, https://doi.org/10.1007/978-1-4842-6908-4_15

I gained the impression that the objectors considered the station a needless extravagance, and that they blocked our proposal on the grounds that they were not going to be in the Gulf long enough to justify such a high expenditure....

Eventually, the front maintained by Paddy Hine and myself, and supported by the Secretary of State, carried the day: Protheroe[3]'s investment was saved and the new British Forces' broadcasting service (BFBS)[4] station was flown out to us – but only after colossal and quite unnecessary expenditure of nervous energy.

Another medium of communication, which I considered vital, was the post. The 'Bluey' – the single-sheet air-mail letter form (as depicted in Figure 15-1[5]) – is a war winner, nothing less.

Figure 15-1. *HM Forces "Blueys"*

---

[3]www.bbc.co.uk/news/uk-wales-22064132

[4]https://about.bfbs.com/

[5]https://armywag.wordpress.com/2011/02/22/bluey-is-the-colour/

Handed out free to servicemen, it induces the warm feeling that at least the Government has given you something for nothing.

It also has the advantage of offering limited space, so that you can fill it up quickly, especially if your writing is large. I myself wrote one to Bridget every day, and during the campaign as a whole phenomenal numbers of "Blueys" were used.

The cost was high – nearly £2 million – but again, the benefit to morale was incalculable.

As a British Forces' Commander, I put what some people might consider a disproportionate amount of time and effort into making sure that the post was as efficient as possible.

The Americans had immense problems with their mail and, to Norman Schwarzkopf[6]'s fury, a letter took four or five weeks to come through from the United States. Ours took more like four or five days and I did everything I could to maintain this kind of service. When a postal strike seemed certain to take place in England, for instance, Paddy Hine arranged a special collection system in barracks in the United Kingdom and Germany, so that Forces' mail by-passed civilian post offices altogether.

Commander British Forces Middle East[7]

Gulf War 1 – Storm Command, 1992[8]

Figure 15-2. *General Sir Peter de la Billière*

---

[6]www.britannica.com/biography/Norman-Schwarzkopf

[7]http://news.bbc.co.uk/1/hi/programmes/breakfast_with_frost/2900539.stm

[8]De, P. (1992). A personal account of the Gulf War. London: Harpercollins.

Introduction

As someone who has both benefited from and have invested in ventures that enhance morale, I can concur as to the benefits which, on the face of it, may appear to provide a limited ROI *(you can see a chronology of my training in Appendix A).*

For example, during my final overseas deployment to Camp Bastion, Afghanistan, following the receipt of a welfare parcel from my daughter, I had been provided with a mascot "Dusty Bear" (as depicted in Figure 15-3[9]).

Dusty Bear

I was sent out to Afghanistan by a 12 yr old little girl so that her dad would not be sad or lonely! However, when I got out here I could see that there was much more for me to do! I will do my part and help out where I can and you can follow my exploits on here!

As you can see there are some very tired boys and girls out here!

Dusty Bear's Photos in Timeline Photos · Mar 19, 2010 ·

Figure 15-3. *Dusty Bear*

It wasn't to be very long before my CIFT colleague (John) would receive a welfare parcel, so that "Dusty" would be joined by "Daisy Bear" (as depicted in Figure 15-4) to continue sharing their adventures.

---

[9]www.facebook.com/public/Dusty-Bear

Figure 15-4. *Dusty and Daisy Bear*

This bear would go on to provide a much-appreciated piece of lighthearted entertainment while providing a means of communication between some of the deployed personnel and their families, and friends, back home.

Taking this beyond the original days of only being able to communicate through the medium of "Blueys," now deployed personnel had access to Internet facilities, and, as a result, these bear adventures could be more interactive, being shared via social media.

The investment had come a long way since the days of my very first deployment to RAF Mount Pleasant, Falkland Islands, in 1992, and during yet another Christmas being separated from my daughter, the benefits provided through the investment in the BFBS facilities proved to provide "priceless" ROI.

There are many similarities between gaining support for investment in services or facilities that enhance morale and to gaining the financial support needed to proportionately invest in Protective Security services or facilities.

Often, Protective Security is seen by many business leaders as being extremely expensive and almost invisible, with a limited ROI.

- If your business has not been compromised, been the victim of a successful cyber-attack, or suffered a data breach, what is the justification for continual investment in enhancing the organization's defenses?

However, on the flip side, what are the potential costs of failing to sufficiently invest in the business' defenses and the company facing the potential financial and reputational costs associated with being the victim of a cyber-attack or data breach?

- **$3.86 million** – Global average total cost of a data breach in 2020 (as depicted in Figure 15-5[10])

Figure 15-5. *Ponemon Institute's Cost of a Data Breach*

However, in the Digital Business, failure to continue with appropriate levels of investment can provide the threat actors with the advantage of being elevated onto the higher ground. From this vantage point, they will then scan their horizon, seeking to identify the most vulnerable targets that they can choose to provide them with their best ROI for their efforts.

We often see reports of the continued investments being made by today's cybercriminals, so it is essential that your digital business does the same and identifies their potential enemy interests to ensure that the defenses are appropriate and proportionate enough to continue to provide a sufficient 5 Ds model (as depicted in Figure 15-6).

---

[10]www.ibm.com/security/digital-assets/cost-data-breach-report/#/

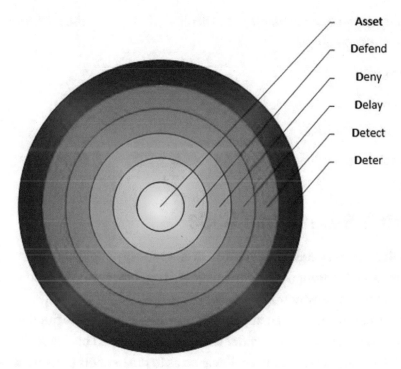

Figure 15-6. 5 Ds model

Unfortunately, unlike the senior military officer's appreciation of the benefits of good morale on their troops, the same may not be so for the knowledge and understanding that your business leaders may possess.

It is essential for you to speak their business language to deliver your "elevator pitch," in the form of a clear and concise business case.

For each investment, you should endeavor to clearly articulate what is needed and what the ROI would be. You should ensure that you avoid the use of complex and technical terms or lengthy justifications.

Do not expect that the decision-makers will know or be interested in the technical details *(that's what they pay you for!)* or have the time to spare to read through lengthy justifications for investment.

- All they are interested in is the context and the answers to their "So What?" questions.

Consequently, one way of helping to articulate this is to use the **PCAN** acronym to help get the message across:

- **P**roblem

- **C**ause

- **A**ctions required

- **N**et benefits

Creating the Business Case

Remember that your key stakeholders are extremely busy people and do not have much time to spare to wade through pages and pages of text; however, you need to get their buy-in and support for any new initiatives.

It will be easier to obtain their support if you are able to provide them with an easily digestible business case, which provides sufficient context and background so that they are better placed to make an informed decision as to the benefits and enhancement it will make to the existing measures and what emerging threats it will help to mitigate against.

Consequently, for those wishing to obtain key stakeholder support, you may wish to consider documenting this in a concise format, using business writing[11] in clear/nontechnical language, for example, delivered in the format of a one- to two-page Business Case Point Brief (as depicted in Figure 15-7).

---

[11]www.thoughtco.com/what-is-business-writing-1689188

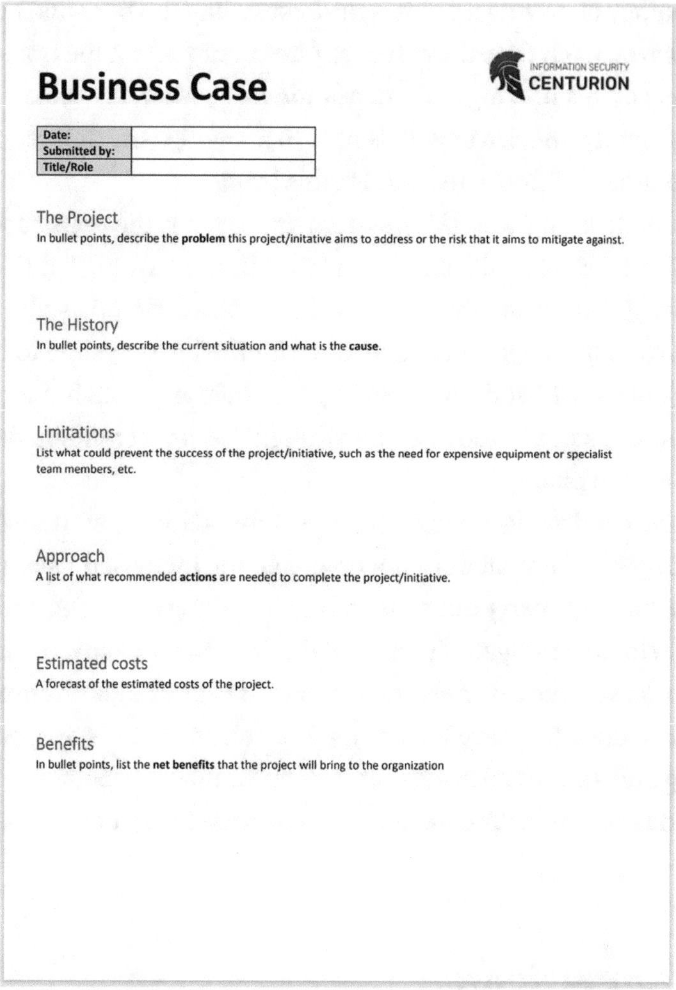

Business Case

INFORMATION SECURITY CENTURION

Date:	
Submitted by:	
Title/Role	

The Project
In bullet points, describe the **problem** this project/initative aims to address or the risk that it aims to mitigate against.

The History
In bullet points, describe the current situation and what is the **cause**.

Limitations
List what could prevent the success of the project/initiative, such as the need for expensive equipment or specialist team members, etc.

Approach
A list of what recommended **actions** are needed to complete the project/initiative.

Estimated costs
A forecast of the estimated costs of the project.

Benefits
In bullet points, list the **net benefits** that the project will bring to the organization

Figure 15-7. *Simple business case template*

Making the Invisible Visible

An often underappreciated, but extremely valuable, practice is the creation of periodic key performance indicators (KPIs) and key risk indicators (KRIs). In essence, you are seeking to export the data from your suite of security tools and audit activities to provide visibility on the benefits these tools and activities are continuing to provide to the business.

Using the analogy of driving a car, it is understanding the benefits the braking system provides to the driver. Each time the driver applies their foot on the brake pedal, they see and feel the effects of this braking system. Additionally, when the brakes start to wear or not to function properly, the driver will be able to recognize the difference in the braking system's performance and the increased risk this brings.

As the wear and tear on the braking system approaches the manufacturer's tolerances, automated senses will alert them (via a brake warning light) of the increased risks to their driving. As a result, the driver can adjust their driving style until they are able to initiate further investigation and arrange for the brake system to be fixed.

The objective of the KPI and KRI reporting is to help key stakeholders to appreciate any threats that have been averted and any inherent risks that remain, despite having mitigation measures in place.

Using the same car driving analogy, you may have a fully operational and effective braking system in place, but that does not eradicate the increased risks associated with situations where you must carry out sudden harsh braking or the requirement to adjust your braking style to help mitigate the risks of driving on snow-covered or icy roads.

The metrics that you provide need to be relevant to your organization and provide context to help articulate the benefits being gained and to help convey when conditions may be changing and additional mitigation measures may be needed.

NIST[12] provides several helpful resources to provide further guidance on making the invisible visible.

Military Comparison

During my 2 years working in the air transport security (ATSy) team, at RAF Aldergrove, we would carry out passenger (PAX) processing for military flights departing the RAF station, as well as the preprocessing of all the RAF Aldergrove's military and civilian passengers, transiting through Belfast International Airport.

To be eligible for the ATSy role, all selected personnel were required to attend a 5-day residential course, at the RAF Police School (as depicted in Figure 15-8), and, later, I was to complete two other civilian equivalent courses – one being attended by PAX processing staff from Belfast International Airport (as depicted in Figure 15-9).

---

[12]https://csrc.nist.gov/projects/measurements-for-information-security/
  standards-guidelines

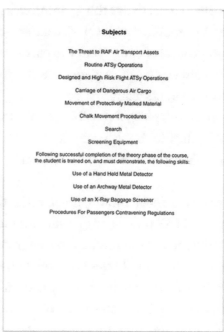

Figure 15-8. *ATSy training certificate*

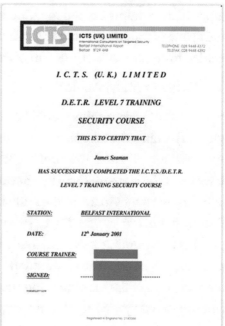

Figure 15-9. *ICTS Aviation Security certificate*

The main objective of this training was to ensure that all ATSy personnel had received the appropriate level of Aviation Security training and had demonstrated an appropriate level of competency to carry out this specialist role.

The team was small, and our role was to provide security support to the resident joint service movements team.

There wasn't really a tangible ROI for this training and role other than success was marked by the number of prohibited assets that were detected and confiscated as well as that the military aircraft departed and arrived at their destination without any security issues.

At the end of each month, the team leader would compile a list of the total number of flights and PAX processed and the number of contraband items that had been seized. These would then be submitted to senior management.

These metrics would then be used to demonstrate the value that the ATSy team were providing to the Protective Security effort for RAF Aldergrove.

This role involved many hours of waiting around, interspersed with sudden bursts of activity to ensure that the surges of PAX to be processed could be done safely, without impeding the departure of the aircraft.

As a small team, we would work closely together and would often play little tricks on each other to help while away the quiet times. Well, one such activity was a game that we made up, which certainly helped to reduce the monotony of the shifts.

During one of the two-person shifts, my colleague (Dave "Shep" Shepherd[13]) and I had decided to create our own version of the game:

- "Where's Wally/Waldo?"

The early and the late shifts would be single crewed, so the game would involve the night shift hiding photocopies *(of various sizes)* of the headshots *(taken from their colleagues' military ID cards)* around the PAX processing and departure areas. The benefit was that the start-up security checks became more interesting and remained thorough, as you sought to avoid the embarrassment of a member of the movements team finding them, before you did, or (worse still) a PAX finding them.

Now, this was working well until that early Saturday morning when I was running late for the first flight departure. Although I did manage to get there in time to open the terminal and prepare the departure lounges for any outbound PAX, I hadn't given myself sufficient time to carry out the PAX processing error.

---

[13]www.gov.uk/government/fatalities/corporal-david-shepherd

Wouldn't you know it, the very first passenger to arrive for their flight back across to England was the officer commanding (OC) the RAF Police *(my Big Boss!)*. I managed to get the movements staff to slow him through their booking in procedures, while I hurriedly scanned round the PAX processing area – recovering three photocopies of my head that had been placed around the PAX processing area by my colleague from the previous late shift.

Phew! Disaster averted, or so I had thought!

It is worth me telling you, at this point, that most of the OC RAF Police weren't the most approachable and struck an air of fear into their RAF Police personnel. Believe me, this OC RAF Police certainly subscribed and embraced this approach and could often be overheard barking out orders from his office, within the RAF Police HQ.

Consequently, it was extremely important to ensure that you were carrying out your duties with the upmost professionalism and discipline. Well, one of the mandated shift start-up duties was to carry out checks of the metal archway detector and X-ray machine.

I hadn't had time to do these checks!

I managed to get both the metal archway and X-ray machines powered up right before the OC RAF Police came around the corner. Just his very presence incited a feeling of fear and nervousness. However, if you did your job properly and in a professional manner, there was never any issue.

I politely welcomed the OC RAF Police and asked him to remove any metallic items from his pockets and to place his bag on the conveyor belt of the X-ray machine and instructed him to wait for my instruction to step through the archway metal detector. Next, I pressed the button to activate the X-ray's conveyor belt to process the OC RAF Police's baggage, and suddenly as the conveyor belt came around, from underneath the belt appeared an A2-sized photocopy of my head *(which had been taped to the underside)*.

Panic!

The supersized image of my face had come toward me before going into the dark abyss of the X-ray baggage screening area. However, not before my keenly sighted boss had seen that something had been stuck to the belt.

He demanded to know what he had seen and waited for this suspicious thing to reappear from the depths of the X-ray machine. While we waited, I pretended that I had not seen anything, and for what seemed to be an eternity, we waited for the belt to come back around *(I'm sure that my heart and breathing stopped as we waited)* and reveal its hidden treasures that would seal my inevitable fate!

Fortunately, despite waiting for more than 5 minutes, the X-ray machine saved my skin and never revealed its treasures to my boss, and, in fact, during the remainder of my time on ATSy duties, at RAF Aldergrove, this X-ray machine never gave up the secret for what happened to my supersized headshot.

However, although this incident gave "Shep" hours of amusement (as I recalled the tale of my near miss), another benefit I gained from this experience was a greater appreciation for the ROI of ensuring that I started my future early shifts in plenty of time to carry out all the mandatory start-up checks.

My training and experiences working in this ATSy team were to continue to provide additional ROIs, through the remainder of my RAF Police career, during assignments in support of operations at RAFO Thumrait, Oman, Royal Ascot at York (RAF Linton On Ouse), and even as I waited for my flight in the Air Terminal, Camp Bastion, enroute (for the "decompression" phase) to Cyprus, at the conclusion of an intensive 6-month counter intelligence field team (CIFT) deployment.

Well, during what was to be my very last ATSy task of my RAF Police career, I had checked in my hold baggage, had been gone through PAX processing (by the resident RAF Police ATSy team), and was waiting for my departure.

I was approached by the resident Warrant Officer 2 (WO2) Joint Services of the movements team ("Chez") *(who, during my time on the RAF Aldergrove ATSy team, had been a junior member of the movements team)* and asked me if I could assist with the processing of some late arrival PAX. The resident ATSy team had already departed, and these PAX had been allocated "compassionate" travel and needed to get on this flight, but the delay in waiting for the resident ATSy team to return could impact the planned flight departure.

Of course, I was happy to oblige an old colleague from our time working together at RAF Aldergrove.

In fact, that was not to be the end of that adventure, as I jokingly asked whether he would be willing to wind up my other waiting fellow RAF Police colleagues with an announcement that their flight would be delayed by 24 hours.

Of course, now that he was in a senior management role, he was never going to accommodate my request. However, you should be careful what you wish for!

Around 20 minutes later, "Chez" returned to the departure's waiting area, looked straight at me, and with a wry smile disappointedly shook his head, while clearly (under his breath) muttering some profanities toward me.

The next thing, "Chez" stood in front of all the waiting outbound PAX (including my RAF Police colleagues), announcing that because of a huge fire[14] (as depicted in Figure 15-10[15]), within the Camp Leatherneck compound, the smoke was obscuring the runway, preventing the safe night departure of our aircraft and, as a result, the flight would be delayed by 24 hours!

Figure 15-10. *Fire in Camp Bastion, Afghanistan*

However, the next night, along with "Dusty," "Daisy," and my fellow RAF Police colleagues, we would board our flight to RAF Akrotiri, Cyprus, where we would enjoy the opportunity to unwind and destress (as depicted in Figure 15-11[16]), before returning home to our friends and families.

---

[14]https://youtu.be/87AKfh4tB5k

[15]www.facebook.com/LeatherneckFirefighters

[16]www.facebook.com/public/Dusty-Bear

Figure 15-11. *Postdeployment decompression*

This was to be the conclusion of my final ever overseas deployment, during my career in the RAF Police.

Prior to and not knowing about my final overseas deployment, I had decided to start my transition away from the RAF Police by commencing 4 years of studies for the MSc, with Loughborough University,[17] on the topic of Security Management.

Believe me when I say that trying to balance studying and delivering assignments (grasping any spare minute to conduct research or the one morning per week in the Expeditionary Forces Institute (EFI)[18] typing up the assignments *(hoping not to be disturbed by my colleague "John" for the call to respond to an incident)*) while providing 24/7 CIFT capabilities proved to be very demanding and stressful, but the final reward of (being able to demonstrate the transfer of my skills and experiences gained from my RAF Police career) achieving the MSc (as depicted in Figure 15-12) proved to be a well-deserved ROI.

---

[17]www.lboro.ac.uk/study/postgraduate/masters-degrees/
[18]https://military.wikia.org/wiki/Navy,_Army_and_Air_Force_Institutes

Figure 15-12. *MSc graduation*

Within 2 years of leaving the RAF Police, the skills, experiences, and knowledge gained through my 22-year career proved to be beneficial in helping me to gain further industry certifications, with the achievement of attaining the ISACA Certified Information Security Manager (CISM) and Certified in Risk and Information Systems Control (CRISC) qualifications and being accepted by the Chartered Institute of Information Security (CIISec)[19] for the NCSC Certified Cyber Professional (CCP) scheme, certified as a Senior Practitioner for the role of Information Risk Advisor (SIRA).

---

[19]www.ciisec.org/

Building BRIDGES

After many customer complaints regarding the lack of digital products provided, a challenger bank is seeking to develop and implement new digitalized customer offerings. Once again, this is reviewed using the **BRIDGES** acronym.

Business Context

Unlike many of the mainstream banks, this challenger bank has been slow to embrace the digital revolution, and now the business leaders have initiated the requirement to provide their customers with a digital mobile banking application.

Their wish is to have this well-designed, aesthetically pleasing, and developed application to enhance their customers' online banking experience and to have the mobile banking application developed, implemented, and available for the customers to use within the next 12 months.

Risk and Resilience

As a traditional banking operation, this challenger bank has little or no personnel with experience of building mobile banking applications, and, given the high number of reported vulnerable banking applications *(e.g., half of mobile banking applications vulnerable to fraud data theft*[20]*)*, they do not wish to introduce new attack surfaces with inherent vulnerabilities.

They wish to benefit from the safe introduction of their mobile banking application, without suffering too many disadvantages[21] and being regarded as a damn vulnerable bank (as depicted in Figure 15-13[22]).

---

[20]https://cisomag.eccouncil.org/flaws-in-mobile-banking-apps/

[21]https://inoxoft.com/what-is-mobile-banking-advantages-and-disadvantages-of-mobile-banking/

[22]https://hacker-gadgets.com/blog/2020/11/27/damn-vulnerable-bank-vulnerable-banking-application-for-android/

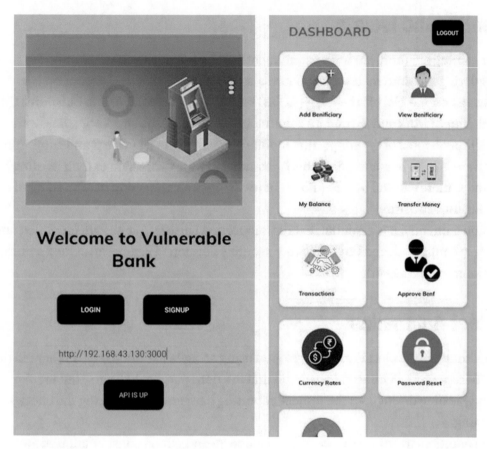

Figure 15-13. *Damn vulnerable bank*

Consequently, as part of this project, they want to ensure that the following security objectives are considered:

1. Minimize the attack surface.

2. Establish software protection mechanisms.

3. Establish secure software operations.

4. Establish effective secure software lifecycle management practices.

Identify and Isolate

After gaining an improved understanding of the complexities and risks, and considering the shortened project timescales, they decide that the best option is to choose a commercial off-the-shelf (COTS) banking application[23] and to outsource the development work and to procure some cloud services for the supporting hardware.

Although most of the supporting mobile application development and supporting hardware is to be outsourced, as this is intended to be an extension to their existing bank offerings, there will still be a requirement to establish a connection back to some of the existing infrastructure.

Consequently, it is essential that the supporting hardware assets are identified and securely configured, and the software is securely developed against an agreed software development framework.

Detect Anomalies

Even though the project is to be developed using an agile methodology, it is agreed that key checkpoints will be established and that the third parties shall carry out regular security testing throughout the project, reporting back any issues during the checkpoint reporting.

In addition, to ensure that security became an embedded consideration of the project, before the mobile application is to go live, it will be independently penetration tested, and any vulnerabilities (above the risk appetite levels) will need to be remediated.

Consequently, the senior management agree that for the safety and security of their consumers, despite the aggressive timescales, the mobile banking application will not go live until the project is formally signed off by a senior member of their risk team.

Govern Processes

Even though the project is to use mobile banking application COTS and be mostly outsourced, the business decides to allocate the same level of oversight and reporting that they would expect from an internally resourced project.

---

[23]www.getapp.com/industries-software/mobile-banking/

Evaluate Security Controls

During the project lifecycle, there will be periodic evaluations against a combination of agreed industry secure software development and security frameworks, for example:

- Payment Card Industry Data Security Standard (PCI DSS)[24]

- Payment Card Industry Software Security framework[25]

- OWASP Mobile Security Testing Guide (MSTG)[26]

- Software Assurance Forum for Excellence in Code (SAFECode) Fundamental Practices for Secure Software[27]

The results will be reviewed, contextualized, and reported into the periodic checkpoints for further deliberation and risk assessment, with all identified risks being recorded in the risk register.

Survive to Operate

Additionally, while the project is under development, the key stakeholders are to consider the implications and contingency plans for if the new mobile application were to be compromised.

For example, what contingencies can be implemented in the event of an outage of the existing supporting mainframe (managed by a third-party supplier), which then prevents the processing and transmission of the essential data sets that the mobile banking application is heavily reliant on?

---

[24]www.pcisecuritystandards.org/document_library#agreement

[25]www.pcisecuritystandards.org/documents/PCI-Secure-Software-Standard-v1_0.pdf?agreement=true&time=1607592369792

[26]https://owasp.org/www-project-mobile-security-testing-guide/

[27]https://safecodedev.wpengine.com/wp-content/uploads/2018/03/SAFECode_Fundamental_Practices_for_Secure_Software_Development_March_2018.pdf

- Does the existing service-level agreement (SLA) need to be reviewed and updated to reflect more stringent recovery point objectives (RPO)[28] and recovery time objectives (RTO),[29] relating to the disaster recovery planning[30] critical mainframe?

  - What is an acceptable timeframe for the mobile banking application to be unavailable?

  - What is the potential impact on the bank's customers?

  - Will the potential damage to the bank's reputation, as the result of an outage, be greater than from not having a mobile banking application?

  - What other banking services could be impacted by a single outage to this critical mainframe asset?

Reality Bites

An important component of outsourcing is to understand the value of the services being delivered by a third party and to gain the appropriate levels of assurances from our critical suppliers.

In May 2020, a large and well-known supplier (Blackbaud) to charities, nonprofits, foundations, and universities from the United States, Canada, the United Kingdom, and the Netherlands was significantly impacted following a ransomware attack on this critical supplier.

It has been reported that, during this attack, almost 200 organizations and millions of individuals may have been impacted by the attack on this supplier.

---

[28]www.ibm.com/services/business-continuity/rpo

[29]www.ibm.com/services/business-continuity/rto

[30]www.precisely.com/blog/data-availability/calculate-rpo-rto-disaster-recovery

Additionally, although Blackbaud was subject to the attack in May 2020 and managed to prevent the attackers from encrypting all the data assets, it was not before the attackers managed to extract some of their data[31] and they did not inform their customers until July 2020.[32]

As a result of this attack, and in seeming attempt to safeguard their reputations and to "Survive to Operate," Blackbaud is purported to have paid the attackers a ransom fee, as well as one of the clients (a United States University) paying the attackers an additional **$1.4 million**.[33]

To date, it is estimated that this ransomware attack has cost Blackbaud an additional $3.6 million[34] to the ransom fee, and they have at least 23 other class action lawsuits pending.[35]

- **Were Blackbaud's clients naïve?**

- **Did these organizations identify Blackbaud as one of their critical/valuable suppliers?**

- **Did they assume that their supplier had adequate defenses in place?**

- **Were they carrying out sufficient due diligence of their suppliers?**

- **Were their third-party management practices proportionate?**

- **Did they believe and rely on what they read on Blackbaud's website** (as depicted in Figure 15-14[36])?

---

[31]www.bleepingcomputer.com/news/security/blackbaud-ransomware-gang-had-access-to-banking-info-and-passwords/

[32]www.blackbaud.com/newsroom/article/2020/07/16/learn-more-about-the-ransomware-attack-we-recently-stopped

[33]www.theregister.com/2020/07/17/blackbaud_paid_ransomware/

[34]www.postandcourier.com/business/cyberattack-has-cost-blackbaud-3-6m-so-far-as-sc-firm-faces-law-enforcement-inquiries/article_5bcca8e0-1df8-11eb-a35a-83455c6abb57.html

[35]www.bleepingcomputer.com/news/security/blackbaud-sued-in-23-class-action-lawsuits-after-ransomware-attack/

[36]www.blackbaud.com/security/security

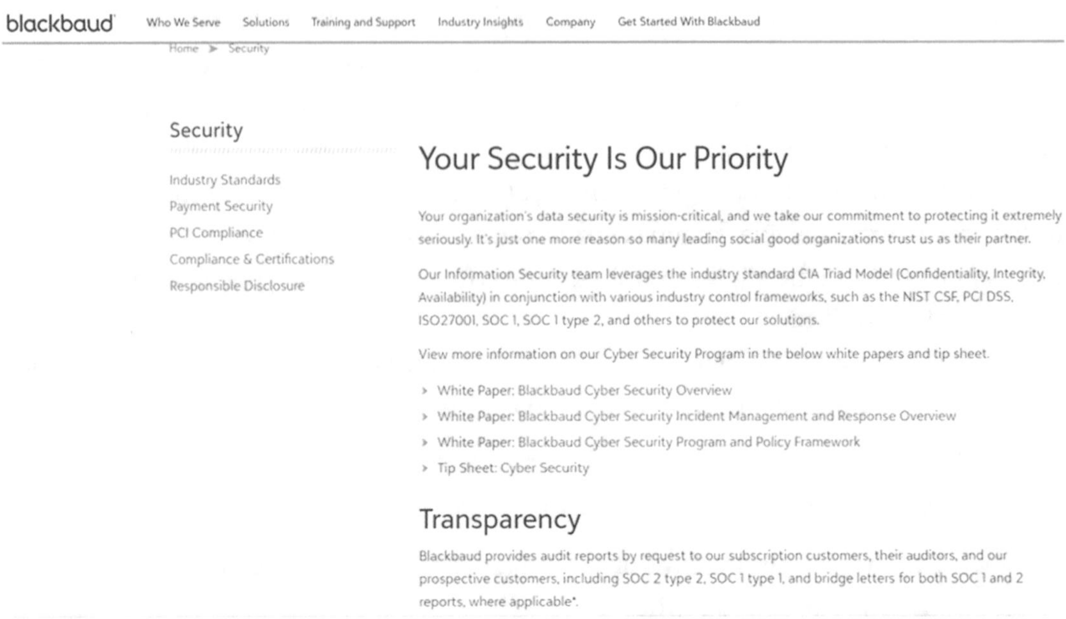

blackbaud   Who We Serve   Solutions   Training and Support   Industry Insights   Company   Get Started With Blackbaud

Home ▶ Security

Security

Industry Standards

Payment Security

PCI Compliance

Compliance & Certifications

Responsible Disclosure

Your Security Is Our Priority

Your organization's data security is mission-critical, and we take our commitment to protecting it extremely seriously. It's just one more reason so many leading social good organizations trust us as their partner.

Our Information Security team leverages the industry standard CIA Triad Model (Confidentiality, Integrity, Availability) in conjunction with various industry control frameworks, such as the NIST CSF, PCI DSS, ISO27001, SOC 1, SOC 1 type 2, and others to protect our solutions.

View more information on our Cyber Security Program in the below white papers and tip sheet.

› White Paper: Blackbaud Cyber Security Overview
› White Paper: Blackbaud Cyber Security Incident Management and Response Overview
› White Paper: Blackbaud Cyber Security Program and Policy Framework
› Tip Sheet: Cyber Security

Transparency

Blackbaud provides audit reports by request to our subscription customers, their auditors, and our prospective customers, including SOC 2 type 2, SOC 1 type 1, and bridge letters for both SOC 1 and 2 reports, where applicable*.

Figure 15-14. *Blackbaud security web page*

Key Takeaways

- Calculating the potential ROI from various Protective Security initiatives can be extremely difficult to do.

- The demonstration of the return may take many years to (or may never) materialize.

- Investments should be aligned to any emerging risks and threats that are identified during the risk management process.

- The most difficult ROI to create a tangible benefit from is the investment in training of an organization's human assets.

- When creating a business case for a new or enhanced Protective Security initiative, it is worthwhile looking at the broader picture to identify any ancillary investments that may be needed, for example:

  - Implementing or changing to a new security solution?

  - Have you considered any familiarization or specialist training requirements needed to support the effective use of the new solution?

- Within the Protective Security field, many of the initiatives can be virtually invisible to senior management. Consequently, it is essential that (where possible) you can export data sets from these initiatives to help to visualize the resulting benefits.

- Investment in outsourced services should be treated the same as any other Protective Security initiative and be subject to periodic KRI and KPI reporting.

APPENDIX A

A Lifetime in Protective Security

The Early Years

The RAF Ethos is the distinctive character, spirit and attitude of the RAF which inspire our people to face challenge, and on occasion, danger.

It is underpinned by tradition, spirit de corps and a sense of belonging.

It encompasses the will to contribute to the delivery of effective air power that arises from confidence in the chain of command, trust in colleagues and equipment, respect for individuality, sustainment of high professional standards and the courage to subordinate personal needs for the greater good.

Air Publication 1 Booklet

Ethos, Core Values and Standards of the Royal Air Force, 2002

Introduction

Before diving straight into the topic of Protective Security, I think that it would be beneficial for you to gain an understanding on my career journey through the Royal Air Force (RAF) and how it helped me to gain a greater understanding of the term Protective Security.

© Jim Seaman 2021
J. Seaman, *Protective Security*, https://doi.org/10.1007/978-1-4842-6908-4

Dictionary Definition[1]

The organized system of defensive measures instituted and maintained at all levels of command with the aim of achieving and maintaining security.

There are many terms that are used in the security industry (e.g., Cyber Security, IT Security, Network Security, Data Protection, Information Security, Security Risk Management, Cyber Resilience, etc.). However, what all these terms have in common is their focus on the protection of a specific type of asset (e.g., Cyber Security = cyberspace-facing assets, IT security = Information Technology assets, Information Security = securing important information, etc.).

This is where the military's use of the term "Protective Security" may be a differentiator, as this is focused on proportionately protecting those assets that are deemed to be valuable/critical.

Although Protective Security is normally associated with the protection of critical national infrastructure, the principles (as described by the CPNI[2]) can be applied to help you protect your valuable business assets:

- **Deter** – Stop or displace the attack

- **Detect** – Verify an attack, initiate the response

- **Delay** – Prevent the attack from reaching the asset (including measures to minimize the consequences of an attack)

- **Mitigate (deny)** – Minimize the consequences of an attack against your site

- **Response (defend)** – Actions to prevent the goal of the attack being completed

The purpose of this book is to help you to gain a greater understanding how this knowledge of this concept and my experiences can assist you to develop appropriate ethos, core values, and standards for your Digital Business operations.

---

[1]www.thefreedictionary.com/protective+security
[2]www.cpni.gov.uk/protecting-my-asset

You will see how embedding a good security culture at the core of your organization will be extremely beneficial to your business, as you grow an increasing dependency of assets that are essential to maintaining your success and that if compromised could have a detrimental effect on your productivity or reputation.

To gain an appreciation of the invaluable lessons and experiences I have gained through my 22-year career in the RAF Police, this appendix will provide you with an overview of the challenging and rewarding times I have experienced.

Life Before a Career in Protective Security

I was just like any teenager (Figure A-1) growing up as part of a middle-class family, the middle child with an older brother and a younger sister. Just like most teenagers, I did not really know what career I had wanted to pursue.

Figure A-1. *Me as a teenager, alongside my elder brother*

However, I do recall that one summer afternoon, when I was around 13 years of age, being sat in the back of my uncle's red Ford Escort and my aunty asking me what I would like to be when I grew up.

Having just seen the RAF Police Dog Demonstration Team, performing at the Royal Tournament (Figure A-2[3]), my response was

I want to be an RAF Police Dog handler!

Figure A-2. *1984 Royal Tournament screenshot*

Additionally, at that time, my cousin was a Corporal (Cpl) Flight Simulator technician, in the Royal Air Force, and my elder brother had been looking to join the RAF Regiment *(however, something that, despite meeting all the criteria needed, he decided not to pursue)*.

While at King's High School, I was provided with many opportunities to explore what life in the UK military might be like. The first was a very civilized visit to the school by the RAF Careers Roadshow, where very well-presented caravan and RAF personnel showed the students what life in the RAF would be like – all very civilized!

---

[3]https://youtu.be/ivhX3uPgeJA

Another was the opportunity to attend Queen Elizabeth Barracks, Strensall, York, United Kingdom, for a one-day British Army experience day. Now, this was carried out on a cold winter's day in December.

The morning commenced with briefings and an outline of the disciplinary rules, one of which was that the students were NOT to place their hands in their pockets. Any failure to follow these rules would result in a punishment.

The morning consisted of briefings on Army life and a 1-hour outdoor circuit training session. The air was crisp and fresh, and the winter sunshine was just starting to warm the morning's frost from the stretch of grass, upon which we were put through our paces.

Having completed an intense hour of exercise, we were to shower and change out of our sportswear into appropriate warm outdoor clothing. It was then time to head off to the cook house for "chow" (food). Like lost sheep, we just followed each other into this very daunting open room, where we had to line up in front of this line of hot food counters to receive a selection of hot food. With just 20–30 mins to make our way down the food line, find an empty table, and eat our food (all while being observed and talked about by these young men, wearing military uniforms), it was extremely stressful. However, we all managed to shovel down our food within the allocated time, to be ready for the next session – a classroom session.

At around 1430 hrs (2:30 that afternoon), we were taken out to the outdoor assault course, where we were faced with a variety of different obstacles. Each student received a briefing before being instructed to attempt to scale each of the physically demanding obstacles (as shown in Figure A-3[4]).

Figure A-3. *Strensall obstacles*

---

[4]www.craven-college.ac.uk/news/public-services/public-services-students-train-strensall-army-barracks/

Now, it is important to put yourself in my shoes. My chosen attire for this part of the day (which I thought would have been appropriate) was hiking boots, hiking socks, denim jeans, and a T-shirt with a woolen jumper over the top.

By around 3:15 pm, we were three quarters of the way around the assault course, and while stood being briefed on a log water crossing (Figure A-4[5]), already dripping wet, fatigued, and cold, the Army instructor noticed that the thumb of my right hand was resting in my front jeans pocket.

Figure A-4. *Strensall assault course*

The next thing I knew was the "shock and awe" of the instructor being nose to nose shouting instructions from me to lie down on my back, into the dirty, cold water channels, beside the log crossings. I was to do ten underwater sit-ups.

---

[5]https://earth.google.com/web/search/barracks+near+Strensall,+York,
+UK/@54.02454339,-1.03312956,25.60809282a,113.20622108d,35y,15.96013477h,59.634919
67t,360r/data=CigiJgokCb36ypfVKkBAES2F4mEGGOBAGWG4YcaNOlBAIaqKOKHNKFBA

Of course, being that teenager who didn't want to be embarrassed in front of his schoolmates, I asked, *"How will I know when to come up?"*

The instructor replied, *"You'll know!"*

I climbed down into the icing cold water, placed a hand on each of the logs to either side of me, and emerged my upper torso into the icy, murky depths. After holding my breath, for what appeared to be an eternity, I felt a bone-crushing sensation to the finger joints of my right hand, as the instructor had applied his weight through his military-issued boots to my hand – clearly, this was my signal to sit up out of the water. However, my reaction to this unexpected pain was to shout underneath the water and so ingesting a mouthful of the cold stagnant water.

After repeating this, on another nine occasions, my mind was made up – from the three branches of the UK military system (British Army,[6] Royal Navy,[7] and Royal Air Force[8]), the British Army was not going to be for me. If I were to pursue a life in the UK military, it was between the Royal Navy (Senior Service) and the Royal Air Force.

Of course, having a surname like mine, you might have thought that I would have had a strong desire to join the Royal Navy – but if you think about it, this could have become very confusing:

- **Able Seaman[9] Seaman**

Decision made, I was to look at pursuing my ambition to fulfill a career in the Royal Air Force, as an RAF Police dog handler.

After attending an RAF Careers Roadshow (which had visited my high school), I had learned that the minimal entry age to join the RAF Police was 17 years and 3 months. Consequently, after finishing high school at the age of 16, I needed to be doing something in the meantime.

---

[6]www.army.mod.uk/

[7]www.royalnavy.mod.uk/

[8]www.raf.mod.uk/

[9]www.royalnavy.mod.uk/careers/roles-and-specialisations/services/surface-fleet/
seaman-specialist

I enrolled at the New College Pontefract, United Kingdom, where I studied Art, Economics, and Sports Studies. However, the only lessons I enjoyed was the practical lessons in Sports Studies and the Art lessons. At the end of the first year, during the 6-week summer break, I started working fulltime for my brother (Head Chef) in the kitchen of a public house – The King's Arms, Heath Common, Wakefield, West Yorkshire, United Kingdom (Figure A-5[10]).

Figure A-5. *King's Arms*

For the entire 6 weeks, I would make a return cycle journey the 7.3 miles each way.

This was pretty much the end of the journey for my continued studies at the New College, as on my return to the second year in September, I was 17 years and 3 months old, and after experiencing a period where I enjoyed receiving a regular weekly salary, I started my application to join the Royal Air Force.

Wearing my best trousers, shoes, shirt, and tie, I made my journey to my nearest RAF Careers Information Office (CIO), in Leeds. Here, I started my application to join the RAF Police. I still recall the RAF recruiter having to change every application form, where I had written that my trade choice was RAF Police dog handler. The recruiters were reminding me that RAF Police was the trade choice and that dog handler was a specialist area within the RAF Police trade.

---

[10]https://earth.google.com/web/search/Kings+Arms,+Heath+Common,
+UK/@53.67464747,-1.46250046,52.08027708a,0d,36.86593403y,72.77221738h,88.
01876467t,0r/data=CigiJgokCS_vVomAAOtAEaH1maEYAOtAGXXEyU5UdvC_IQaoMHXtj_C_
IhoKFjJBWG9uQ2NjUkFqVDBuTO9BRjZZREEQAg

After numerous mental, fitness, and medical tests, at the end of November 1988, I was selected suitable to join the RAF, and the very next day following my attestation into the RAF, I was to be on a train to RAF Swinderby to commence my 6-week basic military skills training.

However, an event happened just 3 weeks before I was due to start in the Royal Air Force, which could have "pulled the rug from under my feet" and stopped my dreams of joining the Royal Air Force. As a young adult, I enjoyed pretending to be an "of age" male and being able to walk into a public house and order some alcohol.

Unfortunately, the influence of alcohol impairs your judgment and helps you act in a manner that you do not normally do so. Well, on this fateful night, I was to frequent a local establishment (The Rustic Arms (as depicted in Figure A-6[11])), which was approximately 2 miles from my home.

Figure A-6. *The Rustic Arms*

I had been in the Rustic Arms, with a couple of friends from the sixth form college. One lived at the bottom of the lane from the public house, while the other had his own vehicle (a green mini van (as depicted in Figure A-7[12]). Consequently, at the end of the night, despite me being aware that my friend had had a couple of pints of ale, I accepted a lift home.

---

[11]www.pubsgalore.co.uk/pubs/41088/

[12]www.carandclassic.co.uk/car/C1065451

Figure A-7. *Green Mini Van*

The drive was only 2 miles. What was the risk? What could go wrong?

Well, just 600 meters from the Rustic Arms, my friend had driven too fast for the road conditions, and as he tried to turn into a sharp right-hand bend, his mini van would fail to keep traction with the road and would drive straight off into a small ditch, running along the side of the road.

During this crash, I would break a bone in my big toe, after the mini's engine came through the firewall into the passenger footwell.

Unfortunately, this was not to be the last occasion when I was to make such a mistake, and around 6 years later, I would make the same mistake. However, the next time, the green British vehicle would be far larger, would be traveling far quicker, and the bend and the ditch (in the Falkland Islands) would be significantly more dangerous. As a result, I would not get off so lightly the second time.

Fortunately, the broken bone would not impact my dream of joining the Royal Air Force.

Unknown to me at the time, joining the Royal Air Force was to be the start of a long, varied, and challenging career within the field of Protective Security.

Training for a Career in Protective Security
Basic Training

Now all trades, except for the RAF Regiment, had to undergo 6 weeks of basic military training before going on to their specialist trade training courses. Anyone who has watched military-based films or TV programs (e.g., *Full Metal Jacket*,[13] *Heartbreak Ridge*,[14] *Private Benjamin*,[15] etc.) might think that this type of basic military training was far-fetched – believe me when I say they are not.

I and two others from the Leeds CIO had got on the train from Leeds train station, heading for Newark train station. We were highly excited but nervous teenagers, embarking on a completely new chapter in our lives and careers. On arrival at Newark train station, we were greeted by the politest Cpl, who helpfully directed us to get on to a Royal Air Force bus transport (similar to the image in Figure A-8[16]), where our luggage was safely stowed away, we took our seats, and we set off on the 20-minute or so bus ride.

---

[13]www.imdb.com/title/tt0093058/

[14]www.imdb.com/title/tt0091187/?ref_=nv_sr_srsg_0

[15]www.imdb.com/title/tt0081375/?ref_=nv_sr_srsg_0

[16]http://miliblog.co.uk/?p=1422

Figure A-8. *RAF bus transport*

To this day, I'm still not sure what happened along the journey, but as we entered the gates to RAF Swinderby (as depicted in Figure A-9[17]), the previously polite and gentle Cpl had made a complete 180-degree change, turning into an aggressively swearing drill instructor.

It was as though we had passed through some invisible barrier that changed the very nature of this human being.

I started to think, was this his alter ego or would I need to have two sides to my character?

- A military persona

- A civilian persona

This was the commencement of the "de-civilianization" process, where they gradually remodel you into a member of the RAF branch of the military – instilling discipline, respect, a sense of urgency, a commitment for completing something, teamwork, leadership, and responsibility.

---

[17]https://mapio.net/images-p/7427876.jpg

Figure A-9. *Main gate at RAF Swinderby*

These characteristics remain engrained into anyone who has donned a military uniform and undergone the military's realignment training.

There's a well-known saying, which has never been more relevant:

You can take the person out of the military, but you will never take the military out of the person!

Suddenly, my new chosen career had taken a distinct change for the worse. However, this was only the beginning of what was to become. Basic military training was soon to become a real shock to my system, learning how to shine shoes, to march, and to carry out basic military skills, so that at the end of the 6 weeks (see Figure A-10), I could "pass out" and move on to commence my trade training.

Figure A-10. *Basic recruit*

Basic training was a complete shock to my system, as my body, mind, and spirit had to endure long days of intensive physical and mental challenges. In fact, the only respite during this intensive 6 weeks was the 1-hour lessons with the RAF Padre (Chaplain).[18] Basically, the Padre's role was to provide spiritual support, strength, and guidance while providing a valuable source of personal wellbeing and guidance.

The Padre session was a saving grace for us all, as it was 60 minutes where we could just relax and destress. Don't ever tell the Padre *(although I very suspect that he already knew)* but I'm sure that I never managed to stay awake for longer than his opening sentence or two.

To successfully complete the basic training, there were several challenges that needed to be attained.

---

[18]www.raf.mod.uk/recruitment/roles/roles-finder/personnel-support/chaplain

For example:

- **Military knowledge** – Achieving the passing score for several tests, based upon the military awareness lessons.

- **Fitness** – Jogging out as a unit one and a half miles and then returning with a timed best-effort solo run. The target was to achieve this in under ten and a half minutes.

- **Skill at arms** – Being able to safely operate a L1A1 Self-Loading Rifle[19] and achieve the required shooting scores (as depicted in Figure A-11).

Figure A-11. *Self-Loading Rifle skills*

- ***Military skills training (MST)*** – Deployed to RAF North Luffenham to undergo a period of tests, such as digging and defending a "Fox Hole" from invading enemy forces and responding to a nuclear, biological, or chemical attack[20] (as depicted in Figure A-12).

---

[19]www.militaryfactory.com/smallarms/detail.asp?smallarms_id=129
[20]www.youtube.com/watch?v=BNNHN9CT62Y

Gas, Gas, Gas!

Mask in Five to stay alive.

Mask in Nine - just in time!

Figure A-12. *Military skills training*

- **Military drill** – Marching in time, as a Flight as part of a Squadron, with precision and timing.

During my basic training, I was assigned to 5 Flight, which was later known as "Sgt Fosbury's Final Fighting Fifth." We were to be Sgt Fosbury's very last group of trainees, as he was to retire at the end of this 6-week training program. Consequently, we had to be the **BEST** Flight of the Squadron during every test and inspection – NO PRESSURE there then!

On a freezing cold morning, at the end of January 1989, I marched out onto the parade square, with a sense of pride and achievement, to the sounds of the accompanying RAF Band and under the observation of the Squadron's proud family members (see Figure A-13).

Figure A-13. *Basic recruit graduation, with my father and younger sister*

My first objective had been successfully achieved, and I was now on my career journey into the world of Protective Security *(however, I still was oblivious to this)*. Next objective was to pass my driving training course at RAF St Athan.

Driver Training

After a short break, back home, I was off on the train to RAF St Athan, South Wales, where I would receive approximately 2 weeks of driver instruction. In the first week, I was being taught how to drive, around the streets and hills of South Wales, in a Series 3 Land Rover (as depicted in Figure A-14[21]), to pass my driving test and obtain a UK driving license.

---

[21]www.defender-landrover.co.uk/2016/06/landrover-series-3-ex-military-88.html

To become a member of the RAF Police, it was essential that we were qualified to drive the RAF Police vehicles (as depicted in Figure A-15[22]) to ensure that we could carry out mobile patrols and to rapidly respond to incidents. In the late 1980s, this was included into the basic RAF Police training. However, today, any RAF Police candidates need to have already attained a full UK driving license.[23]

Figure A-14. *Series 3 Land Rover*

[22]https://hmvf.co.uk/topic/20683-raf-police-land-rover-90/

[23]www.raf.mod.uk/recruitment/roles/roles-finder/force-protection/raf-police?gclid=C jwKCAjw_Y_8BRBiEiwA5MCBJieN_73g8uBNK735tPOQN1S54TtKKcywR6zAAjCAgU8PqED4XAuBLxoCen oQAvD_BwE

Figure A-15. *RAF Police Land Rover*

Having successfully achieved this, the next phase was an advanced driving phase, including controlling a skid on the skid pan, night driving, first-line servicing, motorway driving, solo drive and navigation, and so on.

With my shining new license in my hand and a new set of skills in my knowledge bank, I was all packed up and on my way to commence the next phase of my journey – RAF Police basic training at RAF Newton.

RAF Police Training

The RAF Police training consisted of two phases, the Blue phase *(7 weeks: Police training)* and the Green phase *(6 weeks: Level 7 Infantry (special weapons protection))*, all to be held at the RAF Police School, at RAF Newton, Nottinghamshire.

Oh boy! If I had thought that the basic training was a shock to my system, that was nothing in comparison to the RAF Police training. This was all about discipline, mental toughness, fitness, and "setting the bar higher" than nearly all the other trades. In the RAF Police, we had to be regarded as being "beyond reproach" so that we were set an exemplary standard for the rest of the RAF.

This was to be 13 weeks of a seemingly relentless hell!

Blue Phase

This phase of the RAF Police training commenced at the start of March 1989 and was to really test my resolve with extremely intensive lessons on Service Law, weekly knowledge tests, daily inspections *(even requiring that the wooden floors, within Flintham Block, be manually buffed, so that they shone like a shiny new penny)*, and increasingly demanding fitness challenges.

In Figure A-16, you can see me on my bed space, hard at my studies, during a lunchtime period.

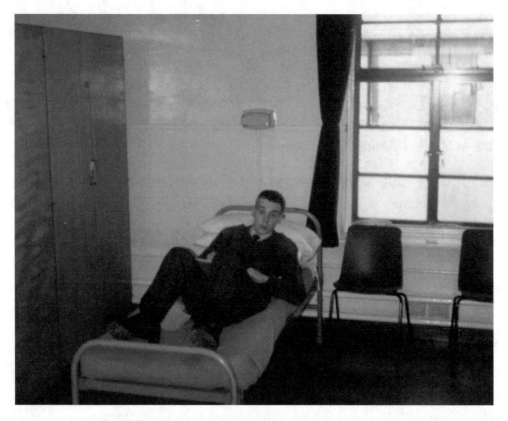

Figure A-16. *Studying hard*

Green Phase

Well, once again, I was going to be shocked by the changing tempo of the training. Having successfully completed the "Blue phase," we were handed over to our RAF Regiment instructors (Cpls Chapman and Arden – both being fitness freaks!).

This is really where the Protective Security journey was to commence. We were to endure 7 weeks of basic infantry training to ensure that we had all the skills needed to protect "special weapons" (SW) storage and movement.

I recall that, during this phase of training, it had been incredibly hot with what seemed like endless sunshine, which did not help given that all the physical activities and the mock "special weapons" training facility were on the other side of the airfield, from the RAF Police training hangar.

If we were to be carrying out physical training drills, our RAF Regiment instructors would insist that, as a course, we would "tactically advance to battle (tab)[24]" out there and back (as depicted in Figure A-17[25]).

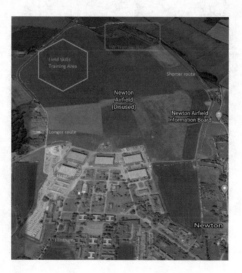

Figure A-17. *RAF Newton*

[24]www.forces.net/military-life/fun/british-military-slang-or-phrases-you-need-know
[25]https://earth.google.com/web/search/RAF+Nwton/@52.96654839,-0.98428274,50.22897082a,2253.86393006d,35y,-82.60616322h,45.01047825t,0r/data=Cig iJgokCf80qEuK1kpAEdeus11K1kpAGXSPaBHGWfe_IXGEGOBmZve_

Our only respite was if we were to be carrying out convoy counter ambush drills (as depicted in Figure A-18[26]) or on the rare occasions that we were lucky enough to enjoy the use of the vehicles (see Figure A-19).

Figure A-18. *Convoy counter ambush drills*

---

[26]https://royalairforcepolice100years.weebly.com/my-books.html

Figure A-19. *The joys of vehicular travel*

I can recall a couple of eventful occasions, during the Green phase, when I would have very much appreciated the use of a Land Rover.

The first was on our return from the "Respirator Test Facility." Having completed our immediate action (IA) drills and experiencing the effects of the CS gas, we had to tab (aka loaded march[27]) back, in full patrol wear (as depicted in Figure A-18), to the RAF Police School hangar.

Not long after setting off on the return leg, along the shorter route back, I felt a second wave effect from the CS gas just as my foot fit a hole in the airfield perry track. The next thing I knew, I had adopted the prone position with my hands and face being buried into the gritty road surface. Before I could comprehend what had happened, I had one of the Regiment instructors shouting directly into my ear. As I had descended to the ground, I had neglected to keep hold of my rifle and received the punishment of doing several push-ups, ensuring the grazes to the palms of my hands spent sufficient time to absorb some more road surface dirt.

The second incident will remain forever etched into my memories. It was a sizzling hot afternoon, and we were to tab out to the SW Training Site. On arrival, in teams of three or four, we had to pick up and carry several heavy wooden frames and sandbags to the Field Skills Training area (as depicted in Figure A-20[28]).

---

[27]https://military.wikia.org/wiki/Loaded_march

[28]www.reddit.com/r/guns/comments/2tvs9t/why_do_most_military_rifles_
  designed_before_wwii/

Figure A-20. *Bayonet training*

The objective of this physical training session was to demonstrate our aggression to the RAF Regiment instructors. While being taught the correct way to thrust our bayonets into the sandbag dummies, we were informed that any wooden frames that remained intact, afterward, would need to be carried back to the store. As you can imagine, this had more than the desired effect, and every wooden frame was demolished through our pure aggressive attacks.

After this exercise was complete, we all moved on to the next training exercise *(health and safety would have had a field day, if it were to happen today!)* which involved learning how to defend against an enemy's bayonet charge. However, with no sandbag dummies remaining and with only the aging "flak vest" for protection, and using the same aggression, we were to carry out these drills on one another, using scabbarded bayonets.

After around three lunges, parries, and thrust *(you've guessed it)*, with his full strength and weight behind his bayonet thrust, the very tip of the colleague's bayonet scabbard connected with a worn part of my "flak vest" *(approximately the size of a ten pence piece[29] (24.5mm), as depicted in Figure A-21).*

---

[29]https://onlinecoin.club/images/coins/United_Kingdom/ec0fc478-f5c9-4031-8e4f-acffaca741f3.jpg

Figure A-21. *10p coin*

The next thing I knew, I felt a sharp pain to the left-hand side of my rib cage. However, I was able to compose myself, and after the RAF Regiment instructors had realized what had happened, I was taken for a medical examination, where it was revealed that I had fractured the bottom two rib bones of my rib cage. I was given strong painkillers and told to be careful.

However, this is not as easy as it sounds. The following morning, I was practice firing the Self-Loading Rifle on the 25-meter range, in the prone position (as depicted in Figure A-22[30]), where you need to lie with your left arm outstretched and which enhances the effect of the rifle's recoil to the left-hand side.

Figure A-22. *Prone shooting position*

---

[30]www.hunter-ed.com/national/studyGuide/Firing-Positions-Prone/201099_92888/

With every shot fired, the pain in my ribs was excruciating, and, as a result, I was struggling to achieve the required shooting scores. Once again, I was taken back to the station Medical Center, where the doctor stated that there was little that could be done for such an injury and that my only choices were to struggle on with the aid of even stronger pain medication or to be backflighted.[31] I chose the first option.

As it turns out, the course had access to a fleet of Land Rovers. However, the RAF Regiment instructors preferred to run the course out and back to do the training rather than use the vehicles that were available to them. On the plus side, I completed my Green phase of training in the best physical condition that I had ever been *(having lost 9.5 kgs/21 lbs and reducing my 1.5 mile run time to 8 mins, 35 secs, when during basic training I was struggling to get the time to under 10 mins, 30 secs)* and successfully completed my RAF Police training (as shown in Figures A-23 and A-24), with the first posting being an RAF Police dog handler, at RAF Brize Norton.

Figure A-23. *In my RAF Police No.1 uniform*

---

[31]Backflighted is where a student's training is put on hold, and they are then put onto a later course.

Figure A-24. *RAF Police passing out*

However, before my posting, I needed to successfully complete a 7-week RAF Police dog handler course, so I was to remain at RAF Newton for several weeks more.

During this training, I was allocated an 18-month-old, lanky, German Shepherd named "Tyson." Back then, many of the working police dogs were mostly untrained donations from members of the public. Consequently, these training courses needed to train both the dog handlers and the dogs at the same time. The training consisted of getting the dogs to successfully "walk to heel," negotiate an obstacle course, show aggression, scent a hidden intruder, and arrest an intruder *(halting the intruder progress by biting and holding onto them)*.

Unfortunately, during the final week of the training, Tyson lost his aggression and would not commit to the arrest of an intruder, instead choosing to run around the intruder, barking. With Tyson being deemed unsuitable to "pass out" from the training course, he was rejected as being a suitable RAF Police working dog, and I had to stay on at RAF Newton, so that I could reteam with a 4-year-old German Shepherd, named Jacob (Figure A-25).

Figure A-25. Jacob

Now, Jacob had already completed his training course and been deployed with a handler to RAF St Mawgan, Cornwall. However, after developing a long-term stomach illness, he had been returned to the RAF Police Dog Training School to convalesce and recover from his illness.

Commencing a Career in Protective Security

In August 1989, I had finally completed the 8 months of training needed to be posted to my very first active role, providing nighttime Physical Security dog patrols for the protection of RAF Brize Norton's critical assets. A night patrol would consist of patrolling either two flight lines or an explosive storage area (ESA).

An effective RAF Police dog patrol was deemed to be the equivalent of deploying eight- to ten-armed service personnel, having enhanced hearing and night vision and the ability to detect the scent in the air of a potential intruder up to 1–1.5 kilometers away. In addition to this, being able to pursue an intruder at speeds of approximately

30mph and being able to go up hills, over gaps, and around corners make them a formidable weapon to deploy over expansive airfields, such as RAF Brize Norton (as depicted in Figure A-26[32]).

Figure A-26. *RAF Brize Norton*

Being such a formidable weapon, each year the patrol teams needed to be evaluated and granted an operational license. This was achieved through an annual one-day "Station Efficiencies" competition, where each team was scored for their proficiency across a range of disciplines (obedience, obstacles, intruder arrest).

In my very first year, I was a nervous wreck, and having been selected for the morning evaluation, I was relieved to have got through everything. However, that was not to turn out to be the case, as this rookie 19-year-old dog handler had scored enough points to be joint first place, along with an extremely seasoned dog handler *(who had over 10 years' "Station Efficiencies" experience).*

Consequently, there needed to be a decider so that first and second places could be confirmed. The decider was to be the negotiation of one of the obstacles, and the more senior dog handler insisted that he should be the one to choose which obstacle this could be.

As predicted, he chose the "A-Frame" (as shown in Figure A-27), as this was the one that his dog has been flawless on, just a few hours earlier.

---

[32]https://earth.google.com/web/search/RAF+Brize+Noprton/@51.74368233,-
1.58942345,80.86564198a,2722.55374206d,35y,28.92375312h,59.98661327t,-0r/
data=CigiJgokCVce-RpFfkpAEZRieziheUpAGQDgVioQFe-_ITYtAiqMLvC_

Figure A-27. *A-Frame*

The objective was that the handler should approach the "A-Frame," with their dog at heel, before getting the dog to sit in front of the obstacle. The handler must then send his dog *(the dog negotiates the obstacle, on the command of their handler, without the handler needing to move from their location)*. Having negotiated the obstacle, on the handler's command to "sit," the dog will sit on the other side of the obstacle and wait for the handler's recall command.

Upon hearing the recall command, the dog will return over the obstacle to sit directly in front of their handler. To conclude the exercise, the handler then commands their dog to "heel round," and the dog will move around their handler to sit perfectly in line, to the left-hand side of their handler.

That's how it is supposed to be done. However, in the morning session, Jacob *(perhaps picking up on my anxiety)* had gone over the obstacle okay, but on the recall had decided to run around the obstacle to return to me.

It was not looking good for me, but at least the pressure had been taken away from me.

A coin was tossed to decide who went first, and the senior handler won the call and opted that he would go first. Now, the senior handler had always had an air of arrogance about him, which grew knowing that he was competing against a "rookie" and whose dog had already flawlessly negotiated the very same obstacle. As he negotiated the obstacle, once again, he was flawless. That was until his dog sat after the "heel round" and flopped his backend out – a half point drop.

Nothing less than perfect would mean first place for me. That afternoon, Jacob was on point and carried out the move to perfection. There was an eruption from the observing crowd, as Jacob finished off the move with a perfectly straight sit, against my left-hand side.

This team relationship continued to grow, with us being selected to participate in the Provost Marshal's Annual Working Dog Trials – the top 22 dog teams from the year competing against one another, over 6 days, across a number of different disciplines (e.g., night patrols, hangar search, wind scent, obedience, obstacles, cross-country, two-intruder arrest) – during the following two years, and achieving fifth place in each of these years (see Figure A-28).

Figure A-28. *Provost Marshal's UK Trials*

During my posting to RAF Brize Norton, there were three notable events that spring to mind, one of which was an extremely traumatic event that was to have an impact on the rest of my life.

Deployment to RAF Bentley Priory

My very first deployment was to provide enhanced Physical Security by patrolling the grounds surrounding the Bentley Priory mansion. There was a high risk from domestic terrorism, and the Secretary of State for Defense (1989–1992) was to attend an event, along with other high-ranking attendees. Working alternate evening and night shifts with another dog handler, from RAF Lyneham, our job was to ensure that the perimeter remained protected from this known threat.

This deployment was mostly uneventful.

As he had been approaching a roundabout, when he tried to apply the brake, he had not realized that his boots had been muddy from patrolling the mansion gardens, so his foot slipped off the brake pedal – resulting in him crashing into the side of the other road user.

High-Profile Dog Patrol for the President of the United States

During President Bill Clinton's visit to Oxford University, in June 1994, I was tasked to spend the day providing a high-profile airfield dog patrol, in order to provide an enhanced perimeter defense for Air Force One (see Figure A-29[33])

---

[33]www.raf.mod.uk/our-organisation/stations/raf-brize-norton/documents/80th-anniversary-brochure/

Figure A-29. *Air Force One*

First Overseas Deployment: RAF Mount Pleasant, Falkland Islands

At just 22 years of age, I was deployed to the Dog Section, at RAF Mount Pleasant, on the Falkland Islands. This is where an event would happen that would have an impact on me for the rest of my life.

Now, it is important to understand that life for dog handlers deployed to the Falkland Islands was vastly different to life back home. It was very much a "Work Hard, Play Hard" ethic that was adopted by all the dog handlers.

After the long flight, on an RAF TriStar aircraft, from RAF Brize Norton *(with a short stopover for refuel at the RAF base on the Ascension Island)*, I arrived on the Falkland Islands in the afternoon, in late November 1992.

Within the first 24 hours, I had experienced all the conditions associated with the four seasons (snow, hail, high winds, heavy rain, and sunshine).

The next morning, I commenced my quick reteam with a German Shepherd dog called Kai. Now, he was a machine who thrived on the thrill and excitement of carrying out an arrest *(a pure War Dog!)*. However, if he were ever to break loose from his leash or kennel, he would sprint off and not be seen for hours on end.

I should have suspected that just how much of a machine he was, when I realized that the entire night shift had opted to stay up to watch me do my very first arrest with Kai. During the briefing, the Dog Section Sgt had suggested that I use a long leash during the first release. However, thankfully, I insisted on using a short leash.

After taking Kai for a short walk, I was ready for the training exercise. Now it is important to note that the "criminals" who were to be bitten would wear padded trousers and jacket for their protection (*consisting of two layers of underlay felt and a black hessian covering, hand sown together with white string* (as depicted in Figure A-30)).

Figure A-30. *Padded dog attack suit*

This was to help protect the "criminal" from being injured from the dog attacking them at speeds of up to 30mph and with a bite pressure of around 120 pounds per square inch. However, the dog handler was not afforded such protection!

This exercise was to mimic something that might happen while on patrol. The dog team would discover in the distance an unauthorized individual (the criminal) acting suspiciously. The handler would issue a warning challenge, and at this point the "criminal" would shout, turn, and run. The handler would repeat the challenge again and wait for around 3 seconds to allow the "criminal" to stop. When the "criminal" did not stop, the handler would release their dog.

Believe me, as the "criminal," there are a few things as undaunting as running away from an attack dog in full pace pursuit. You hear the dog's paw sounds getting closer, louder, and louder, and the noise of the dog's breath and snarling getting louder and closer, before there's a 3-second silence.

This is the time that you prepare yourself for the inevitable. The silence represents the point where the attack dog has committed itself and has now launched itself at you. The next thing the "criminal" feels is the impact of a 40–45 kilogram German Shepherd dog hitting them at 30mph and applying its 120 pounds, per square inch, of bite pressure to their padded suit.

It is highly likely that the "criminal" will end up being forcibly taken to the ground, with the attached German Shepherd dog trying to rip and tear away the padded suit.

Now, Kai loved this chase so much that he was very reluctant to let go after hearing the handler's commands to end the arrest. Consequently, I would need to repeat the command while giving the short leash a sharp tuck to reenforce the command. This was typically where the carnage ensued, as Kai would spit out the "criminal" and turn his attention to his handler. Building up speed, he ran at me, launching himself with his mouth wide open, revealing his sharp, slightly yellowed 42 teeth, ready to tear through my unprotected flesh.

Fortunately, having chosen to use the shorter leash, Kai was unable to reach his full speed. This allowed me time to quickly turn to the side and catch him in a headlock, tucked between my arm and rib cage, where I held him until he had calmed down enough to be released.

For the onlooking dog handlers, who were on the opposite side, they were unsighted and were not aware that Kai had not bitten me but that I had in fact got him in a headlock, so they were under the impression that I had been bitten and were preparing to take me for medical aid.

As you can see from Figure A-31,[34] the use of a canine makes for any effective security control, helping to deter, detect, or detain an intruder.

---

[34]https://ukdefencejournal.org.uk/dogs-war-raf-use-paws-ground/

Figure A-31. *A dogged defense*

Having aptly demonstrated that Kai and I were a compatible team, we could then be assigned to a shift. Being that this was the summertime, in the Falklands, the shift patterns were 4 night shifts patrolling the most sensitive areas (as depicted in Figure A-32[35]) and 4 days off duty.

[35]https://earth.google.com/web/search/RAF+Mount+Pleasant/@-51.88055308,-58.46574251,16.75397454a,8927.55884664d,35y,9.74902863h,60.01239373t,-0r/data=CigiJgokCcQWqcx-5UlAEXmETKqG3UlAGer0f1Z6MPi_Ie-a5F01xvm_

Figure A-32. *RAF Mount Pleasant*

To say that the activities, for the recovery days back then, were extremely limited would be an understatement. Consequently, we would spend 2 days out of the 4 days doing continuation training (CT), and the rest of the time would be in the gym or watching videos in the communal TV room.

Now, I say watching videos because there was no TV as you might know it. TV came through the broadcast of video recordings of UK TV. For example, on a Sunday evening, we would get our places in the communal TV room long before the program that we wanted to watch, so the Sunday evening consisted of sitting through an episode of ITV's *Bullseye* (see Figure A-33[36]) so that we could have our place to watch an episode of the BBC's *Noel's House Party* (see Figure A-34[37]). These programs would have aired in the United Kingdom on Saturday and had been recorded on video cassettes to be put on the next flight to RAF Mount Pleasant. When there was nothing of interest to watch on the TV service, we had the opportunity to go to the welfare facility ("The Oasis") to take a loan from their video library.

Figure A-33. *Bullseye*

[36]http://ukgameshows.co.uk/ukgs/Bullseye
[37]http://ukgameshows.co.uk/ukgs/Noel%27s_House_Party

Figure A-34. *Noel's House Party[38]*

Other than the Monday evening, when all the drinking establishments would be closed, the accepted normal was to spend your evenings off work visiting these many drinking establishments and partaking in copious amounts of alcohol.

It was on one of these visits that I made an error of judgment that would end up having an impact on the rest of my life. A visit to the 1312 Sqn bar, on Saturday, January 9, 1993, would result in my never completing another night shift at RAF Mount Pleasant.

Along with the rest of my shift and a group of other Police personnel and some of the physical training instructors (PTIs), we started our social activities in the RAF Police Club, before touring some of the other drinking establishments and finishing the night at the 1312 Sqn bar (see overview in Figure A-35).

---

[38]http://ukgameshows.co.uk/ukgs/Noel%27s_House_Party

Figure A-35. *RAF Mount Pleasant overview*

With hindsight or had I had carried out a risk assessment of the situation, I would have chosen an alternative option to the decision I made on that night.

At the conclusion of the night of socializing, the group needed to return to our accommodation, via the route indicated in yellow. We had one of the parties who had volunteered to drive us back in their V8 military Land Rover.

However, there were too many of us to all fit into the single vehicle, so half the group waited for alternative transport to come. I took the decision to squeeze into the V8 military Land Rover, along with the other 12 people.

Now, overloaded, the driver *(who, unknown to me, had been drinking alcohol)* set off at pace (approximately 60mph) on the drive back to the accommodation *(shown by the yellow line in Figure A-35)*. Inside the vehicle, everyone was merrily enjoying themselves having consumed several alcoholic beverages.

It was only 5 km back to the accommodation (as depicted in Figure A-36); what harm could it do? What were the risks?

Figure A-36. *Return journey*

The return route consisted of a flat tarmac road, adjoined by 6-feet-deep storm ditches just 6 inches from the side of the road. The conditions were dry, but the road had no street lighting, so that the only illumination was from a vehicle's headlights. Approximately, halfway along the road, there was an upward incline which adversely cambered to the right and where it was common for oncoming vehicles to clip this corner, coming over the brow of this bend on the opposite side of the road (as depicted in Figure A-37).

Figure A-37. *Adverse camber*

Imagine the scene; you're traveling at speed in the back of a long wheel-based Land Rover, fitted with side-facing bench seats *(I'm sat on someone's lap)* and no seatbelts. The next thing I know is that there's a sudden appearance of headlights ahead of us, and the vehicle suddenly swerves violently to the right and then to the left.

The next thing that I remember was coming to (being completed disoriented), being found lying at the side of the road, by Hez (my Dog Section shift colleague). Beforehand, Hez had managed to get himself free from being trapped under the rear wheel of the vehicle (*which had been balancing in the ditch*), before running off in a blind panic, then composing himself and running back to the crash site. The next thing that I remember is standing up and trying to flag down a passing vehicle (*whilst waiting for recovery (for some reason) Hez and I had been laughing hysterically at the whole situation*). Eventually, an ambulance and a Sherpa Minibus arrived on the scene.

The more seriously injured were instructed to get into the ambulance and all others into the Minibus. At this point, I was completely oblivious to my injuries and so climbed into the back of the Minibus, on a side bench on the left-hand side. I was then joined by my shift mate, Hez, who sat alongside me to my right.

I suddenly felt the sensation of what appeared to be cold fluid run down the right side of the back of my neck. I turned to Hez to ask him whether I had cut my head. I could tell from his immediate reaction that this was something more than just a minor cut or graze to my head. Because of the effect of the alcohol that I had consumed during the evening, I could feel no pain; however, Hez's reaction soon changed both of our moods as we were whisked off to the medical facility.

On arrival at the medical facility, I was prepared for an immediate helicopter transport to Stanley hospital – something that I remember being a comedy of errors, as the stretcher they used to transport me from the medical facility would not fit in the RAF helicopter, and then on arrival at Stanley hospital, the stretcher used in the helicopter was not suitable for transport into the hospital.

Following a night of observation, to allow the alcohol to wear off, the next morning I was prepared for surgery. During the accident, I had fractured the right-hand side of my skull, torn a patch of skin and hair from the right side of my head, and a lacerated right ear.

During the operation, I received a skin graft to the right side of my head and 42 stitches to reattach my ear to my head.

Although I was the only vehicle occupant who needed emergency transport to the local hospital facility for surgery, I was not the only person to be injured. The injuries included fractured ribs, fractured collarbones, head injuries, as well as several other minor injuries. However, when you see the damage sustained by the Land Rover, you can gain a greater appreciation of just how lucky we all had been (see Figure A-38).

Figure A-38. *Post-crash Land Rover*

Figure A-38. *(continued)*

The primary impact for me was after a 3-week period of recovery in the hospital, that was the end of my deployment, and in February 1993, I was flown back to the United Kingdom.

The secondary impact of this incident was that the Dog Section was depleted and that RAF Mount Pleasant were unable to continue with their planned military exercise or with their planned seven-a-side rugby tournament *(as the occupants of the vehicle had been key stakeholders).*

After the mandatory 3-week postdeployment leave, I returned to RAF Brize Norton where I was remained on light duties (day shifts) for the remainder of the summer and only returning to dog handling duties in September 1993.

In the longer term, I have since discovered that I also sustained a fractured neck and that the force that caused the injuries has also left me with permanent scarring to my brain tissue. The medical procedures in the early 1990s were focused on treating the visible physical injuries, and any invisible injuries *(arthritis and constant aches and pains in my upper spine and neck)* or the psychological effects of this traumatic event are things that I have had to cope with myself. (Note: It was not until I was referred to private medical specialists that they discovered that I had fractured my neck (discovered in 1996) and suffered a brain injury (discovered in 2017), as noted by the neurologist's notes (as depicted in Figure A-39).

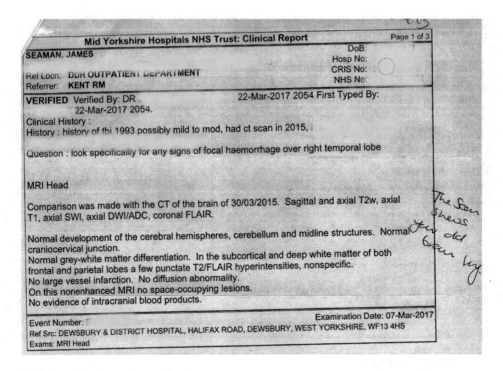

Mid Yorkshire Hospitals NHS Trust: Clinical Report   Page 1 of 3

SEAMAN, JAMES   DoB:
    Hosp No:
Ref Locn: DDH OUTPATIENT DEPARTMENT   CRIS No:
Referrer: KENT RM   NHS No:

VERIFIED Verified By: DR .   22-Mar-2017 2054 First Typed By:
    22-Mar-2017 2054.

Clinical History :
History : history of tbi 1993 possibly mild to mod, had ct scan in 2015,

Question : look specifically for any signs of focal haemorrhage over right temporal lobe

MRI Head

Comparison was made with the CT of the brain of 30/03/2015. Sagittal and axial T2w, axial T1, axial SWI, axial DWI/ADC, coronal FLAIR.

Normal development of the cerebral hemispheres, cerebellum and midline structures. Normal craniocervical junction.
Normal grey-white matter differentiation. In the subcortical and deep white matter of both frontal and parietal lobes a few punctate T2/FLAIR hyperintensities, nonspecific.
No large vessel infarction. No diffusion abnormality.
On this nonenhanced MRI no space-occupying lesions.
No evidence of intracranial blood products.

    Examination Date: 07-Mar-2017
Event Number:
Ref Src: DEWSBURY & DISTRICT HOSPITAL, HALIFAX ROAD, DEWSBURY, WEST YORKSHIRE, WF13 4HS
Exams: MRI Head

Figure A-39. Redacted medical notes

On my return to normal duties, Jacob and I returned to provide protection for RAF Brize Norton's critical assets. However, this was to be Jacob's final winter of active service as during the next annual efficiency evaluation, it became clear that Jacob was struggling to judge distances, and after a veterinary evaluation, he was diagnosed with bilateral cataract. Subsequently, he was retired from the RAF and became my pet, and I was reteamed with a dog named Tyson, from RAF Northolt (see Figure A-40).

Figure A-40. *Tyson*

He was to accompany me on my next posting to RAF Marham, Norfolk. However, I was still to conclude my time at RAF Brize Norton by placing third in the Southern Area Dog Trials (see Figure A-41).

Figure A-41. *Southern Area Dog Trials, RAF St Mawgan, Cornwall*

The posting to RAF Marham came as the RAF embarked toward the end of the Cold War era. However, it still housed several mission-critical and high-value assets that needed to be protected by RAF Police dog patrols, and, as a result, the Dog Section was twice the size of RAF Brize Norton and with a considerably larger footprint to protect (as depicted in Figure A-42[39]).

---

[39]https://earth.google.com/web/search/RAF+Marham/@52.64030158,0.54300848,
17.75231686a,1887.67547515d,35y,36.40349436h,60.04788787t,-0r/data=CigiJgokCfQFhj
n75OnAESldSGqh6UnAGXujTRkXPU3AIfcOxbLGPO3A

Figure A-42. *RAF Marham footprint*

Just 12 months later, I would be on the move once again – this time to RAF Leeming, in North Yorkshire, with its differing mission statement, topology, and supporting assets that needed to be protected (as depicted in Figure A-43[40]).

---

[40]https://earth.google.com/web/search/RAF+Leeming/@54.28395826,-
1.53182207,39.95962428a,2021.78977983d,35y,24.70552446h,60.00783174t,0r/
data=CigiJgokCcbOq-E2VkpAEefhIHjAUEpAGSiRigPFHOM_Idz4RzVS4eA_

Figure A-43. *RAF Leeming footprint*

After a short period on dog handling duties (see Figure A-44), I was notified that I was to be promoted, which would result in a change to my Protective Security career.

Figure A-44. *RAF Leeming Dog Section*

Continuing My Career in Protective Security

In May 1997, following my promotion course and what I thought would be the end of the dog handling phase of my Protective Security career came the posting to the South of England. Here, I was to take up the role of the Deputy Guard Commander, responsible for the supervision of the Policing and Security details, across the four dispersed sites *(Accommodation, Main-Site, NATO, Satellite)* of RAF Oakhanger (as depicted in Figure A-45).

Figure A-45. *RAF Oakhanger Main-Site*

My role, here, required me to ensure that adequate access control was in place, physical security measures remained effective, periodic security patrols and checks were carried out, and effective incident response activities were enabled.

I soon missed the challenges and excitement of my time as a dog handler, and so it was not long before I was requesting a move to a more challenging location.

The RAF were very quick to oblige, and by the following September, I found myself moving to RAF Aldergrove, Northern Ireland (as depicted at Figure A-46[41]).

---

[41]https://earth.google.com/web/search/RAF+Aldergrove/@54.64927049,-6.21949694,
76.75469211a,3676.75789273d,35y,24.75685657h,45.01963651t,-0r/data=CigiJgokCYNOmO
j5jOlAEcSLAIOajklAGSJzKo4Hjuy_IcaOk6uRF-2_

Figure A-46. *RAF Aldergrove*

This was a real step up in the world of Protective Security, knowing that there was a real and present domestic terrorism threat. I started this posting in the role as one of Deputy Shift Commanders, establishing regular security patrols and ensuring that effective controls were in place at all the applicable internal and external checkpoints.

However, 12 months later, my Protective Security career was to take another direction *(adding to my knowledge and experiences)* with an assignment onto RAF Aldergrove's air transport security (ATSy), where I would remain for another 2 years.

My ATSy role was to carry out security processing of all military personnel and their families, passing from RAF Aldergrove through Belfast International Airport (BIA). Additionally, the ATSy team would security process all Infantry personnel returning to their parent unit, on RAF aircraft, following their completion of an operational tour of duty. The lengths they would go to to conceal their prohibited items were shocking.

In fact, I recall one individual who attempted to smuggle through a live round of ammunition within their hold baggage. While carrying out an X-ray of their military-issued Bergen, I noticed an anomaly within a military-issued angle torch (as depicted in Figure A-47). On further inspection, I discovered that inside the battery space, they had placed an empty shotgun case, and inside the empty shotgun case was a live round of ammunition. The contraband was immediately confiscated, and after a debriefing with the individual's regimental sergeant major (RSM), it was agreed that I would leave any disciplinary action in their capable hands.

Figure A-47. *Military-issued torch*

Within minutes, I was hearing loud shouting coming from the open hangar area. As I went to investigate, I saw that the shouting was coming from the very same RSM, and circling around the hangar was the same offending passenger. He was busy running around the perimeter of the hangar, with their offending Bergen being held aloft, with their arms fully outstretched above their head.

I don't think the RSM was impressed, and I don't think that the offending individual will make the same mistake again!

Another memory I can recall from my time at RAF Aldergrove was the time I was assigned to be part of the perimeter security detail for the Maze Prison (as depicted in Figure A-48[42]). Basically, the RAF Police and RAF Regiment were tasked to provide additional Protective Security support for the prison. This involved 24-hour shifts (6 hours tower and patrols, 6 hours immediate response/recover), followed by 24 hours off duty.

Figure A-48. *Maze Prison*

The craziest thing was the logistic planning that went into it. The shifts would meet at RAF Aldergrove, where they had to climb into the back of one of three windowless "pantech" lorries (as depicted in Figure A-49[43]), to be driven to the Maze Prison.

---

[42]https://hmsmazelongkesh.wordpress.com/2016/04/13/first-blog-post/

[43]www.mygreennow.org/solution-for-entrepreneurs-looking-for-hgv-drivers/

Figure A-49. *Pantech lorry*

The crazy part was the military transport's (MT) decision of the color of "pantech" that they would choose to use – one red, one white, and one blue.

Knowing that my time at RAF Aldergrove would be limited to just 3 years, toward the end of this time, I sought to challenge myself with the opportunity of broadening my Protective Security skills and applied for the Close Protection preselection course. I can honestly say that this was the most physically demanding week that I had ever experienced.

The evaluation week started on the Sunday afternoon, where you were to report for a welcome briefing, wearing a formal suit and tie. After the briefing came the first physical evaluation – "21s." This consisted of

- A 2-mile run

- Straight into 30 press-ups, 30 sit-ups, 30 squat thrusts

- **30-second forced rest**

- 50-meter sprint

- Down to one knee and load up a pistol magazine with ten blank rounds

- 50-meter return sprint

- Straight into 30 press-ups, 30 sit-ups, 30 squat thrusts

- **30-second forced rest**

- 50-meter sprint

- Load the magazine into a pistol and fire the ten rounds

- 50-meter return sprint

- Straight into 30 press-ups, 30 sit-ups, 30 squat thrusts

- **30-second forced rest**

- 50-meter fireman's lift sprint with a body and negotiating a hurdle at the 25-meter point

All had to be completed within **21 minutes**!

The rest of the week consisted of daily fitness tests (e.g., Mon, at 0700, squad run and outdoor circuits, PM - house bricks circuit (*basically, a circuit while carrying two house bricks*); Tues, at 0700, obstacle course, PM - boxing circuits; Weds morning – 10 km timed cross-country run; Thurs morning – log run; and Fri morning – swimming circuit)s. When you were not doing fitness tests, you were being evaluated on your weapon safety skills, qualifying on the range, being tested on your first aid skills, and being taught the basic drills of Close Protection (as depicted in Figure A-50[44]).

---

[44]http://pixel8tor.co.uk/web_design/tpw/photo11.htm

Figure A-50. *RAF Police Close Protection*

The objective was to provide effective protection against any threats to the "Principle," with the "Principle" being deemed as a high-value asset.

Fortunately *(as it would turn out)*, I did not manage to complete the assessment week, as on the Thurs AM log run, while running as a pair and carrying a heavy log, I went over on my ankle and was unable to continue. This was to be the event that changed my Protective Security career path.

One of my last memories of my ATSy role, at RAF Aldergrove, was being on duty at the very same time that the 9/11 attacks took place, and all the US-bound aircraft were suddenly diverted into RAF Aldergrove and BIA.

Following my 3 years at RAF Aldergrove, in October 2001, I was posted back to an RAF base in North Yorkshire, where I was posted into the role of the Deputy Shift Commander at an initial flight training school – RAF Linton On Ouse (as depicted in Figures A-51[45] and A-52[46]).

Figure A-51. *RAF Linton On Ouse*

[45]https://earth.google.com/web/search/RAF+Linton+On+Ouse/@54.0447855,-1.2570891, 15.34163641a,1653.78531365d,35y,34.02054901h,59.99598748t,-0r/data=CigiJgokCVk5gw hdV0tAEVvxHu4DUUtAGffe5vDvnxjAIQtKVx-wARnA

[46]https://earth.google.com/web/search/RAF+Linton+On+Ouse/@54.04147006,- 1.24409924,19.61241169a,0d,55.5535862y,13.67006403h,77.92513101t,0r/data=CigiJgok CVk5gwhdV0tAEVvxHu4DUUtAGffe5vDvnxjAIQtKVx-wARnAIhoKFmRVbXZQOGU2bnRtRjNxVlJjVVFpS 1EQAg

Figure A-52. *Main access/egress – RAF Linton On Ouse*

Life at RAF Linton Ouse was to be very different, with the focus being on the control of access, security patrols, and out-of-hours security checks.

During this time, from December 2001 to April 2002, I was on a 4-month detachment to be a Shift Commander at RAFO Thumrait (as depicted in Figure A-53), providing police and security to the deployed Air Operations, in support of Operation Enduring Freedom.[47] You would not believe what the additional predeployment training consisted of:

- Military skills training in the hills of North Yorkshire, United Kingdom

  - *Anyone who has experienced camping in the hills of North Yorkshire, at the end of December, will understand that this is far from being like in the deserts of Oman.*

---

[47]https://edition.cnn.com/2013/10/28/world/operation-enduring-freedom-fast-facts/index.html

Figure A-53. *RAFO Thumrait*

Now, this was only my second ever overseas deployment, and "oh boy!" had things changed. Let me take a little time to explain the working and living conditions.

My role was the shift supervisor for a team of RAF Police, who were responsible for manning a control of access/egress point, carrying out return police and security patrols and processing outbound aircraft passengers. Part of my role was to ensure that the RAF Police Ops room was manned 24 hours a day, 7 days a week, so that there was someone there to ensure that a rapid response could be actioned for any incidents. Additionally, I had the responsibility for the deployed armory (ensuring the safe and secure issue/receipt and storage of the RAF Police and Aircrew weapons and ammunition).

During the day, I had a little more flexibility to get out and about as I could get cover from the "head shed" personnel. However, during the night shifts, this was far more difficult, and I would often be spending 12 hours behind the Operations desk. During the deployment, the shifts consisted of two 12-hour day shifts, two 12-hour night shifts, and two recovery days.

When describing the facilities that were available to us, I can only say that they were extremely limited. If you think of everything being housed within temporary tent-like structures, you might have an idea of the conditions.

For example:

- The accommodation consisted of a non-air-conditioned green canvas 24ft x 18ft military-issued tent (as depicted in Figure A-54[48]).

Figure A-54. *British military tent*

- The passenger processing facility consisted of two of the green canvas tents (one for inbound and one for outbound), and all baggage searches were carried out by hand, in an open/uncovered area (often at the height of the day).

- The "cook house" consisted of the same style of tents connected, with the tent sides removed and several bench seats and tables within.

- The ablutions were a porta-cabin, so that if you needed to use them during the night, you needed to put on your "desert" boots *(having turned them upside down to ensure that there were no scorpions or spiders inside first)* and walk outside your tent to them.

- The shower facilities consisted of several smaller 12ft x 12ft green canvas tents, and on the base were a few wooden pallets. As part of your deployment kit, you were issued with a single "solar shower bag" (as depicted in Figure A-55).

---

[48]www.anchorsupplies.com/ex-british-army-24-x-18-frame-tent-super-grade.html

Figure A-55. *5-gallon solar shower bag*

- There were two large air-conditioned white "super" tents, one with limited gym equipment and weights, and the other was for recreation (VHS player and TV, reading library and sofas, etc.).

- There were a few five-a-side football pitches, which consisted of an open flat area of desert, 3ft side/end panels, and five-a-side goal posts.

- Other than this, we were granted the use of the RAF Omani Squash Court *(literally, a non-air-conditioned breeze block building in the middle of the desert)* and an outdoor swimming pool.

As you might imagine, the living and work conditions were harsh, and, as a result, it was important to keep yourself busy and to take advantage of any luxuries that may be available. One such luxury was the daily "Happy Bus" that you could book a place onto to spend a day beside the pool of a hotel in Salalah. Initially, my shift would go down on the second recovery day, but soon this would extend to the first sleeping recovery day.

Additionally, it was inevitable that in such high tempo working and living environments, people would start to get annoyed with one another.

I recall one such incident when a member of my shift had been playing five-a-side football on the afternoon before going on to the night shift. Now, I do not know the full story behind what happened during the football game, but I do know that this individual was not too pleased with something the Officer Commanding the RAF Police detachment had done.

All through the night, he remained angry about the previous afternoon's events and vented his anger on the officer's thermal mug – basically, taking it off the hook of the mug board and running the rim of the mug down the crack of his bum. No harm done, as I had intended to clean the mug prior to the arrival of the officer the next morning. However, one thing led to another, and after getting distracted with the nightly tasks, I completely forgot about this incident. Well, you may well have guessed it, but the following morning while rushing around to get everything read to hand over to the day shift, the officer arrived and asked if while doing everything else, I could make them a morning cup of tea.

Of course, at this point, I was on autopilot and made them their tea and only remembered the previous evening's incident, at the point that this officer said:

Cheers Jim, this is the best cup of tea, ever!

This deployment was extremely challenging and rewarding, but like all the other experiences of being in the military, it helps you to grow both personally and professionally.

At the conclusion of the deployment, I returned to RAF Linton On Ouse and, after a few months, was selected to return to the RAF Police School to complete a 10-week residential specialist counter intelligence (CI) training course.

The objective of this course was to teach the CI students how to apply the contents from the three volumes of the Defence Manual of Security (Joint Services Publication 440 (JSP 440)[49]) for the proportionate protection of valuable military assets:

- **Volume 1** – The principles of protective security, the responsibilities of those concerned with applying them, and physical security policy

- **Volume 2** – Personnel security policy including the vetting system, line manager responsibility, and travel security

- **Volume 3** – Guidance and policy on the security of Communications and Information Systems (CIS)

The JSP 440 defined Protective Security as being

---

[49]http://wla.1-s.es/uk-mod-jsp-440-2001.pdf

The protection of assets from compromise. Compromise can be a breach of:

a. *Confidentiality. The restriction of information and other valuable assets to authorized individuals (e.g., protection from espionage, eavesdropping, leaks and computer hacking).*

b. *Integrity. The maintenance of information systems of all kinds and physical assets in their complete and usable form (e.g., protection from unauthorized alteration to a computer program).*

c. *Availability. The permitting of continuous or timely access to information systems or physical assets by authorized users (e.g., protection from sabotage, malicious damage, theft, fire and flood).*

In assessing integrity and availability, consideration must be given to both the direct and indirect consequences of compromise.

For example, the theft of a personal computer may be of limited direct consequence as such equipment can be relatively cheaply replaced. The loss of the information contained on the computer may have significant indirect consequences, particularly if no arrangements have been made for backup storage of the information it contains.

Additionally, an asset was defined as

Anything of value, either tangible or intangible that is owned or used by an organization or business. They can be documents and information; material such as buildings, equipment, valuables or cash; operating systems or personnel.

Material assets can have different degrees of value, as defined by the protective markings.

On successful completion of the CI course, I would return to the RAF Police School to complete additional Computer Security level 1 and level 2 courses and go on to complete almost a decade of postings working in CI:

- Station CI, RAF Linton On Ouse

- CI Ops (Central), RAF Cranwell

  - **2005** – Force Protection dog handler, Basra Airfield, Iraq (as depicted in Figure A-56)

Figure A-56. *With Air dog "Snap," at Basra Airfield, Iraq*

- **2006** – Force Protection counter intelligence field team, Exercise Steadfast Jaguar, Cape Verde (as depicted in Figure A-57[50])

---

[50]www.nato.int/multi/photos/2006/m060623a.htm

Figure A-57. *Exercise Steadfast Jaguar*

- **2007** – Force Protection CIFT, Kandahar Airbase, Afghanistan (as depicted in Figure A-58)

Figure A-58. *CIFT Kandahar*

- Station Counter Intelligence Operations, RAF Leeming

- Counter Intelligence Operations (North), HMS Caledonia

  - **2008** – Force Protection CIFT, Camp Bastion, Afghanistan (as depicted in Figure A-59)

Figure A-59. *CIFT Bastion*

The decade of CI training and experience, along with the other 22 years' military service in the RAF Police, has proved to be invaluable for transitioning across to the corporate sector.

However, the objective of this book is not to focus on compliance against a specific industry standard (e.g., PCI DSS, ISO/IEC 27001:2013, NIST, CIS 20 CSCs, etc.) or to focus on such concepts as Cyber Security, Cyber Resilience, Information Security, IT Security, Computer Security, Physical Security, Personnel Security, Risk Management, Data Privacy, Data Protection, and so on but to incorporate all these concepts into the term Protective Security, where the focus is on protecting those assets that are considered to be most valuable, from the business context.

- Safeguarding against

  - **Confidentiality**

  - **Integrity**

  - **Availability**

  - **Accountability**

  - **Authentication**

  - **Nonrepudiation**

A Chronology of Protective Security Development

Introduction

During my military career, I have received much investment and support into my professional and personal development. This, in turn, became the strong foundation for my eventual transition from Protective Security in the RAF Police to a career in the field of Cyber/Information Security within the corporate sector.

To put this level of investment and support into context, I thought you would appreciate a chronology of my development journey.

Premilitary Service

Before joining the Royal Air Force, I was your typical teenage boy who never really applied himself to learning and as a result only managed to average academic achievements, with only five recognized education awards (English, Mathematics, French, Geography, and Art).

However, that was all to change because of embarking in a career in the RAF Police.

Military Service
1989

- **RAF basic training course** – Six-week military skills training at RAF Swinderby, England

- **RAF driver training course** – Two-week driver training at RAF St Athans, Wales

J. Seaman, *Protective Security*, https://doi.org/10.1007/978-1-4842-6908-4

- **RAF Police basic training course** – Seven-week police training, followed by six-week infantry training, at RAF Newton, England
- **RAF Police dog handler training course** – Seven-week police dog handling at RAF Newton, England

1997

- **RAF general service training one (GST 1) course** – Two-week RAF promotion training at RAF Halton, England
- **RAF Police further training (FT) course** – Two-week RAF Police promotion training at RAF Halton, England

1999

- **RAF Police air transport security (ATSy) training course** – One-week RAF Police aviation security and passenger screening/processing training at RAF Halton, England

2000

- **Short University professional development training course** – One-week studying about practical management at Nottingham University, England

2001

- **UK Government aviation security training course** – One-week Department of the Environment, Transport, and the Regions (DETR) level 1 and level 7 security course, with the international consultants on targeted security (ICTS), at Belfast International Airport

2002

- **NEBS Management training course** – Distance learning introductory certificate in Management

- **RAF Police Counter Intelligence training course** – Eight-week protective security training at RAF Halton, England

- **RAF Police national investigative interviewing training course** – One week learning how to carry out investigative interviews at RAF Halton, England

2004

- **RAF Police computer security phase one (CompSy 1) training course** – Two-week introduction to computer security

- **Learning Tree International advanced technology course** – One-week introduction to system and network security

- **RAF Police computer security phase two (CompSy 2) training course** – Three weeks enhanced to computer security awareness

- **Reflex Magnetics Disknet Pro Administrator training course** – Short course on the administration of the Reflex Disknet Pro software at London, England

2005

- **Short University professional development training course** – One-week course about "Terrorism: Causes, Trends, and Responses" at the University of Bradford, England

- **Short University professional development training course** – One-week course about "Hard and Soft Security" at the University of Southampton, England

- **Higher National Certificate (HNC) in Computing** – Two-year evening classes studying "computer platforms, systems analysis, software constructs and tools, computer solutions, computer implementation project, networking, data analysis and database design, visual programming, human computer interface, and multimedia and Internet development" at York College, England

- **RAF Police specialist training course** – One-week training into "Intelligence Development" and "Internet Research and Investigations" with Focus Group, held at RAF Henlow, England

2006

- **Online Defense portal training course** – Distance learning course about "Microsoft Access 2003 and the Web"

- **Online Defense portal training course** – Distance learning course about the insider risk, "an inside job"

- **Online Defense portal training course** – Distance learning course about business continuity, "Business Continuity Awareness"

- **Online Defense portal training course** – Distance learning course about fraud, "Fraud Awareness"

- **Online Defense portal training course** – Distance learning course about data protection, "Data Protection (Handle with Care)"

- **Online Defense portal training course** – Distance learning course about the employment equality, "Equality and Diversity"

- **Short University professional development training course** – One-week course about an "Introduction to World Politics" at the University of Bristol, England

- **RAF Police specialist training course** – One-week training into "Level Two Source Handling" with Kent Police College, England

- **RAF Police specialist training course** – Two one-week trainings into the "National Special Branch Core Training Program" with the South West regional intelligence cell (RIC), Weston-super-Mare, England

2007

- **Short University professional development training course** – One-week course about "International and Regional Institutions: Coalitions and Areas of Conflict" at the University of Southampton, England

- **Short University professional development training course** – One-week course about "International Relations: The Nature and Conduct of War, Since 9/11" at the University of Southampton, England

- **RAF Police specialist training course** – One-week training into the "Digital Camera Handling" at the Defense College of Intelligence, RAF Cosford, England

- **Online Defense portal training course** – Distance learning course about how to conduct productive meetings, "Effective Meetings"

2008

- **RAF Health and Safety training course** – Three-day training on how to conduct and deliver health and safety risk assessments

- **Short University professional development training course** – One-week course about "The War on Terror and the US Role in the Contemporary World" at the University of Leeds, England

- **Short University professional development training course** – One-week course about "European Security" at the University of Bradford, England

- **Institute of Leadership and Management (ILM) training course** – A short course for a level 3 award in leadership

2009

- **Clarity Advanced Leadership and Management training course** – A short course learning how to write effective employee appraisals

- **RAF Management and Leadership training course** – Three-week intermediate management and leadership, Chartered Management Institute (CMI) level 4 and 5 training course, at RAF Halton, England

- **RAF Police trade management training two (TMT 2) course** – Two-week RAF Police senior management training at the Defense Police School, Southwick Park, near Portsmouth, Hampshire, England

2010

- **Online Defense portal training course** – Distance learning course about how to conduct productive presentations, "Delivering a Presentation"

2011

- **Online Defense portal training course** – Distance learning course about how to document security, "Defense Document Handling Security"

- **APM Group Project Management training course** – One-week PRINCE2 Foundation learning about effective project management

2008–2012

- **Master of Science degree university training course** – Four-year distance learning to achieve a Master of Science award, in relation to Security Management, with Loughborough University

Postmilitary Service

After leaving the Royal Air Force, I went on to successfully transfer my skills across to the corporate sector.

2012

- **Master of Science degree university training course** – Final year of four-year distance learning to achieve a Master of Science award, in relation to Security Management, with Loughborough University

- **ISACA Certified Information Security Manager (CISM)**[1] – Self-study into the domains of Information Security Governance, Information Risk Management, Information Security Program Development and Management, and Information Security Incident Management

2013

- **ISACA Certified in Risk and Information Systems Control (CRISC)**[2] – Self-study into the domains of IT risk identification, IT risk assessment, risk response and mitigation, and risk and control monitoring and reporting

- **Payment Card Industry Security Standards Council (PCI SSC) Qualified Security Assessor (QSA)** – Four-day course covering the Payment Card Industry Data Security Standard (PCI DSS), held in Florida, United States

2014

- **Communications-Electronics Security Group (CESG) accreditation** – Selected to enter the CESG listed adviser scheme (CLAS) as an accredited consultant

---

[1]www.isaca.org/credentialing/cism
[2]www.isaca.org/credentialing/crisc

2019

- **Cyber Management Alliance[3] NCSC-Certified Cyber Incident Planning and Response Course[4]** – One-day course and remote proctored exam
- **Cyber Management Alliance Building and Optimizing Incident Response Playbooks[5]**

2020

- **RiskLens[6] factor analysis of information risk (FAIR)[7] analysis fundamentals** – Distance learning course into the fundamentals of risk analysis using the FAIR methodology for quantitative risk assessments
- **RiskLens FAIR Analyst Learning Path** – Distance learning modules furthering my knowledge and understanding of the risk analysis using the FAIR methodology for quantitative risk assessments

Summary

As you can see, this level of training and experience, gained through military service, is something that you may not appreciate and is something that is extremely difficult to convey across to prospective employers in a two-page resume/curriculum vitae (CV).

In addition, there is also the mandatory common core skills (CCS) training, for example, weapons training, live firing, first aid, survive to operate, firefighting, and so on.

However, I hope that this brief chronology of some of the training that I obtained from my military career will help you to better appreciate some of the investments that are made to ensure effective "Defense of the Crown."

All of this could be a beneficial bonus to any business that embraces the employment of ex-military personnel.

---

[3]www.cm-alliance.com/

[4]www.cm-alliance.com/training/cipr-cyber-incident-planning-response/

[5]www.cm-alliance.com/training/cipr-playbooks

[6]www.risklens.com/

[7]The Importance and Effectiveness of Quantifying Cyber Risk (fairinstitute.org)

Bibliography

Business Context

- Farkas, I. (2019). Zero Day, Zero Budget: Information Security Management Beyond Standards. 1st ed. Imre Farkas.

- Saïd El Aoufi (2011). Information security economics. Norwich: Tso.

- Miller, P. (2014). The digital renaissance of work: delivering digital workplaces fit for the future. Farnham, Surrey, England ; Burlington, Vt, USA: Gower.

- Murdoch, R. (2018). ROBOTIC PROCESS AUTOMATION: guide to building software robots, automate repetitive tasks.

- Mary Cecelia Lacity and Willcocks, L. (2018). Robotic process and cognitive automation: the next phase. Stratford-Upon-Avon, Warwickshire: Sb Publishing.

- King, R. (2018). Digital workforce: reduce costs and improve efficiency using robotic process automation. Erscheinungsort Nicht Ermittelbar] Rob King.

- Information Systems Audit and Control Association (2016). ISACA privacy principles and program management guide. Rolling Meadows, Ill.: Isaca.

- Aiken, M. (2016). The cyber effect: a pioneering cyberpsychologist explains how human behavior changes online. London: John Murray.

- Clark, N. and Nixon, C. (2015). Professional services marketing handbook: how to build relationships, grow your firm and become a client champion. London ; Philadelphia: Kogan Page.

© Jim Seaman 2021
J. Seaman, *Protective Security*, https://doi.org/10.1007/978-1-4842-6908-4

- W Chan Kim and Renée Mauborgne (2015). Blue ocean strategy: How to create uncontested market space and make the competition irrelevant. Massachusetts: Harvard Business School Publishing Corporation.

- Mullins, L.J. (2007). Management and organisational behaviour (paperback and internet access card). Harlow: Pearson Education Limited.

- Managing successful projects with PRINCE2. (2009). London: Tso (The Stationary Office), Cop.

- Loginov, M. (2018). CISO: Defenders of the Cyber-Realm. 1st ed. Great Britain: Ascot Barclay Publishing.

- Bonney, B., Hayslip, G. and Stamper, M. (2016). CISO desk reference guide: a practical guide for CISOs. San Diego, Ca: Ciso Drg Joint Venture Pub.

- Bonney, B., Hayslip, G. and Stamper, M. (2018). CISO desk reference guide: a practical guide for CISOs. San Diego: Ciso Drg Joint Venture Publishing, Cop.

- Ferriss, T. (2011). Escape the 9-5, live anywhere and join the new rich. Vermilion.

Risk Management

- Dehghantanha, A., Conti, M., Tooska Dargahi and Springerlink (Online Service (2018). Cyber Threat Intelligence. Cham: Springer International Publishing.

- Borodzicz, E.P. (2005). Risk, crisis and security management. West Sussex, England ; Hoboken, Nj: J. Wiley & Sons.

- Waters, D. (2015). Supply chain risk management: vulnerability and resilience in logistics. London: Kogan Page.

- Young, C.S. (2010). Metrics and methods for security risk management. Amsterdam ; Boston: Syngress/Elsevier.

- Freund, J. and Jones, J. (2015). Measuring and managing information risk: a fair approach. Oxford: Elsevier, Cop.

- Slovic, P., Earthscan and Routledge (2014). The perception of risk. Abingdon, Oxon ; New York: Earthscan From Routledge, Dr.

- Talbot, J. (2019). Security Risk Management: Aide-Memoire. 1st ed. Sydney, NSW, Australia: SERT Pty Ltd.

- (2016). Security and Risk Management: Critical Reflections and International Perspectives. 1st ed. London, UK: Centre for Security Failures Studies Publishing.

- Broder, J.F. and Tucker, E. (2012). Risk analysis and the security survey. Amsterdam ; Waltham, Ma: Butterworth-Heinemann.

- Blyth, M. (2015). Risk and security management: protecting people and sites worldwide. Hoboken, N.J.: Wiley.

- Risk Scenarios: Using COBIT 5 for Risk. (2014). Isaca.

- Advanced persistent threats: how to manage the risk to your business. (2013). Isaca.

- Haber, M.J. and Hibbert, B. (2018). Asset attack vectors: building effective vulnerability management strategies to protect organizations. Berkeley, Ca: Apress.

- Haber, M.J. (2020). *IDENTITY ATTACK VECTORS: implementing an effective identity and access management solution.* S.L.: Apress.

- Haber, M.J. and Hibbert, B. (2018). Privileged attack vectors: building effective cyber-defense strategies to protect organizations. New York, Ny: Distributed To The Book Trade Worldwide By Springer Science+Business Media.

- Hassan, N.A. and Rami Hijazi (2018). Open Source Intelligence Methods and Tools. Berkeley, Ca: Apress.

Identify and Isolate

- American Institute of Certified Public Accountants (2018). Guide: SOC 2 reporting on an examination of controls at a service organization relevant to security, availability, processing integrity, confidentiality, or privacy. New York, N.Y.: American Institute of Certified Public Accountants.

- Information Systems Audit and Control Association (2014). IT control objectives for Sarbanes-Oxley: using COBIT 5 in the design and implementation of internal controls over financial reporting. Rolling Meadows, Il: Isaca.

- Ramos, M.J. (2008). The Sarbanes-Oxley section 404 implementation toolkit: practice aids for managers and auditors. Hoboken, N.J.: Wiley.

- Ross, R. (2013). Security and Privacy Controls for Federal Information Systems and Organizations (NIST SP 800-53, Revision 4). 1st ed. 50 Page Publications.

- Katzer, M.A. (2018). Securing Office 365: masterminding MDM and compliance in the cloud. Berkeley, California: Apress.

- Buchanan, W. (2017). Cryptography. Gistrup, Denmark: River Publishers.

- James, S. (2019). PRACTICAL CRYPTOGRAPHY IN PYTHON: learning correct cryptography by example.

- Haunts, S. (2019). Applied Cryptography in .NET and Azure Key Vault: A Practical Guide to Encryption in .NET and .NET Core. Berkeley, Ca: Apress.

- Vasantha Lakshmi and Springerlink (Online Service (2019). Beginning Security with Microsoft Technologies: Protecting Office 365, Devices, and Data. Berkeley, Ca: Apress.

- Stouffer, K., Falco, J. and Scarfone, K. (2011). Guide to Industrial Control Systems (ICS) Security – Supervisory Control and Data Acquisition (SCADA) systems, Distributed Control Systems (DCS), and other control system configurations such as Programmable Logic Controllers (PLC). S.L.] 50 Page Publ.

- Kobes, P. and Vde-Verlag Gmbh (2020). Guideline Industrial Security IEC 62443 is easy. Berlin Vde Verlag.

- Ginter, A. (2018). SCADA security: what's broken and how to fix it. Calgary: Abterra Technologies.

- Bodungen, C.E., Singer, B.L., Shbeeb, A., Hilt, S. and Wilhoit, K. (2017). Hacking exposed, industrial control systems: ICS and SCADA security secrets & solutions. New York ; Chicago ; San Francisco: McGraw Hill Education.

- Seaman, J. (2020). PCI DSS: an integrated data security standard guide. S.L.: Apress.

- Williams, B.R. and Chuvakin, A. (2012). PCI compliance: understand and implement effective PCI data security standard compliance. Waltham, Ma, USA: Elsevier/Syngress.

- Lacey, D. (2015). A Practical Guide to the Payment Card Industry Data Security Standard (PCI DSS). 1st ed. Illinois, United States: Isaca.

- Isaca (2013). Configuration Management: Using COBIT 5. Isaca.

- Information Systems Audit and Control Association (2014). Vendor management using COBIT 5. Rolling Meadows, Il: Isaca.

- Gilman, E. and Barth, D. (2017). Zero trust networks: building secure systems in untrusted networks. Sebastopol, Ca: O'Reilly Media.

- Gordon Fyodor Lyon (2008). Nmap network scanning: official Nmap project guide to network discovery and security scanning. Sunnyvale, Ca: Insecure.com, Llc.

- Hutchens, J. (2014). Kali Linux network scanning cookbook: over 90 hands-on recipes explaining how to leverage custom scripts and integrated tools in Kali Linux to effectively master network scanning. Birmingham, UK: Packt Publishing.

- Vacca, J.R. (2010). Network and system security. Burlington, Ma: Syngress/Elsevier.

- Knapp, E.D. and Joel Thomas Langill (2015). Industrial network security: securing critical infrastructure networks for smart grid, SCADA, and other industrial control systems. [online] Waltham, Ma: Syngress. Available at: `https://dl.acm.org/citation.cfm?id=2746460` [Accessed 29 May 2019].

- Anderson, R.J. (2008). Security engineering: a guide to building dependable distributed systems. Indianapolis, Ind.: Wiley.

- Baker, P.R. and Benny, D.J. (2016). The Complete Guide to Physical Security. Auerbach Publications.

Detect Anomalies

- Bejtlich, R. (2019). The practice of network security monitoring: understanding incident detection and response. Vancouver, B.C.: Langara College.

- Brown, S.A. and Brown, M. (2011). Ethical issues and security monitoring trends in global healthcare: technological advancements. Hershey, Pa: Medical Information Science Reference.

- Sanders, C. and Smith, J. (2014). Applied network security monitoring: collection, detection, and analysis. Amsterdam ; Boston: Syngress, An Imprint Of Elsevier.

- Andreĭ Miroshnikov (2018). Windows security monitoring: Scenarios and patterns. Indianapolis, In: John Wiley & Sons Inc.

- Liska, A. (2003). The practice of network security: deployment strategies for production environments. Upper Saddle River, Nj: Prentice Hall Ptr.

- Fry, C. and Nystrom, M. (2009). Security monitoring. Farnham: O'Reilly.

- Ghorbani, A.A., Lu, W. and Mahbod Tavallaee (2010). Network Intrusion Detection and Prevention: Concepts and Techniques. New York, Ny: Springer US.

- Flammini, F., Setola, R. and Giorgio Franceschetti (2016). Effective surveillance for homeland security: balancing technology and social issues. Boca Raton: Chapman & Hall/Crc.

Govern Process

- Tricker, R.I. (2015). Corporate governance: principles, policies and practices. Oxford: Oxford Univ. Press.

- Information Systems Audit and Control Association (2017). Implementing a privacy protection program: using COBIT 5 enablers with the ISACA privacy principles. Rolling Meadows, Ill.: Isaca.

- Fay, J. (1999). Model security policies, plans, and procedures. Boston: Butterworth-Heinemann.

- King, N. and Anderson, N. (2002). Managing innovation and change: a critical guide for organizations. London: Thomson.

- Leron Zinatullin (2016). The psychology of information security: resolving conflicts between security compliance and human behaviour. Ely, Cambridgeshire: IT Governance Pub.

- Levit, A. (2019). Humanity works merging technologies and people for the workforce of the future. London, United Kingdom New York Kogan Page.

- Hayden, L. (2016). People-Centric Security: Transforming Your Enterprise Security Culture. 1st ed. New York, United States: McGraw Hill Education.

- Person, R. (2013). Balanced scorecards & operational dashboards with Microsoft Excel. Indianapolis, In: Wiley.

- Peter De Tender, Rendon, D., Erskine, S. and Springerlink (Online Service (2019). Pro Azure Governance and Security: A Comprehensive Guide to Azure Policy, Blueprints, Security Center, and Sentinel. Berkeley, Ca: Apress.

Evaluate Security Controls

- Mcnab, C. (2017). Network security assessment: know your network. Sebastopol, Ca: O'Reilly Media, Inc.

- Weidman, G. (2014). Penetration testing: a hands-on introduction to hacking. San Francisco: No Starch Press.

- Oakley, J.G. (2019). Professional Red Teaming Conducting Successful Cybersecurity Engagements. Berkeley, Ca: Apress.

- Deviant Ollam (2012). Practical lock picking: a physical penetration tester's training guide. Waltham, Ma: Syngress/Elsevier.

- Watson, G., Mason, A.G. and Ackroyd, R. (2014). Social engineering penetration testing: executing social engineering pen tests, assessments and defense. Amsterdam ; Boston: Syngress, An Imprint Of Elsevier.

- Daniel, C. (2012). Reader-Friendly Reports: A No-nonsense Guide to Effective Writing for MBAs, Consultants, and Other Professionals. McGraw-Hill.

- Sennewald, C.A. (2004). Security consulting. Oxford: Elsevier Butterworth-Heinemann.

- Sennewald, C.A. (2013). Security consulting. Boston: Butterworth-Heinemann.

- Bencie, L. (2014). Global security consulting: how to build a thriving international practice. Mountain Lake Park, Md: Mountain Lake Press.

Survive to Operate

- Conboy, N., Jan Van Bon and Stationery Office (Great Britain) (2017). Service rescue!: an implementation and improvement guide for incident management. Norwich: The Stationery Office.

- Thompson, E.C. (2018). *Cybersecurity Incident Response: how to contain, eradicate, and recover from incidents*. New York Apress.

- Niranjan Reddy (2019). Practical Cyber Forensics: An Incident-Based Approach to Forensic Investigations. New York Apress.

Cybersecurity

- Dafydd Stuttard, Pinto, M. and Pauli, J.J. (2012). *The web application hacker's handbook: finding and exploiting security flaws*. Indianapolis, Ind.: John Wiley & Sons.

- Sullivan, B. and Liu, V. (2012). Web application security: a beginner's guide. New York: McGraw-Hill.

- Wear, S. (2018). BURP SUITE COOKBOOK: practical recipes to help you master web penetration testing with burp suite.

- Kim, P. (2015). The hacker playbook 2: practical guide to penetration testing. North Charleston, South Carolina: Secure Planet, Llc.

- Kim, P. (2018). The hacker playbook 3: practical guide to penetration testing. North Charleston, South Carolina: Secure Planet, Llc.

- Hacking: the Art of Exploitation. (2007). Erscheinungsort Nicht Ermittelbar: No Starch Press, US.

- Carey, M.J. and Jin, J. (2020). Tribe of hackers blue team: tribal knowledge from the best in defensive cybersecurity. Indianapolis, In: John Wiley & Sons, Inc.

- Jin, M.J. (2020). TRIBE OF HACKERS SECURITY LEADERS: tribal knowledge from the best in cybersecurity... leadership. S.L.: John Wiley & Sons.

- Carey, M.J. and Jin, J. (2019). Tribe of hackers Red Team: tribal knowledge from the best in offensive cybersecurity. Indianapolis, Indiana: John Wiley & Sons.

- Jin, M.J. (2020). TRIBE OF HACKERS SECURITY LEADERS: tribal knowledge from the best in cybersecurity... leadership. S.L.: John Wiley & Sons.

- Engebretson, P. (2013). The Basics of Hacking and Penetration Testing: Ethical Hacking and Penetration Testing Made Easy Ed. 2. Syngress.

- Franke, D. (2016). Cyber security basics: protect your organization by applying the fundamentals. Don Franke.

- Hayslip, G. (202AD). The Essential Guide to Cybersecurity for SMBs. 1st ed. San Diego: CISO DRG Publishing.

- Prabath Siriwardena (2020). Advanced API security: OAuth 2.0 and beyond. Berkeley, California: Apress.

- Oakley, J.G. (2020). Cybersecurity for space: protecting the final frontier. California: Apress.

- Copeland, M. (2011). Cyber Security on Azure an IT professional's guide to Microsoft Azure Security Center. New York, Ny Apress, Springer Science+Business Media.

- Donaldson, S.E., Siegel, S.G., Williams, C.K. and Aslam, A. (2018). *Enterprise cybersecurity study guide: how to build a successful cyberdefense program against advanced threats*. Berkeley, California: Apress.

- Wilson, Y. and Abhishek Hingnikar (2019). Solving identity management in modern applications: demystifying OAuth 2.0, OpenID connect, and SAML 2.0. San Francisco, California: Apress.

- Parker, C. (2018). Firewalls Don't Stop Dragons A Step-by-Step Guide to Computer Security for Non-Techies. Berkeley, Ca: Apress.

- Waschke, M. (2017). *Personal cybersecurity: how to avoid and recover from cybercrime.* Bellingham, Washington: Apress.

- Oakley, J.G. (2019). Waging cyber war: technical challenges and operational constraints. Berkeley, California: Apress.

Counter Terrorism

- Staniforth, A. and Police National Legal Database (2009). Blackstone's counter-terrorism handbook by Andrew Staniforth. Oxford: Oxford University Press.

- Corbin, J. (2002). Al-Qaeda: in search of the terror network that threatens the world. New York: Thunder Mouth Press/Nation Books.

- Dershowitz, A.M. (2008). Why Terrorism Works: Understanding the Threat, Responding to the Challenge. Yale University Press.

- Post, J.M. (2009). The mind of the terrorist: the psychology of terrorism from the IRA to al-Qaeda. New York: Palgrave Macmillan.

- Silke, A. (2011). The psychology of counter-terrorism. London ; New York: Routledge.

- Hoffman, B. and Ebrary, I. (2006). Inside terrorism. New York, N.Y. ; Chichester: Columbia University Press.

- Brigitte Lebens Nacos (2007). Mass-mediated terrorism: the central role of the media in terrorism and counterterrorism. Lanham, Md.: Rowman & Littlefield.

- Silke, A. (2004). Research on terrorism: trends, achievements & failures. London ; Portland, Or: Frank Cass.

Crime

- Staniforth, A., Babak Akhgar and Police (2017). Blackstone's handbook of cyber crime investigation. Oxford, United Kingdom: Oxford University Press.

- Molan, M.T., Lanser, D. and Bloy, D. (2003). Modern criminal law. London ; Sydney ; Portland (Or.): Cavendish.

- Molan, M.T., Lanser, D. and Bloy, D. (2000). Bloy and Parry's principles of criminal law. London: Cavendish.

- Maguire, M., Morgan, R. and Reiner, R. (2007). The Oxford handbook of criminology. Oxford ; New York: Oxford University Press Inc.

- Card, R. (2008). Card Cross and Jones criminal law. London: Oxford University Press.

Military and Warfare

- Sunzi (2014). The art of war. New York: Black & White Classics.

- Antulio J Echevarria, II (2017). Military strategy: a very short introduction. New York: Oxford University Press.

- Black, J. (2020). Military Strategy: A Global History. Yale University Press.

- Proctor, I. (2014). The Royal Air Force in the Cold War, 1950–1970. Barnsley: Pen & Sword Aviation.

- Mick Haygarth (2019). From the Cold War to the War on Terror: the personal story of an RAF armourer and engineer from nuclear weapons to bomb disposal. Barnsley ; Havertown, Pa: Frontline Books.

- Annett, R. (2010). Lifeline in Helmand: RAF front-line air supply in Afghanistan - 1310 flight. Pen & Sword Books Ltd.

- Farrell, T., Frans P B Osinga and James Avery Russell (2013). Military adaptation in Afghanistan. Stanford (Calif.): Stanford Security Studies, Cop.

- T Robert Fowler (2016). Combat mission Kandahar: the Canadian experience in Afghanistan. Toronto: Dundurn.

- Silinsky, M. (2014). The Taliban: Afghanistan's most lethal insurgents. Santa Barbara, Ca: Praeger Security International.

- NATO military forces, strategy, structure and operational handbook. (2009). Washington DC Etc.: International Business Publications, USA, Cop.

- Morris, R. (2000). The biography of Leonard Cheshire, VC, OM. Viking.

- Davies, S. (2018). RAF POLICE – Snowdrop Humour. 1st ed. Independently Published.

- Davies, S.R. (1997). Fiat justitia: a history of the Royal Air Force Police. London: Minerva.

- Davies, S. (2017). Royal Air Force Police in the Line of Fire. Independently Published.

- Davies, Stephen R. (2017) RAF Police Whitecap Two-Five. Independently Published.

- Davies, S.R. (2008). Those bloomin' Snowdrops!: a lighthearted look at life in the RAF Police. Bognor Regis: Woodfield Pub.

- Davies, S. R. (2017). A Concise Global History of the RAF Police 1918–2018. Independently Published.

- Davies, S. (2006). RAF Police Dogs on Patrol: An Illustrated History of the Deployment of Dogs by the Royal Air Force. 1st ed. Bognor Regis: Woodfield Publishing.

Index

A

Access control, 527, 528, 534
Access management (AM), 577, 578
Account types, 535
Additive manufacturing, 415
Advanced drug manufacturing plant, 415
Aircraft damage analysis, 605
Air power, 222
Air transport security (ATSy), 30, 622
Annualized loss exposure (ALE), 150
APEC privacy framework, 105
API security, 352, 353
Application programming
      interface (API), 351
Asset Definition and Management (ADM),
      570, 571
Asset inventory, 301, 302, 304
Asset management, 161
    banking, 166
    crypto, 163
    electronic/digital data storage and
        transmission, 163
    encryption, 163
    encryption classes, 165
    hardcopy data assets, 161, 162
    jewelry stores, 166
    KISS model, 161
    protection, 163
    security container
        classes, 163, 164

security document box, 162
    storage container, 161, 162
Asset risk views, 196
ATLAS supplier questionnaire, 471
Attacks, supply chain, 450
Attack vectors, 29, 346, 347
Audit trail, 535
Australian Protective Security, 17
Auto ecommerce, 239
Automated code analysis, 516
Autonomous robots, 414
Availability, 403

B

Base commanders, 275
Base defense, 273
Bayonet training, 662
Bell-LaPadula, 291
Bespoke Office 365 login
      web page, 558
Biba Model, 292
BLACK network, 296
Blackbaud security, 636
Board-driven risk, 442
Braking system, 427
Branch security officers (BSyOs), 59
British military tent, 699
Business alignment, 442
Business-as-usual (BAU), 200
Business case, 620, 621

J. Seaman, *Protective Security*, https://doi.org/10.1007/978-1-4842-6908-4

Printed in the United States
by Baker & Taylor Publisher Services